FEMINIST THOUGHT

■

FEMINIST THOUGHT

—■—

A Comprehensive Introduction

Rosemarie Tong
Williams College

First published 1989 in the United States of America by Westview Press, Inc.
First published in the United Kingdom by Unwin Hyman Ltd.

Reprinted 1992 (twice), 1993, 1994, 1995, 1997
by Routledge
2 Park Square, Milton Park, Abingdon, Oxon, OX14 4RN

Transferred to Digital Printing 2006

British Library Cataloguing in Publication Data
A catalogue record for this book is available from the British Library

Library of Congress Cataloguing in Publication Data
A catalogue record for this book is available from the Library of Congress

ISBN 0-415-07874-1

Publisher's Note
The publisher has gone to great lengths to ensure the quality of this
reprint but points out that some imperfections
in the original may be apparent

In memory of my husband,
Paul ki-king Tong

Contents

CONCLUSION:
STANDPOINTS AND DIFFERENCES   235

Acknowledgments

I am indebted to numerous students and colleagues and wish to thank them for whatever contribution this book may make. In particular, I owe thanks to Michael Weber, Antje Haussen Lewis, Elaine Freedman, and Nancy Gannon for assisting me with the editorial review of some of this book's preliminary drafts. Michael catalyzed me to rethink liberal feminism and pointed me toward some sections of Marx and Freud that are particularly interesting from a feminist point of view. Antje and Elaine enabled me to reconsider some of my interpretations of radical, psychoanalytic, and existential feminism. Because of their insights, I was saved several trips down the proverbial blind alley as well as numerous trips to the library. I also owe special thanks to Amy Jeffress. Chapter 7 was written largely in the spirit of collaboration with her. For this experience of intellectual partnership, I am truly grateful. The ultimate reward of teaching is the opportunity to be taught by one's students.

This book is much better for the thoughtful comments and criticisms of Alison Jaggar, Virginia Held, Eleanor Kuykendall, Christine Di Stefano, Sandra Bartky, Nancy Holmstrom, and Joyce Trebilcot, all of whom read one or more chapters. In addition, Kathryn Jackson and Meredith Michaels read the entire manuscript and forced me to improve and clarify my arguments at many points. I am grateful to all of them. I wish I could say that I took all the excellent advice I was given, but limitations of time, energy, and insight sometimes worked against the process of revision.

For preparation of the manuscript, I owe many thanks to Stefano Donati's patient proofreading. Because the book went through at least six revisions, Donna Chenail, Peggy Bryant, Shirley Bushika, and Lori Tolle experienced firsthand Nietzsche's "eternal recurrence." Without these four women, this book would never have come close to meeting its deadline. I also with to thank the staff at Westview Press, particularly Spencer Carr. His firm flexibility and unfailing support were there when I most needed them.

Finally, I wish to thank President Francis C. Oakley and Dean John Reichert. Their financial and collegial support eased the writing of this book as did the cheerful encouragement of my two sons, Paul and John, ever willing to take care of themselves.

Rosemarie Tong

---■---

Introduction:
The Varieties of Feminist Thinking

ABOUT EIGHT YEARS AGO, WHEN I DECIDED to develop at Williams College a course entitled "Introduction to Feminist Theory," several of my colleagues had two predominant and for the most part inconsistent reactions. One colleague branded the course "a political polemic." It turned out that he saw feminist theory as a monolithic ideology into which unsuspecting students would be indoctrinated. Another colleague criticized the course for almost opposite reasons: He saw nothing theoretical about feminist theory at all. Echoing many early critics of feminist thought, he described it as a random mixture of complaints pointing out, but scarcely analyzing, the subjugation of women.[1] After much discussion, and with the help of the Williams Women's Studies Committee, I finally persuaded my skeptical colleagues that feminist theory is not one, but many, theories or perspectives and that each feminist theory or perspective attempts to describe women's oppression, to explain its causes and consequences, and to prescribe strategies for women's liberation. The more skillfully a feminist theory can combine description, explanation, and prescription, the better that theory is.

Feminism, like most broad-based philosophical perspectives, accommodates several species under its genus. No short list could be exhaustive, but many, although by no means all, feminist theorists are able to identify their approach as essentially liberal, Marxist, radical, psychoanalytic, socialist, existentialist, or postmodern. I understand each of these to be a partial and provisional answer to the "woman question(s)," providing a unique perspective with its own methodological strengths and weaknesses. What continues to fascinate me, however, is the way in which these partial and provisional answers intersect, joining together both to lament the ways in which women have been oppressed, repressed, and suppressed and to celebrate the ways in which so many women have

1

"beaten the system," taken charge of their own destinies, and encouraged each other to live, love, laugh, and be happy *as women*.

Because so much of contemporary feminist theory defines itself in reaction against traditional liberal feminism, liberalism is the obvious place to begin a survey of feminist thought. This perspective received its classic formulation in Mary Wollstonecraft's *A Vindication of the Rights of Woman*[2] and in John Stuart Mill's "The Subjection of Women."[3] Its main thrust, an emphasis still felt in contemporary groups such as the National Organization for Women, is that female subordination is rooted in a set of customary and legal constraints that blocks women's entrance and/or success in the so-called public world. Because society has the false belief that women are, by nature, less intellectually and/or physically capable than men, it excludes women from the academy, the forum, and the marketplace. As a result of this policy of exclusion, the true potential of many women goes unfulfilled. If it should happen that when women and men are given the same educational opportunities and civil rights, few women achieve eminence in the sciences, arts, and professions, then so be it. Gender justice, insist liberal feminists, requires us, first, to make the rules of the game fair and, second, to make certain that none of the runners in the race for society's goods and services is systematically disadvantaged; gender justice does not also require us to give the losers as well as the winners a prize.

But is this feasible? Marxist feminists think it impossible for anyone, especially women, to obtain genuine equal opportunity in a class society where the wealth produced by the powerless many ends up in the hands of the powerful few. With Friedrich Engels,[4] they claim that women's oppression originated in the introduction of private property, an institution that obliterated whatever equality the human community had previously enjoyed. Private ownership of the means of production by relatively few persons, originally all male, inaugurated a class system whose contemporary manifestations are corporate capitalism and imperialism. Reflection on this state of affairs suggests that capitalism itself, not just the larger social rules under which men are privileged over women, is the cause of women's oppression. If all women—not just the relatively privileged or exceptional ones—are ever to be liberated, the capitalist system must be replaced by a socialist system in which the means of production belong to one and all. Because, under socialism, no one would be economically dependent on anyone else, women would be economically freed from men and therefore equal to them.

Radical feminists, however, believe that neither their liberal nor their Marxist sisters have gone far enough. They argue that it is the patriarchal system that oppresses women, a system characterized by power, dominance, hierarchy, and competition, a system that cannot be reformed but only ripped out root and branch. It is not just patriarchy's legal and political structures that must be overturned; its social and cultural institutions (especially the family, the church, and the academy) must also go.

Although radical feminist writings are as distinct as they are myriad, one of their frequent themes is the effect of female biology on woman's self-perception, status, and function in the private and public domains. In order to avoid confusion, it is important to distinguish this feminist inquiry from the antifeminist dictum that biology is women's unfortunate and unchanging destiny. When conservatives say that biology is destiny,[5] they mean that (1) people are born with the hormones, anatomy, and chromosomes of either a male or a female; (2) females are destined to have a much more burdensome reproductive role than are males; (3) males will, other things being equal, exhibit "masculine" psychological traits (for example, "assertiveness, aggressiveness, hardiness, rationality or the ability to think logically, abstractly and analytically, ability to control emotion"), whereas females will, other things being equal, exhibit "feminine" psychological traits (for example, "gentleness, modesty, humility, supportiveness, empathy, compassionateness, tenderness, nurturance, intuitiveness, sensitivity, unselfishness");[6] and (4) society should preserve this natural order, making sure that its men remain "manly" and its women "womanly." In contrast to conservatives, radical feminists have no interest in preserving the kind of "natural order," or biological status quo, that subordinates women to men. Rather, their aim is to question the concept of a "natural order" and to overcome whatever negative effects biology has had on women and perhaps also on men.[7]

Initially preoccupied with the enslaving aspects of women's biology and psychology,[8] most radical feminists came to view women's biology (especially their reproductive capacities) and the nurturant psychology that flows from it as potential sources of liberating power for women.[9] What is oppressive is not female biology per se, but rather that men have controlled women as childbearers and childrearers. Thus, if women are to be liberated, each woman must determine for herself when to use or not to use reproduction-controlling technologies (for example, contraception, sterilization, abortion) and reproduction-aiding technologies (for example, artificial insemination by donor, in vitro fertilization, contracted motherhood);[10] and each woman must also determine for herself how and how not to rear the children she bears.[11]

Not all radical feminists focus on the biological origins of women's oppression, however. Indeed, most focus instead on the ways in which gender (masculinity and femininity) and sexuality (heterosexuality versus lesbianism) have been used to subordinate women to men. Although radical feminists seldom separate their discussions of gender and sexuality, preferring instead to discuss the sex/gender system in toto,[12] moments of emphasis do punctuate their writings. As we shall see, many radical feminists, like many liberal feminists, have at some time or other espoused a nurture theory of gender differences according to which masculine and feminine traits are almost exclusively the product of socialization or the environment[13] (think here of Margaret Mead, who after studying three primitive societies—the Arapesh, the Mundugumor, and the Tschambuli— found both Arapesh sexes "feminine," both Mundugumor sexes "masculine," the female Tschambuli "masculine," and the male Tschambuli "feminine"[14]). Unlike liberal feminists, however, who tend to deemphasize men's power over women and who quite often suggest "that men are simply fellow victims of sex-role conditioning,"[15] radical feminists insist that male power, in societies such as ours, is at the root of the social construction of gender.

At first, some radical feminists reasoned that if, to their own detriment, men are required to exhibit masculine characteristics only and if, to their own detriment, women are required to exhibit feminine characteristics only, then the solution to this problem is to permit each and every person to be androgynous—that is, to exhibit a full range of masculine *and* feminine qualities. Men should be permitted to explore their "feminine" dimensions and women their "masculine" ones. No human being should be forbidden the sense of wholeness that comes from being both male and female. But after more reflection on the concept of androgyny, many radical feminists concluded that androgyny is not really a liberation strategy—at least not for women.[16] Some antiandrogynists argued that the problem is not femininity in and of itself, but rather the low value that patriarchy assigns to female qualities such as nurturance, emotion, gentleness, and the like. They maintained that if we can just value the "feminine" as much as the "masculine," women's oppression will be a bad memory. Other antiandrogynists disagreed, insisting that femininity has to be the problem because it has been constructed by men for patriarchal purposes. In order to be liberated, women must give new gynocentric meanings to femininity. Femininity should no longer be understood as those traits that deviate from masculinity. On the contrary, femininity should be understood as a way of being that needs no external reference point. Still other antiandrogynists, reverting back to a "nature theory," argued that despite patriarchy's imposition upon all women of what amounts to a false, or inauthentic, *feminine* nature, many women have nonetheless unearthed a true, or authentic, *female* nature. Full personal freedom for a woman consists, then, in her ability to renounce her false feminine self in favor of her true female self.

It is difficult to fully appreciate all the nuances of radical feminist thought on gender. But it is even more difficult to adequately represent all that radical feminists have had to say about sexual oppression—about

male sexual domination and female sexual submission. Through pornography, prostitution, sexual harassment, rape, and woman battering,[17]
through foot binding, suttee, purdah, clitoridectomy, witch-burning, and
gynecology, men have controlled women's sexuality for male pleasure.[18]

At first, many radical feminists believed that in order to be liberated,
women must escape the confines of heterosexuality and create an exclusively
female sexuality through celibacy, autoeroticism, or lesbianism.[19] Alone,
or with other women, a woman can discover the true pleasures of sex.
More recently, some radical feminists have argued that no specific kind
of sexual experience should be prescribed as *the* best kind for a liberated
woman.[20] Each and every woman should be encouraged to experiment
sexually with herself, with other women, and even with men. As dangerous
as heterosexuality is for a woman within a patriarchal society—as difficult
as it can be for a woman to know when she truly wants to say "yes"
to a man's sexual advances—she must feel free to follow the lead of her
own desires.

Sexuality also plays a crucial role in psychoanalytic feminist theory,
but in a markedly different way. Whereas for radical feminists, the
centrality of sexuality emerges "from feminist practice on diverse issues,
including abortion, birth control, sterilization abuse, domestic battery,
rape, incest, lesbianism, sexual harassment, prostitution, female sexual
slavery, and pornography,"[21] for psychoanalytic feminists, the centrality
of sexuality arises out of Freudian theory and such theoretical concepts
as the pre-Oedipal stage and the Oedipus complex.

Psychoanalytic feminists find the root of women's oppression embedded
deep in her psyche. Originally, in the pre-Oedipal stage, all infants are
symbiotically attached to their mothers, whom they perceive as omnipotent. The mother-infant relationship is an ambivalent one, however,
because mother at times gives too much—her presence overwhelms—
and at other times gives too little—her absence disappoints. The pre-
Oedipal stage ends with the Oedipus complex, the process by which the
boy gives up his first love object, mother, in order to escape castration
at the hands of father. As a result of submitting his id (or desires) to
the superego (collective social conscience), the boy is fully integrated
into culture. Together with his father he will rule over nature and woman,
both of whom contain a similarly irrational power. In contrast to the
boy, the girl, who has no penis to lose, separates slowly from her first
love object, mother. As a result, the girl's integration into culture is
incomplete. She exists at the periphery or margin of culture as the one
who does not rule but is ruled, largely because, as Dorothy Dinnerstein
suggested, she fears her own power.[22]

Because the Oedipus complex is the root of male rule, or patriarchy,
some psychoanalytic feminists suggest that it is an invention of men's

imagination—a psychic contraption that everyone, especially women, should escape.[23] Others object that unless we are prepared to pull the string that unravels society, we must accept some version of the Oedipus complex as the experience that integrates the individual into society. In accepting *some* version of the complex, wrote Sherry Ortner, we need not also accept the Freudian version, according to which authority, autonomy, and universalism are labeled "male" and love, dependence, and particularism are labeled "female."[24] These labels, which attach more value to being male than to being female, are not essential to the Oedipus complex. Rather, they are simply the consequences of a child's actual experience with men and women. As Ortner saw it, dual parenting—as recommended also by Dorothy Dinnerstein and Nancy Chodorow[25]—and dual participation in the work force would change the gender valences of the Oedipus complex. Authority, autonomy, and universalism would no longer be the exclusive property of men; and love, dependence, and particularism would no longer be the exclusive property of woman.

But we are far from exhausting the riches of the feminist tradition. Simone de Beauvoir's *The Second Sex,* probably the key theoretical text of twentieth-century feminism, offered an existentialist explanation of woman's situation.[26] De Beauvoir argued that woman is oppressed by virtue of "otherness." Woman is the Other because she is *not*-man. Man is the self, the free, determining being who defines the meaning of his existence, and woman is the Other, the object whose meaning is determined for her. If woman is to become a self, a subject, she must, like man, transcend the definitions, labels, and essences limiting her existence. She must make herself be whatever she wants to be.

The task of weaving these several strands of feminist theory together seems to have been taken up most effectively by socialist feminists. In *Woman's Estate,* for example, Juliet Mitchell argued that women's condition is *overdetermined* by the structures of production (from Marxist feminists), reproduction and sexuality (from radical feminists), and the socialization of children (from liberal feminists).[27] Woman's status and function in all of these structures must change if she is to achieve anything approximating full liberation. Furthermore, as Mitchell made clear in her later book, *Psychoanalysis and Feminism,*[28] woman's interior world (her psyche) must also be transformed (as emphasized by psychoanalytic feminists), for without such a change, improvements in her exterior world will not liberate her from the kind of patriarchal thoughts that undermine her confidence (as emphasized by existentialist feminists).

Another powerful attempt to achieve a synthesis within feminist thought has been made by Alison Jaggar. Although conceding that each and every feminist perspective acknowledges the conflicting demands made on women as wives, mothers, daughters, lovers, and workers,[29] Jaggar insisted that what is unique about socialist feminism is its concerted effort to interrelate the myriad forms of women's oppression. Jagger used the unifying concept of alienation to explain how under capitalism, everything (work, sex, play) and everyone (family, friends) that could be a source of woman's integration as a person instead becomes a cause of her disintegration. Like Mitchell, Jaggar insisted that there are only complex explanations for female subordination. Once again, the emphasis of socialist feminism is on unity and integration, both in the sense of integrating all aspects of women's lives and in the sense of producing a unified feminist theory.

But these attempts to find integration and agreement, to establish one specifically feminist standpoint that could represent how women see the world have not gone without challenge.[30] Postmodern feminists regard this whole enterprise as yet another instantiation of "phallocentric" thought. It is typical "male thinking" to seek the "one, true, feminist story of reality."[31] For postmodernists, such a synthesis is neither feasible nor desirable. It is not feasible because women's experiences differ across class, racial, and cultural lines. It is not desirable because the One and the True are philosophical myths that have been used to club into submission the differences that, in point of empirical fact, best describe the human condition. That feminism is many and not one is to be expected because women are many and not one. The more feminist thoughts we have, the better. By refusing to center, congeal, and cement their separate thoughts into a unified truth too inflexible to change, feminists resist patriarchal dogma.

As attractive as the postmodern approach to feminism may be, some feminist theorists worry that an overemphasis on difference may lead to intellectual and political disintegration. If feminism is to be without any standpoint whatsoever, it becomes difficult to ground claims about what is good for women. It is a major challenge to contemporary feminism to reconcile the pressures for diversity and difference with those for integration and commonality. We need a home in which everyone has a room of her own, but one in which the walls are thin enough to permit a conversation, a community of friends in virtue, and partners in action. Only such a community can make feminist ethics and politics possible.

Contemporary feminists are not shrinking from this challenge. Indeed, it struck me many times, as I wrote and rewrote this book, just how artificial are the boundaries between the various feminist perspectives. It is enormously difficult to assign with confidence a "label" to many of the theorists discussed in this book. Is Juliet Mitchell, for example, a Marxist feminist? She does, after all, sometimes write as if *the* cause of women's oppression is the fact that we live in class society. Or do the powerful psychoanalytic themes of her later work persuade us instead that she is more of a psychoanalytic than a Marxist feminist? Or does her emphasis upon the overdetermination of women's oppression make her a socialist feminist? For my part, I finally decided to treat her twice, emphasizing *Psychoanalysis and Feminism* in the chapter on psychoanalytic feminism and *Woman's Estate* in the chapter on socialist feminism, but others might easily and just as reasonably have chosen differently.

But even as we recognize that these categories can be both limiting and distorting, I continue to believe that they serve a useful analytic purpose. These categories have helped me, for example, to locate myself on the spectrum of feminist thought—to recognize that at different stages of my life I have been far more liberal than radical, and vice versa; and that I am simultaneously attracted to both socialist and postmodern feminism but for very different reasons. Although I presently find it enormously difficult to assign to myself any one feminist label, this is because I find something valuable in each of the feminist perspectives to which I have been introduced. Perhaps this is a sign that the labels are obsolete. Then again, it may only be a sign that my feminism is not as consistent and coherent as it ought to be or, more sympathetically, a sign that I am growing as a thinker.

I have tried as much as possible to present the weaknesses as well as the strengths of each of the feminist perspectives presented here. In so doing, I have aimed not so much at *neutrality* as I have at *respect*. Each of these views has made a rich and lasting contribution to feminist thought, and it would be ungrateful and dishonest to denigrate any in the process of making a case for another. Readers looking for one "winning" view at the end of this book, a champion left standing after an intellectual free-for-all, will be disappointed. All these perspectives cannot be equally correct, and my own views and preferences will show along the way, but there is no need here for a definitive "final say." There is always, and there will be here, room for growth, improvement, reconsideration, expansion—for all those intellectual processes that free us from the authoritarian trap of "having to know it all."

But even though I allow for a generous voice, it is still necessary to speak, and as I speak throughout this book, I am painfully aware that I do not speak for womankind, for feminists, or for any wider circle at all. I speak out of a specific background of experience, as do we all, and I have tried very hard to avoid two possible mistakes: that of accepting an analysis simply because it resonated with my own experience and that of rejecting an analysis simply because it clashed with my own experience. Certainly, I have tried to avoid the trap of either accepting or rejecting a feminist theory merely on the basis of its ability or inability to fit an abstract, armchair analysis of "universal's woman's" experience.

Finally, this book is truly an *introduction* to some major themes in feminist thought. Anyone steeped in feminist theory and practice will immediately recognize just how partial and provisional it is. Limitations of time and space often forced me to sacrifice depth and/or breadth, and my own scholarly background and interests undoubtedly imposed other limitations. I hope that the shortcomings will spur others to do the job better someday. But my overriding hope is that each reader will be prompted to experience the power of a woman thinking herself into the fullness of her being.

CHAPTER ONE

———— ■ ————

Liberal Feminism

LIBERALISM, THE SCHOOL OF POLITICAL THOUGHT from which liberal feminism has evolved, is in the process of reconceptualizing, reconsidering, and restructuring itself,[1] which makes it difficult to determine the status of liberal feminist thought. If we wish to gauge the accuracy of Susan Wendell's provocative claim that liberal feminism has largely outgrown its original political base,[2] then we must survey the state of contemporary liberal thought and decide for ourselves whether liberal rhetoric does in fact resonate with feminist oratory. □

THE ROOTS OF LIBERAL FEMINISM

Alison Jaggar, in *Feminist Politics and Human Nature,*[3] observed that liberal political thought holds a conception of human nature that locates our uniqueness as human persons in our capacity for rationality. The statement that reason distinguishes us from other creatures is relatively uninformative, so liberals have attempted to define reason in various ways, stressing either its *moral* aspects or its *prudential* aspects. When reason is defined as the ability to comprehend the rational principles of morality, then the value of individual autonomy is stressed. In contrast, when reason is defined as the ability to calculate the best means to achieve some desired end, then the value of self-fulfillment is stressed.[4]

Whether liberals define reason largely in moral or prudential terms, they nevertheless concur that a just society allows individuals to exercise their autonomy and to fulfill themselves. The "right," liberals assert, must be given priority over the "good."[5] In other words, our whole system of individual rights is justified because these rights constitute a framework within which we can all choose our own separate goods, provided that we do not deprive others of theirs. Such a priority defends religious freedom, for example, neither on the grounds that it will increase the general welfare nor on the grounds that a godly life is inherently

11

worthier than a godless one, but simply on the grounds that people have a right to practice their own brand of spirituality. The same holds for all those rights we generally identify as fundamental.

The proviso that the right takes priority over the good complicates the construction of the just society. For if it is true, as most liberals claim, that resources are limited and that each individual, even when restrained by altruism,[6] has an interest in securing as many available resources as possible, then it will be a challenge to create political, economic, and social institutions that maximize the individual's freedom without jeopardizing the community's welfare.

When it comes to state interventions in the private sphere (family or domestic society),[7] liberals agree that the less we see of Big Brother in our bedrooms, bathrooms, kitchens, recreation rooms, and nurseries, the better. We all need places where we can, among family and friends, shed our public personae and become our "real" selves. When it comes to state intervention in the public sphere (civil or political society),[8] however, a difference of opinion emerges between so-called classical, or libertarian, liberals on the one hand and so-called welfare, or egalitarian, liberals on the other.[9]

For classical liberals, the ideal state protects civil liberties (for example, property rights, voting rights, freedom of speech, freedom of religion, freedom of association) and, instead of interfering with the free market, simply provides all individuals with an equal opportunity to determine their own accumulations within that market. For welfare liberals, in contrast, the ideal state focuses on economic justice rather than on civil liberties. As this more recent group of liberals sees it, individuals come to the market with differences based on initial advantage, inherent talent, and sheer luck. At times, these differences are so great that some individuals cannot take their fair share of what the market has to offer unless some adjustments are made to offset their liabilities. Due to this perceived state of affairs, welfare liberals call for such positive government intervention in the economy as legal services, school loans, food stamps, low-cost housing, Medicaid, Medicare, Social Security, and Aid to Families with Dependent Children so that the market does not perpetuate or otherwise solidify huge inequalities.

Although many nineteenth-century liberal feminists fit the classical, or libertarian, mold, most twentieth-century liberal feminists fit the welfare, or egalitarian, mold. In fact, when Susan Wendell (not a liberal feminist) described contemporary liberal feminists, she wrote, "I can safely say that liberal feminism is not committed to socialism, or it would be socialist feminism. Liberal feminists usually are, however, committed to major economic re-organization and considerable redistribution of wealth, since one of the modern political goals most closely associated with liberal feminism is equality of opportunity, which would undoubtedly require and lead to both."[10]

An egalitarianism that worries about all women's basic needs is probably more feminist than a libertarianism that is concerned only about a few women's rights. In this chapter, therefore, my aim in part is to determine whether liberal feminism is truly becoming more feminist, or whether this is simply wishful thinking on the part of those feminists who wish to affirm all schools of feminist thought, including those schools that have at times come close to celebrating male paradigms as human paradigms. □

HISTORICAL DEVELOPMENT
OF LIBERAL-FEMINIST THOUGHT

To discuss liberal feminism only in the context of some liberal feminists is, of course, a political choice and in this case one that reveals my candidates for the title of "quintessential liberal feminist." But it is also an analytic choice, a recognition that at times depth of treatment is preferable to breadth. Thus, my choices of Mary Wollstonecraft, John Stuart Mill, Harriet Taylor, and Betty Friedan are both politically charged and analytically motivated, as is my desire to focus on a group such as the National Organization for Women. I have chosen these liberal feminists because the drift of their thought is away from some of the less feminist assumptions of classical liberalism and toward some of the more feminist assumptions of welfare liberalism. Although this progression is by no means constant—*some* of Betty Friedan's work is a case in point[11]—it is certainly steady enough to warrant our continued interest in, and support for, the liberal feminist goal of "a just and compassionate society in which freedom flourishes."[12]

Liberal Feminism in the Eighteenth Century:
The Same Education for Women as for Men

In *The Radical Future of Liberal Feminism,* Zillah Eisenstein reminded us that Mary Wollstonecraft (1759–1799) was writing at a time when the economic and social position of European women was in decline. Up until the eighteenth century, productive work (work that generated an income from which a family could live) had been done in and around the family home by women as well as men. But then the forces of industrial capitalism began to draw labor out of the private home and into the public workplace. At first, this process of industrialization moved slowly and unevenly, leaving its strongest impact on married, bourgeois women. These women were the first to find themselves left at home with little productive, or income-generating, work to do. Married to relatively wealthy professional and entrepreneurial men, these women had no incentive to work productively outside the home or, in those cases where they had several servants, even "nonproductively" inside it.[13]

In reading *A Vindication of the Rights of Woman*,[14] we see how affluence worked against eighteenth-century married, bourgeois women. Wollstonecraft compared these "privileged" women (whom she hoped to inspire to a fully human mode of existence) to members of "the feathered race," birds confined to cages who have nothing to do but plume themselves and "stalk with mock majesty from perch to perch."[15] To be a middle-class lady is, according to Wollstonecraft, to sacrifice health, liberty, and virtue for whatever prestige, pleasure, and power a husband can provide. Kept women are enervated women. Because they are not allowed to exercise outdoors lest they tan their lily-white skin, they lack healthy bodies. Because they are not permitted to make their own decisions, they lack liberty. And because they are discouraged from developing their powers of reason—given that a great premium is placed on indulging self and gratifying others, especially men and children—they lack virtue.

Although Wollstonecraft did not use terms such as "socially constructed gender roles," she denied that women are, by nature, more pleasure seeking and pleasure giving than men. She reasoned that if men were confined to the same cages women find themselves locked in, they would develop the same characters.[16] If denied the chance to develop their rational powers, to become moral persons who have concerns, causes, and commitments beyond personal pleasure, men would become overly "emotional," a term Wollstonecraft tended to associate with hypersensitivity, extreme narcissism, and excessive self-indulgence.

Given her generally negative assessment of emotion and the extraordinarily high premium she placed on reason as the capacity that distinguishes human beings from brutes, it is no wonder that Wollstonecraft abhorred Jean-Jacques Rousseau's *Emile*.[17] In this classic of educational philosophy, Rousseau portrayed the development of rationality as the most important educational goal for boys but not for girls. Rousseau was committed to sexual dimorphism—that is, to a belief that "rational man" is the perfect complement for "emotional woman," and vice versa.[18] As he saw it, men should be educated in virtues such as courage, temperance, justice, and fortitude, whereas women should be educated in virtues such as patience, docility, good humor, and flexibility. Thus, Rousseau's ideal male student, Emile, studies the humanities, the social sciences, and the natural sciences, while Rousseau's ideal female student, Sophie, dabbles in music, art, fiction, and poetry, all the while refining her homemaking skills. Rousseau's hope was that the development of Emile's mental capacities will make him a rational, moral, self-governing, self-sufficient citizen and husband/father and that the development of Sophie's sensitivities will create in her an understanding, responsive wife and a caring, loving mother.

Wollstonecraft agreed with Rousseau's projections for Emile, but not with his projections for Sophie. Drawing no doubt upon her familiarity with certain middle-class ladies, she predicted that Sophie will be a detriment rather than a complement to her husband. Fed a steady diet of "novels, music, poetry, and gallantry," Sophie will become a creature of sensation, a slave to her passions.[19] Her sensibilities tingling, her passions erupting, her emotions churning, she will show no sense in performing her wifely and, especially, motherly duties.

Wollstonecraft's cure for Sophie was to let her, like Emile, be provided with a real education, one that sharpens and focuses her mind and gives her a chance to develop her rational and moral capacities, her full human potential. Initially, Wollstonecraft phrased her argument on behalf of Sophie's real education in utilitarian terms that stressed the social benefits likely to result from educational parity between men and women. Unlike emotional and dependent women, who are always shirking their domestic duties and indulging their carnal desires, rational and independent women tend to be "observant daughters," "affectionate sisters," "faithful wives," and "reasonable mothers."[20] The truly educated woman is able to manage her household—especially the children—"properly."[21] She wastes neither her time nor her energy on idle entertainments.

It would be a mistake, however, to think that Wollstonecraft's arguments on behalf of educational parity between men and women were all utility based. On the contrary, the view she usually took in *A Vindication* was remarkably akin to Immanuel Kant's view in *Groundwork of the Metaphysic of Morals*—namely, that unless a person acts autonomously, he or she is acting as less than a fully human person.[22] Wollstonecraft insisted that if rationality is the capacity that distinguishes brute animals from human persons, then unless girls are brute animals (a description that most men will probably resist when it comes to their own mothers, wives, and dauthers), women as well as men have this capacity. Thus, society owes girls the same education as boys simply because all persons deserve an equal chance to develop their rational and moral capacities so that they can achieve personhood.

Again and again, Wollstonecraft celebrated reason, usually at the expense of emotion. As Jane Roland Martin said, "in making her case for the rights of women . . . [Wollstonecraft] presents us with an ideal of female education that gives pride of place to traits traditionally associated with males at the expense of others traditionally associated with females."[23] It did not occur to Wollstonecraft to question the value of traditional male traits. Nor did it occur to her to blame children's lack of virtue on their absentee fathers who should be summoned, in her view, only when "chastisement" is necessary.[24]

The strength of Wollstonecraft's analysis was that she wanted women to be treated as, and to act as, autonomous decisionmakers. *A Vindication* was not so much a plea for political and economic liberty for women as an argument that women share the same rational human nature men do. Wollstonecraft recognized that it is in women's interest to be economically independent of men, but she provided women with few recommendations about how to achieve such a state of affairs.[25] Similarly, she recognized that in order to be legally independent of men, women need the same civil liberties as men have; but no sooner did she assert this than she went on to say that, practically speaking, it does not really matter whether women get voting rights or not because the whole system of legal representation is, after all, a corrupt and "convenient handle for despotism."[26]

Despite the limitations of her analysis, Wollstonecraft did present a vision of a woman, strong in mind and body, who is not a slave to her passions, her husband, or her children. For Wollstonecraft, the ideal woman is less interested in fulfilling herself—if by self-fulfillment is meant any sort of pandering to duty-distracting desires—than in exercising self-control.[27] In order to liberate herself from the oppressive roles of emotional cripple, petty shrew, and narcissistic sex object, a woman must, Wollstonecraft believed, obey the commands of reason and discharge her wifely and motherly duties faithfully.

What Wollstonecraft most wanted for woman is personhood. Woman is not, she asserted, the "toy of man, his rattle," which "must jingle in his ears whenever, dismissing reason, he chooses to be amused."[28] In other words, woman is not what the philosopher Kant called a "mere means," or instrument, to someone else's happiness or perfection. Rather, woman is what Kant called an "end," a rational agent whose dignity consists in having the capacity for self-determination.[29] To treat someone as a mere means is to treat her as less than a person, as someone who exists not for herself but as an appendage to someone else. So, for example, if a husband treats his wife as no more than a pretty indoor plant, he treats her as an object that he nurtures merely as a means to his own delight. Similarly, if a woman lets herself be so treated, she lets herself be treated in ways that do not accord with her status as a full human person. Rather than assuming responsibility for her own development and growing into a mighty, although gnarled, redwood, she forsakes her freedom and lets others make of her a stunted, although beautiful, bonsai tree.

Presumably, a real education—that is, the same education as is provided to a man—will allow a woman to assume responsibility for her own development and growth. But unless society also provides the equally educated woman with the same civil liberties and economic opportunities a man has, she will be able to exercise her hard won autonomy only within the private, or domestic, realm. As welcome as such a development would be, Wollstonecraft glossed over its limits.

Liberal Feminism in the Nineteenth Century: The Same Civil Rights and Economic Opportunities for Women as for Men

Writing approximately one hundred years later, John Stuart Mill and Harriet Taylor Mill joined Wollstonecraft in celebrating rationality. But they conceived of rationality both morally—as autonomous decision-making—and prudentially—as self-fulfillment, or using your head to get what you want. That their understanding of rationality differed from that of Wollstonecraft is not surprising because Mill and Taylor believed that the ordinary way to maximize aggregate utility (happiness/pleasure) is to permit individuals to pursue whatever they desire, provided of course that they do not hinder or obstruct each other in the process. Mill and Taylor also differed from Wollstonecraft in insisting that if we are to achieve sexual equality, or gender justice, then society must not only give women the same education as men; society must also provide women with the same civil liberties and economic opportunities that men enjoy.

Like Mary Wollstonecraft, who twice attempted suicide, refused marriage until late in life, and had a child out of wedlock, John Stuart Mill and Harriet Taylor led fairly unconventional lives. They met in 1830 when Harriet Taylor was already married to John Taylor and was the mother of two sons (a third child, Helen, would be born later). Harriet Taylor and J. S. Mill were immediately attracted to each other, both intellectually and emotionally, and they carried on a close, arguably Platonic relationship for twenty years, until the death of John Taylor, whereupon they married. During the years before her husband died, Harriet Taylor and Mill routinely saw each other for dinner and frequently spent weekends together along the English coast. John Taylor agreed to this arrangement in return for the "external formality" of Harriet residing "as his wife in his house."[30]

Due to their unorthodox bargain with John Taylor, Harriet Taylor and Mill found the time to author, separately and/or jointly, several essays on sexual equality. Although there is much scholarly debate about who deserves credit for which specific ideas in the essays they co-authored, it is generally agreed that they collaborated on the 1832 "Early Essays on Marriage and Divorce," that Harriet Taylor Mill was the primary author of the "Enfranchisement of Women" (1851), and that John Stuart

Mill was the primary author of "The Subjection of Women" (1869). As we shall see, the question of these works' authorship is significant because Taylor's views tended to be more explicitly feminist than Mill's.

Given their personal situation, it is not surprising that Mill and Taylor should have written essays on marriage and divorce laws. What *is* surprising is that they did not always agree on which legal reforms are in women's, and also children's, best interests. Taylor insisted that when a couple divorces, the mother should assume responsibility for the childrearing. Thus, Taylor, who left unchallenged traditional assumptions about the relative strength of maternal versus paternal ties, cautioned women to have few children. In contrast, Mill urged couples to marry late, have children late, and live in extended-family or commune-like situations so that, should divorce occur, the rhythm of the affected children's lives will not dramatically alter. An even greater difference between Taylor and Mill was evident in the issue of women's participation in the work force. Mill contested Taylor's view that in order to be fully liberated, a woman actually needs to work outside the home. As he saw it, so long as a woman is permitted to enter and leave the labor market at will, she is already fully liberated.[31]

Although Taylor, like Mill, adhered to many traditional assumptions about women's maternal nature and role, she nonetheless disagreed with his contention that the liberated woman's occupation is to "adorn and beautify" rather than to "support" life.[32] In the "Enfranchisement of Women," Taylor argued that sexual inequality is the result not of nature's decrees but of society's customs and traditions. This fact, according to Taylor, will become apparent to all as soon as women are given the following:

1. *Education* in primary and high schools, universities, medical, legal, and theological institutions.
2. *Partnership* in the labors and gains, risks, and remunerations of productive industry.
3. *A coequal share* in the formation and administration of laws—municipal, state, and national—through legislative assemblies, courts, and executive officers.[33]

Whereas Mill stressed education and a coequal share in his essays, Taylor frequently stressed partnership. Mill believed that even given the same education, economic opportunities, and civil liberties as men, women will still choose marriage and motherhood over other, competing occupations. But Taylor believed that if given free reign, "numbers" of women may trade in the "career" of marriage and motherhood for something else. If the choice for a woman is between devoting her life "to one *animal* function and its consequence"[34] on the one hand, and writing great books, discovering new worlds, and building mighty empires on the other, she may be easily prompted to choose a career in the arts, business, or politics instead of the "career" of marriage and motherhood.

Although the foregoing passage suggests that Taylor believed a woman had to choose between wifing and mothering on the one hand and working outside the home on the other, other passages in "Enfranchisement" indicate she believed a woman had a third option: namely, to add a career outside the home to her domestic career. The institution of marriage, asserted Taylor, can be made equal only if a woman, by virtue of her employment, first has a real chance to remain husbandless and, second, once married, has the confidence and sense of entitlement that come from contributing "materially to the support of the family."[35] Decidedly unimpressed by Mill's 1832 argument that women's economic equality would depress the economy and subsequently lower wages,[36] Taylor insisted that it is psychologically vital that every woman work, regardless of financial necessity: "Even if every woman, as matters now stand, had a claim on some man for support, how infinitely preferable is it that part of the income should be of the woman's earning, even if the aggregate sum were but little increased by it, rather than that she should be compelled to stand aside in order that men may be the sole earners, and the sole dispensers of what is earned."[37] In short, in order to be the partners rather than the servants of their husbands, wives must earn an income outside of the home.

In insisting that married as well as single women work, Taylor demonstrated her concern for gender equality in marriage but betrayed her classism. Zillah Eisenstein reminded us that by the second half of the nineteenth century, even most "middle-range middle-class women" could afford only one servant to help them do an amount of work that "was more than enough to keep two women busy."[38] Taylor glossed over this fact because the women who, according to her vision, will combine career and marriage will also have available to them a "panoply of domestic servants," presumably working-class females, to assist them.[39] Apparently, Taylor overlooked the problems inherent in this approach to the so-called double day, not the least being that it sets up invidious class distinctions among women. Only an upper-middle-class woman, wealthy enough to hire several relatively disadvantaged women, stands a realistic chance of combining career and marriage successfully.

Like Wollstonecraft, then, Taylor was writing not so much to all women as to a certain class of married women whose economic advantages would allow them to work outside the home without in any way jeopardizing the quality of life within it. But despite her classism, Taylor's analysis of women's oppression was more clearly woman centered than was Mill's. He tried to establish in "The Subjection of Women" that if women are recognized as fully rational and worthy of the same civil liberties and economic opportunities as men, society will reap benefits— public-spirited citizens for itself, intellectually stimulating spouses for husbands, a doubling of the "mass of mental faculties available for the higher service of humanity," and a multitude of very happy women.[40] Although Mill's arguments against the subjugation of women did not, according to political theorist Susan Okin, strictly require that he prove that women are men's exact equals—indeed most of the projected benefits of women's liberation could accrue even if women were somewhat less capable than men—he felt obliged to make a strong case for sexual equality.[41] Unlike Wollstonecraft, who tended to downplay the exceptional woman and put no "great stress on the example of a few women who, from having received a masculine education, have acquired courage and resolution,"[42] Mill used the exceptional woman to strengthen his case that all the differences claimed to exist between men and women are differences of average. No one who knows anything about human history, said Mill, can argue that *all* men are stronger and smarter than *all* women. That the average woman cannot do something that the average man can do does not justify a law or taboo that bars all women from attempting that something.[43]

According to Mill, even *if* all women are worse than all men at something, this still does not justify forbidding them from trying to do that thing anyway, for "what women by nature cannot do, it is quite superfluous to forbid them from doing. What they can do, but not so well as the men who are their competitors, competition suffices to exclude them from."[44] Although Mill believed that women are in fact men's equals, that they will fare quite well in any and all competitions with men, he conceded that there may be some biological sex differences between males and females. Like Wollstonecraft, however, he denied that there are intellectual and/or moral differences between men and women: "I do not know a more signal instance of the blindness with which the world, including the herd of studious men, ignore and pass over all the influences of social circumstances, than their silly depreciation of the intellectual, and silly panegyrics on the moral, nature of women."[45]

Like Wollstonecraft, Mill was quick to see that society has set up an ethical double standard that hurts women. Most of the "virtues" extolled in women are, in fact, negative character traits that impede women's progress toward personhood. This is equally true for an ostensibly negative trait (helplessness) or an ostensibly positive trait (unselfishness). Mill suggested that because women's concerns are confined to the private realm, the typical woman is preoccupied with her own concerns and those of her immediate family. She overestimates her family's wants and needs and underestimates those of society in general. As a result, her unselfishness takes the form of what is best described as extended egoism. Although she will spare no effort to further her husband's career and will work herself to exhaustion to put her children through school or to marry them off to good families, the typical wife's and mother's charity begins and ends at home. This is not the kind of unselfishness utilitarians such as Mill value. They value the kind that motivates people to take into account the good of the whole society as well as the good of the individual person or small family unit. Mill believed that were a woman given the same education as a man—that is, were she taught to pay attention to the universals as well as the particulars, to the forest as well as the trees—then she would develop genuine unselfishness. This belief explains Mill's passionate pleas for universal suffrage. One excellent way to introduce a woman to the larger picture is to give her the vote. Because morally responsible citizens assume that when it comes to forging public policy, collective good is more important than individual good, voting will remind women that even if charity begins at home, it must not end there.[46]

Mill went further than Wollstonecraft in challenging men's alleged intellectual superiority. Whereas Wollstonecraft admitted that even though men's and women's intellectual abilities are of the same *kind,* there is a possibility that women cannot attain the same *degree* of knowledge as men,[47] Mill argued that any intellectual achievement gap between men and women can be explained by man's more thorough education and by his privileged position. In fact, Mill was so eager to establish that men are not intellectually superior to women that he tended to err in the opposite direction by valorizing and celebrating women's attention to details, use of concrete examples, and intuitiveness.[48]

Given his high regard for woman's intellectual abilities, and given his admission that woman's time-consuming, energy-depleting, and concentration-fragmenting duties as wife and mother hold her back from success in the professions, it is curious that Mill, unlike Taylor, still believed that in the best possible world—with marriage a free contract between real equals, with legal separation and divorce easily available to wives, and with jobs open to women living outside the husband-wife relationship—most liberated women will continue to choose the career of family over other competing careers.

> Like a man when he chooses a profession, so, when a woman marries, it may in general be understood that she makes choice of the management of a household, and the bringing up of a family, as the first call upon her exertions, during as many years of her life as may be required for the purpose; and that

she renounces not all other objects and occupations, but all which are not consistent with the requirements of this.[49]

The reality as Mill saw it, then, is that with few exceptions, voluntary "wifing" and "mothering" are not simply a career but a full-time one at that.

Although Taylor's reflections on women's attitudes toward career-marriage tensions probably mirror reality more accurately than Mill's do, Taylor, like Mill, was ultimately a reformist, not a revolutionary. Taylor had the same blind spot Mill had—an unawareness that fathers are just as responsible for, and perhaps capable of, rearing their children as are mothers. To be sure, by insisting that women as well as men should work outside the home, Taylor did challenge the division of labor within the family, whereby the man earns the money and the woman manages its use; but Taylor's challenge to this familial status quo did not go far enough because she failed to link the flow of women into the public sphere to a counterflow of men into the private sphere. In my view, were husbands to parent alongside their wives, and were domestic duties equally divided, then neither husbands nor wives would have time for eight or more hours of work outside the home. Until the couple's children were school age, part-time employment would be the norm.

Liberal Feminism in the Twentieth Century: The Pluses and Minuses of Treating Women and Men the Same

Anyone who has read Wollstonecraft's *Vindication*, Taylor's "Enfranchisement," and Mill's "Subjection" cannot help but agree with Zillah Eisenstein that Betty Friedan's 1963 book, *The Feminine Mystique*,[50] was in some ways less "radical" than Wollstonecraft's, Taylor's or Mill's. Despite Friedan's implicit understanding of woman as a powerless sex class, she often wrote as if individual women can, through sheer effort, advance to the ranks of the powerful sex class known as "man."[51] Her tendency, at least in *The Feminine Mystique*, was to forget that this is easier said than done, so long as men are generally in charge of hiring and promoting.

According to Friedan, the "feminine mystique"—that is, the idea that women can find satisfaction exclusively in the traditional role of wife and mother—has left women, at least middle-class, suburban, white, heterosexual housewives, feeling empty and miserable. Deprived of meaningful goals, these women dust and polish their furniture as if they were Sisyphus rolling an enormous boulder up a steep hill only to have it roll down again. As if it were a sacred duty, they buy every conceivable labor-saving device, believing that the increase in efficiency will make them more competent homemakers. Soon their days are filled with empty time. To make this empty time seem meaningful they, consciously or unconsciously, convince themselves that they cannot possibly execute their wifely and motherly duties without expert advice. What the house-bound woman hopes to hear from the experts—from the legion of doctors, gynecologists, obstetricians, clinicians, pediatricians, counselors, psychiatrists, and ministers—is that being a wife and mother is a full-time job, the most important a woman can ever undertake.

Sometimes, however, not even the experts can convince her this job is a big enough challenge. Frustrated and frazzled, bored and beleaguered, she may turn to sex in hopes of finding the spice that makes life palatable and perhaps even delectable. She will paint her face and pad her breasts, sharpen her sexual techniques, girdle and strap the reality of her body into the image and likeness of a Hollywood starlet. She will do all this and more, according to Friedan, in the hope that sex will set her free. What she fails to realize is that her desire for sex is not really her own. Rather, it has been manufactured by the media not only as an opiate to dull her consciousness—to make her content with a boring existence—but also as a poison to spoil whatever meaningful relations she could have with her husband and children.[52]

Friedan's cure for suburban housewives' addiction to motherhood and wifehood was work outside the home. She warned that unless women in the United States get college educations and then use them productively in the full-time, public work force, they will be driven to strange manias and deep depressions. Friedan also cautioned that stay-at-home mothers do their children little good. Smothered as they are by the obsessive-compulsive love of their mothers, all children, but especially boys, grow up passive and immature. Therefore, even if contemporary, "liberated" women want to stay at home with their husbands and children, they should not be allowed to do so. Their partial absence will make their husbands and children into better people.[53]

Clearly, Friedan was not asking women to sacrifice marriage and motherhood for a high-powered career. "The assumption of your own identity, equality, and even political power does not mean you stop needing to love, and be loved by, a man, or that you stop caring for your own kids."[54] The error in the feminine mystique was its claim that women, if they wish to be normal as well as moral, ought to choose marriage and motherhood over career. But to think, as Mill and even Wollstonecraft did, that a woman who is a wife and mother has no time for a career is to limit her development as a full human person. Being a wife and mother, suggested Friedan, need make very few claims on a woman's time. Once a woman sees housework for what it is—something

to get out of the way, to be done "quickly and efficiently"—and sees
marriage and family for what it is—a part of her life, but not all of
it—she will find plenty of time and energy to develop her total self in
"creative work" outside the home.[55] Any woman, with just a bit of help,
can meet all of her wifely, motherly, and professional obligations without
hiring that team of domestic helpers Taylor suggested.

Although *The Feminine Mystique* helped explain why marriage and
motherhood are not enough for a certain kind of woman and why this
kind of woman needs to work outside the home, it failed to address a
whole host of issues deeper than "the problem that has no name"—
Friedan's tag for the dissatisfaction of the suburban, white, educated,
middle-class, heterosexual housewife in the United States. In particular,
The Feminine Mystique failed to consider just how difficult it would be
for even privileged women to combine marriage and motherhood with
a career unless major structural changes were made within, as well as
outside, the family. Like Wollstonecraft, Taylor, and Mill before her,
Friedan sent women out into the public realm without summoning men
into the private domain.

In *The Second Stage*,[56] written nearly a quarter century after *The
Feminine Mystique*, Friedan did consider the difficulty of combining
marriage and career. If women in the 1960s were victims of the *feminine*
mystique, said Friedan, then women in the 1980s were victims of the
feminist mystique.

> In the first stage, our aim was full participation [of the women's movement],
> power and voice in the mainstream. But we were diverted from our dream.
> And in our reaction against the feminine mystique, which defined women
> solely in terms of their relation to men as wives, mothers and homemakers,
> we sometimes seemed to fall into a *feminist* mystique which denied that core
> of women's personhood that is fulfilled through love, nurture, home.[57]

What diverted women from their dream in the 1960s and 1970s was,
according to Friedan, "sexual politics." She claimed it is counterproductive
for women to insist that all men are misogynistic pornographers, pimps,
sexual harassers, rapists, and woman batterers; such "man hating" is
unwarranted. In her estimation, not only do many men like and love
women; many women like and love men. Any feminism that fails to
recognize these facts will, of necessity, fail.

In addition to giving up sexual politics, women in the second stage
of the women's movement will have to cure themselves of the "feminist
mystique." In reaction to the feminine mystique of the 1960s, victims
of the 1980s feminist mystique embraced what Friedan perceived as a
destructive "male" model that was no better for women than it was for

men. Although many of these career women succeeded in becoming just as powerful and wealthy as career men, they are no happier than are the women who never got over the feminine mystique. In interviewing a large sample of these career women, Friedan repeatedly noted their disappointment at, and disillusionment with, the rewards of "success."

> I was the first woman in management here. I gave everything to the job. It was exciting at first, breaking in where women never were before. Now it's just a job. But it's the devastating loneliness that's the worst. I can't stand coming back to this apartment alone every night. I'd like a house, maybe a garden. Maybe I should have a kid, even without a father. At least then I'd have a family. There has to be some better way to live. A woman alone . . . [58]

A quarter century ago, Friedan would have advised this woman to go ahead and have that child because it is "easy" for an efficient woman to combine career and family. Today, as she watched Superwoman racing around on her way to a breakdown, Friedan admitted that no matter how efficient a woman is, career-marriage combinations are anything but easy. Superwoman, Friedan contended, seeks to be both the quintessential wife and mother—the *woman* who is slave to her husband and children, who not only meets but also anticipates their every need—and the quintessential careerist—the *man* who is slave to his boss, who consistently arrives to work early and stays late. What Superwoman forgets is that she cannot serve two masters and still have any time for herself.

Rather than urging Superwomen to retreat back into the private sphere from which they emerged in the mid-1960s, Friedan exhorted them and all women to (1) get the women's movement going again and (2) work with men for changes in public values, leadership styles, and institutional structures, which will enable all persons to achieve personal fulfillment, we must suppose, in the "mainstream."

Friedan's program for getting the women's movement going again was, as we shall see, vulnerable to several attacks, the first being that it did not go far enough in challenging the assumption that women are "responsible for the private life of their family members."[59] In criticizing Friedan's push for flextime, where employees are permitted to arrange their starting and leaving hours, Zillah Eisenstein observed: "It is never clear whether this arrangement is supposed to ease women's double burden (of family and work) or significantly restructure *who* is responsible for childcare and *how* this responsibility is carried out."[60] Eisenstein suspected that women, not men, will be the ones to take advantage of flextime and that gradually flextimers will come to be devalued as workers who are not really serious about their jobs.

In all fairness to Friedan, however, she did explicitly argue in *The Second Stage* (written after Eisenstein's book) that when solutions to the double day (a full-time career coupled with full-time wifing and mothering) are billed as "woman's benefits," they tend to reinforce the wrongheaded idea "that home and family belong to women's sphere rather than being a joint responsibility."[61] Unlike Wollstonecraft, Taylor, and Mill, Friedan seemed to advocate a balance of women's assimilation into the workplace with a counterassimilation of men into the family. Although this transition period will be a difficult one for men in particular, Friedan believed that men are ready for it. A majority of men in the United States already want, she wrote, to spend more time with their children, run less strenuously in the rat race, and develop their inner selves. For these men, women's liberation is men's liberation because at last a husband does not have to be "just a breadwinner."[62] No one either wants to, or has to, run the rat race anymore, observed Friedan.[63] Two part-time salaries, one earned by the husband and one earned by the wife, leave both mother and father ample time for home, children, and recreation.

Friedan's projections were perhaps too optimistic. Whereas some couples are willing and able to stop running the rat race, others are able but not willing, and still others are willing but not able. Although *The Second Stage* was filled with the testimony of overworked, underloved professionals who want to work less and enjoy life more, the pages of the *New York Times* routinely celebrate the lives of workaholic couples who are willing to sacrifice their entrails to the Moloch of material success. Whether people are as attracted to beta lifestyles as Friedan maintained is at least open to debate. Moreover, just because a couple wants to enjoy life more by working fewer hours does not mean they can afford to do this. Two physicians may live very well on two part-time salaries, but two short-order cooks cannot.

In many ways, the difference between the Betty Friedan of *The Feminine Mystique* and the Betty Friedan of *The Second Stage* is the difference between a classical liberal on the one hand and a welfare liberal on the other. In *The Second Stage,* Friedan reminded her readers that single mothers living on welfare, widowed homemakers living on social security, and divorced women living on substantially reduced incomes cannot be said to have the same opportunities to compete in the marketplace as do women who are fully supported by men. If equal opportunity is society's goal, insisted Friedan, then the government must provide single mothers, as well as widowed and/or divorced homemakers, with an adequate subsidy.[64]

Clearly, Friedan has been moving away from her 1960s espousal of gender-neutral laws as the type most likely to achieve quality between the sexes toward a 1980s advocacy of more gender-specific laws. In 1986, she joined a coalition supporting a California law requiring employers to grant as much as four months unpaid leave to women disabled by pregnancy or childbirth. In taking this stand, she alienated those members of the National Organization for Women who believed that to treat men and women equally should mean to treat them in the same way. If men should not receive special treatment on account of their sex, then neither should women. According to Friedan, this line of reasoning, which she herself pressed in the 1960s, is misguided. It asks the law to treat women as "male clones," when in fact, "there has to be a concept of equality that takes into account that women are the ones who have the babies."[65]

If Friedan is right, then liberalism is wrong to deny the differences between men and women, to press for gender-neutral laws and/or gender-blind policies. Thus, the task of the liberal feminist is to determine not what liberty and equality are for abstract rational persons, but what liberty and equality are for concrete men and women. This is a difficult and dangerous task, for, as Rosalind Rosenberg has stated, "If women as a group are allowed special benefits, you open up the group to charges that it is inferior. But, if we deny all differences, as the women's movement has so often done, you deflect attention from the disadvantages women labor under."[66]

Is there really a way to treat women and men *differently* yet *equally* without falling into some version of the pernicious "separate but equal" approach that characterized official race relations in the United States until the early 1960s? Or must liberal feminists work toward the elimination of differences as the first step toward true equality? If so, should women become like men in order to be equal with men? Or should men become like women in order to be equal with women? Or should both men and women become androgynous, each person combining the correct blend of positive masculine and feminine characteristics in order to be equal with every other person?

Whereas *The Feminine Mystique* pushed women to become like men, *The Second Stage* encouraged society to recognize the difference between the sexes until that day when men and women become androgynous human beings. Throughout *The Second Stage,* Friedan came close to replacing feminism with humanism. She repeatedly urged women to work *with* men and even *for* men if that will produce a truly human society. In a recent article about getting the women's movement "moving" again, she even urged women to move beyond "women's issues" in order "to redeem our democratic tradition and turn our nation's power to the interests of life."[67] But can feminism move beyond "women's issues" and remain feminism? Is it not premature to instruct women to become humanists, when the very notion of "human being" is still contested as male defined?

These are questions Friedan neither articulated nor addressed. But she is not the first liberal feminist who has found traditional humanism attractive. In their own distinct ways, what Wollstonecraft, Taylor, and Mill all wanted for women was personhood, full membership in the human community. The hypothesis that the ends and aims of feminism may, after all, be identical with those of humanism is a controversial one, but worth keeping in mind as we consider recent trends in liberal feminism.

Contemporary Directions in Liberal Feminism

Betty Friedan is just one of thousands of women who can be classified as liberal feminists. As Zillah Eisenstein has noted, Elizabeth Holtzman, Bella Abzug, Eleanor Smeal, Pat Schroeder, and Patsy Mink are liberal feminists, as are many other leaders and members of the National Organization for Women and the Women's Equity Action League.[68] Although these women are sometimes divided, they do agree that the single most important goal of woman's liberation is sexual equality, or, as it is sometimes termed, gender justice. What liberal feminists wish to do is free women from oppressive gender roles—that is, from those roles that have been used as excuses or justifications for giving women a lesser place, or no place at all, in the academy, the forum, and the marketplace. Liberal feminists argue that patriarchal society thinks women are ideally suited only for certain occupations—teaching, nursing, and clerking—and are largely incapable of other tasks—ruling, preaching, and investing. Whereas male-centered society deems appropriate for women those jobs that require traits associated with the feminine personality— ego-effacement and other-directedness—it deems appropriate for men those jobs that require traits associated with the masculine personality— self-confidence and self-aggrandizement. Liberal feminists claim that this type of gender stereotyping is terribly unequal and must be remedied if the goals of liberalism are to be realized for men as well as for women.

First, the argument proceeds, this conflation of *sex* and *gender* assumes that women lack the qualities necessary for those jobs typically associated with men, and vice versa. (For our purposes, the term *sex* refers to chromosomes [XX or XY], hormones, and anatomical structures; the term *gender* refers to personality traits and behavior patterns associated with the cultural constructs "masculinity" and "femininity" respectively.[69]) Consequently, all women are assumed a priori to be unqualified for many jobs in U.S. society; and in the past at least, it has not been considered wrong to pass legislation specifically barring women from such "masculine" jobs as mining and bartending or preventing women from working the night shift and/or overtime. Although most of this de jure gender discrimination is largely a memory today, de facto gender discrimination lingers on. Faced between voting for a male or a female candidate, for example, many voters unreflectively vote "male" on the grounds that women are too emotional—jittery, flighty, high-strung—to steer the ship of state. For similar reasons—if a "gut feeling" can be deemed a reason— employers prefer to hire men for certain positions, even when women are at least as qualified.

It is sometimes argued that men, no less than women, are the victims of de facto discrimination; that even if the law has always been kind to men, other vehicles of social control have not. Thus, we hear complaints about the parents who consistently refuse to hire male baby-sitters and about the nursery schools that are never able to find "qualified" men to fill their staff positions. Although liberal feminists are willing to sympathize with men who have found it difficult to pursue child-centered careers because of de facto discrimination, they nonetheless observe that the kind of de facto discrimination that men experience is not nearly as systematic as the kind that women experience. Society remains structured in ways that favor men and disfavor women in the competitive race for the goods with which our society rewards us: power, prestige, and money.

In focusing on those structural impediments to women's progress— obstacles that range from inhospitable, environmental features such as the smell of pipes, rococo chairs, and tweed jackets, to the lack of easily accessible, well-run, affordable child care facilities—contemporary liberal feminists disagree about how to eliminate these hurdles. Classical liberal feminists believe that after discriminatory laws and policies have been removed from the books, thereby formally enabling women to compete equally with men, not much else can be done about the fact that "birds of a feather will flock together"—that is, that a male senior professor, for example, will be more favorably disposed toward a male candidate than toward an equally qualified female candidate.

In contrast, welfare liberal feminists argue that government action should be taken to break up that "old flock (gang) of mine," especially when the failure to make feathers fly results in asymmetrical gender ratios such as the one that characterized Harvard University's senior art and sciences faculty in the early 1970s: 483 men and not one woman.[70] Society, these feminists claim, should not only compensate women for past injustices but should also eliminate socioeconomic, as well as legal, impediments to women's progress today. Thus, welfare liberal feminists advocate that female applicants to schools and jobs either be selected over *equally* qualified white male applicants (so-called preferential admissions or hiring) or (2) selected over *more,* as well as equally, qualified white male applicants, provided that the female applicants are still able to perform adequately (so-called reverse discrimination).[71] However, welfare liberal feminists believe that policies of preferential hiring and reverse discrimination are compatible with the essential values of liberalism only if they are regarded as transitional measures whose justification ceases when women have de facto as well as de jure equality with men.

We may think the only meaningful liberal feminist approaches to combating gender discrimination are the classical and welfare approaches, both of which rely heavily on legal remedies. But recently, some liberal feminists have provided us with another approach. This last is a conceptual approach that counteracts the inclination to think less of a person on account of that person's gender. The concept I refer to here is that of the androgynous person (from the Greek words for male [*andro*] and female [*gyn*] respectively. If we think the issue through, one fundamental way to ensure that no person will be discriminated against on account of his or her gender is to guide persons to exhibit both masculine and feminine gender traits and behaviors. Were we all androgynous, there would be no impetus to discriminate against someone simply on the basis of gender. (Presumably, there is no good reason to go so far as to mix and match male and female chromosomes, hormones, and anatomical structures—to create not only androgynous but hermaphroditic persons—unless, of course, the only way to end discrimination on the basis of sex as well as on the basis of gender is to genetically engineer persons who are neither all male nor all female but partially male and partially female. This, however, is a subject that goes beyond the boundaries of this book.)

Discussions of sex differences, gender roles, and androgyny have helped focus liberal feminists' drive toward liberty, equality, and fairness for all. According to Jane English, terms such as *sex roles* and *gender traits* denote "the patterns of behavior which the two sexes are socialized, encouraged, or coerced into adopting, ranging from 'sex-appropriate' personalities to interests and professions."[72] Boys are instructed to be masculine, girls to be feminine. Psychologists, anthropologists, and sociologists tend to define "masculine" and "feminine" in terms of prevailing cultural stereotypes, which are influenced by racial, class, and ethnic factors. Thus, to be masculine in the middle-class, white, Anglo-Saxon, Protestant United States is, among other things, to be rational, ambitious, and independent; and to be feminine is, among other things, to be emotional, nurturant, and dependent. To be sure, even within this segment of the population, exceptions to the rule will be found. Some biological males will manifest feminine gender traits, and some biological females will manifest masculine gender traits. But these individuals will be "exceptional" or "deviant." No matter what group of people (for example, working-class Italian Catholics) is under scrutiny, then, gender-role stereotyping will limit the individual's possibilities for development as a unique self. The woman who displays characteristics that her social group regards as "masculine" will be penalized together with the man who displays characteristics his social group regards as "feminine." She will be viewed as less than a *real* woman; he, as less than a *real* man.[73]

It is in order to liberate women, and also men, from the culturally constructed cages of masculinity and femininity that many liberal feminists advocate the formation of androgynous personalities.[74] Some liberal feminists favor monoandrogyny—the development of a single, or unitary, personality type that embodies the best of prevailing masculine and feminine gender traits. For example, Carolyn Heilbrun argued that in Western thought there is a long tradition defining the human as combining the best qualities of men and women. "Androgyny," said Heilbrun, " . . . seeks to liberate the individual from the confines of the appropriate. . . . [It] suggests . . . a full range of experience open to individuals who may, as women, be aggressive, as men, tender; it suggests a spectrum upon which human beings choose their places without regard to propriety or custom."[75] Psychologist Sandra Bem added that the brightest and most accomplished people register as highly androgynous on her personality scale. They possess, she said, a full complement of traditional female qualities—nurturance, compassion, tenderness, sensitivity, affiliativeness, cooperativeness—along with a full complement of traditional male qualities—aggressiveness, leadership, initiative, competitiveness.[76] (Recall once again that this list of traditional qualities probably needs to be modified depending on the racial, class, and ethnic characteristics of the group under consideration.) Other liberal feminists resist monoandrogyny and instead advocate polyandrogyny—the development of multiple personality types, some of which are totally masculine, others totally feminine, and still others a mixture.[77] Whether liberal feminists advocate monoandrogyny or polyandrogyny, however, they tend to agree that a person's biological sex should in no way determine his or her psychological and social gender. □

CRITIQUES OF LIBERAL FEMINISM

In recent years, liberal feminists have been reassessing their own position. In particular, they have recognized their tendency to accept male values as human values. In addition, they have been criticized by nonliberal feminists on a number of grounds, particularly their tendency to overemphasize the importance of individual freedom over that of the common good and their tendency to valorize a gender-neutral humanism over a gender-specific feminism.[78] Because criticisms of liberal feminism such as these provide valuable insights into the deeper structure of liberal feminism, they are worth careful consideration.

A Communitarian Critique of Liberal Feminism

Jean Bethke Elshtain is a controversial political theorist who has debated with many feminists the nature and function of the family. Although Elshtain's opponents claim that she is a neoconservative intent on redrawing the nineteenth-century boundary between a private "female" domain and a public "male" domain, Elshtain insists that this is not her intention. Rather, her purpose is to point out to liberal feminists that their emphasis on the priority of the individual over the community prevents people from coming together.[79] According to Elshtain, "There is no way to create real communities out of an aggregate of 'freely' choosing adults."[80] Her dissatisfaction with what she perceives as the liberal feminist position on the individual-community balance is coupled with dissatisfaction with what she perceives as the liberal feminist position on so-called male values. Elshtain accuses the Friedan of the 1960s— and, to a lesser extent, Wollstonecraft, Mill, and Taylor—of equating male being with human being, "manly" virtue with human virtue. In her critique, "Why Can't a Woman Be More like a Man?" Elshtain identified what she considered liberal feminism's three major flaws: (1) its claim that women *can* become like men if they set their minds to it; (2) its claim that most women *want* to become like men; and (3) its claim that all women *should* want to become like men, to aspire to masculine values.

With respect to the first claim—that women *can* become like men— Elshtain pointed to the liberal feminist belief that most differences between men and women are the products of culture rather than biology, of nurture rather than nature. Although Elshtain did not herself attempt to resolve the nature-nurture controversy, she faulted liberal feminists for having avoided it. Elshtain called this avoidance irresponsible and said it derived from a stubborn refusal among liberal feminists to entertain the possibility that some sex differences are biologically determined or from a fear that some questions about such differences are better left unasked because the answers could be used to justify the repression, suppression, and oppression of women. For these two reasons, many liberal feminists have, in Elshtain's estimation, become "excessive environmentalists"—that is, people who believe that their identities are the nearly exclusive product of socialization.[81] For Elshtain, environmentalists believe in nurture, not nature. But, she wondered, are all differences between men and women merely the product of culture? Can nature really be totally transcended?

Although she wanted to avoid both the reactionary position of contemporary sociobiologists—according to whom all of society is rooted in biology—and the sentimental speculations of some nineteenth- and also twentieth-century feminists—according to whom women are, by nature, morally better than men[82]—Elshtain accepts the view that some sex-based differences cannot be erased overnight without doing violence to the personal identities of the men and women so transformed. Her point is less that we must recognize as innate certain biological and psychological differences between men and women and more that unless we wish to do what Plato suggested in *The Republic*—namely, banish everyone over the age of twelve and begin an intensive program of centrally controlled and uniform socialization from infancy onward— we cannot hope, in just a few generations, to eliminate these differences between men and women. In sum, women *cannot* be like men unless they are prepared to commit themselves to the kind of social engineering and behavior modification that is incompatible with the spirit, if not also the letter, of liberal law.[83]

Liberal feminism also has a tendency, claimed Elshtain, to overestimate the number of women who *want* to be like men, who *want* to abandon roles such as "wife" and "mother" for roles such as "citizen" and "worker." Elshtain dismissed the claim that any woman who wants, more than anything else, to be a wife and mother is a benighted and befuddled victim of patriarchal "false consciousness." Patriarchy, in Elshtain's estimation, is simply not powerful enough to make mush out of millions of women's minds. If it were, she reasoned, we would be unable to provide a cogent explanation for the emergence of feminist "true consciousness" out of pervasive patriarchal socialization. What is more, it is not self-evident that "wifing" and "mothering" are, properly speaking, roles; and if they *are* roles, they are certainly not the kind a woman can shed as easily as a cat can shed hair.

> Mothering is *not* a "role" on par with being a file clerk, a scientist, or a member of the Air Force. Mothering is a complicated, rich, ambivalent, vexing, joyous activity which is biological, natural, social, symbolic, and emotional. It carries profoundly resonant emotional and sexual imperatives. A tendency to downplay the differences that pertain between, say, mothering and holding a job, not only drains our private relations of much of their significance, but also over-simplifies what can or should be done to alter things for women, who are frequently urged to change roles in order to solve their problems.[84]

Any woman whose *identity* is that of wife and mother is likely to become either angry or depressed if after investing years of her blood, sweat, tears, and toil in becoming and being a wife and mother, she is told that "wifing" and "mothering" are merely roles, and problematic ones at that. It is one thing to tell a woman she should change her hairstyle; it is quite another to tell her she should get a more meaningful identity.

Finally, as Elshtain saw it, liberal feminists are wrong to sing "a paean of praise to what Americans themselves call the 'rat race,'"[85] to suggest that either women or men *should* absorb traditional masculine values. Articles written for women about dressing for success, making it in a man's world, being careful not to cry in public, avoiding intimate friendships, being assertive, and playing hardball serve only to erode what may, after all, be best about women—their learned ability, according to Elshtain, to create and sustain community through involvement with friends and family. Women ought not to unlearn these lessons. Rather than encouraging each other to mimic the traditional behavior of successful men, who spend a minimum of time at home and a maximum of time at the office, women ought to work toward the kind of society in which men, as well as women, have as much time for friends and family as for business associates and professional colleagues.

Although she came close here to forwarding the problematic thesis that every wife and mother is the Virgin Mary in disguise, Elshtain insisted that maternal thinking "need not and must not descend into the sentimentalization that vitiated much Suffragist discourse."[86] Fearing that full participation in the public sphere would threaten female virtue, the suffragists reasoned that "the vote" alone was a way for women to reform the evil, deceitful, and ugly public realm without ever having to leave the supposed goodness, truth, and beauty of the private realm. As Elshtain saw it, had the suffragists not constructed a false polarity between male vice and female virtue, between the evil public world and the good private world—had they instead realized that the world we live in is one in which virtue and vice coexist and in which the public and private worlds intermingle—then they might have marched into the public world and then refused to leave it until it had absorbed whatever was in fact good about the private world from which they had come.[87]

A Socialist Feminist Critique of Liberal Feminism

One of the most recent criticisms of liberal feminism has been advanced by Alison Jaggar in *Feminist Politics and Human Nature*. Like Elshtain, Jaggar criticized liberal feminists for being too eager to adopt male values. However, her main criticism of liberal feminism was aimed at its conception of the self as a rational, autonomous agent. According to Jaggar, this is a fundamentally male conception. Because it is not obvious what is specifically male about rationality, autonomy, or agency, Jaggar's claim needs some elaboration.

To the degree that they put emphasis on the ability of humans to act rationally and autonomously, liberal feminists, in Jaggar's classification, are "normative dualists"—thinkers committed to the view that the functions and activities of the mind are somehow better than those of the body.[88] Eating, drinking, excreting, sleeping, and reproducing are not, according to this view, quintessential human activities because members of most other animal species also engage in them. Instead, what is special about human beings is their capacity to wonder, imagine, and comprehend, that seems to set them apart from the rest of animal creation.[89]

Jaggar speculated that because of the original sexual division of labor, mental activities and functions were increasingly emphasized over bodily activities and functions in Western liberal thought. Given his distance from nature, his undemanding reproductive and domestic roles, and the amount of time he was consequently able to spend cultivating the life of the mind, man tended to devalue the body, regarding it as a protective shell whose contours had little to do with his self-definition. In contrast, given her close ties to nature, her heavy reproductive and domestic roles, and the amount of time she consequently had to spend caring for bodies, woman tended to value the body, viewing it as essential to her personal identity. Because men have traditionally been the philosophers, observed Jaggar, their way of seeing themselves has come to dominate Western culture's collective history of ideas. As a result, all liberals, male or female, nonfeminist or feminist, tend to accept as truth the priority of the mental over the bodily, even when their own daily experiences contradict this belief.

Liberal feminism's adherence to normative dualism is problematic, according to Jaggar, not only because it leads to a devaluation of bodily activities and functions, but also because it usually leads to both political solipsism and political skepticism. (Political solipsism is the belief that the rational, autonomous person is essentially isolated, with needs and interests separate from, and even in opposition to, those of every other individual. Political skepticism is the belief that the fundamental questions of political philosophy—in what does human well-being and fulfillment consist, and what are the means to attain it?—have no common answer.) Thus, the immediate result of emphasizing mind over body, self over others is, apparently, a set of political attitudes and behaviors that put an extraordinary premium on liberty—on the rational, autonomous, independent, self-determining, isolated, separated, unique person being able to think, do, and be whatever he or she deems worthy.[90]

The liberal feminist who is both a normative dualist and a political solipsist fails, as Jaggar saw it, to recognize that all rational human persons are always and already in human community. As a result, the only satisfying explanation he or she can offer for *why* and *how* individuals form community is the contractarian one. Individuals are drawn together when they discover that they cannot attain their separate, conflicting ends by themselves—that they need to stop waging the war of all against all if they are to survive, let alone thrive. Thus, individuals contract, actually or hypothetically, to cede only as much of their liberty as they must in order to achieve as many of their own goals as possible.

Jaggar criticized political solipsism, this notion of the selfish self forced into community, on essentially empirical grounds. Once again, she emphasized that political solipsism is a male concept and that it is puzzling that liberal feminists should accept it. Women, who spend their lives weaving webs of human relationship and defining themselves and others in terms of these relationships, are not likely to think that individuals are prior to the community in any meaningful sense of the term *prior.* Any woman who has experienced pregnancy knows that a child is related to others even before it is born. The baby does not—indeed could not— exist as a lonely atom prior to subsequent entrance into the human community. Human infants are born helpless and require great care for many years. Because this care cannot be adequately provided by a single adult, humans live in social groups wherein resources are shared so that together they can bring their offspring to maturity. "Human interdependence," said Jaggar, "is . . . necessitated by human biology, and the assumption of individual self-sufficiency is plausible only if one ignores human biology."[91] Thus, she insisted, what liberal political theorists need to explain is not why isolated individuals come together but why communities ever dissolve. Competition, not cooperation, is the mystery.

To add force to her empirical argument, Jaggar observed that political solipsism makes no sense conceptually. Here she invoked Naomi Scheman's point that political solipsism requires belief in abstract individualism.[92] The abstract individual is one whose emotions, beliefs, abilities, and interests can supposedly be articulated and understood without any reference whatsoever to social context. Kant's person is this type of abstract individual—a pure reason unaffected/uninfected by either the empirical-psychological ego or the empirical-biological body. However, Kant's philosophy notwithstanding, we are not *abstract* individuals; we are *concrete* individuals able to identify certain of our physiological sensations as ones of sorrow, for example, only because we are "embedded in a social web of interpretation that serves to give meaning"[93] to our twitches and twinges, our moans and groans, our squealings and screamings. What is more, apart from this interpretive grid we are *self-less;* that is to say, our very identities are determined by our socially constituted wants and desires. We are, fundamentally, the selves our communities have created, a fact that challenges the U.S. myth of the self-sufficient individual.

Political skepticism collapses together with political solipsism, for it, too, depends on an overly abstract and individualistic conception of the self. Autonomy suggests that human beings are capable of choosing their ends, and as indicated earlier, the *right* to pursue one's ends is more important in the liberal tradition than the *goodness* of such ends. Thus, liberals, especially classical liberals, argue that the state must refrain as much as possible from citing any specific conception of human well-being and fulfillment as *the* good for one and all. In other words, the state is to serve as a traffic cop who, without passing judgment on drivers' stated destinations, simply makes sure their cars do not collide. But Jaggar believed that human biology has something to say not just against political solipsism but against political skepticism as well. Our choice of ends is not absolutely arbitrary. Whether we like it or not, human biology and psychology dictate a basic set of human wants and needs, and societies that ignore these wants and needs do not generally endure. Assuming that we want to endure, we should criticize so-called voluntary master-slave and sadomasochistic relationships, for example, on the grounds that because such relationships operate in defiance of what usually count as the basic psychological and physical wants and needs of persons, they are unlikely to thrive, even if they do manage to survive.[94] Thus, as Jaggar saw it, what makes an end "good" is not simply that someone has freely chosen it. This may be a necessary condition for its goodness, but certainly not a sufficient one. According to Jaggar, unless an end contributes, in some small way, to human surviving and thriving, it is probably bad. Thus, there are reasons for traffic cops not only to keep traffic moving but also to block off certain roads.[95] □

CONCLUSION

One way to react to the limitations of liberal feminism is to dismiss theirs as a bourgeois, white movement. In essence, this is precisely what Ellen Willis did in her 1975 article, "The Conservatism of *Ms.*" Willis faulted *Ms.* magazine, one of the chief organs of liberal feminism, for imposing a pseudofeminist "party line." After enumerating several points in this "line," Willis noted that their cumulative emphasis is a denial of women's pressing need to overthrow patriarchy and capitalism and an affirmation of women's supposed ability to make it in the system. Whatever *Ms.* has to offer women, insisted Ellis, it is not feminism.

At best, *Ms*'s self-improvement, individual-liberation philosophy is relevant only to an elite; basically it is an updated women's magazine fantasy. Instead of the sexy chick or the perfect homemaker, we now have a new image to live up to: the liberated woman. This fantasy, misrepresented as feminism, misleads some women, convinces others that "women's lib" has nothing to do with them, and plays into the hands of those who oppose any real change in women's condition.[96]

Willis's criticism may have been on target at the time, but *Ms.* has changed in the last decade. Its editors have been featuring articles that show, for example, how both classism and racism intersect with sexism, doubling and even tripling the oppression of some women. With some notable exceptions,[97] liberal feminists are moving away from their traditional belief that almost every woman can liberate herself "individually" by "throwing off" her conditioning and "unilaterally" rejecting her traditional sex roles.[98] Indeed, an increasing number of liberal feminists are willing to concede that individual actions *and* social structures prevent many, if not most, women from securing *full* liberation. In her qualified defense of liberal feminism, Susan Wendell wrote that in her experience, most liberal feminists believe that even a modest goal such as "creating equal employment opportunity for women" will require fairly ambitious means, such as "giving girls and boys the same early education and ending sex prejudice, which in turn will require major redistribution of resources and vast changes in consciousness."[99] Sexual equality cannot be achieved through women's willpower alone. Also necessary are major alterations in the deepest social and psychological structures.

Liberal feminism is by no means passé; it may even have the "radical future" Eisenstein predicted. For all its limitations, its strengths are undeniable. We owe to liberal feminists many, if not most, of the educational and legal reforms that have improved the quality of life for women. It is doubtful that without liberal feminists' efforts, so many women could have attained their newfound professional and occupational stature. To be sure, there is more to feminism than educational and legal reforms aimed primarily at increasing women's professional and occupational position. But such reforms are to be neither trivialized nor memorialized as *past* accomplishments. Liberal feminists still have much work to do before *all* women's educational, legal, and professional/ occupational gains are entirely secure.

CHAPTER TWO

— ■ —

Marxist Feminism

ALTHOUGH MARXIST FEMINISTS HAVE MUCH in common with socialist feminists (see Chapter 6), at least one major point divides these two traditions. Whereas socialist feminists believe that gender and class play an approximately equal role in any explanation of women's oppression, Marxist feminists believe that class ultimately better accounts for women's status and function(s). Under capitalism, they say, bourgeois women will not experience the same kind of oppression that proletarian women will. What is distinctive about Marxist feminism, then, is that it invites every woman, whether proletarian or bourgeois, to understand women's oppression not so much as the result of the intentional actions of individuals but as the product of the political, social, and economic structures associated with capitalism. □

SOME MARXIST CONCEPTS AND THEORIES: THEIR FEMINIST IMPLICATIONS

The Marxist Concept of Human Nature

Just as the liberal concept of human nature is present in liberal feminist thought, the Marxist concept of human nature is present in Marxist feminist thought. As I noted in Chapter 1, liberals believe that what distinguishes human beings from other animals is a specified set of abilities, such as the capacity for rationality and/or the use of language; a specified set of practices, such as religion, art, science; and a specified set of attitude and behavior patterns, such as competitiveness and the tendency to put self over other. Marxists reject this liberal theory of human nature, emphasizing instead that what makes us human is that we produce our means of subsistence. We are what we are because of what we do—specifically, what we do to meet our basic needs in productive activities such as fishing, farming, and building. Unlike bees, beavers, and ants, whose activities are governed by instinct, we create ourselves in the process of intentionally, or consciously, transforming and manipulating nature.[1]

In his *Introduction to Marx and Engels,* Richard Schmitt cautioned that the statement "Human beings create themselves" is not to be read as "Men and women, *individually,* make themselves what they are." Rather, it is to be read as "Men and women, through production, *collectively* create a society that, in turn, shapes them."[2] This emphasis on the collective accounts for the Marxist view of history. For the liberal, the ideas, thoughts, and values of individuals account for change over time. For the Marxist, material forces—that is, the production and reproduction of social life—are the prime movers in history. In the course of articulating this doctrine of how change takes place over time, a doctrine usually termed *historical materialism,* Marx stated that "the mode of production of material life conditions the general process of social, political, and intellectual life. It is not the consciousness of men that determines their existence, but their social existence that determines their consciousness."[3] In other words, Marx believed that a society's mode of production—that is, its forces of production (the raw materials, tools, and workers that actually produce goods) plus its relations of production (the ways in which the production process is organized)—generates a superstructure (a layer of legal, political, and social ideas) that, in turn, bolsters that mode. So, for example, Americans think in certain characteristic ways about liberty, equality, and freedom *because* their mode of production is capitalist.

Like Marxists in general, Marxist feminists also believe that social existence determines consciousness. "Women's work is never done" is for Marxist feminists more than an aphorism; it is a description of the *nature* of woman's work. Always on call, a woman forms a conception of herself that she would not have if her role in the family and at the workplace did not keep her socially and economically subordinate to men. Thus, Marxist feminists believe that to understand why women are oppressed in ways that men are not, we need to analyze the links between women's work status and women's self-image.[4]

The Marxist Theory of Economics

To the degree that Marxist feminists believe that women's work shapes women's thoughts and thus "female nature," they also believe that capitalism is a system of power relations as well as exchange relations. When capitalism is viewed as a system of exchange relations, it is described as a commodity or market society in which everything, including one's labor power, has a price and all transactions are fundamentally exchange transactions. When capitalism is viewed instead as a system of power relations, it is described as a society in which every kind of transactional relation is fundamentally exploitative. Thus, depending on one's emphasis, the worker-employer relationship can be looked at as either an exchange relationship in which equivalents are freely traded—labor for wages—or as a workplace struggle where the employer, who has superior power, coerces workers to labor ever harder for no discernible increase in wages.

Whereas the liberal views capitalism primarily as a system of voluntary exchange relations, the Marxist views capitalism primarily as a system of exploitative power relations. According to Marx, the value of any commodity that is produced for sale is determined by the amount of labor, or actual expenditure of human energy and intelligence, necessary to produce it.[5] More precisely, the value of any commodity is equal to the *direct* labor incorporated in the commodity by the worker, plus the *indirect* labor stored in the worker's artificial appendages—that is, the tools and machines that were made by the direct labor of his or her predecessors.[6] Because all commodities are worth exactly the labor necessary to produce them, and because the worker's labor power (capacity for work) is a commodity that can be bought and sold, the value of the worker's labor power is exactly the cost of whatever it takes (food, clothing, shelter) to maintain him or her throughout the work day. But there is a difference between what the employer pays the worker for his or her capacity to work (labor power) and the value that the worker actually creates when he or she puts these capacities to use in producing commodities.[7] Marx termed this difference *surplus value* and from it employers derive their profits. Thus, capitalism is an exploitative system because employers pay workers only for their labor power, without also paying them for the actual expenditure of human energy and intelligence that is taken out of them and transferred into the commodities they produce.[8]

At this point, it is natural to ask how the employer can induce workers to labor for more hours than are necessary to produce the value of their subsistence, especially when workers receive no compensation for this extra work. Why do not workers, after supplying the employer with labor value equal to the cost of their own subsistence, quit working? The answer, as Marx explained in *Capital,* is that employers have a monopoly on the means of production. Thus, workers must choose between being exploited and having no work at all. Just to survive, they must consent to wage contracts in which they are exploited. The liberal fiction that workers as well as employers routinely enter into mutually beneficial and freely signed contracts is shattered with the realization that capitalism is just as much a system of power relations as it is one of exchange relations. Workers are "free" to contract with employers only in the sense that no one is holding a gun to their heads as they sign on the dotted line. But even this small level of freedom is circumscribed, indeed negated, by the fact that because workers do not own the means of production, they must work for those who do. Thus, by virtue of their monopoly over factories, tools, land, means of transportation, and communication, employers are able to force workers to labor under exploitative conditions.

Significantly, there is another, less-discussed reason why employers are able to exploit workers under capitalism. According to Marx, capitalist ideologues lead workers and employers to focus on capitalism's surface structure of exchange relations.[9] As a result of this ideological ploy, termed by Marx the *fetishism of commodities,* workers gradually convince themselves that even though their money is very hard earned, there is nothing inherently wrong with the specific exchange relationship into which they have entered because life, in all its dimensions, is simply one colossal system of exchange relations.

Marxist feminists agree that conceiving of capitalism as merely a system of exchange relations obscures the fact that it is also a system of power relations. The fact that capitalist ideologues defend quasicontractual relations such as prostitution and surrogate motherhood as exercises of free choice is no accident, insist Marxist feminists. What these ideologues obscure are the power dynamics that better explain what is really behind these arrangements. When a woman chooses to sell her sexual or reproductive services only because she has nothing else of comparable value to sell in the marketplace, chances are that her choice is more coerced than free.

The Marxist Theory of Society

Like the Marxist analysis of power, the Marxist analysis of class has provided feminists with some of the conceptual tools necessary to understand women's oppression. Marx observed that every political economy—be it the primitive communal state, the slave epoch, the precapitalist, or bourgeois society—contains the seeds of its own destruction. To this rule, Marx thought, capitalism is no exception. Within capitalism, there are enough internal contradictions to generate a class division so severe that it will overwhelm the very system that produced it. On the other hand, there is the class of wealthy, property-owning employers; on the other hand, the class of poor, propertyless workers. Whereas the employer lives in luxury, the worker lives in squalor, receiving only a subsistence wage for laboring to exhaustion under inhumane factory conditions. To the degree that these classes become conscious of themselves *as* classes, class struggle inevitably ensues and ultimately topples the system that produced these very classes.[10]

It is important to emphasize the dynamic nature of class. Classes are not something that simply appear. They are slowly, and often painstakingly, formed by similarly situated people who share the same wants and needs. According to Marx, these people initially have no more unity than "potatoes in a sack of potatoes,"[11] but through a long and complex process of struggling together about issues of local, and later national, interest to them, they gradually become a unity, a true class. Because class unity is such a hard-won achievement, its importance cannot be overstated. As soon as a group of people is fully conscious of itself as a class, that group becomes extremely difficult to prevent from achieving its fundamental goals.

Class consciousness is clearly the opposite of false consciousness, which is a state of mind that impedes the creation and maintenance of true class unity by deceiving exploited people into thinking they are not really exploited and therefore are capable of acting and speaking as if they were just as free and equal as their exploiters. The bourgeoisie are especially adept at fooling the proletariat. Thus, for example, Marxists discredit egalitarian, or welfare, liberalism as a ruling-class ideology that tricks workers into falsely believing that at least some members of the bourgeoisie are concerned about the best interests of the proletariat. As Marxists see it, programs such as Medicare, Medicaid, and Aid to Families with Dependent Children serve only to impede the formation of a real working *class*. Overly grateful for these small sops, workers are less able to perceive just how bad their lot in life really is. As a result, they begin to perceive reality not with their own eyes but with those of the ruling class, and thus they are soon trapped within the status quo.

Given that Marxist feminists, like most feminists, are eager to bring women together, it is clear why Marxist teachings on class, class consciousness, and false consciousness play such a large role in Marxist feminist thought. Much debate within the Marxist feminist community has centered on the question, Do women per se constitute a class? On the one hand, given that some women are the wives, daughters, friends, or lovers of *bourgeois* men, whereas other women are the wives, daughters, friends, and lovers of *proletarian* men, it appears that women do not constitute, in the strict Marxist sense, a single class. On the other hand, most women's domestic experiences bear enough similarities to motivate unifying struggles such as the wages for housework campaign (see the section on "The Wages for Housework Campaign"). By struggling to have domestic work recognized as real work, many women have gained a consciousness of themselves as a "class" of workers, labeling as *false* the consciousness that calls it inappropriate to view wifely and motherly duties as work, merely because they are done out of love.[12]

By keeping the Marxist conceptions of class and class consciousness in mind, we can understand another crucial concept in both Marxist and Marxist feminist social theory—alienation. Like many Marxist terms, *alienation* is difficult to capture in a succinct dictionary definition. But in his book, *Karl Marx,* Allen Wood suggested that we are alienated "if we either experience our lives as meaningless or ourselves as worthless, or else are capable of sustaining a sense of meaning and self-worth only with the help of illusions about ourselves or our condition."[13] Robert Heilbroner added that alienation is a profoundly fragmenting experience. Things and/or persons who are, or should be, connected in some significant way are instead viewed as separate; and, as Heilbroner saw it, this sense of fragmentation, of meaninglessness, is particularly strong under capitalism.

As a result of invidious class distinctions and the highly specialized and highly segmented nature of the work process (think here of an assembly line or a government bureaucracy), human existence loses its unity and wholeness in four basic ways. First, workers are alienated from the *product* of their labor. Not only do workers have no say in what commodities they will or will not produce, but the fruits of their labor are snatched from them, so that the satisfaction of determining when, where, how, and to whom these commodities will be sold is denied them. In short, what should partially express and constitute their being-as-workers confronts them as a thing apart, a thing alien.[14]

Second, workers are alienated from *themselves* because when work is experienced as something unpleasant to be gotten through as quickly as possible, it is deadening. When the potential source of a worker's humanization becomes the actual source of his or her dehumanization, the worker is bound to undergo a major psychological crisis.

Third, workers are alienated from *other human beings* because the structure of the capitalist economy encourages—indeed forces—workers to see each other as competitors for jobs and promotions. When the potential source of the worker's community (the other as cooperator, as friend, as someone to be with) becomes the actual source of his or her isolation (the other as competitor, as enemy, as someone to avoid), the worker is bound to lose identification with those who have, at least in part, constituted his or her identity.

Fourth and finally, workers are alienated from *nature* because the kind of work they do and the conditions under which they do it make them see nature as an obstacle to their survival. This sets up an opposition where, in fact, a connectedness should exist—the connectedness among all elements in nature. Thus, the elimination of alienation, a return to a humane kind of labor, is an important justification for the overthrow of capitalism.[15]

In building on the idea that in capitalist society human relations take on an alienated nature in which "the individual only feels himself or herself when detached from others,"[16] Ann Foreman has argued that this state of affairs is worse for women than it is for men.

> The man exists in the social world of business and industry as well as in the family and therefore is able to express himself in these different spheres. For the woman, however, her place is within the home. Men's objectification within industry, through the expropriation of the product of their labour, takes the form of alienation. But the effect of alienation on the lives and consciousness of women takes on even more oppressive form. Men seek relief from their alienation through their relations with women; for women there is no relief. For these intimate relations are the very ones that are the essential structures of her oppression.[17]

As Foreman saw it, women's alienation is profoundly disturbing because women experience themselves only as the fulfillment of other people's needs. Foreman worried that in the absence of their families' and friends' needs of them, women have no sense of self. Thus, one of the primary tasks of Marxist feminism is to create the kind of world in which women will experience themselves as whole persons, as integrated rather than fragmented, or splintered, beings.

The Marxist Theory of Politics

Like those of economics and society, the Marxist theory of politics also offers to Marxist feminists an analysis of class that promises to liberate women from the forces that oppress them. In fact, much of Marxist thought is devoted to sketching a blueprint that will guide workers, be they male or female, as they struggle first to constitute themselves as a class, then to effect the transition from capitalism to socialism, and finally to achieve communism: full community and complete freedom.

As I noted previously, class struggle takes a certain form within the workplace because the interests of the employer are not those of the workers. Whereas it is in the employer's interests to use whatever tactics may be necessary (harassment, firing, violence) to get workers to work ever more effectively and efficiently for ever lower wages, it is in the workers' interests to use whatever countertactics may be necessary (slow-downs, sick time, strikes) to limit the extent to which their labor power is converted into actual labor and thereby to limit the employer's profits.

The relatively small and everyday class conflicts that occur, in this instance, within the capitalist workplace serve as preliminaries to the full-fledged, large-scale class struggles that, according to Marx, undergird the progress of history. Should workers, on account of their common exploitation and alienation, achieve class consciousness, they will be able to fight their employers for control over the means of production (for example, the nation's factories). If workers manage to take over the means of production, then a highly committed, politically savvy, well-trained group of revolutionaries (Marx called them the "vanguard of the revolution") will be able to marshall a broad-based attack against every political and economic structure of capitalism. If successful, this attack will lead to the replacement of capitalism with socialism, a political economy in which workers are neither exploited nor alienated; and, if all goes according to plan—if people under socialism learn how to cooperate—then communism, "the complete and conscious return of man himself as a social, that is, human being,"[18] will come into existence.

Under capitalism, Marx suggested, people are largely free to *do* what they want to do within the confines of the system, but they have little say in determining those confines, which make them behave like self-interested egoists. "Personality," said Marx, "is conditioned and determined by quite definite class relationships."[19] What Marx meant by this epigram, explained Richard Schmitt, is the following:

> Inasmuch as persons do certain jobs in society, they tend to acquire certain character traits, interests, habits, and so on. Without such adaptations to the demands of their particular occupations, they would not be able to do a great job. A capitalist who cannot bear to win in competition, or to outsmart someone, will not be a capitalist for long. A worker who is unwilling to take orders will not work very often. In this way we are shaped by the work environment, and this fact limits personal freedom for it limits what we can choose to be.[20]

In contrast to the persons living under capitalism, persons living under communism are free not only to *do* but also to *be* what they want because they have the power to structure the system that shapes them.

If we read between these lines, we can appreciate another of Marxism's major appeals to women: its promise to reconstitute human nature in ways that preclude all the pernicious dichotomies that have made slaves of some and masters of others. Marxism also promises to make people free, a promise that women would like to see someone keep; and, indeed, there is something very liberating about the idea of women and men constructing together the social structures and social roles that will permit both genders to realize their full human potential.

Although this brief introduction to some frequently discussed Marxist concepts does not do justice to the richness of the Marxist tradition, it does help us pinpoint the major task of the Marxist feminist: namely, to give feminist vision to the originally "sex-blind" categories and concepts of Marxist thought. Indeed, as Michèle Barrett has written, the main goal of the Marxist feminist is "to identify the operation of gender relations as and where they may be distinct from, or connected with, the processes of production and reproduction understood by historical materialism."[21] What accounts for the dynamic nature of Marxist feminist thought, then, is that human beings remain in flux, moving both through space and through time. As long as the mode of production and systems of appropriation and exploitation keep changing, the Marxist feminist will need to relate these changes to developments in the organization of sexuality, domestic production, and the household. To the degree that this intricate relationship is understood and transformed, women will be set free from the material conditions that have traditionally impeded their progress toward a nonexploitative and nonalienated mode of existence. □

FRIEDRICH ENGELS: *THE ORIGIN OF THE FAMILY, PRIVATE PROPERTY, AND THE STATE*

Although the fathers of Marxism have not taken women's oppression nearly as seriously as workers' oppression, some of them have offered explanations for why it is that women are oppressed qua women. With Marx's apparent blessing, Engels wrote *The Origin of the Family, Private Property, and the State* (1845), in which he showed how changes in the material conditions of people affect the organization of their family relations. He argued that before the family, or structured conjugal relations, there existed a primitive state of "promiscuous intercourse"[22]—a total free-for-all where every woman was fair game for every man and vice versa. All were essentially married to all. As the product of natural selection, suggested Engels, various kinds of blood relative were gradually excluded from consideration as eligible marriage partners.[23] As fewer and fewer women in the tribal group became available to any given man, individual men began to put forcible claims on individual women as their personal possessions. As a result, the pairing family, in which one man is married to one woman, came into existence.

Noting that when a man took a woman, he came to live in *her* household, Engels interpreted this rape-like act not as a sign of women's subordination but as a sign of women's economic power. Because women's work was vital for the tribe's survival,[24] and because women produced most of the material goods (for example, bedding, clothing, cookingware, tools) that could be passed on to future generations, Engels concluded that early pairing societies were probably matrilineal (inheritance and lines of descent traced through the mother).

In a digression, Engels speculated that pairing societies were probably not only matrilineal but also matriarchal (women have political and social as well as economic power).[25] But his main, and certainly less debatable, point remained that whatever status woman had in times past, it was derived from her position in the household, the primitive center of production.[26] Only if the site of production changed would she lose her superior position.[27] This, claimed Engels, was precisely what happened. The "domestication of animals and the breeding of herds" led to an entirely new source of wealth for the human community.[28] Because men were in control of the tribe's animals (Engels did not tell us *why*),[29] the relative power of men and women shifted in favor of men, as they were able to meet the tribe's milk and meat needs by raising not only enough animals but an actual surplus.

This surplus constituted an accumulation of wealth that men could use as a means of intergens exchange. Now that men possessed more than enough of a valuable socioeconomic good, the issue of inheritance took on major significance for them. Inheritance, directed through the mother's line, was originally a minor matter of the bequest of a "house, clothing, crude ornaments and the tools for obtaining and preparing food—boats, weapons and domestic utensils of the simplest kind."[30] As production outside the household began to outstrip production within it, the traditional sexual division of labor between men and women, which had supposedly arisen out of the physiological differences between the sexes—specifically, the *sex act*[31]—took on new social meanings. As men's work and production grew in importance, not only did the value of women's work and production decrease; so, too, did their status within society. Because men now possessed something of much more value than what women possessed, and because men, for some unexplained reason, suddenly wanted *their own* children to get *their* possessions, they exerted enormous pressure to convert society from a matrilineal one into a patriarchal one. As Engels phrased it, mother right had "to be overthrown, and overthrown it was."[32]

Engels regarded this conversion as pivotal in its impact on women's position in society because the "overthrow of mother right" constituted *"the world-historic defeat of the female sex."*[33] Having produced and staked a claim to wealth, man took control of the household, reducing woman to the "slave" of his carnal desire and a "mere instrument for the production of his children."[34] In this new familial order, the husband rules by virtue of his economic power, which led Engels to say of the husband that "he is the bourgeois and the wife represents the proletariat."[35]

Engels believed that because man's control of woman is rooted in the fact that he, not she, controls the property, the oppression of women will cease only with the dissolution of the institution of private property.

The emergence of private property and the shift to patrilineage also explains for Engels the transition to the monogamous family. Because women give birth, the mother of any child is always known. However, the identity of the father is never certain because a woman could have been impregnated by a man other than her husband. To secure their wives' marital fidelity, men supposedly seek to impose an institution of compulsory monogamy on women. Ideally, husbands should be as monogamous as their wives, but patriarchal society does not *require* marital fidelity from its men. Thus, according to Engels, the sole purpose of the institution of monogamy is to serve as a vehicle for the orderly transfer of a father's private property to his children. Male dominance, first in the form of patrilineage and then of patriarchy, is simply the result of the class division between the propertied man and the propertyless woman. Engels commented that monogamy was "the first form of the family to be based not on natural but on economic conditions,"[36] which suggests that the monogamous family is the product not of love and commitment but of power plays and economic exigencies. Only the elimination of class society—of women's economic dependence on men— will allow men and women to enter marriages based on love.

Given that monogamous marriage is a social institution that has nothing to do with love and everything to do with private property, Engels argued that if wives are to be emancipated from their husbands, women must first become economically independent of men. In fact, the first presupposition for the emancipation of women is "the reintroduction of the entire female sex into public industry"; the second is the socialization of housework and childrearing.[37]

Interestingly, Engels believed that proletarian women experience less oppression than do bourgeois women. As he saw it, the bourgeois family consists of a relationship between a husband and a wife in which the husband agrees to support his wife provided that she promises to remain sexually faithful to him and to reproduce only his legitimate heirs. Engels was not one to mince words: "This marriage of convenience often enough turns into the crassest prostitution—sometimes on both sides, but much more generally on the part of the wife, who differs from the ordinary courtesan only in that she does not hire out her body, like a wageworker, on piecework, but sells it into slavery once for all."[38]

Unlike the bourgeois marriage, the proletarian marriage is not, in Engels's estimation, a mode of prostitution because the material conditions of the proletarian family differ substantially from those of the bourgeois family. Not only is the proletariat's lack of private property significant in removing the primary male incentive for monogamy—namely, the reproduction of legitimate heirs for one's property—but the general employment of proletarian women as workers outside the home leads to a measure of equality between husband and wife that, according to Engels, provides the foundation of true "sex-love." In addition to these differences, the household authority of the proletarian husband, unlike that of the bourgeois husband, is not likely to receive the full support of the legal establishment. For all these reasons, Engels concluded (according to Barrett) that in the proletarian home, all "the material foundations of male dominance had ceased to exist (other than in the form of residual brutality)."[39]

Although Engels's *Origin* remains influential in Marxist feminist thinking on the family and women's oppression, its failings have not gone unnoticed. Jane Flax, who writes within the Marxist tradition, has recently argued that the book is in several ways a flawed analysis of women's oppression. Engels began the *Origin* in a promising enough way, asserting both that "the ultimate determinants of all history" are "the production and reproduction of life" and that kinship, understood as the system that determines with whom it is permissible to have sexual relations, is the organizing matrix of society.[40] Having paid his respects to the reproduction of life, however, Engels quickly reoriented his analysis to the production of life, which remained for him the primary means of comprehending class struggle and, hence, historical movement. As a result, Engels explained the overthrow of "mother-right" simply as a change in the mode of production; community property is overthrown by private property. But given that community property is associated with *women* and private property with *men,* Flax suspected that the overthrow of mother-right (*if,* indeed, it ever existed) probably reflected a change in the mode of reproduction at least as much as in the mode of production. "The overthrow of matriarchy was a political as well as economic revolution in which men as men subdued or destroyed the privileged (or perhaps equal) position of women for a number of historically possible reasons (such as men discovering their role in reproduction and/or asserting control over reproduction)."[41]

What was even more worrisome than Engels's slighting of reproduction-of-life factors, insisted Flax, was his belief that there was an original sexual division of labor. Without explaining how this came to be, Engels simply stated that in the tribe women were charged with the care of the household, whereas men provided food and engaged in productive work. As I mentioned, the sexual division of labor originated, for Engels as well as for Marx, from the "division of labor in the sexual act."[42] But, as Alison Jaggar pointed out, "if we take this remark seriously, it implies that, no matter how much society may seek to abolish the division of labor, such divisions are always likely to re-emerge so long as 'the division of labor in the sexual act' remains."[43] Even if there is nothing inherently wrong with a sexual division of labor, the fact remains that in every culture women's work, regardless of its nature, is seen as less valuable than men's work.[44] We must suspect, therefore, that the sexual division of labor, rooted in the institution of heterosexuality, is at least as responsible for women's oppression as is the institution of private property—a point that Engels failed to address and that led him to valorize the proletariat family/marriage over the bourgeois family/marriage. Thus, it is not clear that the program for women's liberation that begins with women's entrance into public industry, continues with women's domestic labor being taken over by service industries, and peaks in class struggle against capitalist exploiters, will, in and of itself, end women's oppression. □

CONTEMPORARY MARXIST FEMINISM

Marxist theory appears to have little room for questions that deal directly with women's reproductive and sexual concerns (contraception, sterilization, and abortion; pornography, prostitution, sexual harassment, rape, and woman battering), and as a result Marxist feminists have tended to focus on women's work-related concerns. In so doing, they have helped us understand, among other things, how the institution of the family is related to capitalism; how women's domestic work is trivialized as not *real* work; and, finally, how women are generally given the most boring and low-paying jobs. As we shall see, even if the nature and function of woman's work are not complete explanations for gender oppression, they are at least very convincing partial ones.

The Family, or Household, Under Capitalism

Prior to industrial capitalism, the family, or household, was the site of production. Parents, their children, and assorted relatives all worked together to reproduce themselves generationally as well as transgenerationally; and the work women did—cooking, canning, planting, preserving, childbearing, and childrearing—was as central to the economic activity of this extended family as the work men did. But with industrialization and the transfer of goods production from the private household to the public workplace, women, who for the most part did not initially enter the public workplace, were regarded as "nonproductive" in contrast to "productive," wage-earning men.

To regard women's work—the production of people—as nonproductive when compared to men's work—the production of things—is, according to Engels's theory, a failure to understand what the term *production* includes.[45]

> According to the materialistic conception, the determining factor in history is, in the final instance, the production and reproduction of immediate life. This, again, is of a twofold character: on the one side, the production of the means of existence, of food, clothing and shelter and the tools necessary for that production; on the other side, the production of human beings themselves, the propagation of the species. The social organization under which the people of a particular historical epoch live is determined by both kinds of production.[46]

Engels's words notwithstanding, even in contemporary socialist countries there is a tendency to conceive as "unproductive" the very large job of reproducing the labor force—a job for which women in socialist, as well as capitalist, countries are primarily responsible. As a result, investment in the socialization of domestic work and child care is, in Hilda Scott's words, "the Cinderella of every socialist budget."[47] While socialist planners endlessly debate the wisdom of diverting funds away from industrial and military development and toward socialized housework and child care, socialist women, she wrote, wait to be freed of the burdens of the double day.

If women's work is the Cinderella of the socialist budget, it is also the neglected stepdaughter of the capitalist budget. As much as it can, capitalism needs to keep women working "for free" in the household, even when it also needs them working for low wages in the workplace. Marx and Engels had predicted that under capitalism, the whole of the working class, including women and children above a very low age, would have to enter the public work force in order to together earn a family wage. With no one left within the household, or family, to reproduce the labor power of working-class men, men as well as women and most children "would be exploited *individually* as wage labourers reproducing their own individual means of consumption/reproduction."[48] A proletarian revolution would then be easy to foment because virtually all of the working class would be feeling the direct results of exploitation.

Although Marx and Engels correctly predicted that working-class women and even children would enter the work force, they failed to realize that as victims of false consciousness, working-class people would react to their increasing exploitation under capitalism not by revolting but by gradually removing first their children and then their women from the work force in an effort to approximate the bourgeois life-style. Liberal reformist laws banned children from the workplace and limited the number of hours women, especially pregnant women, could spend there. At the same time, the unions strove to increase men's wages so that they could bring home a "family wage" singlehandedly. Although unmarried women were still welcome in the workplace, more and more they found themselves doing there the equivalent of women's work: sewing, weaving, ironing, nursing, teaching, cleaning. Married women were also welcome in the workplace from time to time, especially during the world wars when women were permitted to do men's as well as women's work. For the most part, however, working-class women stayed at home with their children, while their husbands went to work.

The Socialization of Domestic Labor
Versus Wages for Housework

What angered many Marxist feminists most about the description of the nature and function of women's work under capitalism was its trivialization of women's work. Women were increasingly regarded as mere consumers, as if the role of men was to earn wages and that of women was simply to spend them on "the right products of capitalist industry."[49] But, said Margaret Benston, women are primarily producers and only secondarily consumers. In fact, as Benston saw it, women constitute a class: namely, that class of people "responsible for the production of simple use-values in those activities associated with the home and family."[50]

In claiming that women are the class responsible for the production of simple use-values (things such as meals that are cooked to be eaten by the family rather than to be packaged for sale alongside the Swanson and Armour frozen entrees), Benston wished to make clear that just because a woman does not sell the products of her labor, her work is no less difficult. Benston was concerned that unless a woman is freed from her heavy domestic duties, including child care, her entrance into the work force will be a step away from, rather than toward, liberation.

> At all times household work is the responsibility of women. When they are working outside the home they must somehow manage to get both outside job and housework done (or they supervise a substitute for the housework). Women, particularly married women with children, who work outside the home simply do two jobs; their participation in the labor force is only allowed if they continue to fulfill their first responsibility in the home. This is particularly evident in countries like Russia and those in Eastern Europe where expanded opportunities for women in the labor force have not brought about a corresponding expansion in their liberty. Equal access to jobs outside the home, while one of the preconditions for women's liberation, will not in itself be sufficient to give equality for women; as long as work in the home remains a matter of private production and is the responsibility of women, they will simply carry a double work-load.[51]

To introduce a woman into public industry without simultaneously socializing the jobs of cooking, cleaning, and child care is, in Benston's opinion, to make her oppressed condition even worse.

It is conceivable, she conceded, that the socialization of domestic work will lead to a woman's doing the same work outside the home tomorrow as she does inside the home today. A change to communal eating arrangements, for example, might simply mean moving a woman from her small, private, individual kitchen into a large, public, communal one. Benston predicted, however, that even this simple change will represent progress for women. The significance of socializing domestic work is not that it will necessarily free women from it, but rather that it will enable everyone to recognize how socially necessary such work is. As soon as everyone realizes just how difficult domestic work is, society will no longer have grounds for the oppression of women as parasitic people of inferior value. In sum, for Benston, the socialization of private house-keeping and tending children is *the* single factor that will end women's oppression as a group and that will give each and every woman the respect she deserves.

The Wages for Housework Campaign

Some Marxist Feminist Arguments for Waged Housework

Although Benston, in contrast to Engels, assigned priority to the socialization of domestic labor rather than to the en masse entrance of women into public industry, she remained within the orthodox Marxist fold. In "Women and the Subversion of the Community," Mariarosa Dalla Costa and Selma James made the unorthodox Marxist claim that women's domestic work is productive not in the colloquial sense of being "useful" but in the strict Marxist sense of "creating surplus value."[52] No woman has to *enter* the productive work force, for all women are already in it, even if no one recognizes the fact. Women's work is the necessary condition for all other labor, from which, in turn, surplus value is extracted. By providing current (and future) workers not only with food and clothes, but also with emotional and domestic comfort, women keep the cogs of the capitalist machine running.

Given their view of women's domestic work as productive work, it is not surprising that Dalla Costa and James's program for women's liberation differed not only from Benston's but also from Engels's. As these two leaders of the "wages for housework" campaign saw it, women who enter public industry work a double day that begins with paid, recognized work on the assembly line and ends with unpaid, unrecognized work at home. The way to end this inequity, said Dalla Costa and James, is for women to demand wages for housework.

Like other advocates of waged housework, Dalla Costa and James proposed that the state (the government and employers), not individual men (husbands, fathers, and boyfriends), pay wages to housewives[53] because *capital* ultimately profits from women's exploitation.[54] The state, when required to pay women for housework, will not be able to accumulate huge profits while housewives work themselves to the bone for a pittance.

Advocates of waged housework maintain that wages need not take the form of a paycheck. Such wages can be dispensed in the form of payments to welfare mothers for the work they have been doing in the home or in the form of child care for any mother who is overburdened with work. If the state refuses to pay housewives wages, then housewives should strike. According to advocates of waged housework, some housewives (married or single women who are not paid, or not paid enough, for providing services to men and/or children) have already gone on strike. When a woman divorces her husband, she is "refusing the work" that goes along with having a husband around the house. Similarly, when a woman practices contraception or has an abortion, she is refusing to take on the extra work a large family would bring. Finally, when a secretary says "no" to making coffee, or a teacher says "no" to taking her students on extra field trips, or a nurse says "no" to working eighteen-hour shifts, she is refusing to work "for love"—that is, for free. Such rebellions on the part of women have revolutionary potential, for capitalism needs women to produce labor power in men and children.[55]

Some Marxist Feminist Arguments Against Waged Housework

Despite the power of Dalla Costa and James's line of reasoning, the emerging consensus among Marxist feminists outside their immediate circle is that, ultimately, wages for housework is neither feasible nor desirable as a liberatory strategy for women. It is not entirely feasible because even if the state pays out wages to housewives, it will do so in a way that will preserve itself. Contrary to the pipedreams of some wages for housework campaigners, the state has no intention of going under as it pays a salary to housewives that, on several reliable estimates, would exceed the salary of the average woman in the work force two- or threefold.[56] What the state is likely to do, said Barbara Bergmann, is put a special tax on married men, which after it is collected might be distributed to their wives by the Internal Revenue Service. Depending on how large the tax bite was on her husband's dollar—and there is reason to believe that it would be hefty—the wife's paycheck would, insofar as the family's real income is concerned, represent a mere status gain. Alternatively, the state could pay housewives out of its ordinary revenue. If it took this approach, the state would tax everyone regardless of whether he or she was living in a household serviced by a housewife.

The net effect of this scheme would be to overly burden single people and two-earner families who are, on the average, already less well off than single-earner families, where the husband works outside the home and the wife within it. As a result, this scheme would "encourage women to become and remain housewives."[57]

This last point, made by Barbara Bergmann in *The Economic Emergence of Women*, summarizes what many Marxist feminists are finding undesirable about the wages for housework campaign. In the first place, wages for housework would have the effect of keeping a woman isolated in her own home, where she has few opportunities to do other than increasingly trivial work. Carol Lopate observed:

> The decrease in house size and the mechanization of housework have meant that the housewife is potentially left with much greater leisure time; however, she is often kept busy buying, using, and repairing the devices and their attachments which are theoretically geared toward saving her time. Moreover, the trivial, manufactured tasks which many of these technological aids perform are hardly a source of satisfaction for housewives. Max-Pacs may give "perfect coffee every time," but even a compliment about her coffee can offer little more than fleeting satisfaction to the housewife. Finally, schools, nurseries, day care, and television have taken from mothers much of their responsibility for the socialization of their children.[58]

Second, by demanding wages for housework, the housewife would be contributing to capitalism's tendency to commodify everything, including husband-wife and mother-child relationships. Third, being paid for housework would give a woman little incentive to work outside the household. As a result, just when it looked as if it might weaken, the sexual division of labor would actually ossify. Men would feel no pressure to do "women's work," and women would have no incentive to do "men's work."[59]

If breaking down the division of sexual labor is one of the ultimate goals of Marxist feminists, then paying housewives for housework seems at best a distraction and at worst an impediment. It would be far better to take Benston's recommendations and socialize housework and child care. Even if a woman winds up doing "women's work" outside of the home, it will give her an opportunity to work with other women and to form a class consciousness; and if a woman is paid what her work is truly worth, at least some of "women's work" might become appealing to men who can earn a decent wage doing it.

Yet another argument against the wages for housework campaign is that it undercuts the traditional Marxist emphasis on reintegrating women into social production. As Nancy Holmstrom and others see it, the writings of Benston, Dalla Costa, and James, for example, are flawed for at least two reasons. First, it is simply not true that women constitute a class in the Marxist sense of the term *class*. Benston's characterization of women as the class of people who produce simple use-values for home consumption, like Dalla Costa and James's suggestion that, to the extent she serves a man, each and every women belongs to the unitary housewife class, works only if we ignore the class differences that exist among women. Whatever the wife of a millionaire and her maid have in common, it does not seem to be their material conditions. Women, according to Nancy Holmstrom, come in all classes, and although all women are oppressed as women, they are not all equally oppressed. Indeed, as Holmstrom saw it, there are significant differences between the ways in which working-class women are oppressed and the ways in which middle- and upper-class women are oppressed.

> Working class women are super-exploited in their wage work and exploited in their domestic work. In other ways as well they suffer more from sexism than do middle- and upper-class women. They have less reproductive freedom in that they have less access to abortion, contraception and child care, and are often subject to sterilization abuse. They are also more subject to sexual abuse on the job and in the streets. Hence the interests of working-class women are more consistently opposed to sexism as well as capitalism than are the interests of middle- and upper-class women.[60]

In addition to making the arguable claim that women constitute a single class, Benston, Dalla Costa, and James are faulted for a second, equally substantial reason. To the degree that they emphasize the ways in which stay-at-home housewives serve the interests of capital, these three thinkers neglect the ways in which capital also needs women in the work force. Some of the most recent Marxist feminist thought has underscored the fact that fewer and fewer women are exclusively housewives. The material barriers that used to keep women out of the capitalist work force have been lowered. Because of advances in birth control, a woman who wishes to have children is better able to space her pregnancies than in the past; and because of labor-saving devices, convenience foods, and other "timesavers," a woman is able to tend her home in less time than in previous eras.[61] These two developments, combined with the effects of the 1960s women's liberation movement, the increasing need for two incomes, and the proliferation of service-oriented, or women's-work jobs, have contributed to major changes in the composition of the contemporary work force. Today, more than 45 percent of the U.S. work force is female.[62]

The fact that nearly half of the work force is female indicates that capital wants and indeed needs women in the work force. What this bald statistic does not show, however, is that capital wants/needs women in the work force largely because women's work does not command as much compensation as men's work. Moreover, this bald statistic does not show capital's unwillingness to make the lives of women workers easier by providing the kinds of service—especially adequate care for the young, the old, and the infirm—that would release women from the pressures of the double day. Because capital is unwilling to reduce its profits in order to pay workers the kind of wage they need to hire domestic help, workers need to do most of their own cooking, cleaning, and people care.[63] To be sure, the working class could decide not to live in traditional nuclear families, thereby releasing women from the domestic duties associated with this mode of human organization. But for largely ideological reasons, working-class men and women wish to maintain—at least as an ideal—the nuclear family. When domestic work becomes so burdensome that two fully employed people cannot possibly handle it without costly outside help (imagine, for example, if a couple becomes the proud parents of twins, if an aged parent suffers from Alzheimer's disease, or if a beloved adolescent contracts AIDS), chances are that one or the other will drop down to part-time or even no-time employment status. Although there is no abstract capitalist law mandating that the person who drops out of the work force should be female rather than male, in most cases the woman will stay at home if the work to be done there is both time consuming and costly. This state of affairs has two primary causes: (1) as it now stands, because of women's traditional absence from or intermittent participation in the work force, women's wages are generally lower than men's wages (see next section on comparable worth); and (2) historically, the "exigencies of biological reproduction" were such that women often had to leave work as a result of the stresses and strains associated with multiple pregnancies and caring for newborn infants.[64] The best way to destroy this vicious cycle is, in the opinion of many Marxist feminists, to pay women as well as men the wages that would permit all workers, regardless of gender, to work full-time without either men or women being doomed to the double day.

Comparable Worth

The criticisms that have most recently been directed against a preoccupation with the housewife and the inequitable manner in which the sexual division of labor operates in the household have caused many Marxist feminists to refocus attention on the inequitable manner in which this same sexual division of labor operates in the workplace. The overall assessment of these thinkers is that, at least under capitalism, when a woman enters public industry, she tends to do women's work there:

teaching, nursing, clerking, cooking, sewing, and the like. Moreover, as in the household, this work is undervalued, given that, on the average, a woman's salary is less than two-thirds of a man's for comparable work.

Although a feminist does not have to be a Marxist in order to be a comparable worth advocate, Marxist feminists, unlike liberal feminists, for example, see not only *reformist* but *revolutionary* potential in the movement. As an issue, comparable worth is, in the estimation of many Marxist feminists, an opportunity to challenge the market basis of wages— that is, to force us to reconsider why we pay some people so much and others so little.[65] Women in the 1980s, like their 1960s counterparts, earned just sixty-four cents for every dollar that men earned. Even when this wage differential is adjusted for such factors as educational preparation, work experience, or labor force commitment, at least half of the gap between male and female wages goes unexplained. Many social scientists attribute this gap to job segregation according to sex. Women in female-dominated occupations typically earn far less than men in male-dominated occupations. For example, secretaries, 99 percent of whom are female, earn an average of $12,000 annually, whereas truck drivers, 98 percent of whom are male, earn $16,300; and child care workers, 87 percent of whom are female, earn $7,900 annually, whereas mail carriers, 88 percent of whom are male, earn $21,000 annually.[66] But why should a truck driver earn so much more than a nurse or a mail carrier so much more than a child care worker? Is it because truck driving and mail carrying are so much more physically, psychologically, and/or intellectually demanding than nursing and child caring? Or is it because truck drivers and mail carriers are so much more valuable to their respective employers than nurses and child care workers are to theirs? Or is it simply because most truck drivers and mail carriers are *men* and most nurses and child care workers are *women*?

Convinced that a person's gender is the best explanation for why that person's salary is either high or low, comparable worth advocates, be they Marxist or non-Marxist, urge employers to evaluate their employees objectively—that is, without paying attention to their race, class, ethnicity, or gender. In order to evaluate a job or worker objectively, all that the employer needs do is to sum up the "worth points" for the four components found in most jobs: (1) knowledge and skills, or the total amount of information or dexterity needed to perform the job; (2) mental demands, or the extent to which the job requires decisionmaking; (3) accountability, or the amount of supervision the job entails; and (4) "working conditions," such as how physically safe the job is.[67] When Norman D. Willis and Associates used this index to establish the worth points for various jobs performed in the state of Washington, they found the following disparities:

A Food Service I, at 93 points, earned an average salary of $472 per month, while a Delivery Truck Driver I, at 94 points, earned $792; a Clerical Supervisor III, at 305 points earned an average of $794. A Nurse Practitioner II, at 385 points, had average earnings of $832, the same as those of a Boiler Operator with only 144 points. A Homemaker I, with 198 points and an average salary of $462, had the lowest earnings of all evaluated jobs.[68]

After reflecting upon the Willis and Associates' study, a federal court judge in Tacoma, Washington, ruled that the state was in violation of Title VII of the 1964 Civil Rights Act, which prohibits discrimination by type of employment and level of compensation, and that the state of Washington should eliminate pay gaps within its system.[69]

Marxist feminists support comparable worth for two sets of reasons—one having to do with assessing the feminization of poverty, the other with assessing the value of work. Because nearly half of all poor families are headed by women, and because women are the primary recipients of Food Stamps, Legal Services, and Medicaid, if wage-earning women were paid what their jobs are worth, these women would be able to support themselves and their families adequately without being forced, in one way or another, to attach themselves to men as an additional source of income. In reply to the objection that capital will respond to any mandatory hiking of women's wages with "automation, elimination of state programs, and runaway shops to countries in which women still provide a super-exploitable labor force," Marxist feminists concede that comparable worth must be pursued in conjunction with job-security demands, retraining programs, and plant-closing legislation.[70] In reply to the further objection that, like wages for housework, comparable worth will have the effect of keeping women in traditionally female jobs, Marxist feminists observe that as traditionally female jobs offer higher wages, men may be attracted to at least some of them.[71]

In addition to seeing comparable worth as a way to alleviate women's poverty, Marxist feminists see it as a way to equalize wages. Even if comparable worth supporters currently believe it possible to rank jobs on the basis of some set of *objective* criteria or another, over time they will recognize that criteria such as knowledge and skills, mental demands, accountability, and working conditions are, in fact, *subjective*. Teresa Amott and Julie Matthaei have commented that

> if the discussion of what makes work worthy is extended to the grass roots, we may well determine that all jobs are equally worthy. We may decide that workers in unskilled, routinized jobs may be doing the hardest work of all, for such work saps and denies their very humanity. Why should those whose jobs give them the most opportunity to develop and use their abilities also

be paid the most? The traditional argument—that higher pay must be offered as an incentive for workers to gain skills and training—is contradicted by the fact that our highly paid jobs attract many more workers than employers demand. And given unequal access to education and training, a hierarchical pay scheme becomes a mechanism for the intergenerational transmission of wealth privilege, with its historically-linked racism, sexism, and classism.[72]

Whether the value we assign to work is this subjective is certainly debatable. Nevertheless, many Marxist feminists derive satisfaction from the thought that as a result of the comparable worth movement, capitalist assumptions about what kind of work counts as valuable could be seriously, even permanently, undermined. □

CRITIQUES OF MARXIST FEMINISM

Marxist feminists have remained committed to the core teaching of Engels's *Origin*. To a greater or lesser degree, they still urge women to enter public industry, and they still press for the full socialization of housework and child care. What is more, they remain attracted to programs that aim to destroy the family as an *economic* unit—as a structure that serves to bolster the capitalist system. Finally, Marxist feminists—more than any other group of feminists—have made women's economic well-being and independence their primary concern and have focused on the intersection between women's experience as workers and their position in the family.

Although non-Marxist feminists have directed several criticisms against the wages for housework campaign and the comparable worth movement, their main criticism of Marxist feminism has been what they perceive as its simplistic conception of the family and preoccupation with the nature and function of women's work as the only or best means of understanding and ending women's oppression. In the following two sections we see how Jean Bethke Elshtain's communitarian, even traditionalist, critique of Marxist feminists differs from the more sympathetic, but no less thoroughgoing, critique by socialist feminist Alison Jaggar.

A Communitarian Critique of Marxist Feminism

In *Public Man, Private Woman*, Jean Bethke Elshtain was particularly critical of what some Marxist feminists have had to say about the family under capitalism. As she saw it, the family is not simply and finally the Frankensteinian creature of capitalism, manufactured to reproduce labor power at women's expense. Rather, the family is the only place where human beings can still find some love, security, and comfort—indeed, the only place where human beings can still make decisions based on something other than a monetary bottom line.[73]

Elshtain saw the family not only as a capitalist counterculture, but as the best protection against the tendencies of a totalizing state that cannot tolerate diversity of any sort. What most distressed Elshtain about Marxist feminism was what she regarded as its inability to recognize the salutary role the family can play in preserving social diversity. Were the state the only socializing mechanism in society, all individuals would be inculcated with the same set of values. As a result, they would find it difficult to gain a critical perspective on the society that had produced them. An individual family allows for this critical perspective because its values are somewhat idiosyncratic. Pacifist families react to an arms buildup differently than nonpacifist families do; religious families react to prayer in public schools differently than atheist families do; and so on. This is not to say, insisted Elshtain, that an individual family's values are always better than those of society as a whole. Rather, this is to say that if children do not experience the unique texture of their own family's world view, then when children from different families get together, they will have no differences to examine—the kinds of difference that challenge children, and for that matter adults, to recognize that what *is* does not have to be.[74]

Clearly, children were a priority for Elshtain. Although she believed they can derive considerable benefit from contact with a variety of adults, she refused to regard children as a collective blessing in which every adult has an *equal* stake. It is appealing to view children as a group of little people everyone should love, but Elshtain nevertheless believed that something very important is lost in depriving a child of the intimacy that comes from daily contact with one or two adults committed to parenting him or her. Although she conceded the drawback of identifying a child as "*my* child," Elshtain also observed that it is an even greater drawback for a child to belong to everyone in general but to no one in particular.[75]

What is worrisome about Elshtain's critique is that it may play into the stereotypical image some Americans have of "communist" women who bear children only to let dispassionate day care attendants rear them. When Marxist feminists have condemned the family, they have condemned it as an economic unit, not as an emotional unit. No less an authority than Engels spoke eloquently about the future of the family.

What we can now conjecture about the way in which sexual relations will be ordered after the impending overthrow of capitalist production is mainly of a negative character, limited to the most part to what will disappear. But what will there be new? That will be answered when a new generation has grown up: a generation of men who never in their lives have known what it is to buy a woman's surrender with money or any other social instrument of power; a generation of women who have never known what it is to give themselves to a man from any other considerations than real love or to refuse to give themselves to their lover from fear of the economic consequences. When these people are in the world, they will care precious little what anybody today thinks they ought to do; they will make their own practice . . . and that will be the end of it.[76]

Although Engels's words invite Marxist feminists to envision radically new forms of relationships, commitments, households, and communities— "families" in which heterosexuals, homosexuals, and/or lesbians live together—in point of fact what they have most often envisioned is the traditional biological family minus its gender-oppressive features. In truly socialist society, men marry women, but these women are their equals; heterosexual couples have their own *biological* children, but these children are regarded as everyone's *social* children; and people set up individual households even though little in the way of cooking, cleaning, and/or child care goes on in them. Far from rejecting Elshtain's family, then, many a Marxist feminist has actually embraced it as a description of the family under authentic socialism.[77]

A Socialist Feminist Critique of Marxist Feminism

Alison Jaggar's critique of Marxist feminism is written from the perspective of a socialist feminist who worries that Marxist feminists have said too little about women's oppression by *men*. When Marxist feminists speak about women's oppression, they argue that capital is the primary oppressor of women as workers and that men are, at most, the secondary oppressors of women as women. Thus, Jaggar wonders what is specifically feminist about a Marxist feminist analysis and whether it is true that men are merely the secondary, or indirect, oppressors of women. She also wonders whether there is adequate room in a Marxist feminist analysis to express dissatisfaction about those women's issues that are unrelated to the nature and function of women's work.

It concerns Jaggar that Marxist feminists rarely discuss issues related to sex; and that when they do, they tend to compare sex to work—for instance, by comparing not only the pimp-prostitute relation but also the husband-wife relation to the bourgeoisie-proletariat relation, as if male-female relations in marriage and prostitution were exploitative and alienating in precisely the same way as those in employer-employee relationships. Marxist feminists draw these analogies, said Jaggar, because they want "to link the Marxist treatment of women's sex-specific oppression with Marxism's main theoretical system, incorporating domination both

by class and by gender in the same explanatory framework."[78] As Jaggar
saw it, however, Marxist feminists cannot make this important link
because, for all the similarities, exploited workers do not suffer in the
same way as do oppressed wives and/or prostitutes.

In order to disassociate class exploitation from gender oppression,
Jaggar began, interestingly, with a detailed recapitulation of the Marxist
feminist analysis of prostitution and marriage. Because women in a
capitalist system do not have sufficient access to the workplace, in order
to survive they must connect themselves financially to men. In this
respect, Marxist feminists see the difference between a prostitute and a
wife as merely a difference of degree, not of kind. Both sell themselves—
that is, their sexual services and, in the case of wives, also their domestic
and nurturing services—for economic livelihood. Whether this takes the
form of "hustling" or of a "marriage of convenience" is a secondary
issue for Marxists. The wife, according to this view, "differs from the
ordinary courtesan only in that she does not hire out her body, like a
wage-worker, on piecework, but sells it into slavery once and for all."[79]

In describing bourgeois marriage as a form of prostitution, Marx and
Engels implicitly accepted that the services that can be prostituted are
not limited to sexual services. Housework, child care, and emotional
support are also services sold by the prostitute-wife. From this, Jaggar
pointed out, it is only a short step to describing the sale of a number
of other services as types or instances of prostitution.[80] In fact, Marx
asserted exactly this in the *Economic and Philosophical Manuscripts:*
"Prostitution is only a *specific* expression of the *general* prostitution of
the laborer, and since it is a relationship in which falls not the prostitute
alone, but also the one who prostitutes—and the latter's abomination
is still greater—the capitalist, etc., also comes under this head."[81]

This statement certainly gives us insight into the Marxist view of
prostitution. First, it points out that prostitution, like wage labor, is a
class phenomenon. The economic situation of unemployed or underemployed women explains why they, like laborers, sell themselves to
others. Second, it points out that prostitutes are alienated. Just as wage
laborers are estranged from their work, from themselves, and from
humanity itself, so, too, are prostitutes. Selling oneself, whether as a
wife or a prostitute, alienates one from one's work because that work is
being done for another, not for oneself. This concept is particularly
appalling in the case of the prostitute, for what she is selling is what is
closest to her: her body, her sexuality. So, under capitalism, a woman's
sexuality becomes a commodity. This is true for both the wife-prostitute
and for the prostitute proper. For both women, an essential human
capacity is alienating. Like wage laborers, the wife-prostitute and the

prostitute proper become dehumanized, and their value as persons is reduced to their market value.

Inequalities of wealth, then, are the cause of prostitution, just as they are of wage labor. According to traditional Marxist analysis, therefore, the typical prostitute is an unemployed or underemployed female, and the typical patron is an upper- or middle-class male—because only these men have enough money to purchase the sexual services of women other than their wives.[82] As long as there is a bourgeois demand for prostitutes, and as long as most women are paid no wages or inadequate wages, economically dependent women will sell their bodies to men in order to support themselves and, in some instances, their children. Thus, to fight capitalism is also to fight prostitution—whatever form it takes, including marriage—because most women will not have access to meaningful work at a decent wage until the capitalist system that depends upon their exploitation is smashed.

What Marxists stress, said Jaggar, is that the elimination of capitalism is truly necessary for women's liberation. Why then, she asked, have the lives of women in socialist nations not been substantially transformed? Their entrance into the workplace has seldom been accompanied by the full socialization of housework and child care. Women are as likely to work two jobs—"home" *and* "work"—in Eastern Europe as in the United States. What is more, issues of particular concern to women— such as sexual violence against women and reproductive freedom—are likely to rank as low, if not lower, on the priority list of the Central Committee of the USSR as in the Congress of the United States. For reasons like these, many a Marxist feminist has expressed exasperation with her male comrades' single-minded concentration on the problems of the male working class and with their trivialization of issues that specifically touch the lives of women.

The orthodox explanation of why socialist women are not the full equals of socialist men, observed Jaggar, is that sexist capitalist ideologies do not die off immediately; in other words, it takes time for the ideas of formerly capitalist populations to change. As an answer, "residual capitalism" is obviously too glib because women under socialism have, for some time now, been performing the same sorts of auxiliary function they do under capitalism, with socialist institutions benefiting from this continued oppression of women in much the same way that capitalist institutions do. If Marxism is to ensure the liberation of women, then, it must incorporate some understanding of patriarchy as an incredibly powerful and/or tenacious system, one that intersects only incompletely with capitalism. Marxism must recognize, suggested Jaggar, at least the possibility that part of what women in the United States, in the People's Republic of China, in the so-called Third World nations, and in the

Soviet Union have in common is their oppression, *as women,* by men, *as men.*

As Jaggar saw it, socialism cannot claim to wholly eliminate gender oppression. Thus, Marxists who are concerned with women's oppression would do well to identify precisely which kind of oppressive relations a Marxist revolution can overcome and which kind it cannot. Only then will there really be a Marxist *feminism.* □

CONCLUSION

The point is sometimes made that because Marxist feminism has been superceded by socialist feminism—which combines Marxist feminist insights with radical and psychoanalytic feminist insights—there is really no need to dwell on the work of theorists such as Margaret Benston, Mariarosa Dalla Costa, and Selma James. After all, the writing style of these thinkers leaves them open to the criticism that Jean Bethke Elshtain leveled against them; namely, that they are too *technical* for their own good.

> The most compelling example I [Elshtain] can think of against Marxist feminism's infusion of econometric terms into the sphere of family ties and relationships would be to ask any mother whether she would accept "producing the future commodity labor power" as an apt characterization of what she is doing. One's fears and love for children are drained of their meaning, their emotional significance, when they are recast as relations between "reproducers" and "future labor power." By their choice of an abstracted, reductionist language, Marxist feminists confound ordinary language and evade the serious questions that arise when one attempts to express and examine the depth and complexity of family relations. Within the boundaries of econometric discourse, issues that emerge when one takes the human subject and her relations as a starting point simply disappear.[83]

The problem with this type of critique of Marxist feminism is that it tends to throw out the proverbial baby with the bath water. Statements such as "the mode of production determines the lives of women within their households and by locating their position in the social system"[84] may sound abstract, but their meaning is very concrete.

Eli Zaretsky has written a series of articles that detail the ways in which a capitalist mode of production has determined the contours of women's lives. Zaretsky argued that we have grown accustomed to a work-family split, and to a concomitant version of the public-private split, that is peculiar to capitalism. In the days before industrial capitalism, people lived in extended families in largely rural, or agrarian, settings.

Insofar as the project of sustaining everyday life was concerned, the work women did was considered just as important as the work men did. Thus, in the primary activity of life—production—women, no less than men, saw themselves as "insiders," not as "outsiders."

Significantly, this society was patriarchal insofar as women were barred from the realm of freedom, or intellectual discourse (the world of religion, culture, and especially politics) and confined to the realm of necessity, or physical labor (the world of material production). But women still played an important role in the realm of necessity, a role that was essentially the same as that of their male coworkers. Together, men and women brought in the harvest and stored it for many a winter meal, and no one in this kind of patriarchal society—and there are many kinds, some worse than others—thought to question the value of women's work.[85]

With industrialization and the transfer of goods production from the home to the workplace, this brand of patriarchy vanished in the modernized West. Production, which had been conceived as constitutive of the world of necessity, came to be conceived, together with cultural conversation, as constitutive of the world of freedom. Now one would become fully human as easily by producing commodities (economics) as by discoursing on the good, the true, and the beautiful (philosophy and politics). With the transfer of everything thought to be really worth doing to the public realm, and with the en masse movement of men into this world of production, little of socially recognized value remained to be done in the private realm, the world of reproduction. As a result of the valorization of public production over private reproduction, and the concomitant association of men with the public realm and women with the private realm, women were gradually denigrated as second-class citizens and workers.

Given that the modern family—woman as reproducer, man as producer—is a capitalist construction, Zaretsky argued that the liberation of woman requires the elimination of capitalism: "The family cannot be transformed except as a part of the general transformation and destruction of the capitalist economy."[86] The private sphere, so dear to the liberal feminist's heart, is a veritable prison to the Marxist feminist. It subordinates woman by permanently excluding her from the public, productive world and leaving her with a life comprising little more than the emotional support of man who engages in "real" human activity. As Heidi Hartmann suggested, "Just as Engels sees private property as the capitalist contribution to women's oppression, so Zaretsky sees privacy."[87]

Zaretsky was most emphatic that women will not achieve liberation just by entering the labor force. As long as "the family remains the primary institution through which women participate in this society," and thus as long as the family remains in its present form, each and every woman in a familial relationship will be subordinated whether or not she enters the labor force.[88] Zaretsky's solution, then, was to eliminate the family as we know it, to break down the dichotomy between family and work, female and male. To do this, he suggested that women's work be reconceived as productive work in some nontechnical sense of the term *productive*. As a result of this conceptual revolution, women will no longer be regarded as people who dwell outside the public and productive world. Zaretsky argued that once the work of the wife is recognized as being as valuable as the work of her wage-earning husband, then men and women can work together to overcome the pernicious split that capitalism created between the private family and the public workplace. For it is this split that, among other things, pits women against men, convincing women that the enemy is not capital but men. According to Hartmann:

> In Zaretsky's view women are laboring for capital and not for men; it is only the separation of home from workplace, and the privatization of housework brought about by capitalism, that creates the *appearance* that women are working for men privately in the home. The difference between the *appearance*, that women work for men, and the *reality*, that women work for capital, has caused a misdirection of the energies of the women's movement. Women should recognize that they, too, are part of the working class, even though they work at home.[89]

Although Zaretsky did not argue that housework is productive in the strict Marxist sense and that, therefore, housewives are exploited by capital, he did agree that the kind of work women do in the home is essential to capital and that capital oppresses housewives by confining them to the home. In fact, more than most other Marxist feminists, Zaretsky was preoccupied with the isolation and loneliness inherent in a life lived completely in the private sphere—the kind of life led by many suburban wives who spend their days, and nights, with a television set, scads of modern conveniences, and perhaps a preverbal infant or two. What Zaretsky wanted for each woman is, minimally, the sense of self-worth that comes from the realization that the work she does is of value to others and, more specifically, to society as a whole.

Zaretsky is by no means the only thinker who has contributed to new directions in specifically Marxist feminist thought. He is in the company of such theorists as Ann Foreman, Michèle Barrett, Johanna Brenner, Nancy Holmstrom, and Maria Ramos, each of whom has pointed out the many and subtle connections between women's experiences as workers and as family members. It makes more strategic sense, said Brenner and

Holmstrom, to organize working women rather than housewives because the former have more cohesion, social power, and consciousness than the latter. But this does not mean that the only way to organize working women is around exclusively sphere-of-production issues.[90] When V. I. Lenin berated Clara Zetkin for discussing sexual matters, he was failing to appreciate the interconnections between the domestic sphere and the workplace, between a woman's private life and her public life, between reproduction and production.[91] Although some of the concerns working women have are the concerns of any worker (wages, fringe benefits, safety standards), other concerns almost exclusively affect female workers (maternity leave, unequal pay for equal or comparable work, sexual harassment). In addition to these sphere-of-production concerns, Brenner and Holmstrom noted that working women have two additional kinds of concern: those that explicitly link the sphere of production with that of reproduction (for example, child care); and those that all women have *as* women (legal rights, reproductive control/freedom, violence against women).[92]

Because working women are both workers and women, they are ideally situated to make alliances with working-class men and with women who do not work. Given the recent influx of women into the workplace, and given that, for a variety of reasons, women are increasingly unwilling to work "more for less," Marxist feminists are in a position first to develop working women's revolutionary consciousness and then to lead them to revolutionary action. Far from existing at the margins of the revolution, women—especially working women who live in both the workplace and the household—appear to be at the center of it. Marxist feminists hold out the hope that if woman's status and function(s) truly change in the workplace, her status and function(s) in the household will also change, if not today, then tomorrow.

CHAPTER THREE

———————— ■ ————————

Radical Feminism on Reproduction and Mothering

RADICAL FEMINISM IS STILL EVOLVING in several directions at once, and so any attempt to define it is bound to stress some of its aspects more than others. But one way to approach this rich school of feminist thought is to point to radical feminists' insistence that women's oppression is the most fundamental form of oppression. According to Alison Jaggar and Paula Rothenberg, this claim can be interpreted to mean

1. That women were, historically, the first oppressed group.
2. That women's oppression is the most widespread, existing in virtually every known society.
3. That women's oppression is the deepest in that it is the hardest form of oppression to eradicate and cannot be removed by other social changes such as the abolition of class society.
4. That women's oppression causes the most suffering to its victims, qualitatively as well as quantitatively, although the suffering may often go unrecognized because of the sexist prejudices of both the oppressors and the victims.
5. That women's oppression . . . provides a conceptual model for understanding all other forms of oppression.[1]

Although few radical feminists subscribe to all five interpretations of women's oppression, most do agree that it is the first, the most widespread, and the deepest form of human oppression.

Depending on what aspects of women's oppression a radical feminist stresses, she will focus on any one of a number of topics: art, spirituality, food, ecology, reproduction and mothering, gender and sexuality, and so on. In the best possible world—where time and space were unlimited— I would have been able to include chapters on the contributions radical feminists have made to women's culture. During the last twenty years, radical feminists have, in a variety of ways, been creating and celebrating women's religion, science, art, poetry, literature, song, dance, cuisine, horticulture. The list is a long and happy one.

Regrettably, this is not the best possible world, and thus I have made the difficult decision to discuss only those radical feminist writings that are concerned primarily with reproduction and mothering or with gender and sexuality. My selection is motivated by two lines of reasoning. First, more than liberal and Marxist feminists, radical feminists have directed attention to the ways in which men attempt to control women's bodies. Whether this control takes the form of restrictive contraception, sterilization, and/or abortion laws, or of violence directed against women (pornography, sexual harassment, rape, woman battering), it constitutes an especially cruel power play. To the degree that a person is deprived of power over his or her own body, that person is deprived of his or her humanity.

Second, more than liberal or Marxist feminists, radical feminists have explicitly articulated the ways in which men have constructed female sexuality to serve not women's but men's needs, wants, and interests. What women must do, insist many radical feminists, is to reconceive female sexuality, this time in the image and likeness of women. Although this reconception is difficult, it is potentially empowering. Liberated from the Procrustean bed of male-defined and male-controlled female sexuality, women are discovering the richness and diversity of the female body, sensing within it the power of what some have termed "woman spirit rising."

In this chapter, I will focus on some radical feminist analyses of childbearing and childrearing; in the next, on some radical feminist analyses of gender and sexuality. What will become clear, I think, is that no matter what kind of patriarchal system women live under, radical feminist writings inspire women of all races and classes not only to celebrate women's reproductive and sexual powers in bold and new ways but also to use these powers joyously and wisely. □

REPRODUCTION: CURSE OR BOON?

Reproduction as the Cause of Women's Oppression

In *The Dialectic of Sex*, Shulamith Firestone claimed that patriarchy—the systematic subordination of women—is rooted in the biological inequality of the sexes. Firestone's reflections on women's reproductive role led her to a feminist revision of the materialist theory of history offered by Marx and Engels. Although Marx and Engels correctly focused upon class struggle as the driving forces of history, said Firestone, they paid scant attention to what she termed *sex class*.[2] Firestone proposed to make up for this oversight by developing a feminist version of historical materialism in which sex class, rather than economic class, is the central concept.

To appreciate Firestone's co-optation of Marxist method, we have only to contrast her definition of historical materialism with that of Engels. We will remember that Engels defined historical materialism as

> that view of the course of history which seeks the ultimate cause and great moving power of all historical events in the economic development of society, in the changes of the modes of production and exchange, in the consequent division of society into distinct classes, and in the struggles of these classes against one another.[3]

Firestone took Engels's definition and reformulated it as follows:

> Historical materialism is that view of the course of history which seeks the ultimate cause and the great moving power of all historical events in the dialectic of sex: the division of society into two distinct biological classes for procreative reproduction, and the struggles of these classes with one another; in the changes in the modes of marriage, reproduction and child care created by these struggles; in the connected development of other physically-differentiated classes [castes]; and in the first division of labor based on sex which developed into the [economic-cultural] class system.[4]

In other words, for Firestone, the original class distinction is between men and women, and it is a *class* distinction to which orthodox Marxists have paid scant attention.

Firestone's argument is bound to trouble the orthodox Marxist, for she considered relations of reproduction rather than of production to be the driving force in history. If we want to understand why women are subordinate to men, we require a biological, not an economic, explanation. Firestone reminded us, however, that we should attribute the inequality between the sexes not to the observable, biological differences between them, but to the fact that men's and women's differing reproductive roles led "to the first division of labor at the origins of class, as well as furnishing the paradigm of caste discrimination based on biological characteristics."[5]

Because Firestone believed that the roots of women's oppression are biological, she concluded that women's liberation requires a biological revolution, in much the same way that Marx concluded that the essentially economic oppression of workers required an economic revolution.[6] Whereas the proletariat must seize the means of *production* in order to eliminate the economic class system, women must seize control of the means of *reproduction* in order to eliminate the sexual class system; and just as the ultimate goal of the communist revolution is, in a classless society, to obliterate class distinctions, the ultimate goal of the feminist revolution is, in an androgynous society, to obliterate sexual ones. As soon as the biological realities of reproduction are overcome, said Firestone, the fact that some persons have wombs and others have penises will "no longer matter culturally."[7] The only valid distinction between men and women will have been vanquished.

What makes this biological revolution a real possibility is technology. When Firestone wrote *The Dialectic of Sex,* only the reproduction-controlling technologies of contraception, sterilization, and abortion were widely used. Today, eighteen years later, the reproduction-aiding techniques of artificial insemination by donor, in vitro fertilization, and embryo transfer are also quite widely used. Due to these technologies and to legal arrangements such as contracted motherhood, a woman who begets a child need not bear it, and a woman who bears a child need not rear it. Furthermore, as soon as it is possible to beget a child in vitro and bring it to term ex utero, women's role in the reproductive process will be no larger than men's. Women will donate ova to egg banks, and men will donate sperm to sperm banks. After the in vitro union of ovum and sperm, the resulting embryo will be gestated outside of the womb in an artificial placenta; and when the fetus finally reaches full term, any number of caring human beings, male or female, will be able to attend to its needs.

Firestone believed that when women and men stop playing substantially different roles in the reproductive drama, it will be possible to eliminate all sexual roles. She was convinced that these roles have been imposed upon people in order to shore up the biological family. When technology is able to perfect "artificial" ways for people to reproduce, the need for the biological family will disappear and, with it, the need to impose genital heterosexuality as a means of ensuring human reproduction. Lesbianism and male homosexuality will no longer be viewed as freely chosen alternatives to the norm of heterosexuality or as perversions resulting from the degrading influence of capitalist society.[8] Instead, the categories of homosexuality and heterosexuality will be abandoned; and institutionalized sexual intercourse, in which male and female each play a well-defined role, will disappear.

The biological family's demise as a reproductive unit will also spell its demise as an economic unit. Firestone was enough of a Marxist to believe that biology's sexual division of labor has served capitalism well. The fact that women reproduce makes it easy for capitalism to confine women to the private, or domestic, realm and to send men out to labor in the public realm. Over time, the biological family has evolved into an economic unit in which women engage in unpaid productive work and in which women and children engage in the kind of consumption that bolsters the capitalist economy. However, once women no longer have to reproduce, the primary rationale for keeping them at home disappears; and with the entrance of women into the workplace, the family will no longer exist as an economic unit.

Because Firestone was unconvinced, however, that the workplace, as we know it, is a life-enhancing spot for women or for men, she saw women's entrance into it as a stopgap measure. If men and women have been at odds with each other largely because of their confining and distorting reproductive and productive roles, one way to end the war between the sexes is to eliminate both roles by developing technology that can replace them. If technology can eliminate the role of woman-the-reproducer, it can eliminate the role of man-the-producer. In godlike fashion, technology can ensure that no person need "bear children in pain and travail" and that no person need "toil by the sweat of the brow in order to live."[9]

When there are no longer distinct reproductive and productive roles for women and men, Firestone believed it will be possible to overcome all of the relations, structures, and ideas that have always divided the human community: oppressing male/oppressed female, exploiting capitalist/exploited worker, white master/black slave. Firestone envisioned an androgynous culture that will surpass not only the peak experiences of male technological culture and female aesthetic culture, but also combine them into an integrated whole. She saw this development as "more than a marriage, rather an abolition of the cultural categories themselves, a mutual cancellation—a matter-antimatter explosion, ending with a poof! culture itself."[10] What Firestone called for was nothing short of a new creation. Indeed, she commented that "if there were another word more all-embracing than *revolution* we would use it."[11]

Firestone wished to explode masculinity and femininity, but she was convinced that this explosion will not occur unless humans abandon patriarchal *reproduction* as well as capitalist *production*. No matter how much educational, legal, and political equality women achieve, and no matter how many women enter public industry, nothing fundamental will change for women so long as biological reproduction remains the rule rather than the exception. As Firestone saw it, biological reproduction is neither in women's best interests nor in those of the children so reproduced. The joy of giving birth—invoked so frequently in this society—is a patriarchal myth. In fact, pregnancy is "barbaric," and natural childbirth is "at best necessary and tolerable," at worst, "like shitting a pumpkin."[12] Moreover, biological motherhood is the root of further evils, especially the vice of possessiveness that generates feelings of hostility and jealousy among human beings. Engels's *Origin* was incomplete not so much because he failed to account adequately for the production of surplus value, as because he failed to explain why men wish so intensely to pass *their* property on to *their* children. As Firestone saw it, the vice of possessiveness—the favoring of one child over another on account of its being the product of one's own ovum or sperm—is precisely what must be overcome if we are to put an end to divisive hierarchies.

This last point was developed by radical feminist Marge Piercy in her science fiction novel, *Woman on the Edge of Time*.[13] Piercy set the story of her utopia within the tale of Connie Ramos's tragic life. Connie is a late-twentieth-century, middle-aged, lower-class Chicana with a history of what society describes as "mental illness" and "violent behavior." Connie has been trying desperately to support herself and her daughter Angelina on a pittance. One day, when she is near the point of exhaustion, Connie loses her temper and hits Angelina too hard. As a result of this one outburst, the courts judge Connie an unfit mother and take her beloved daughter away from her. Depressed and despondent, angry and agitated, Connie is committed by her family to a mental hospital, where she is selected as a human research subject for brain-control experiments. Just when things could get no worse, Connie is transported by a woman named Luciente to a future world called Mattapoisett—a world in which women are not defined in terms of reproductive functions and in which both men and women delight in rearing children.

What makes Piercy's future world plausible is artificial reproduction. In Mattapoisett, babies are born from what is termed the "brooder." Female ova, fertilized in vitro with male sperm selected for a full range of racial, ethnic, and personality types, are gestated within an artificial placenta. Unable to comprehend why Mattapoisett women have rejected the experience that meant the most to her—physically gestating, birthing, and nursing an offspring—Connie is initially repelled by the brooder. She sees the embryos "all in a sluggish row . . . like fish in the aquarium."[14] Not only does she regard these embryos as less than human; she pities them, for no woman loves them enough to carry them in her own womb and, bleeding and sweating, bring them into the world.

Eventually, Connie learns from Luciente that the people of Mattapoisett did not casually give up biological reproduction for technological reproduction. They did so only when they realized that the loss of biological reproduction was the price to pay for the elimination of sexism as well as racism and classism.

It was part of women's long revolution. When we were breaking all the old hierarchies. Finally there was that one thing we had to give up too, the only power we ever had, in return for no power for anyone. The original production: the power to give birth. Cause as long as we were biologically enchained, we'd never be equal. And males never would be humanized to be loving and tender. So we all became mothers. Every child has three. To break the nuclear bonding.[15]

Thus, as a result of women giving up an apparent monopoly on the power to give birth, the original paradigm for power relations is destroyed, and everyone in Mattapoisett is in a position to reconstitute human relationships in ways that defy the hierarchical ideas of better-worse, higher-lower, stronger-weaker, and, especially, dominant-submissive.

The reason Piercy's utopia is more radical than a Marxist utopia is, then, that the family is eliminated as a biological as well as an economic unit. Individuals possess neither private property nor private children. No one has his or her own genetic child. Children are not the possessions of their biological mothers and fathers, to be brought into this world in their parents' image and likeness and reared according to their idiosyncratic values. Rather, children are precious human resources for the entire community, to be treasured on account of their uniqueness. Each child is reared by three co-mothers (one man and two women or two men and one woman) who are assisted by "kidbinders," a group of individuals who excel at mothering Mattapoisett's children. Childrearing is a communal effort, with each child having access to large-group experiences at child care centers and small-group experiences in the separate dwellings of each of his or her co-mothers.[16]

Initially, Connie doubts that Mattapoisett's system for begetting, bearing, and rearing children is all it is touted to be. She wonders whether co-mothers and kidbinders really love the children they are rearing. But gradually she decides that a biological relationship is not essential to good parenting. Indeed, she eventually agrees that technological reproduction is superior to biological reproduction in that the kind of mothering that flows from it is truly nurturing and unselfish, totally separated from ambivalent feelings of resentment and guilt, and always freely chosen.[17]

Reproduction as the Source of Women's Liberation

A Critique of Marge Piercy

As beautifully as Piercy expressed and modified some of Firestone's more controversial ideas, she, like Firestone, has been challenged by many feminists, including many radical feminists, who insist that it is a mistake for women to give up biological motherhood for ex utero child gestation. Empathizing with Connie's initial reaction of disgust at ex utero gestation, and her initial reaction of bewilderment at Luciente's explanation for why the women of Mattapoisett had to give up the only power they had ever had, Piercy's critics observe that from the point of view of women who are currently living within patriarchy, Mattapoisett is both implausible and unintelligible.[18]

Mattapoisett is implausible for today's women, insist Piercy's critics, because women's oppression is not likely to end if, as Azizah al-Hibri observed, women give up the only source of men's dependence on them: "Technological reproduction does not equalize the natural reproductive power structure—it *inverts* it. It appropriates the reproductive power from women and places it in the hands of men who now control both the sperm and the reproductive technology that could make it indispensable. . . . It 'liberates' them from their "humiliating dependency" on women in order to propagate."[19] Far from liberating women, reproductive technology will further consolidate men's power over women.

In addition to being implausible, Mattapoisett is, in the opinion of Piercy's critics, also unintelligible to today's women—at least its notions of who counts as a mother. In our society, a mother is a woman who is defined *and* defines herself in terms of a nine-month pregnancy, a twenty-four-hour or so delivery, and eighteen years or so of childrearing. There is, insisted Anne Donchin, no "solid ground" upon which women can stand to get a clear fix on what it would be like to be a "co-mother" or a "kidbinder" instead of a *real* mother—that is, a woman who, as Connie says, knows what it means to carry a child nine months "heavy under her heart," to bear a baby "in blood and pain," to suckle a child.[20]

Three Critiques of Firestone and
Other Wholesale Endorsements of Reproductive Technology

To the degree that Piercy's utopian vision has been criticized as implausible and unintelligible, Firestone's analysis has been criticized as a blueprint for woman's further enslavement. Firestone's critics argue that woman's oppression is not caused by "female biology," in and of itself, but rather by man's control of that biology—a control that could become total depending on how reproductive technology is developed.

Male alienation from reproduction. Among the feminists most critical of positions such as Firestone's is Mary O'Brien, who asserted that if woman is to free herself from man's control, she has to understand that the source of her oppression is also the source of her liberation. Despite the fact that the process of reproduction has been a "bitter trap" for woman, it also contains for her untapped "possibilities" and "freedom."[21]

O'Brien analyzed reproduction through the lens of male alienation from reproduction. Patriarchy, she insisted, is man's compensation for and attempt to counteract the alienation of his reproductive consciousness.

Man's alienation from reproduction, and therefore from children, rests on at least three factors. First, the spatial and temporal continuity between the ovum and the resulting child is unbroken, taking place inside the woman's body, whereas the spatial and temporal continuity between the sperm and the resulting child is broken, taking place outside the man's body.[22] Second, women, not men, necessarily perform the fundamental labor of reproduction—pregnancy and birth.[23] Third, a woman's connection to a particular child is certain—she knows, at the moment of birth at least, that it is flesh of her flesh. A man's connection to a particular child, in contrast, is always uncertain—he is never absolutely sure, even at the moment of birth, whether the child is in fact genetically related to him.[24]

From what has been said so far, it is clear that although motherhood can be understood as a lived relationship with a child from the moment of its conception onward, fatherhood cannot be understood in the same way. Think here of artificial insemination by donor (AID), a mode of reproductive technology that discounts genetic fatherhood. If ever a man's seed is totally alienated from him, it is in AID, for the sperm donor has no connection with either the child or the mother. In fact, courts have ruled that an AID child has no natural father, only a legal father—namely, the husband of the woman who gives birth to the child. But noncoitally produced genetic fatherhood, as O'Brien has observed, is not that different from coitally produced genetic fatherhood. In either case, there is only one brief moment—ejaculation or injection—and then the man's role is over, and he is separate from the woman and the child. If this is so—if fatherhood is an artificial, legally created relationship—then as Sara Ann Ketchum argued, there is no natural, extralegal connection that the law ignores when it recognizes only a legal father of an AID child. If, however, fatherhood is in some way a natural relationship, then as a metaphor for genetic fatherhood, AID undermines the parental status of coital as well as noncoital sperm donors.[25]

Because men are aware that their parental status is precarious, they reason that to own women's reproductive labor power is also to own the product(s) of that labor power. Thus, men seek to control women's bodies in order to control those of their children. For this reason, insisted O'Brien, women should be wary of the kind of reproductive technologies Firestone celebrated because they are simply new ways for men to get "something—that is, a child—for nothing."[26]

The power of the mother. Like O'Brien, Adrienne Rich believed that men are jealous and fearful of women's reproductive powers. The jealousy stems largely from men's realization that "all human life on the planet is born of woman," that woman has a unique power to create life.[27] The fear comes primarily from men's sense that women's reproductive powers are somehow mysterious and uncontrollable—that if women can give life, women may also be able to take life.[28] Rich suggested that this feeling, that women are the source of death as well as life, has a material base. As infants, all children are dependent upon their mothers—upon their breasts for milk, their love for protection. At any moment, mothers could withdraw their breasts and their love, thereby leaving their children to die. Thus, from a son's perspective, woman "is first of all the mother who has to be possessed, reduced, controlled, lest she swallow him back into her dark caves, or stare him into stone."[29]

Given their jealousy and fear of women's reproductive powers, men quickly realized, according to Rich, that if patriarchy wishes to survive, let alone thrive, it must restrict the power of the mother. Thus, as soon as they were able to devise the means, men took "birthing" over from women. Male obstetricians replaced female midwives, and hands of iron (obstetrical forceps) replaced hands of flesh (female hands sensitive to female anatomy). In addition, male doctors and psychologists increasingly wrote the rules not only for giving birth but also for being pregnant. Men have told women how to act during pregnancy—when to eat, sleep, exercise, have sex, and the like. Men have even dictated to women how to feel during the process of childbirth—when to feel pain and when to feel pleasure. But, said Rich, these rules frequently clash with a woman's lived experience, and when this happens a woman does not know whether to trust the authority of the doctors or the sensations of her own body. This kind of experience can transform a pregnancy into a profoundly alienating experience. Indeed, Rich wrote that this was precisely what happened in her own case.

> When I try to return to the body of the young woman of twenty-six, pregnant for the first time, who fled from the physical knowledge of her pregnancy and at the same time from her intellect and vocation, I realize that I was effectively alienated from my real body and my real spirit by the institution—not the fact—of motherhood. This institution—the foundation of human society as we know it—allowed me only certain views, certain expectations, whether embodied in the booklet in my obstetrician's waiting room, the novels I had read, my mother-in-law's approval, my memories of my own mother, the Sistine Madonna or she of the Michelangelo *Pieta,* the floating notion that a woman pregnant is a woman calm in her fulfillment or, simply, a woman waiting.[30]

Rich suggested that were women put in charge of pregnancy and childbirth, then these experiences could take on active rather than passive meanings. Women would no longer sit passively waiting for childbirth to occur. Rather, women would actively direct childbirth, regaining control of the pleasures as well as the pains of the experience. In short, pregnancy does not have to feel like "shitting a pumpkin."[31] It can, under ordinary circumstances, feel a great deal more exhilarating and certainly far less dehumanizing.

The desire to control the mother. Recently, some of Rich's ideas have been developed by several radical feminists, including Andrea Dworkin, Margaret Atwood, Gena Corea, and Robyn Rowland. All of these writers believe that reproductive technology poses an enormous threat to whatever powers women still possess and that biological motherhood ought not to be forsaken in favor of artificial motherhood.

Dworkin argued that men value women not as unique individuals but as members of a class who serve them sexually and reproductively. There are, she said, two models that best explain what it means to be a woman within patriarchy: the brothel model, which relates to prostitution, and the farming model, which relates to motherhood. Although people have been led to believe that prostitutes and mothers have nothing in common, in point of fact, claimed Dworkin, they have almost everything in common, which is becoming increasingly clear with the advent of the new reproductive technologies.[32]

The brothel model is, from men's point of view, incredibly efficient. Men get women under their control through alcohol, drugs, hunger, desperation, and manipulation. Made to depend on men not simply for their livelihood but also for their very lives, prostitutes hand over their bodies to men who literally use them up or waste them.[33]

In contrast to the brothel model, the farming model is, from men's point of view, quite inefficient for two reasons. First, it is more difficult for a man to distance himself emotionally from the wife he has brought home to "husband"—that is, "to plow for the purpose of growing crops," where "crops" means "children"—than it is for him to expunge from his consciousness a prostitute whose "services" he bought for a one-night stand. In the same way that a farmer usually forms an intense relationship with his land, a husband usually forms an intense relationship with his wife. Although the husband-wife relationship is severely limited by men's general misogyny, because of the long-term nature of marriage, it is not in any husband's best interest to use up or waste his wife too quickly. A wife, it turns out, is not as easily replaceable as a prostitute is. It makes good sense, therefore, for husbands to take relatively good care of their wives.[34] Second, wives have far more power over their husbands than prostitutes have over their "johns." A "john" can get what he wants from a prostitute—most often an orgasm—with relatively little effort. But a husband can get what he wants from his wife— presumably children—only with considerable effort.

The farming model requires the constant application of force (explicit or implicit, usually a nice combination), incentive, reward; and a lot of plain luck with respect to fertility and reproductive vigor. When a man wants sons, as most do, the inefficiency inherent in the model is particularly emphasized: no matter how many babies she has, there is no certainty that any of them will be male. And, for all the coercion of the farming model, the women subject to it have organized politically, have found ways to seize the time between babies and domestic chores—here and there, now and then—to foment rebellion.[35]

But even if the farming model was less efficient in the past than the brothel model, said Dworkin, this gap is closing with the inception of the new reproductive technologies. As she saw it, technologies such as artificial insemination, in vitro fertilization, sex preselection, embryo transplantation, fetal monitoring, and eventual cloning make the womb the province not of women, but of scientists and doctors who wish to control it. For women to worry about whether these technologies are moral or immoral, good or bad, then, is to worry about the wrong issue. Instead, women should be worrying about whether these technologies are going to be used in order to further consolidate male power, to create a society in which women are not whole persons but mere functions: domestics, sex prostitutes, and reproductive prostitutes.[36]

Dworkin's analysis was the apparent inspiration of Margaret Atwood's *The Handmaid's Tale*,[37] a work of feminist science fiction that stands in stark contrast to Marge Piercy's *Woman on the Edge of Time*. What we see in the Republic of Gilead, Atwood's antiutopia, are women reduced to their respective functions. There are the Marthas, or domestics; the Wives, or social secretaries and functionaries; the Jezebels, or sex prostitutes; and the Handmaids, or reproductive prostitutes. One of the most degrading Gileadean practices, from a women's perspective, consists in the Commanders' engaging in ritualistic sexual intercourse with their Wives. The Wife, who is infertile, lies down on a bed with her legs spread open.[38] The Handmaid, one of the few fertile women in Gilead, then puts her head between the spread-out legs of the wife, whereupon the Commander engages in sexual intercourse not with his Wife but with her Handmaid. Should the Handmaid become pregnant, the child she bears will be regarded as that of the Commander and his Wife. Indeed, on the day the Handmaid gives birth to the child, the Wife will simulate labor pains, and all the other Wives and Handmaids in Gilead will gather round the fortunate Wife and her blessed Handmaid, experiencing through them an ephemeral moment of female bonding—of women's pride, passion, and power.

After one such birth day, the central character, Offred—whose name literally means "to be of Fred"—recalls better times and speaks in her mind to her mother, who had been a feminist leader: "Can you hear me? You wanted a woman's culture. Well, now there is one. It isn't what you meant, but it exists. Be thankful for small mercies."[39] Of course, they are *very* small mercies, for with the exception of birth days—those rare occasions when a Handmaid manages to produce a child—women have little contact with each other. The Marthas, Wives, Jezebels, and Handmaids are segregated from one another, and what contact women do have—even within an assigned class—is largely silent, for women are permitted to speak to each other only when absolutely necessary.

Like Dworkin and Atwood, Gena Corea is also suspicious of what the new reproductive technologies and their concomitant social arrangements promise women. Corea is convinced that because men currently control them, the new reproductive technologies will be used not to empower women but to further consolidate male power. Corea drew implicit analogies between Count Dracula and Dr. Robert Edwards, one of the codevelopers of in vitro fertilization. Just as Dracula never had enough blood to drink, Dr. Edwards never had enough ova upon which to experiment. As a result, he would routinely appear at the hysterectomies his colleagues were performing so that he could secure enough ova for his experiments.[40] Toward the end of her essay entitled "Egg Snatchers," Corea asked:

> Why are men focusing all this technology on woman's generative organs—the source of her procreative power? Why are they collecting our eggs? Why do they seek to freeze them?
>
> Why do men want to control the production of human beings? Why do they talk so often about producing "perfect" babies?
>
> Why are they splitting the functions of motherhood into smaller parts? Does that reduce the power of the mother and her claim to the child? ("I only gave the egg. I am not the real mother." "I only loaned my uterus. I am not the real mother." "I only raised the child. I am not the real mother.")[41]

Robyn Rowland is yet another radical feminist who agreed with Dworkin, Atwood, and Corea that reproductive technology will simply increase men's control over women. Rowland pointed to the work of John Postgate, a British professor of microbiology, as an example of the forms this new power over women may take. Postgate suggested that the best way to curb overpopulation is to develop a pill—the Manchild Pill—that would ensure the conception of male children, thereby eventually creating a scarcity of women and a decline in birth rates. In a matter-of-fact tone of voice, he forecasts that in order to control male access to females (unlucky males could resort to homosexuality and/or to autoeroticism), women will have to be sequestered.[42]

As if visions of future worlds in which women are more tightly controlled by men than ever before are not bad enough, Rowland imagines an even worse scenario: a world in which only a few superovulating women are permitted to exist, a world in which eggs are taken from women, frozen, and inseminated in vitro for transfer into artificial placentae. The replacement of women's childbearing capacity by male-controlled technology would remove women's biological burden, but it would also leave women "without a product" with which "to bargain": "For the history of 'mankind' women have been seen in terms of their value as childbearers. We have to ask, if that last power is taken and controlled by men, what role is envisaged for women in the new world?"[43]

Unlike Piercy, then, Rowland would not urge women to give up the ultimate female power—the power to reproduce. There is, in Rowland's estimation, a difference between the kind of affirming power women exert in bringing new life into the world and the kind of negating power men exert in controlling nature/women through technology. Only those forms of human power that are oppressive need to be forsaken; and, as Rowland saw it, women's reproductive powers are anything but oppressive. If women's power over life is the paradigm for anything, it is for one person's or group's ability to connect with another. □

MOTHERING: LOVE IT OR LEAVE IT?

Although commentators do not always make adequate distinctions between biological and social motherhood, these two dimensions of mothering need to be distinguished. If we accept Jaggar's extension of the term *mothering* to "any relationship in which one individual nurtures and cares for another,"[44] then a person does not need to be a biological mother in order to be a social mother. Nevertheless, patriarchal society teaches us that the woman who bears a child is best suited to rear him or her. In viewing this tenet as one that often places unreasonable demands upon women's bodies and energies, some radical feminists have made strong arguments against biological motherhood. But other radical feminists have challenged these arguments, insisting that no woman should, in an act of unreflective defiance against patriarchy, deprive herself of the satisfaction that comes from not only bearing a child but also playing a major role in his or her personal development. As we shall see, the arguments on both sides of this debate are powerful ones; the issues of the status and function of *female* mothering are enormously complex.

The Case Against Biological Motherhood

There are at least two versions of the initial case against biological motherhood: a weaker, more general version offered by Ann Oakley and a stronger, more specific version offered by Shulamith Firestone. As Oakley saw it, motherhood is a myth based on the threefold belief that "all women need to be mothers, all mothers need their children, all children need their mothers."[45]

The first assertion, that all women need to be mothers, gains its credibility, according to Oakley, from the way in which girls are socialized and from popular psychoanalytic theory, which provides "pseudo-scientific backing" for this process of socialization. If parents did not give their daughters dolls; if the schools, the churches, and the media did not stress the wonders of motherhood; if psychiatrists, psychologists, and physicians did not do everything in their power to transform "abnormal" girls ("masculine" girls who do not want to be mothers) into "normal" girls ("feminine" girls who do want to be mothers), then few girls would grow into women who *need* to mother in order to have a sense of self-worth. As far as Oakley was concerned, the need to mother "owes nothing" to women's "possession of ovaries and wombs" and everything to the way in which women are socially and culturally conditioned to be mothers.[46]

The second assertion, that all mothers need their children, is based on the belief that unless a woman's "maternal instinct" is satisfied, she will become increasingly frustrated. In Oakley's view, there is no such thing as a maternal instinct either in the sense that all normal women experience a desire to have a biological child or in the sense that during and subsequent to pregnancy, there exist hormonally based drives that "irresistibly draw the mother to her child in the tropistic fashion of the moth drawn to the flame."[47] In order to support her contention that the "instinct" for motherhood is "culturally induced" and that the ability to mother is learned, Oakley pointed to studies such as one that observed 150 first-time mothers. Few of these women knew how to breastfeed, and those that did had seen either their own mother or some other female relative nursing a baby.[48] Additionally, Oakley pointed to studies that showed that most women who abuse or neglect their children were themselves abused or neglected as children. Never having seen a woman mothering properly, these women never learned the behavior repertoire this society associates with adequate mothering. Mothers, in short, are not born; they are made.[49]

The third assertion, that children need their mothers, is, according to Oakley, the most oppressive feature of the myth of biological motherhood. Oakley lamented the fact that this assertion contains three assumptions that unnecessarily tie women to children: first, that children need biological, not social mothers; second, that children, especially young children, need the devoted care of their mothers much more than of their fathers; and third, that children need one nurturant caretaker (preferably the biological mother), not many.[50]

As Oakley saw it, each of these three assumptions (in support of the assertion that children need their mothers) is false. First, social mothers are just as effective as biological mothers. Studies have shown, for example, that adopted children are at least as well adjusted as nonadopted children.[51] Second, children do not need their mothers more than their fathers. What a child needs, wrote Oakley, is someone with whom to establish an intimate relationship—a trustworthy and dependable person who will provide the child with consistent care and discipline, recognize and cherish the child's uniqueness, and be there when the child needs him or her.[52] Third, and finally, one-on-one childrearing is not necessarily better than collective socialization or "multiple mothering." Children reared in Israeli kibbutzim, for example, are just as happy, intelligent, emotionally mature, and socially adept as children reared exclusively by their biological mothers in U.S. suburbs.[53]

Given that biological motherhood is not, in Oakley's estimation, a natural need of women, she concluded that it is a cultural construction— a myth with an oppressive purpose. Not wanting to be accused of selfishness and even abnormality, women who would be happier not having children at all become mothers; and women who would be happier sharing their childrearing responsibilities with one or more nurturant adults make of mothering an exclusive and twenty-four-hour-a-day job. No wonder, said Oakley, that so many mothers are unhappy—an unhappiness made all the worse by the fact that for a woman to admit any serious dissatisfaction with mothering is for her to admit failure as a person.

Although Shulamith Firestone's negative assessment of biological motherhood was not that different from Oakley's, it was even harsher in tone. In *The Dialectic of Sex*, Firestone suggested that the desire to bear and rear children is less the result of an "authentic liking" for children and more a "displacement" of ego-extension needs. For a man, a child is a way to immortalize his name, property, class, and ethnic identification; for a woman, a child is a way to justify her homebound existence as absolutely necessary. At times, a father's need for immortality or a mother's need for justification becomes pathological. When this happens, said Firestone, the less than "perfect" child will inevitably suffer.[54]

Firestone believed that if adults had other ways to gratify their egos, many would discover in themselves an authentic desire to live in close association with children. People do not need to be biological parents in order to lead child-centered lives, said Firestone. Ten or more adults could agree, for example, to live with three or four children for a determinate period of time—seven to ten years, or however long children really need a stable structure. During their years together, the people in this household would relate not as parents and children but as older and younger friends. Firestone did not think that adults have a natural desire to be any closer to children than this kind of household arrangement permits. Instead, she believed that adults have been socialized to view biological reproduction as life's raison d'être because without this grandiose sense of mission and destiny, the pains of childbearing and the burdens of childrearing would have proved overwhelming. Now that technology promises to liberate the human species from the burdens of reproductive responsibility, Firestone predicted that women will no longer want to bear children in pain and travail or rear children endlessly and self-sacrificially. Rather, women, and men, will want to spend *some* of their time and energy with and on children.[55]

The Case for Biological Motherhood

Although Adrienne Rich agreed with some of Firestone's analysis, she criticized Firestone for condemning biological motherhood "without taking full account of what the experience of biological pregnancy and birth might be in a wholly different political and emotional context."[56] Throughout her book *Of Woman Born,* Rich sharply distinguished between motherhood as "the *potential relationship* of any woman to her powers of reproduction and to children" and motherhood as "the *institution,* which aims at ensuring that that potential—and all women—shall remain under male control."[57] Rich's distinction was sometimes expressed as the difference between the experience of mothering and the institution of motherhood, or as the difference between *women* deciding who, how, when, and where to mother and *men* making these decisions for women.

Rich agreed with Firestone that biological motherhood, as it has been institutionalized under patriarchy, is definitely something from which women must be liberated. If success is measured in terms of patriarchy's ability to determine not only women's gender behavior but also her gender identity through "force, direct pressure . . . ritual, tradition, law and language, customs, etiquette, education, and the division of labor," then institutionalized biological motherhood is one of patriarchy's overwhelming successes.[58] Men, suggested Rich, have convinced women that unless a woman is a mother, she is not really a woman. Indeed, until relatively recently, patriarchy has kept women convinced that mothering is their one and only job. This view of women's role is, of course, very restricting. It denies women access to the public realm of culture. It also denies women the right to have gynocentric wants and needs. Good mothers are not supposed to have any personal friends or plans unrelated to those of their families. They are supposed to be on the job twenty-four hours a day and love every minute of it. Ironically, observed Rich, it is just this expectation that causes many women to act in anything but "motherly" ways. The constant needs of a child can tax a mother's patience and, with no relief from her husband or any other adult, ultimately make her feel angry, frustrated, and bitter.

> I remember being uprooted from already meager sleep to answer a childish nightmare, pull up a blanket, warm a consoling bottle, lead a half-asleep child to the toilet. I remember going back to bed starkly awake, brittle with anger, knowing that my broken sleep would make the next day hell, that there would be more nightmares; more need for consolation, because out of my weariness I would rage at those children for no reason.[59]

Rich's point was not that women do not love children, but that no person can be expected to remain always cheerful and kind unless that person's own physical and psychological needs are being met.[60]

Rich also argued eloquently that by institutionalizing biological motherhood, patriarchy does its best to corrupt any relationship that could exist between mother and child. Patriarchal psychoanalysts work together with pediatricians to undermine a woman's confidence by blaming her for whatever goes wrong in her children's lives. Rich recounted squabbles with her own husband about the best way to raise their two sons. She also recalled doing it his way even though she knew full well that father did not always know best. Under patriarchy, she wrote, most men have demanded sons for the wrong reasons: "as heirs, field-hands, cannon-fodder, feeders of machinery, images and extensions of themselves; their immortality."[61] What is worse, most husbands have demanded that their wives help them raise their sons to be "real men." Rich happily recalled a seashore vacation she spent with her two boys, but without her husband. While vacationing alone, she and her children lived spontaneously for several weeks, ignoring most of the established rules of patriarchy. They ate the wrong food at the wrong time. They stayed up past the proper bedtime. They wore the wrong clothes. They giggled at silly jokes. Through all of these trespasses, they were enormously happy. Indeed, suggested Rich, were fathers told that they do *not* know best, then mothers would find childrearing energizing rather than enervating, joyful rather than miserable.

As Rich saw it, if women took control of childbearing *and* childrearing, more mothers would be able to experience biological motherhood on their own terms. Rich insisted that no woman is required to renounce, in the name of "liberation," all that female biology has to offer.

> I have come to believe . . . that female biology—the diffuse, intense sensuality radiating out from clitoris, breasts, uterus, vagina; the lunar cycles of men-

struation; the gestation and fruition of life which can take place in the female body—has far more radical implications than we have yet come to appreciate. Patriarchal thought has limited female biology to its own narrow specifications. The feminist vision has recoiled from female biology for these reasons; it will, I believe, come to view our physicality as a resource, rather than a destiny. In order to live a fully human life we require not only *control* of our bodies (though control is a prerequisite); we must touch the unity and resonance of our physicality, our bond with the natural order, the corporeal ground of our intelligence.[62]

According to Rich, Firestone was wrong to argue that female biology is necessarily limiting and that the only way to liberate women from this limitation is through technology. In a patriarchal society, Rich said, the solution to the pains of childbearing is not technology, but rather for a woman to ride with, not against, her body. A woman must not give up on her body before she has had a chance to use it as she thinks best. Likewise, claimed Rich, the solution to the impositions of child-rearing in a patriarchal society is not the renunciation of children; the solution is for each and every woman to rear those children with feminist values.

Reassessing the Pros and Cons of Biological Motherhood

As cogent as Rich's distinction between the institution and the experience of motherhood seems, and as problematic as Firestone's "technological fix" seems, some radical feminists remain unconvinced that there is a safe form of biological motherhood for women to experience—that is, a form of motherhood that does not both change a woman's priorities and narrow her already limited range of alternatives. Jeffner Allen urged women to "evacuate" motherhood: to focus not on the power *to have* children but rather on the power *not to have* children: "At present, and for several thousands of years past, women have conceived, borne, and raised multitudes of children without any change in the conditions of our lives as women. In the case that all females were to decide not to have children for the next twenty years, the possibilities for developing new modes of thought and existence would be almost unimaginable."[63] We may add that were females also to decide not to engage in social motherhood—that is, nurturing, nursing, consoling, counseling, teaching, and tending the old and the young, the sick and the disturbed, the homeless and the disadvantaged—then not only women's but also men's ways of thinking and acting would be fundamentally altered.

Allen's proposal to annihilate motherhood is both exhilarating and disturbing. On the one hand, I envision a woman who has the time and energy to become anyone she wants to be. On the other hand, I conjure up images of old and young people left alone, of sick and disturbed people left suffering, of homeless and disadvantaged people left cold and hungry. Yet I suspect that unless women stop mothering, men will never learn how to mother. According to Adrienne Rich:

> Even if contraception were perfected to infallibility, so that no woman need ever again bear an unwanted child; even if laws and customs change—as long as women and women only are the nurturers of children, our sons will grow up looking only to women for compassion, resenting strength in women as "control," clinging to women when we try to move into a new mode of relationship. As long as society itself is patriarchal—which means antimaterial—there can never be enough mothering for sons who have to grow up under the rule of the Fathers, in a public "male" world separate from the private "female" world of the affections.[64]

Perhaps each and every woman has to deny herself, at least temporarily, the experience of mothering so that the patriarchal institution of motherhood is destroyed once and for all.

The Case of Contracted, or Surrogate, Motherhood

The attention of feminists, especially radical feminists, has recently focused on surrogate, or contracted, motherhood—an arrangement where a third party is hired and required by contract to bear a child to be reared by someone else.[65] The birth mother (the woman whose pregnancy has been contracted for) is either the full biological mother of the child (that is, both the genetic and the gestational mother) or the gestational but not the genetic mother of the child. Marxist and radical feminists have criticized contracted motherhood for at least two reasons: When a woman consents to sell her reproductive services to a married infertile couple, her consent is about as genuine as the "consent" a woman gives when she sells her sexual services to a client; and when society encourages a woman to rent her womb, it comes dangerously close to dehumanizing reproduction by turning it into a mode of commodity production.

Marxist feminists argue that most contracted mothers, like most prostitutes, are much poorer than their clients. Unable to get a decent job, a woman is driven to sell the only thing she has that seems to have any value: her body. To say that a woman "chooses" to do this, says the Marxist feminist, is to say that when a person is forced to choose between being poor and being exploited, she may choose being exploited as the lesser of the two evils. Although Surrogate Parenting Associates has described contracted mothers as "next door neighbor types" who enjoy pregnancy and feel healthier when pregnant,[66] and although some agencies refuse to accept indigent women into their program,[67] some observers—including those who screen surrogacy candidates—have claimed that the poorer a woman is, the better candidate she is for surrogacy. "If a woman is on unemployment and has children to care for, she is not likely to change her mind and want to keep the baby she is being paid to have for somebody else."[68] An even more classist remark has been made by John Stehura, president of the Bionetics Foundation, yet another agency that contracts pregnancies. Stehura has suggested that because the going rate for contracted mothers may be too high for even middle-class couples to pay, the surrogate industry should move either to poverty-stricken parts of the United States, where women would carry fetuses for one-half the standard fee, or to the Third World, where women would accept one-tenth the standard fee.[69]

Radical feminists use the prostitution-surrogacy analogy to underscore several points about "consent" that Marxist feminists do not usually emphasize. They remind us, for example, that even when a well-to-do college graduate decides to work as a high-priced "call girl," it is not entirely clear that her choice is best described as "free." Women, says the radical feminist, are socialized to meet male sexual wants and needs as a matter of duty and pride. In this connection, one feminist prosecutor reported that in her district a man approached several single-parent mothers on welfare with the following proposition: In return for cash payments for them (the mothers) and gifts for their little girls, ages seven to twelve, the mothers would permit him to spend time with their daughters. The mothers agreed, and the daughters spent their after-school hours with "Uncle Charlie," who proceeded to molest them. Gradually, a rivalry developed among the girls, each of them trying to be Uncle Charlie's favorite. Indeed, so attached did they become to him that when one of the mothers finally blew the whistle to the police, the little girls were depressed at the thought of not seeing their Uncle Charlie anymore. The prosecutor predicted that without first-rate counseling, many of the girls would spend much of their lives trying to "turn men on" sexually.[70]

Just as prostitutes are not born but made by a society that teaches girls that if all else fails, they can always gain attention or money by offering their bodies to men, contracted mothers are not born but made by a society that teaches girls that they are *better* than boys because they are so generous, so willing to share all that they have, including their bodies. Although conceding that biological motherhood is a highly valuable activity, some radical feminists caution that because *only* women can give birth, appeals for contracted mothers can constitute something like a "compassion trap" for women.[71] Frequently, the call for contracted

mothers is accompanied by visions of infertile couples who are in desperate
need of someone to help them out of their chronic loneliness. An appeal
is made to generous, loving, altruistic women to step forward to "give
the gift of life," a bundle of joy, to sorrowing, lonely, childless couples.
The fact that approximately one-third of all the women who answer this
appeal have either had an abortion or given up a child for adoption
strengthens the suspicion of many radical feminists that deep and dark
forces are driving women to "choose" surrogacy even when it may not
be in their best interests to do so.[72]

The final and perhaps strongest objection some radical feminists lodge
against surrogate motherhood is that it creates divisions among women.
The first division is the one analyzed earlier—namely, between economically privileged women and economically disadvantaged women. The
former are able to hire the latter in order to meet their reproductive
needs, adding gestational services to the childrearing services that economically disadvantaged women have traditionally provided to economically privileged women. The second division is one Gena Corea envisioned—namely, among childbegetters, childbearers, and childrearers.
According to Corea, the process of reproduction is being segmented and
specialized as if it were simply a mode of production. In the future, no
one woman will beget, bear, and rear a child. Rather, genetically superior
women will beget embryos in vitro; strong-bodied women will bear
these test-tube babies to term; and sweet-tempered women will rear these
newborns from infancy to adulthood.[73] As a result of this division of
labor, a dystopia similar to the one Margaret Atwood described in *The
Handmaid's Tale* could come into existence, complete with the divisive
female-female relationships that, as we saw, characterize it. No woman
is whole in Gilead; all individual women are reduced to parts or aspects
of the monolith, Woman.

Although Corea's analysis and Atwood's novel may dampen enthusiasm
for reproductive technology, some radical feminists insist that, handled
properly, arrangements such as contracted motherhood could bring women
closer together rather than farther apart. Already there are reports of
contracted mothers living in close proximity to the couples who com-
missioned them and sharing the joy of the new life.[74] Such reports bolster
the claim that contracted motherhood can be viewed not as the male-
directed and male-manipulated specialization and segmentation of the
female reproductive process, but as two women getting together—as in
the case of the post-menopausal South African mother who carried her
daughter's in vitro fetus to term—to achieve, in unison, something
neither could do alone.[75]

But even if it is plausible that in a nonpatriarchal society, genetic and
gestational mothers could determine the extent of their interaction with

each other and their children, radical feminists who oppose contracted motherhood note that in a patriarchal society, what we see is not "collaborative reproduction"[76] among women but, rather, court battles between the child's genetic father and the child's genetic and gestational mother.[77] Far from being a commissioning couple's collaborator, the contracted mother is more like the couple's employee, whose terms of employment are set forth in as coercive a contract as possible.[78]

Although the precedent for enforcing contracted motherhood agreements is still relatively weak, many people have voiced the opinion that "a contract is a contract" and that a woman who agrees to bear a child for somebody else must honor the terms of whatever agreement she voluntarily signs.[79] In response to this affirmation of "contract," several state legislatures have proposed bills that would adopt a so-called specific performance approach to breached contracted-motherhood agreements. If passed, these bills would, insist the radical feminists who oppose them, not only deprive genetic and/or gestational mothers of their children but also open women's bodies to all sorts of invasions and intrusions.[80]

Currently, a contracted mother may breach a contract in at least four ways. She may (1) refuse, after all, to be inseminated; (2) either abort or fail to abort the fetus against the commissioning couple's wishes; (3) negligently harm the fetus during the pregnancy; and/or (4) refuse to give up the child at birth.[81] Although there is growing precedent for regarding as criminals women who harm their fetuses by smoking, drinking, or taking drugs during pregnancy,[82] and although several courts have ordered unwilling women to have Caesarean sections for the sake of the fetuses' best interests,[83] most legal observers argue that the right to privacy is still strong enough to preserve women's abortion rights in particular and procreative rights in general. When it comes to forcing the contracted mother to give up the baby she has gestated, however, legal observers are more divided. Some side with the genetic father against the contracted mother even in those instances where she is both the child's genetic and gestational mother.[84]

Radical feminists who oppose contracted motherhood see in the defense of the genetic father's rights a strong reaffirmation of patriarchy. Of concern is the claim, among others, that genetic fathers "unwillingly deprived of access to their children" experience the *same* "feeling of regret and self-betrayal" that contracted mothers feel when they are forced to give up their children.[85] The claim is based on the assumption that genetic fathers and contracted mothers have an equal relationship to their children; but, as many radical feminists see it, such equality does not exist. Because the genetic father in surrogacy is usually distanced from a number of the connections that genetic fathers can ordinarily make with their developing children—following gestational development, attending birthing classes, participating at delivery, caring for the child immediately at birth—the genetic father in surrogacy will have a harder time forging immediate bonds with his child than will the genetic father in nonsurrogacy arrangements. In addition, the kinds of bond a genetic father can establish with his child are inherently more tenuous than those a contracted mother can establish with her child as she carries it to term. Thus, if anyone should have the benefit of a doubt in surrogacy disputes, it is the contracted mother, who, more than the genetic father, stands to be hurt by a forced separation from the child she has brought into the world. □

CONCLUSION

As we have seen in this chapter, reproductive technology raises profound questions about motherhood—about the importance or nonimportance of genetic and gestational links to the children one rears. It also raises troubling questions about power—about who controls reproduction in societies such as ours. Refusing to reproduce and to mother may be the safest course of action for women who wish to escape the snares of patriarchy; but because any such refusal represents, for many women at least, an act of self-denial, there may also be good reason for women to lay claim to those dimensions of reproduction and mothering that have not been distorted by patriarchal socialization. The main problem, of course, is to determine precisely what it is about reproduction and mothering that is, from women's point of view, both power giving and pleasure giving. Whatever the difficulties that may accompany this search, the woman who completes it successfully is unlikely to be disappointed. Rather, she is likely to discover why it is that *she* wants to mother—and how much.

————— ■ —————

CHAPTER FOUR

Radical Feminism on Gender and Sexuality

RADICAL FEMINISTS HAVE TRADITIONALLY taken the lead not only in articulating the "highly elaborate" and "deeply entrenched" nature of the sex/gender system,[1] but also in sketching exit routes out of it. In particular, radical feminists have proposed several ways to free women from the cage of femininity. These proposals have ranged from working toward an androgynous culture in which male and female differences are minimized to replacing male culture with female culture. Similarly, radical feminists have proposed several ways to enable women to escape from the sexual domination of men. These have ranged from transforming the institution of heterosexuality so that neither men nor women play a dominant role to rejecting heterosexuality in favor of celibacy, autoeroticism, or lesbianism. Although much of what they have had to say about sex and gender has also been said by nonradical feminists, radical feminists should be credited with detailing the ways in which men, rather than "society" or "conditions," have forced women into oppressive gender roles and sexual behavior. □

BIOLOGICAL SEX AND PATRIARCHAL GENDER

Androgyny as the Solution to the Patriarchal Imposition of "Femininity" and "Masculinity"

Millett's Sexual Politics

One of the first radical feminists to insist that the roots of women's oppression are buried deep in patriarchy's sex/gender system was Kate Millett. In her *Sexual Politics* (1970), Millett argued that sex is political primarily because the male-female relationship is the paradigm for all *power* relationships: "Social caste supercedes all other forms of inegalitarianism: racial, political, or economic, and unless the clinging to male supremacy as a birthright is finally forgone, all systems of oppression will continue to function simply by virtue of their logical and emotional mandate in the primary human situation."[2] Because male control of the public and private worlds is what constitutes patriarchy, male control must be eliminated if women are to be liberated. But this is no easy task. To eliminate male control, men and women have to eliminate gender—specifically, sexual status, role, and temperament—as it has been constructed under patriarchy.

Patriarchal ideology, according to Millett, exaggerates biological differences between men and women, making certain that men always have the dominant, or "masculine," roles and that women always have the subordinate, or "feminine," ones. This ideology is particularly powerful because through conditioning, men usually secure the apparent consent of the very women they oppress. They do this through institutions such as the academy, the church, and the family, each of which justifies and reinforces women's subordination to men with the result that most women internalize a sense of inferiority to men. Should a woman refuse to accept patriarchal ideology, and should she manifest her mistrust by casting off her femininity—that is, her submissiveness/subordination— men will use coercion to accomplish what conditioning has failed to achieve. Intimidation, observed Millett, is everywhere in patriarchy. The streetwise woman realizes that if she wants to survive in patriarchy, she had better act "feminine," or else she may be subjected to "a variety of cruelties and barbarities."[3]

Millett stressed that despite all the attempts to condition and coerce them, however, women have never been brought under the complete control of men. During the 1800s in particular, women's resistance to men's power took many forms, including the women's movement inaugurated in 1848 at Seneca Falls, New York. This spirited movement helped women gain not only in legal, political, and economic liberties and equalities but also in sexual ones. Nevertheless, the women's movement of the 1800s ultimately failed to liberate women. Because the patriarchal "socialization process of temperament and role differentiation"[4] remained largely intact, reactionaries were able to lead a misogynistic counterrevolution between 1930 and 1960.

Among the reactionaries Millett singled out for particular criticism were D. H. Lawrence, Henry Miller, and Norman Mailer. Hailed as intellectual luminaries, these three authors wrote with such authority that their *descriptions* of relationships in which women are sexually humiliated and abused by men tend to be read as *prescriptions* for sexual conduct.[5] Men and women who read these writers begin to feel inadequate—or at least dull, boring, and decidedly unsexy—if they are not relating to each other in the same way as characters in, for example, Miller's *Sexus*.

> "You never wear any undies do you? You're a slut, do you know it?"
> I pulled her dress up and made her sit that way while I finished my coffee.
> "Play with it a bit while I finish this."
> "You're filthy," she said, but she did as I told her.
> "Take your two fingers and open it up. I like the color of it."
> . . . With this I reached for a candle on the dresser at my side and I handed it to her.
> "Let's see if you can get it in all the way. . . . "
> "You can make me do anything, you dirty devil."
> "You like it, don't you."[6]

To the argument that readers of *Sexus* can tell the difference between fiction and reality, Millett replied that fiction often functions in much the same way that advertising does. The perfectly slim bodies of the models who grace the covers of *Vogue* become standards for the whole of womankind. Nobody has to articulate an explicit law, "Thou shalt mold thine lumpen body in the image of Cheryl Tiegs." Every woman simply knows what is expected of her, what it means to be an adequate woman.

In addition to this literary trio, Millett branded as "reactionary" two other groups: neo-Freudians and Parsonian functionalists. Although Sigmund Freud's openness about sexuality, his willingness to talk about what people do or do not do in the bedroom, initially appeared as a progressive step toward better, more various, and more liberating sexual relations, Millett claimed that his disciples used his writings to "rationalize the invidious relationship between the sexes, to ratify traditional roles, and to validate temperamental differences."[7] In a similar vein, the followers of Talcott Parsons, an eminent sociologist, used his writings to argue that distinctions between masculine and feminine traits are biological/ natural rather than cultural/artificial; and that without rigid gender dimorphism, society could not function as well as it supposedly does. Convinced that gender identities and behaviors are not "an arbitrary imposition on an infinitely plastic biological base," but rather "an adjustment to the real biological differences between the sexes," Parsonian functionalists confidently asserted that women's subordination to men is natural.[8]

Rather than concluding her discussion of male reactionaries on a despairing note, Millett ended it on an optimistic note. Late 1970s women were, she believed, regrouping their forces. Aware that their nineteenth-century predecessors had made some mistakes, these twentieth-century feminists were determined not to repeat history. What Millett observed in contemporary feminism was a determined effort to destroy the sex/gender system—the real source of women's oppression—and to create a new society in which men and women are equals at every level of existence.[9]

Although in 1970, Millett looked forward to an androgynous future, to an integration of separate masculine and feminine subcultures, she insisted that this integration must proceed cautiously with an evaluation of the true human desirability of all masculine and feminine traits. "Obedience," as it has been traditionally exhibited by women, for example, should not be unreflectively celebrated as a desirable female trait; that is, as a trait an androgynous person should recognize as positive and, therefore, seek to possess. Nor is "aggressiveness," as it has been traditionally exhibited by men, to be incorporated into the psyche of the androgynous person as a desirable masculine trait. Androgyny, speculated Millett, is a worthy ideal only if the feminine and masculine qualities integrated in the androgynous person are separately worthy.[10] After all, if we are told that the ideal human combines in himself/herself masculine arrogance and feminine servility, we will be less favorably impressed than if we are told that the ideal human combines in himself/herself the strength traditionally associated with men and the compassion traditionally associated with women. Not only does it seem undesirable to combine in one person the two vices of arrogance and servility—the excess and defect of self-respect, respectively—it also seems impossible, given that they are polar opposites. In contrast, it is not only possible to combine in one person the complementary qualities of strength and compassion; it is also desirable because both qualities are likely to help a person grow and live in community.

French's Analysis in Beyond Power

Like Millett fifteen years earlier, Marilyn French believed that patriarchy is the paradigm par excellence for all modes of oppression; that sexism is prior to all other "isms," including classism and racism. As French saw it, the oppression of women by men leads logically to further systems of domination. If it is possible to justify men's domination of women, it is possible to justify any and all forms of domination. "Stratification of men above women," wrote French, "leads in time to stratification of classes: an elite rules over people perceived as 'closer to nature,' savage, bestial, animalistic."[11] Because French believed that patriarchy is the sine qua non for oppression of any and every kind, she undertook a systematic account of the origins of patriarchy before explaining the enslaving ideology that sustains it—"power-over"—and the liberating ideology that could undo it—"pleasure-with."

After inquiring into the origins of patriarchy, French concluded that early humans lived in harmony with nature.[12] They saw themselves as small parts of a larger whole into which they had to fit if they wanted to live. Based on evidence from primates and the world's remaining "simple societies," French speculated that the first human societies were probably matricentric (mother centered), for it was the mother who probably played the primary role in the group's survival-oriented activities of bonding, sharing, and harmonious participation in nature. Nature was friend; and as sustainer of nature, as reproducer of life, woman was also friend.[13]

As the population grew, however, humans unfortunately found that food became scarce. There was suddenly little available to hunt and/or to gather, and nature was no longer experienced as a generous friend but as a niggardly foe. Nature would have to be drilled, dug, and plowed for whatever bounty "she" was holding back from humans. Thus, humans literally took matters into their own hands, developing techniques to free themselves from the whims of nature. The more control humans gained over nature, however, the more they separated themselves from it physically and psychologically. French commented that because a "distance had opened up between humans and their environment as a result of increasing controls exercised over nature," humans became alienated from nature.[14] Alienation, defined by French as a profound sense of separation, arouses "hostility," which in turn leads to "fear" and finally to "enmity." Not surprisingly, these negative feelings intensified man's desire to control not only nature but also woman, who, on account of her reproductive role, had been associated with nature.[15]

With man's desire to control the monolith "woman/nature"[16] was born patriarchy, a hierarchical system that values power-over. Originally developed to ensure the human community's survival, power-over rapidly became, under patriarchy, a value cultivated simply for the experience of being the person in charge, the lawgiver, the "boss," number one in the "pecking order." French worried that the competitive values of patriarchy will overwhelm the values of cooperation and that competition, untempered by cooperation, will inevitably lead to conflict.[17]

Because French wished to spare the world conflict—particularly as it could, in these times, escalate into a nuclear holocaust—she insisted that "feminine" values must be reintegrated into the "masculine" society patriarchal ideology has created. If we want to see the twenty-first century, said French, we must value in our lives and actions "love and compassion and sharing and nutritiveness [sic] equally with control and structure, possessiveness and status."[18]

Were we to take this last assertion at face value, we could easily infer that, for French, the best society is an androgynous one in which the

historically feminine values of love, compassion, sharing, and nutritiveness
are treasured just as much as the historically masculine values of control,
structure, possessiveness, and status. Yet, a closer reading suggests that
French valued "feminine" values more than "masculine" values and that
any time she affirmed a "masculine" value, it had been subjected to
what Joyce Trebilcot called a "feminist reconceiving"[19]—a linguistic
reinterpretation that may involve a change in the descriptive meaning of
a term, the evaluative meaning of a term, or both.[20] Most of French's
affirmations of masculine values involved a change in their descriptive
meaning. For example, she did not argue that masculine values such as
control and structure, possessiveness and status are inherently evil. Rather,
she argued that the meaning of each of these male values needs to be
reinterpreted. "Structure," for example, is good, provided that it is
intended to interconnect people—not to rank order them.[21] (Of course,
to affirm structure on the condition that it connect humans horizontally
rather than rank them vertically is, arguably, to dramatically alter the
traditional meaning of the term.)

That French's androgyny involved a substantial reinterpretation of most
male/masculine traits, but not of most female/feminine traits, became
increasingly clear throughout *Beyond Power*. At times, French came close
to asserting that to the degree that humanness was identified with
"masculinity" in the past, it should be identified with "femininity" in
the future because a masculine world is less fully human than a feminine
one.[22]

Based as it is on the value of power-over, by which French meant the
domination by one group or person of all others, the masculine world
can accommodate only those values that serve it. It has room for "true
grit," "doing what you have to do," and "the end justifying the means,"
but no room for "knowing when to stop," savoring the "best things in
life" (which, we are told, are "for free"), or reflecting on process as
well as product. Thus, to be a total man, or patriarch, is not to be a
full human being but to be what Dorothy Dinnerstein, a psychoanalytic
feminist, termed a minotaur—"[the] gigantic and eternally infantile
offspring of a mother's unnatural lust, [the] male representative of mindless,
greedy power, [who] insatiably devours live human flesh."[23]

In contrast, the feminine world, based as it is on the value of pleasure-
with, by which French meant the ability of one group or person to affirm
all others, can accommodate all sorts of values, including those derived
from what we generally view as opposite sources. Pleasure, insisted
French, can be derived from self as well as others, from the body as
well as the mind, from the simple and bucolic as well as the complex
and urbane. French saw pleasure as a very broad and deep concept, able

to accommodate all of the enriching experiences we believe a full human person should have.[24]

Although French advanced pleasure as an androgynous value (one that is *human* enough to encompass both traditionally masculine and traditionally feminine approaches to life), in point of fact, pleasure may ultimately be as feminine as power was masculine. French's new androgynous person may really be a fully actualized woman. To be truly human seems, for French, to be fully woman: a combination of all that was traditionally good about being a woman and all that could have been good about being a man had these traits been developed along matricentric rather than patriarchal lines. So, for example, power is bad not in and of itself, but only when it appears as power-over. When it appears as power-to it is good and humanizing. "Power-to," wrote French, "refers to ability, capacity, and connotes a kind of freedom," whereas power-over "refers to domination."[25]

Whereas power-to is constructive, power-over is destructive. Power-to seeks to create and to further pleasure for everyone; power-over seeks to destroy and spread pain. Thus, according to French, we must foster power-to and use it to further goals of human survival, and we must reject power-over insofar as it has catapulted Western, postmodern societies into the lead of a march toward Armageddon. French admitted that power-to cannot exist without power-over. Power-to is the result of community support networks that allow persons to succeed at something the community considers worthy. To succeed, each person needs both individual talent and communal resources to nurture that talent; neither is sufficient alone. But communal resources are limited; and the price of one person's success may be another person's failure. The process of actualizing human potentiality is necessarily competitive at some level or another, and this competition implies power-over. Because of the inevitability of some form of competition, French envisioned a world without any domination whatsoever as an unattainable ideal toward which we should nonetheless strive. By exposing, as best we can, the pain inherent in power-over, we can open the way for the pleasure inherent in power-to.

Clearly, French's conception of androgyny was very different from Millett's. For Millett, at least the Millett who wrote *Sexual Politics,* constructing the androgynous person consisted in identifying and then combining the most positive masculine and feminine traits. This is a contentious process because what is a positive feminine trait for a patriarchal, Parsonian functionalist is not usually one for a radical feminist. No feminist is going to celebrate female passivity, for example. For French, the process of analyzing masculine and feminine traits with respect to their desirability as positive human traits was similar. However, she was ultimately unconvinced that under patriarchy, there are any unambiguously positive masculine traits for the androgynous person to possess. To be sure, she saw that there are positive terms for masculine traits (for example, independence), but patriarchy has so distorted the meaning of these terms that the behaviors and attitudes to which they currently refer are negative. Thus, before any masculine trait can be made part of the androgynous person, there must be a rectification of terms. Positive meanings, and therefore positive referents, must be supplied for positive-sounding masculine terms. Only then can the construction of the androgynous person proceed.[26]

Going Beyond Androgyny: Female Culture as the Ultimate Solution to the Patriarchal Imposition of "Femininity" and "Masculinity"

Like Kate Millett and Marilyn French, Mary Daly challenges patriarchy's construction of gender. As Daly sees it, oppressive gender roles will be deconstructed as a result of a revolution that, she predicts, will begin with dissident women. This emphasis on women's revolutionary role eventually takes Daly far beyond the possibility of an acceptable androgyny at the end of any road that begins in patriarchy. Although Daly begins her journey in *Beyond God the Father* with a plea for androgyny, she ends it in *Pure Lust* with a spirited defense of "wild," "lusty" and "wandering" women—women who no longer desire to be androgynous and who prefer to identify themselves as radical lesbian feminist separatists.

Daly's Beyond God the Father

Although Daly's thought has evolved in ways that seem to distance her from the thoughts she expresses in *Beyond God the Father* and *Gyn/Ecology*, her thoughts in *Pure Lust* defy temporality (any convenient splitting of her thinking into past, present, and future modalities). Thus, I prefer to use the present tense when I write about Mary Daly's thinking, which moves comfortably forward and backward in time, refusing to be bound by the literary and stylistic conventions that manage to limit most of us.

In her first major work, *Beyond God the Father*, Mary Daly focuses on God as the paradigm for all patriarchs, arguing that unless He is dethroned from both men's and women's consciousness, women will never be empowered as full persons.[27] An off-repeated idea in *Beyond God the Father* is that if anyone ever had a power-over complex, it is the transcendent God we meet in Judaism, Islam, and especially Christianity. God is so remote and aloof that He dwells in a place, Heaven, that is beyond Earth, reminding us that ultimate power-over also implies absolute separation-from. A transcendent God, observes Daly, is a God who thinks in terms of I-It, subject-object, or self-other relationships; and what is most unlike this transcendent God, this total being, is the natural world He called into existence out of total nothingness. Thus, woman, who is associated with nature on account of her reproductive powers, plays "It," object, and other not only to God's "I," subject, and self but also to that of His image and likeness: man.

Given that this old, transcendent God rejects women, Daly wishes to replace Him with a new, immanent god. Dwelling within the universe as opposed to outside of it, an immanent god thinks in terms of I-Thou, subject-subject, or self-self relationships, and the natural world is as much a part of him as he is of it. Thus, women are at least equal to men before this god, who Daly describes as Be-ing.[28]

One of the main ways in which I-It thinking is reflected in patriarchal society, says Daly, is through the institution of rigid masculine and feminine gender roles that polarize the human community into two groups. Because men collectively perceive and define women as the second sex, each man becomes an I, or self, and each woman becomes an It, or other. One way, then, to overcome I-It thinking, and the transcendent God who thinks I-It thoughts, is to break down gender dimorphism by constructing the androgynous person, who is neither "I" nor "It" but beyond both forms.

Daly's few comments about androgyny in *Beyond God the Father* suggest that it was not destined to remain her favored approach (in any form) to women's liberation. Daly contrasts her conception of androgyny with the "pluralist" and the "assimilation" conceptions forwarded by other, mainly liberal, feminists.[29] According to the pluralist model, men and women have complementary traits, the separateness of which represents no problem provided that they are equally valued; thus, once this valuation is secured, women will experience the same liberty and equality that men do. According to the assimilation model, women can achieve full personhood only in concert with men. To free themselves from oppression, women who are ready, willing, and able to develop masculine traits should be permitted and even required to do so.

Daly rejects these liberal feminist approaches to gender polarity because neither asks itself whether masculinity and/or femininity are ideas worth preserving. This is, of course, a question Daly shares with French, but whereas French seemed interested in reinterpreting, or "feminizing," *masculine* traits, Daly is intent on reinterpreting—although certainly not on "masculinizing"—traditional *feminine* traits, including many of those that struck French as unproblematic. What Daly suggests is that positive feminine traits such as love, compassion, sharing, and nutritiveness need to be carefully distinguished from their excesses—the sort of masochistic feminine "virtues" for which they are frequently mistaken. Loving is good, but under patriarchy it can become, for women, a form of total self-sacrifice, or martyrdom. Thus, Daly believes that the construction of the truly androgynous person cannot and must not begin until women say "no" to the values of the "morality of victimization." Out of this "no," says Daly, will come a "yes" to the values of the "ethics of personhood."[30] By refusing to be the other, by becoming a self with needs, wants, and interests of her own, woman will put an end to the game of man the master/woman the slave, a game that cannot, after all, be played without slaves. Once this pernicious game is stopped— once sexism is trumped—all other "isms" will come tumbling down as well. All classifications, labels, and categories will be overcome, and a new being will come into existence: the whole person, the androgynous person.

Daly's Arguments in Gyn/Ecology

In *Beyond God the Father*, Daly observes that the Unholy Trinity of Rape, Genocide, and War combined in their one patriarchal person the legions of sexism, racism, and classism. In *Gyn/Ecology*, she enhances this claim, arguing that this Unholy Trinity, this single patriarchal person, has but one essential message: necrophilia, defined as "obsession with and usually erotic attraction toward and stimulation by corpses, typically evidenced by overt acts (as copulation with a corpse)."[31] Whereas Daly argues in *Beyond God the Father* that a woman cannot thrive so long as she subscribes to the morality of victimization, in *Gyn/Ecology* she cautions that a woman cannot even survive so long as she remains in patriarchy. Not only are men out to oppress women's minds, they are out to oppress women's bodies through such practices as Hindu suttee, Chinese foot binding, African female circumcision, European witch burning, and Western gynecology.[32]

In *Gyn/Ecology*, Daly rejects three words she had used in *Beyond God the Father:* God, androgyny, and homosexuality. She rejects the term *God* because it signals death to woman and blocks her "life-loving be-ing." She rejects the term *homosexuality* because it neglects lesbians and suggests that same-sexed love is the same for women as for men. Finally, she rejects the term *androgyny* because it twists words and conveys something like "John Travolta and Farrah Fawcett-Majors scotch-taped together."[33]

Daly's rejection of androgyny in *Gyn/Ecology* is the result of her having thought through to its logical conclusion the assumption that reproduction, gender, and sexuality are constructed under patriarchy. If patriarchy has constructed "femininity"—if it has constructed Mary and Eve, the madonna and the whore, the positive feminine qualities of nurturance, compassion, and gentleness and the negative feminine qualities of pettiness, jealousy, and vanity—then there is good reason for women to reject everything for which these labels stand. "Femininity," asserts Daly, "is a man-made construct, having essentially nothing to do with femaleness."[34]

According to critic Ann-Janine Morey-Gaines, Daly uses Jerzy Kosinski's image of the "painted bird" to articulate in detail the differences between "femininity" and "femaleness." In Kosinski's tale of the same name, a keeper imprisons a nondescript bird simply by painting its feathers with a glittering color. Eventually, the bird is destroyed out of jealousy by her ordinary and natural-looking contemporaries. Daly reverses Kosinski's image. She suggests that when it comes to women, the ordinary, natural-looking birds (which Daly calls "wild females"), not the painted birds (which Daly looks upon as tamed, domesticated, feminized females), are the ones who suffer. For Daly, painted birds are those women who permit "daddy" to deck them out in splendor, to "cosmeticize" and perfume them, to girdle and corset them. They are also sent out by "daddy" to destroy real, natural women—those who refuse to be what the patriarchs want them to be, who insist on being themselves no matter what, who peel patriarchal paint off their minds and bodies.[35] In Daly's words, the "painted bird functions in the anti-process of double-crossing her sisters, polluting them with poisonous paint."[36] The courageous natural woman, on the other hand, is "attacked by the mutants of her own kind, the man-made women."[37]

For Daly, flying is the antidote to painting. The natural woman does not take off the paint only to become vulnerable. Rather, she "takes off"; she "sends the paint flying back into the eyes of the soul-slayers"; she "soars . . . out of the circle of Father Time" and flies "off the clock into other dimensions."[38] She is flying free of mutant fembirds (those women who have permitted themselves to be constructed by patriarchy). She is also flying free of the power of patriarchal language and, therefore, patriarchal values. Thus, the last section of *Gyn/Ecology* is a dictionary of new language. In Daly's terms, "hags," "spinsters," and "haggard heretics" "unspook" traditional language and simultaneously "spin" into being new language and themselves. Terms for women that have a pejorative connotation in patriarchal language take on celebratory meanings in Daly's language. For example, a hag is not what Merriam-Webster defines her to be: namely, "an ugly, repulsive old woman, especially an evil and malevolent one." Rather, a hag is a woman who sees through and rejects patriarchal culture's demand for submissiveness, obedience, and complicity.

In many ways, Daly's adamant rejection of androgyny leads her precisely to where Friedrich Nietzsche's transvaluation of values led him: to a redefinition of what is good and what is bad, counter to prevailing notions of good and bad. In *On the Genealogy of Morals,* Nietzsche contended that there are two basic kinds of moralities: master and slave. In a master morality, good and bad are equivalent to noble and despicable respectively. To be good is to be on top of the world. To be bad is to be repressed, oppressed, suppressed, or otherwise downtrodden. Significantly, the criteria for goodness articulated in the slave morality are the polar opposites of the criteria for goodness articulated in the master morality. Those who espouse a slave morality extol qualities such as kindness, humility, and sympathy as virtues and denigrate qualities such as assertiveness, aloofness, and pridefulness as vices. Whereas weak and dependent individuals are regarded as saints, strong and independent individuals are regarded as sinners. By the standards of slave morality, then, the good man of the master morality is evil and the bad man is good.

Motivated by an all-consuming resentment (*resentiment*) of the masters, the slaves gradually develop a negative psychic attitude toward what Nietzsche believed is the most natural drive of a human being: the will to power. As Nietzsche saw it, not only do the slaves have no desire for power; they have no desire for life. Fearful of conflict, of challenge, of charting the course of their destinies, the slaves wish to be complacent in their mediocrity. Nietzsche found them profoundly boring. But he also found them incredibly dangerous, for they seem intent on clogging Western civilization's arteries with sugar plums, placebos, and the milk of human kindness.

> For this is how things are: the diminution and leveling of European man constitutes *our* greatest danger, for the sight of him makes us weary.—We can see nothing today that wants to grow greater, we suspect that things will continue to go down, down, to become thinner, more good-natured, more prudent, more comfortable, more mediocre, more indifferent, more Chinese, more Christian—there is no doubt that man is getting "better" all the time.
>
> Here precisely is what has become a fatality for Europe—together with the fear of man we have also lost our love of him, our reverence for him, our hopes for him, even the will to him. The sight of man now makes us weary.[39]

In order to stop this will to impotence, mediocrity, and death, Nietzsche maintained that there must again occur a transvaluation of all values. By this he did not mean the creation of a new set of moral values. Rather, he meant to declare war upon the accepted slave values of his time, which he identified as the values of Judaism, Christianity, democracy, and socialism—any philosophy or theology that asks the individual to sacrifice himself/herself for the greater good of the community. Because slave morality is, according to Nietzsche, a perversion of the original, natural morality/psychology of the masters, transvaluation must consist in rejecting the slave morality/psychology. Transvaluation implies that all the stronger, or master, values still exist but now go unrecognized under false names. So, for example, the will to power appears under false names such as cruelty, injury, appropriation, suppression, exploitation. These names are false because, having been distorted by the slaves, they do not connote what the masters originally meant, which had everything to do with affirming life and nothing to do with embracing death.[40]

Daly is Nietzschean not because she posits two types of morality—a superior female morality and an inferior male morality—but because she insists that when it comes to women, she whom the patriarch calls evil is in fact good, whereas she whom the patriarch calls good is in fact bad. Thus, if a woman is to escape the traps men have laid for her— if she is to assert her power, to be all that she can—then she must realize that it is not good for her to sacrifice, deny, and deprive herself for the sake of the men and children in her life. In other words, what *is* good for women, insists Daly, is precisely what patriarchy identifies as evil for women. For example, Daly insists that it is good for a woman to be a hag.

> *Hag* is from an Old English word meaning harpy, witch. Webster's gives as the first and "archaic" meaning of *hag:* "a female demon: FURY, HARPY." It also formerly meant: "an evil or frightening spirit." (Lest this sound too negative, we should ask the relevant questions: "Evil" by whose definition? "Frightening" to whom?) A third archaic definition of *hag* is "nightmare." (The important question is: Whose nightmare?) *Hag* is also defined as "an ugly or evil-looking old woman." But this considering the source, may be considered a compliment. For the beauty of strong, creative women is "ugly" by misogynistic standards of "beauty." The look of female-identified women is "evil" to those who fear us. As for "old," ageism is a feature of phallic society. For women who have transvaluated this, a Crone is one who should be an example of strength, courage, and wisdom.[41]

Clearly, by the time she wrote *Gyn/Ecology*, Daly had rejected the "ideal" of androgyny. Rather, the image of the "wild female" must capture the thoughts of the woman who would actualize her full potential. To become a whole person, to make contact with her true, natural self, a woman need only strip away the false identity—femininity—that patriarchy has constructed for her. (We are left wondering, however, whether this true, natural self is an original self that existed before both patriarchy and matriarchy or whether it is the *counterfactual* self that would have been constructed had women and men lived in matriarchies rather than patriarchies.)

Values in Pure Lust

In *Pure Lust,* Daly continues her transvaluation of values. In this book about woman's power, Daly extends French's analysis of power-to. It is this power that men have been feeding on, making women grow thin, weak, frail, even anorexic. In order to grow strong, women must resist the trap of androgyny. Utterly dependent upon their God-given helpmates, patriarchs promise "androgyny" in a last-ditch effort to keep women by their sides. "Come, join forces with us. Masculinity and femininity together!" Daly turns a deaf ear to this plea, for she sees it as just a ploy on the part of men to appropriate for themselves whatever is best about women. Daly reminds us that at the end of the film *Tootsie,* after the lead character's maleness had been disclosed (he had been posing as a female television star named Dorothy), he tells Julie, a woman he had befriended in his incarnation as Dorothy, that he actually *is* Dorothy. "The message clearly is one of cannibalistic androgynous maleness. Little Dustin, whom Julie had loved but rejected because she believed he was a woman, incorporates the best of womanhood—like Dionysius and Jesus before him."[42] Androgyny, as Daly articulates it in *Pure Lust,* means that whatever is female is subsumed or even consumed by whatever is male. Instead of submitting to the gynocidal process of androgyny, women must spin new, powerful self-understandings, radically apart from men and their will to subsume and consume women.

What is most impressive about *Pure Lust* is that in it, Daly surpasses whatever Nietzsche managed to accomplish in his transvaluation of values. Daly not only gives new *prescriptive,* or evaluative, meanings to terms; she gives them new *descriptive* meanings at the same time. The term *lust* is a case in point. Daly writes that "the usual meaning of *lust* within the lecherous state of patriarchy is well known. It means 'sexual desire, especially of a violent self-indulgent character: LECHERY, LASCIVIOUS-NESS.' "[43] Lust, then, is evil, but only because we live in a patriarchy with its slave morality, which resents women. Lust has other, nonpa-triarchal, good meanings such as "VIGOR," "FERTILITY," "CRAV-ING," "EAGERNESS," and "ENTHUSIASM."[44] Lusty women wander and wonder in a hundred directions at once. Indeed, the lusty women of *Pure Lust* are the wild females of *Gyn/Ecology,* the women who refuse to be domesticated by men. For the domesticators, the benevolent fathers, the wise patriarchs, Daly has no tolerance. She names their society a "sadosociety," which is "formed/framed by statutes of studs, decrees of drones, canons of cocks, fixations of fixers, precepts of prickers, regulations of rakes and rippers . . . bore-ocracy."[45] Daly has no use for the petrified language of patriarchy and refers to it only with the aim of investing words such as witch and father with drastically new meanings in a drastically new field of values. To imply that Jefferson is a stud, Reagan a drone, the Pope a cock, and Tip O'Neill a rake and ripper is to speak of, and to speak out, a world of values radically different and separate from those of patriarchy.[46]

The whole of *Pure Lust* constitutes a transvaluation of the terms with which the moral character of men and, especially, women are judged. It is also a detailed analysis of the passions that can affect women's journey to a rich state of being Daly describes as Be-Longing, Be-Friending, and Be-Witching.[47] Daly contrasts genuine, or bona fide, passions—love, desire, joy, hate, aversion, sorrow, hope, despair, fear, and anger—with plastic passions on the one hand and potted passions on the other.

In contrast to genuine passions, which spur women on to action, plastic passions leave women passive and deprived of a sense of purpose. The plastic passions of guilt, anxiety, depression, hostility, bitterness, resentment, frustration, boredom, resignation, and, interestingly, fulfillment enervate women. Daly's contrasting of the plastic passion of fulfillment with the real passion of joy is particularly instructive. She claims that fulfillment is the "therapeutized perversion" of joy. A fulfilled woman is "filled full," "finished," "fixed" just the way patriarchy likes her. Because she is so "totaled," she cannot live the "e-motion of joy." She lacks the energy to move/act purposely.[48] Fulfillment, says Daly, is another term for Betty Friedan's "problem that has no name"—having a comfortable home, a successful husband, a wonderful child . . . but no joy.[49]

Another set of pseudopassions Daly analyzes are what she calls "potted passions." These passions are more real than plastic, but, like bonsai trees, their growth is stunted. To better understand the phenomenon Daly has described, we have only to compare a real orange tree with one of those miniature versions people are prone to purchase for their homes come January. Love, for example, may be a "many splendored thing," but when it is potted, packaged, and sold as "romance," women are duped into settling for its illusion rather than its reality.[50] There is, of course, something tragic about settling for so little when there is so much to be had. Nietzsche hoped that the advent of the *übermensch* (overman) would unleash the potential in people for greatness. Similarly, Daly hopes Elemental Women will inspire their sisters to release themselves from the pots and plastic molds that block their passions. Once woman's passions are released, no patriarchal morality will be able to restrain her volcanic and tidal forces. She will be pure, positive spinster. □

FEMINIST SEXUALITY

To the same degree that socially constructed gender and reproductive roles restrict a woman's identity and behavior, socially constructed sexual roles make it exceedingly difficult for a woman to identify and develop her own sexual desires and needs. As many radical feminists see it, sexuality is the crucial issue in feminism because "aggression and the 'need' to dominate form a routine part of what is accepted as [normal] male sexuality."[51] Male violence against women is normalized and legitimized in sexual practices through the assumption that when it comes to sex, men are by nature aggressive and dominant, whereas women are by nature passive and submissive.

Because male dominance and female submission are the norm in something as fundamental as sexuality, they become the norm in other contexts as well. As most radical feminists see it, women will never be men's full political, economic, and social equals until heterosexual relations are entirely egalitarian—a state of affairs not likely to be achieved so long as women's sexuality is interpreted in terms of men's sexuality— as if Eve had indeed been made only to service Adam's every want and need.

This last point was the impetus for Catharine MacKinnon's essay, "Feminism, Marxism, Method and the State: An Agenda for Theory," in which she argued that sexuality is *the* locus of male power. Gender, the socially constructed dynamic of male domination and female submission, is rooted in the institution of heterosexuality.[52] Each and every element of the female gender stereotype is sexually charged. "Softness," for example, is a gender trait associated with women; it is sexually charged because, as MacKinnon defined it, "softness" is "pregnability by something hard."[53]

Like Firestone, MacKinnon worked with traditional Marxist arguments, using them to make analogies between the oppression of workers and the oppression of women. Work is important in Marxist theory, because through work people shape not only their material environment but also their personal identities. Thus, to deprive people of the products of their work is to separate them from what literally constitutes their identity. Analogously, sexuality is important in feminist theory because woman's personal identity is very bound up with her sexuality. Unfortunately, what is most her own (sexuality) is "most taken away."[54] This point cannot be overemphasized. It is similar to one that has previously been made by Carolyn M. Schafer and Marilyn Frye. In their analysis of rape, Schafer and Frye appeal to the notion of a domain. A domain is where a person lives. At the center of this domain is a set of "person-properties" (for example, the ability to reason, the capacity for self-awareness, the ability to deliberate and make choices) and their physical location, the body. Away from the center of this domain are the things and spaces the person uses as he or she engages in thought and action. To violate the center of a person's domain is to inflict maximum harm upon him or her. Since rape is "a use of a person which involves tampering with parts of its self which are for most people centrally rather than peripherally involved in their personal identity,"[55] it is the kind of crime that threatens to disintegrate a woman—that is, to make her less of a person by depriving her of bodily autonomy. In rape—and also in incest, sexual harassment, prostitution, and pornography—a man takes a woman's sexuality, as it is mediated through her body, and through his action proclaims that women's sexuality is *for men*—for what men want and need.[56]

To say that women's sexuality is for men but that men's sexuality is not for women is to say something that would probably not occur to the ordinary person on the street. Because radical feminists believe that most people mistake appearances for reality when it comes to sexuality, they challenge the ordinary person's eyesight. "Look," says the radical feminist, "and see for yourself who has the upper hand in all heterosexual relationships—it is man." "For whom does prostitution exist?" "For whom does pornography exist?" "Who rapes whom?" "Who harasses whom?" "Who batters whom?" And so on. Thus, unlike the liberal feminist, who believes that given the correct legal and political institutions, heterosexual relations will be voluntary, egalitarian, and just, and unlike the Marxist feminist, who insists that given the right economic institutions, heterosexual relations will not be exploitative, alienating, or oppressive, the radical feminist believes that women will always remain subordinate to men unless sexuality is reconceived and reconstructed. The extent to which radical femininists part company with both liberal and Marxist feminists regarding the issue of sexuality—and the significance of this divergence—becomes clearer upon a close analysis of those kinds of relationship that are, for example, depicted in pornography. □

PORNOGRAPHY AS SYMPTOM AND SYMBOL OF MALE-CONTROLLED FEMALE SEXUALITY

In recent years, pornography has become one of the central issues in radical feminist literature. On account of the widespread use and increasingly antifemale tone of pornography, radical feminists have identified it as an especially pernicious factor in promoting male dominance. Thus, they have sought to expose pornography for what it really is—the intentional degradation and subordination of women to men—and to seek either legal and/or extralegal measures to eliminate it. The analysis and the solution offered have sparked considerable debate within as well as outside the feminist community and have led to serious disagreements between radical and liberal feminists concerning the feasibility/desirability of strict legal controls on pornography. By attending to these disagreements, we will come to understand just how difficult it is to free female sexuality from the conceptual grid of male sexuality.

The Prefeminist Debate on Pornography

Pornography, or sexually explicit material consisting in graphic pictorial depictions and verbal descriptions of sexual organs and various modes of coitus, has always been a matter for debate in the United States. In general, the debate has been staged between cultural conservatives brandishing the sword of public morality and civil libertarians waving the flag of individual liberty.

Relying on the principles of legal moralism[57] and legal paternalism,[58] cultural conservatives traditionally argued, first, that good sex is always heterosexual, usually takes place in marriage, and is, if at all possible, oriented toward procreation; second, that sexually explicit material activates all those polymorphous perverse snakes deep within us that threaten to undo civilization in general and each of us in particular; third, that sexually explicit material is either not real speech, because it is a noncognitive mode of expression appealing not to brains but to penises and the like, or, if real speech, then lacking in serious literary, artistic, political, or scientific value and therefore undeserving of First Amendment protection; and, finally, that the law ought to serve as morality's handmaiden, protecting it from the forces of the flesh that would, if they only could, devour it.

Relying on the harm principle[59] and, to a lesser extent, the offense principle,[60] civil libertarians traditionally argued, first, that good sex is a matter of aesthetics, not ethics, of taste, not virtue; second, that sexually explicit material invites us to try out a variety of sexual experiences and to overcome any number of our unhealthy Puritanical and Victorian sexual inhibitions; third, that sexually explicit material is real speech with a socially valuable message—"Cast off your old, tired, and repressive sexual mores and delight in the erotic celebration of the body"; and, finally, that the law ought to serve simply as a system of green and red lights that permits each of us to get our sexual satisfaction whenever, wherever, however, and with whomever or whatever we please, provided that no one, with the possible exception of ourselves, is either harmed or egregiously offended in the process.

The Feminist Debate on Pornography

In the 1970s, a woman's voice shattered the predictable format of the debate between conservatives and libertarians. This voice sang neither the conservative praises of public morality nor the libertarian praises of individual freedom; rather, it pleaded for equality for women. As feminist antipornographers saw it—and here I am primarily referring to radical feminists, although it must be noted that many other kinds of feminists were and still are members of groups such as Women Against Pornography and Woman Against Violence in Pornography and the Media—pornography was not so much about sex per se as about male power exerted against females in the context of heterosexual relations.

Feminist Antipornographers
and the Case Against Pornography

Relying on the harm principle, specified this time as harm done to women, feminist antipornographers noted that there are two kinds of sexually explicit depictions or descriptions—*erotica* (from the Greek *eros,* love or a creative principle) and *thanatica* (from the Greek *thanatos,* death or a destructive principle).[61] Although both erotica and thanatica are forms of sexually explicit speech, there are two crucial differences between them: (1) whereas erotic representations show sexual relationships between fully consenting, equal partners who identify emotionally with each other, thanatic representations show sexual relationships in which full consent, real equality, and emotional identification are absent; and (2) whereas erotica encourages both men and women to treat each other as full human persons, thanatica encourages men in particular to treat women as mere objects. Because of these two crucial differences, feminist antipornographers have argued that whatever First Amendment protection thanatica (hereafter referred to as pornography, thanatic pornography, or violent pornography) has, it is overridden by the likelihood that it harms women: specifically by promoting sexual harassment, rape, and woman battering, and generally by degrading them.

Although most feminist antipornographers believe there is a continuum from pulpy romance novels, which tell stories of thinly disguised male domination and female submission, to soft-core magazines such as *Playboy,* which feature depictions of quivering young bunnies disrobing in front of elderly Great White Hunters, to hard-core magazines such as *Bondage,* which highlight scenes of men torturing women (for example, shots of businessmen systematically applying hot irons, scissors, torches, and knives to the breasts and vaginas of their secretaries),[62] feminist antipornographers have in the main directed their campaigns against the "easy cases." These have included films such as *Snuff,* in which a woman, in order to satiate a man's bloodthirsty sexual desires, is treated to a fate worse than hanging and quartering. If any sexually explicit depictions and descriptions may be legally regulated, feminist antipornographers maintain that it is those where the inequalities between coercing, abusing men and coerced, abused women are too blatant to be explained away as freely chosen, sadomasochistic fun and frolic.

At this point the predictable objection is made that although there may be legal grounds for restricting forms of pornographic behavior such as sexual harassment, rape, and woman battering, these grounds cannot be invoked to restrict representations of such behavior because pornographic depictions and descriptions are not harmful per se. To this objection feminist antipornographers have made two basic replies: (1) although in and of itself pornography is not harmful in the way that sexual harassment, rape, and woman battering are, it encourages people (men) to behave in these harmful ways; and (2) pornography *is* in and of itself harmful because it defames and/or discriminates against women.

The first argument—that pornography causes violent behavior toward women—is, of course, based on the belief that thought leads to action, a widely held belief that is nevertheless enormously difficult to prove. Two presidential commissions, one in 1970, the other in 1986, investigated the matter and came up with conflicting results. Whereas the 1970 Lockhart Commission on Obscenity and Pornography concluded that there is "no evidence . . . that exposure to explicit sexual materials plays a significant role in the causation of delinquent or criminal behavior among youth or adults,"[63] the 1986 Meese Commission on Pornography concluded that there is evidence of a causal link between at least violent pornography and aggressive behavior toward women.[64] Significantly, both commissions drew heavy criticism. The 1970 commissioners were criticized for having relied too heavily on the work of Donald L. Mosher, who admitted that he usually showed his test subjects erotica rather than thanatica, the implication being that erotic sights dispose men to treat women gently.[65] Similarly, the 1986 commissioners were criticized for having relied almost exclusively on the work of Edward Donnerstein, who almost always showed his subjects violent pornography, the implication being that thanatic sights dispose men to treat women abusively.[66] Ironically, Donnerstein himself complained that the Meese Commission drew unwarranted conclusions from his research. Although Donnerstein never repudiated the 1986 report, he publicly commented that, in all likelihood, graphic violence, not explicit sex, triggers aggressive attitudes in spectators: "If you take out the sex and leave the violence, you get the increased violent behavior in the laboratory setting . . . . If you take out the violence and leave the sex, nothing happens."[67]

Given that there is so much uncertainty about the precise causal relationship between seeing *x* and doing *x,* no matter what recommendations an executive commission or legislative body makes about pornography, the judiciary is unlikely to support the motion. Despite some backsliding now and then, the U.S. Supreme Court's commitment to free speech is so strong that without proof positive that pornography incites men to sexually abuse women as immediately as tinkling bells cause Pavlovian dogs to salivate, the Court will not ban depictions of sexually abused women as it has the yelling of "fire" in a crowded theater. For this reason, feminist antipornographers have more recently argued not that pornography constitutes a "clear and present danger" to women, but that it constitutes a harm to women akin either to defamation or to a civil rights violation.

The defamation argument is reasoned as follows: Defamatory communications are those that damage a person's reputation by expressing to third parties thoughts that either diminish the esteem in which the defamed party is held or excite adverse feelings or opinions against him/her. Because pornographic films such as *Snuff* defame women by telling a deep and vicious lie about them—that they are all crazed masochists who crave sexual abuse—then women as individuals and perhaps as a group may bring civil suits against pornographers.

There are at least three problems with this approach. First, it is not clear that pornographers flash images of sexually abused women across the screen in order to make statements, defamatory or otherwise, about women. According to many students of film, the typical pornographer is not Bertolt Brecht trying to get across an important social message. On the contrary, the typical pornographer does not intend to *state* anything in particular when he creates images of women who plead to be tortured or killed during sexual exchanges with men. The pornographer realizes that people who patronize XXX porn films come not to be educated, but to release or relieve their sexual tensions. Thus, he provides them with the mechanisms that will, if all goes well, carry off the effluvia of socially banned sexual expressions into the realm of fantasy.[68]

Second, even if it could be established that most pornographers do intend to communicate women-degrading messages to their audiences— that is, that they mean to activate against women the brains as well as the penises of the audience—the objection will be made that Anglo-American law simply has no way to handle cases of group defamation. Traditionally, the law of defamation is concerned with the protection of an individual's reputation, not with that of a group's, especially an unwieldy and huge group like women.[69]

Third, even if it could be established that women as a group are defamed by pornography, a group defamation approach would open the floodgates to all manner of lawsuits. If women can sue the creators and purveyors of pornography for depicting and describing women as sexually warped masochists, then women can sue the producers of television commercials that portray women as rather unintelligent housewives who agonize over which laundry detergent to use. If women can initiate such suits, then industrialists can sue leftists who claim "all capitalists are bloodsuckers," and Latin-Americans can sue the producers of "Miami

Vice" for conveying the impression that most Latinos spend their weekends shipping cocaine to the homes of the rich and the famous. And so on, ad infinitum, until everyone is suing someone and our courts collapse under the strain.

In contrast to the group defamation approach to pornography, which is rooted in tort law, the civil rights approach to pornography is rooted in antidiscrimination law. This approach has been advanced by Andrea Dworkin and Catharine MacKinnon, who defined pornography as

> the graphic sexually explicit subordination of women through pictures or words that also includes women dehumanized as sexual objects, things, or commodities; enjoying pain or humiliation or rape; being tied up, cut up, mutilated, bruised, or physically hurt; in postures of sexual submission or servility or display; reduced to body parts, penetrated by objects or animals, or presented in scenarios of degradation, injury, torture; shown as filthy or inferior; bleeding, bruised, or hurt in a context that makes these conditions sexual.[70]

Premised as it is on inequality, pornography leads men (and to some degree women) not only to think less of women, but to treat women as second-class citizens, as less than full, human persons. For this reason, MacKinnon and Dworkin argued that pornography can and ought to be controlled as a civil offense, a civil rights violation. Any woman—or man, child, or transsexual used in the place of a woman—should be granted a legal cause of action if she is coerced into a pornographic performance, has pornography forced on her, or has been assaulted or attacked because of a particular piece of pornography. Further, any woman should be able to bring suit against traffickers in pornography on behalf of all women.[71]

Although MacKinnon and Dworkin were quite successful in their attempts to have antipornography ordinances passed in Minneapolis and Indianapolis, these ordinances were ultimately declared unconstitutional by the Supreme Court.[72] What added to the bitterness of MacKinnon and Dworkin's defeat was the fact that the Feminist Anti-Censorship Taskforce (FACT), an alliance of mostly, although certainly not exclusively, liberal feminists, was partially responsible for it.

Feminist Anti-Antipornographers
and the Case Against Pornography's Censorship

Given that the feminist case against censoring pornography is a largely *liberal* feminist case, it is not surprising that in one way or another, it is a defense of First Amendment speech rights. Groups such as FACT have, in general, faulted the MacKinnon-Dworkin Anti-Pornography Ordinance on account of the vagueness of its central terms. They complain, for example, that the phrase "sexually explicit subordination of women" has no fixed meaning. One woman may think that "sexually explicit subordination" applies only to rape scenes; another, to scenes of sexual harassment; and still another, to any depiction of heterosexual intercourse where the man is on top and the woman is on the bottom.[73]

In a detailed critique of the MacKinnon-Dworkin Ordinance, FACT discussed at some length the film *Swept Away* in an effort to show just how difficult it is to decide whether or not a particular scene or set of scenes is depicting the sexually explicit subordination of women. In essence, the film tells a story of domination and submission. An attractive, upper-class woman and a brawny, working-class man are shown, during the first half of the film, as *class* antagonists and then, during the second half of the film, as *sexual* antagonists when they are stranded on an island and the man exacts his revenge by repeatedly raping her. Initially, she resists him, but gradually she falls in love with him and, eventually, he with her. Because scenes in *Swept Away* clearly present the woman character as a victim of sexual humiliation who then apparently grows to enjoy it, the film could easily have been suppressed under the MacKinnon-Dworkin Anti-Pornography Ordinance. According to FACT, however, such suppression would have represented censorship of the worst sort because critical and popular opinion of the film varied, ranging from admiration to repulsion. Whereas the reviewer for *Ms.* wrote that "'Swept Away' comes to grips with the 'war' between the sexes better than anything" she had ever read or seen, the reviewer for *The Progressive* wrote that he did not know what was "more distasteful about the film— its slavish adherence to the barroom credo that what all women really want is to be beaten, to be shown who's boss, or the readiness with which it has been accepted by the critics."[74] Apparently, suggested FACT, if two film critics see the images and hear the words of *Swept Away* so differently, contextual factors must ultimately explain their divergent interpretations.

Significantly, MacKinnon conceded that context and interpretation *do* inescapably determine the effect of sexual text and images; but she insisted that FACT was wrong to assume that in this culture there exists a multiplicity of contexts, each of which can provide a different interpretation for a given sexual text or image. There is instead in this culture only one context, only one lens—that of male domination and female subordination—through which all sexual texts and images are filtered. Films such as *Swept Away*, insisted MacKinnon, can be interpreted only as yet another depiction of a woman's social subordination accomplished through the means of hierarchy, objectification, submission, and violence.[75]

Unconvinced that there is only *one* way to interpret films such as *Swept Away,* many liberal feminists, some of whom belong to FACT, have challenged each clause of the MacKinnon-Dworkin Anti-Pornography Ordinance. Because it is difficult to prove that a man assaulted a woman *because* he saw a specific pornographic film, liberal feminists doubt the efficacy of the ordinance's assault clause—a legal strategy that has already been tested without success. In the ill-fated 1978 case of *Olivia N.* v. *National Broadcasting Company, Inc.,* a minor girl brought a civil suit against NBC, claiming that a TV drama program, "Born Innocent," had stimulated some of her female classmates to inflict injury on her by raping her with a bottle. The suit alleged that these young girls had viewed a similar rape scene in the television drama and that the scene had caused them to decide to perform a similar act against her. The case also alleged that the producers or distributors of media products— books, magazines, films, or TV programs—portraying sexual violence should be held legally responsible for a victim's injury if the media product stimulated a consumer of the product to inflict injury on an innocent victim. Because of constitutional barriers, however, Olivia N. was not able to recover damages. NBC's defense lawyers argued that although speech directed toward inciting or producing imminent lawless action is not protected by the First Amendment, NBC did not through its broadcast of a rape scene *intend* any such action. Nor, on the basis of available social psychological research, could NBC even have reasonably *foreseen* the kind of violent action that might follow a screening of "Born Innocent." Despite NBC's victory, however, and, as a concession in the direction of MacKinnon and Dworkin, liberal feminists observe that as our understanding of the media's impact on human behavior grows, those responsible for portraying sexual violence may find it increasingly difficult to plead lack of reasonable foresight.[76]

To the degree that liberal feminists object to the assault clause because it is inefficacious, they object to the force clause because it is ambiguous. There is, they argue, no clear line between forcing pornography on a woman and inviting her to use it. MacKinnon objected that this line is perfectly clear. Men force pornography on women when they use it to intimidate women into leaving jobs that are "men's jobs"; when they use it as a "How-to Manual" for wives so that they will learn what "normal" women like and do; when they literally wallpaper their bedrooms with it; and when they use it as the subject matter for translation in language and literature classes.[77] Conceding that MacKinnon's *examples* of pernicious impositions of pornography are helpful, some liberal feminists still fault her for not identifying adequate *criteria* for separating these pernicious impositions from nonpernicious ones. We can imagine, they say, a husband who consistently encourages his wife to engage in some sexual experimentation on the grounds that unless he, or someone, encourages her to do so, she will remain a captive of her parochial-school inhibitions. As liberal feminists see it, we need to know what to say about this man, and we will not be able to say anything decisive about his conduct unless we can make a distinction between what would constitute appropriate urgings (persuasion) on his part and what would constitute inappropriate badgerings (force).

Liberal feminists also find the coercion clause, as drafted, problematic because in their estimation it renders meaningless any distinction between consent and nonconsent. In defense of the consent clause, MacKinnon noted that child pornography may currently be removed from public view on the grounds that such material harms the involved children (*New York* v. *Ferber*).[78] Not only do pornographers frequently abuse child models, but "kiddie-porn" flicks constitute a permanent and usually damaging record of a child's past participation in the porn industry, a past participation made worse by circulation to an ever-widening circle of porn devotees. But if this reasoning persuades us to ban child porn, insisted MacKinnon, it should also persuade us to ban adult porn. After all, was not harm done to Linda Marchiano when her then-husband and manager coerced her, sometimes at gunpoint, to engage in repeated acts of fellatio in front of the camera of *Deep Throat*? Is not harm still being done to Linda Marchiano each time *Deep Throat* is shown and an audience wrongly believes that Linda Marchiano is in real life what she appears to be in the film—namely, the sexually voracious and promiscuous Linda Lovelace?[79]

In general, liberal feminists answer "yes" to MacKinnon's questions, noting that if we care about women, we must support legislation that would enable the Linda Marchianos of the world to sue the maggots who feed off their bodies. However, liberal feminists caution that this does not mean we must agree with MacKinnon that consent is a fake concept—that conditions such as "signing a contract, showing no resistance, and being paid for pornographic performances" fail to show that a woman consented to be a porn model.[80] For if women are incapable of consent, what entitles them to be treated less paternalistically than children? If *maternalism* is permissible when it comes to a woman's sexual decisions, why is *paternalism* impermissible when it comes to a woman's workplace and schoolplace decisions? Women either have or do not have the capacity to consent, and no one can afford to remain undecided on the issue.

Of all the provisions of the ordinance, however, the trafficking clause gives liberal feminists the most problems. Although liberal feminists concede that the assault, force, and coercion clauses could be reworked in ways that would preserve liberty, equality, and fairness for everyone involved in a pornography suit, they see little possibility of so reworking the trafficking clause. Under this clause, absent any showing of harm to herself or to women in general, a woman may secure an injunction against the distribution, sale, exhibition, or production of any sexually explicit item that fits MacKinnon and Dworkin's definition of pornography.[81] In other words, any woman could secure an injunction against the sale of *Playboy* at the corner grocery, if the local Human Rights Commission were persuaded that the photos in it graphically depict the sexual subordination of women by showing them as sexual objects, things, or commodities. In order to secure such an injunction in the name of all women, neither the woman in question nor any other women need have been forcibly squeezed into a bunny suit, been forced to read or imitate the contents of *Playboy* magazine, or been sexually assaulted as a result of some man's desire to feast on bunny stew. Given what they regard as the vagueness of MacKinnon and Dworkin's pornography definition, liberal feminists worry that the trafficking clause may have the effect of limiting the free speech of bad sexist boys as well as good feminist girls. They fear, in other words, that conservatives could use MacKinnon's and Dworkin's pornography definition to secure injunctions against sexually explicit feminist texts.

But even if MacKinnon and Dworkin could answer all these liberal feminist criticisms, they would still have to answer the additional criticism that men—not men who take the place of women but *men*—are also demeaned, degraded, and defamed by pornography. MacKinnon was particularly impatient with this objection. She was frustrated by the fact that each time society is confronted with sexual harassment, rape, or battering, society's excuse is that it happens to men, too. If women are raped, so are men. If women are sexually harassed, so are men. If women are battered, so are men. Why, wondered MacKinnon, do so many of us fail to see what is so obvious: namely, that far fewer men than women are harmed in these ways?[82]

MacKinnon's frustration is not difficult to appreciate. After all, radical feminists such as MacKinnon and Dworkin noticed what we all should have noticed years ago: namely, that the pornographic imagination focuses on the bodies of women far more than on those of men. With rare exceptions, pornography—and, for that matter, sexual harassment, rape, and battering—is something men do to women. Nevertheless, claim liberal feminists, there is a world of difference between pointing out this distressing asymmetry and insisting, as MacKinnon and Dworkin did, that pornography is *central* to women's subordination. To suggest that pornography contributes to women's oppression more than does lack of access to good jobs, affordable child care, and quality education, is, insist liberal feminists, to suggest something about which the typical woman on welfare can only shake her head in disbelief.[83]

The debate between MacKinnon and Dworkin on the one hand and liberal members of FACT on the other is but one moment in a long discussion within the feminist community about the pleasures and dangers of sex. At the Barnard Sexuality Conference in 1982, an argument broke out between feminist antipornographers and, for lack of a better term, feminist sexual libertarians—many of whom were lesbian sadomasochists but some of whom were simply avid readers of *Harlequin* romances, subscribers to *Vogue* magazine, or traditional heterosexuals who enjoyed being submissive every once in a while. The sexual libertarians called the antipornographers "prudes." The feminist antipornographers denied this, arguing that they had nothing against sexual material on account of its explicitness, excessive candor, "unnaturalness," and/or prurience. They were not opposed to erotica, where the term denotes depictions and descriptions of women being integrated, constituted, or focused during loving or at least life-affirming sexual encounters, but to thanatica, where the term denotes depictions and descriptions of women being disintegrated, dismembered, or disoriented during hate-filled or even death-driven sexual encounters. Significantly, the sexual libertarians were not impressed by these disclaimers. They objected to any type of erotica/thanatica distinction on the grounds that it suggests that the only good sex is *vanilla* sex—that is, gentle, "touchy-feely," side-by-side (no one on the top or the bottom), altogether pretty sex. Why, asked the sexual libertarians, should we limit women, or anyone else for that matter, to a particular brand of sex? If women are given free rein, some may choose rocky-road sex (encounters where pain punctuates pleasure, for example). In any event, the sexual libertarians asserted that under no circumstances should a woman be told that if she wants to be a feminist, then only certain sorts of sexual encounter are for her. If women's sexuality is as "absent" as Catharine MacKinnon said it is, then it is premature for anyone to decide what that sexuality is.[84]

Interestingly, some lesbians were among the first to argue against being limited to vanilla sex. But as soon as groups such as Samois[85] started to engage in sadomasochistic practices, they were harshly criticized by most members of the radical feminist community for mimicking heterosexual S&M (total male dominance and complete female powerlessness in their sexual lives).[86]

In their own defense, some members of Samois claimed that, unlike heterosexual S&M, lesbian S&M involves the eroticization not of dominance and powerlessness, but rather of pain, a physical sensation that within certain limits can be particularly stimulating sexually. Other members of Samois disagreed, insisting that like heterosexual S&M, lesbian S&M does involve the eroticization of dominance and powerlessness, but that this ordinarily antifeminist eroticization becomes fem-

inist when used as a means to achieve feminist goals. By playing at
sadism (dominating) and masochism (being dominated) in the fantasies
of their private lives, lesbians can learn how to overcome the forces of
domination in the realities of their public lives.

Although radical feminists opposed to lesbian S&M do not necessarily
object to the eroticization of pain, they do object to anyone, lesbian or
not, eroticizing dominance and powerlessness. If the testimony of many
ex-lesbian-sadomasochists is accurate, then lesbian S&M is not always
cathartic therapy; S&M is often behavior that reinforces the very tendencies
it is supposed to eradicate. That so many lesbians who practice S&M
scoff at the vanilla, or affectional, sex they used to enjoy suggests that
S&M is a learning, even an addictive, experience.[87]

Although a practitioner of lesbian S&M can defend herself by asserting
that what she and her friend do behind closed bedroom doors is their
own business, Audre Lorde, a black lesbian feminist, asserted that try
as a woman might, she cannot close her bedroom doors. "The erotic,"
said Lorde, "empowers, nourishes and permeates all of our lives."[88] What
lesbian couples do in their own homes is not their *own* business, but
rather everyone's business: "It is a fallacy of liberal individualism that
any behavior is purely personal. Whatever we do takes place in a social
context and has an effect upon other human beings. To degrade someone,
even with that person's expressed consent, is to *endorse* the degradation
of persons. It is to affirm that the abuse of persons is *acceptable*."[89]

Lesbian S&M is, of course, not a practice in which a significant
number of lesbians engage, but it is a mode of sexual exploration, and
the debate about it represents the attempt, particularly by radical feminists,
to reassess the pleasures and dangers of sex for all women. This reas-
sessment occurs as feminists strive to claim sexuality as a realm of power
for themselves, a realm in which women can control their own situation.
Like power, with its aspects of domination and creation, sexual experience
can be dangerous, *and* it can be pleasurable. Just as power-over and
power-to are not independent of one another, the dangers and pleasures
of sex cannot be neatly separated from one another. Thus, there are those
radical feminists who emphasize that the pursuit of pleasure is and has
been fundamentally dangerous for women. By emphasizing the dangers
of sex, however, these feminists risk precluding any movement toward
a sexuality—including a heterosexuality—that promises "pleasure, agency,
and self-definition" for women.[90]

Forward movement requires feminists to scrutinize what society labels
"good sex" (heterosexual, married, monogamous, procreative, noncom-
mercial, in pairs, in a relationship, same generation, in private, no
pornography, bodies only, vanilla) and what it labels "bad sex" (homosexual, unmarried, promiscuous, nonprocreative, commercial, alone

or in groups, casual, cross-generational, in public, pornography, with manufactured objects, sadomasochistic).[91] Sometimes, as perhaps in the case of lesbian S&M, the experiment will falter, even fail. But other times it will succeed. □

LESBIANISM AS PARADIGM FOR FEMALE-CONTROLLED FEMALE SEXUALITY

Radical feminists generally agree that, with the arguable exception of S&M, lesbian sexuality does serve as a paradigm for female sexuality— the kind of sexuality that meets women's own needs and fulfills their own desires. In contrast to both liberal and Marxist feminists, radical feminists view lesbianism as much more than a purely personal decision; they see it as an outward sign of an internal rejection of patriarchal sexuality. Indeed, many radical feminists argue that in order to make a complete commitment to feminism, a woman has to be or become a lesbian. Charlotte Bunch, for example, refused to accept heterosexuals as full-fledged feminists because "the very essence, definition, and nature of heterosexuality is men first."[92] Bunch explained that it is male society that defines lesbianism as a personal choice because it is not in the interest of men to recognize lesbianism as having any political implications: "For the Lesbian-Feminist, it [sex] is not private; it is a political matter of oppression, domination, and power."[93] The implications of lesbianism extend beyond the sexual realm, as "lesbianism is a threat to the ideological, political, and economic basis of male supremacy."[94] With these beliefs about the nature of heterosexuality and the impact of lesbianism, it follows that Bunch believed that only lesbians can be serious feminists and that lesbianism is best understood as a revolutionary rejection of all male-defined institutions.

Despite uncompromising voices such as Bunch's, not all radical lesbian feminists dismiss heterosexual feminists as pseudofeminists. Indeed, many radical lesbian feminists point out that despite sporadic outbreaks of recrimination, there is a mutually beneficial conversation between lesbianism and feminism. What lesbianism and feminism share is an affirmation of women's community and a desire to see each woman actualize her capacities to like, feel affection for, and love other women. Because women preferring the companionship of women to that of men is a thing unheard of (or at least unspoken of) in patriarchy, an insistence on strong relationships between and among women is what puts lesbians and feminists in alliance against the "fathers."

Even though feminism and lesbianism are linked together in many ways, their relationship is not *necessarily* binding. Many lesbians do not label themselves "feminists." Particularly when a lesbian has a liberal political orientation and/or is not an active critic of the institutions of career, family, religion, she is likely to assert that "the person I sleep with just happens to be a woman" or that "my sex life is my private business." In the context of other life choices, this nonpolitical attitude must be recognized as reasonable and functional. If success in a woman's public life depends upon discretion about her private life, it makes no sense for her to be vocal about her lesbianism. When public life and private life are disconnected, as they are *supposed* to be in our society, they can be and are often most easily pursued separatedly. This state of affairs depends, of course, upon liberal tolerance of lesbianism as an alternative sexual preference. The frequent absence of this tolerance in reality pressures lesbian women to be political, to struggle for gay rights, to "come out of the closet." Harassment of lesbians and hostility toward public displays of affection between women can have two effects: the suppression of lesbianism or the growth of lesbian identity and community. The distinction between nonpolitical and political here is a distinction between silence and protest.[95]

Radical lesbian feminists claim that the choice to be political, to protest, is a choice that yields both negative and positive consequences. On the one hand, living as an avowed lesbian can mean being in conflict with one's friends, family, and community and leading a life of relative poverty because, with few exceptions, a manless woman is, in this society, a poor woman.[96] On the other hand, living as an avowed lesbian can lead to a feeling of integrity and wholeness. A political lesbian need not divide her life into public and private, with silence on one side and possible shame on the other. Having no desire to be discreet, she can actively participate in women's communities and collectives that will provide her with goods, services, and companionship that are largely unavailable in a society where the lesbian is generally out of sight and, therefore, out of mind. Freed of the need to conform to patriarchy's rules about what counts as "good" or "normal" sex for women, the political lesbian finds herself able to begin understanding her own oppression as well as the oppression of other types of people whom patriarchy wishes to control. This expanded consciousness can provide the broad base that oppressed social groups need in order to unite into a coalition powerful enough to effect liberation for each of its members.

If lesbianism shares so much with feminism and other political agendas, then why are some lesbians separatists? Why would lesbians isolate themselves instead of joining forces with other oppressed groups? To find possible reasons, it is important to understand what separatism and lesbian separatism mean.

Rather than beginning with either an excuse or justification for lesbian separatism, it may be useful to approach separatism as something that all people—and particularly those concerned with social change—practice. Every person participates in a multitude of social relations, some of them consciously, some of them not. Once we begin to question our place in society, we are led to ask how, where, and in what ways we participate in it. To reject some relations—to resist paying income tax for nuclear weapons, to divest from South Africa, or to be a conscientious objector, for example—is to engage in noncooperation, in nonpartici-pation, in *separatism*. Change often requires that we cease to comply with an objectionable relation and instead transform it or develop an alternative to it. Indeed, separation can be an imperative if we find ourselves the oppressed person in a relation.

What distinguishes *feminist* separatism from separatism in general is, as Marilyn Frye wrote, that it is a separation "from men and from institutions, relationships, roles and activities which are male-defined, male-dominated and operating for the benefit of males and the maintenance of male privilege—this separation being initiated or maintained at will, *by women*."[97] Thus, simply by refusing to approve the status quo for women, feminists can be said to separate themselves from the patriarchal society endorsing this status quo. More deliberately, by creating women's spaces—such as the consciousness-raising groups of the 1970s, rape crisis centers, all-women social events, battered women's shelters, and women's art galleries—feminists can be said to be engaging in acts of separatism. Of course, some feminists go further in their attempts to break down male supremacy and to restore to women the power of defining themselves and, even more importantly, of controlling access to themselves. They refuse to change their career plans simply because the men in their lives ask them to; they refuse to have sexual intercourse with their boyfriends or husbands on demand; they refuse to say "yes" simply because the men in their lives wish they would. In sum, as Frye saw it, "access" is the crucial battle to be fought in the struggle for women's liberation from patriarchy, for the "Patriarchal Imperative" teaches that "males *must have access* to women."[98] Women must remove (redirect, reallocate) goods and services from men in order to weaken, and even destroy, patriarchal power.

Because the most vital goods and services that women have provided for men are immediately or ultimately sexual in nature, it is not surprising that a call for *feminist* separatism frequently leads to a call for *lesbian* separatism (nonparticipation in the institution of heterosexuality). This nonparticipation can be uncompromising, as it was for Charlotte Bunch and Jill Johnston, both of whom insisted that women cannot be free of patriarchal control so long as women are sexually involved with men.[99] But this call for nonparticipation in heterosexuality can be interpreted less absolutely, as it was by Adrienne Rich, who believed that all feminist women—including heterosexual women—are, to the extent that they desire to identify with other women, lesbian: "It is the lesbian in us who drives us to feel imaginatively, render in language, grasp the full connection between woman and woman. It is the lesbian in us who is creative, for the dutiful daughter of the fathers in us is only a hack."[100] Thus, for Rich, lesbianism is a potential, a matter of degree. Women constitute a "lesbian continuum," a "range—through each woman's life and throughout history—of woman-identified experience," including experiences of "primary intensity between and among women," of sharing, and of bonding.[101] What was crucial for Rich was not so much that women withdraw their affections from men as that women transfer them to other women.

As I have analyzed the phenomenon of separatism so far, lesbian separatism is simply a further development of feminist separatism, with neither degree of separatism being overall better or more correct. Whether it is lesbian or not, a separate space for women represents a chance for women to withdraw from the demands of men in order to find, in the words of Mary Daly, "wholeness."[102]

Among radical feminist lesbians, Daly is not unique in portraying men as the fragmenters of female unity. Nor is she alone in believing that "the healing response to this condition is the providing of a *context* that affirms precisely that form which women under patriarchy have been dissociated, that is, identification as Wild, Original women."[103] Daly views patriarchy as squelching women's true selves, which makes it imperative for women to destroy the "myths, names, ideologies, and social structures" men have used to constrict the female body of imagination.[104] Given that these concepts and structures constitute the existing sociocultural milieu, it is no surprise that Daly instructs feminists to withdraw not only from the institution of heterosexuality but from all patriarchal institutions: churches, schools, professional organizations, and the family.

Whatever appeal the idea of total isolation and independence from men may have, most feminist separatists are less radical than Daly. They argue that absolute separatism from men is neither feasible nor ultimately desirable for women. It is not feasible, said the authors of *No Turning Back*, for example, because "even if a group of lesbians builds a completely isolated self-supporting community deep in the country, the money to buy that land must still either be earned or inherited from the system, and the women are still subject to the laws of the state and the nation."[105] Absolute separatism is not desirable because "women will destroy patriarchy by confronting it, not by isolating themselves from it."[106] □

CRITIQUES OF RADICAL FEMINISM

In the last two chapters, we have discussed radical feminist views on reproduction, biological motherhood, gender, and sexuality. Although radical feminists are highly esteemed in the feminist community, some have been criticized for their claims about the goodness of women's nature and the evilness of men's nature. Whether these criticisms are justified is, of course, a decision for us to make.

Woman's Biology: Is It the Root of Her "Goodness"?

Speaking from a socialist feminist standpoint, Alison Jaggar began her critique of radical feminists by complimenting them on their materialism. They pay attention to woman's body. By systematically reflecting on human reproductive biology, radical feminists have brought sexuality, childbearing, and childrearing practices into the domain of politics. Whereas reproduction, gender, and sexuality have been virtually ignored in Western political theory and denied in Western political practice, they are the central topics of radical feminism. However, Jaggar contended, in attending to the body as the primary conceptual framework for feminist analysis, some radical feminists have developed a rather deterministic picture of human nature, conceiving of biology as an unchanging and fixed given. Jaggar argued to the contrary that biology is as changing and moving as the environmental forces with which it interacts. For example, sex differentiation is minimal in many social groups in which women are as tall, broad-shouldered, and narrow-hipped as men. In our own society and others like it, however, sexual dimorphism is exaggerated. Jaggar attributed the smaller shape of women in societies such as ours to women's history. Because of their inferior social status, women have had a poorer diet nutritionally than men have had. Women are smaller than men not so much because nature has made them so, but because culture has. We must, insisted Jaggar, understand human beings as the historical product of the interplay between environment and biology, between culture and nature. Thus, it is not the case that women's biology will yield the same set of imperatives across space and time. Biology is only one of the constituents of woman's identity.

Although it may be true that, in a moderately harsh environment and with little technology, social survival depends on infant care by women, it does not follow that infants must be cared for by women where bottle feeding is available or where other kinds of productive work do not require heavy physical labor or long absences from home. We may say, if we wish, that the human biological constitution requires a certain form of social organization *within certain material circumstances.* But we cannot universalize from this to what is required in other circumstances.[107]

In short, woman's biology is not in and of itself a prescription for her gender and sexuality; at most, it is a recommendation.

According to Jaggar, however, several radical feminists have theorized that women's biology leads to a definite female psychology and, by parity of reasoning, that men's biology leads to a definite male psychology. Although Jaggar conceded that radical feminists sometimes differ in identifying these specific gender psychologies, she observed that they also have many assumptions in common. Radical feminist psychology, believed Jaggar, sometimes consists simply in identifying men with power-over, rationality, and aggression and identifying women with power-to, emotionality, and nurturance. Because men's drive to exert power over everything and everyone in their world has so often taken the form of suppressing the pride and passion of women, radical feminists maintain that women have developed a resultant false consciousness that sadly perceives the qualities associated with females as less desirable than those associated with males. Radical feminists, said Jaggar, have fought against this false consciousness as a psychology of oppression. Not only are female qualities not less desirable than male qualities; they are more so.

Although Jaggar conceded to radical feminists the point that under most historical conditions, nurturance, for example, is probably preferable to aggression, she was troubled by the insistence that it is *always* preferable. She was even more troubled by the radical feminist position that locates psychological qualities such as nurturance and aggression in female and male biology respectively. Because Jaggar rejected the theory of biological determinism, she had no reason to believe that by nature all men are one way and all women another, or even that *most* men are one way and *most* women another. The historical interplay of biology and environment makes this man the way he is and this woman the way she is.

Jaggar's historical materialist explanation of biology and psychology led her to an unequivocal rejection of any universal assertions about men and women. As she saw it, not all men are victimizers, and not all women are victims. The fact that radical feminists themselves are able to escape their false consciousness, even under the system of patriarchy, is evidence of this. If patriarchy were, indeed, all pervasive and totalizing, radical feminism could never have obtained the space it needed to develop. Moreover, even a cursory sketch of history shows that all men do not oppress all women in the same ways. To say that they do is to ignore the historical realities of class and race. To suggest, for example, that a poor, male hired hand on a rich white woman's ranch is oppressing her because he has the physical power to rape her and is not oppressed by her even though she is paying him at best a subsistence wage is to suggest something at most partially true. Likewise, to say that a white woman who loses out in a job competition to a slightly less qualified black man is discriminated against, all the while ignoring the ways in which she participates in his oppression, is to close our eyes to the complexity of the situation. This is the cost of using a single model to explain a world that is hardly uniform.[108]

Jaggar did not, however, want to dismiss the reality of male dominance. Rather, she wanted feminists to speak about it in very specific and concrete terms, resisting as much as possible the tendency to indulge in generalities and abstractions. She drew on the work of Michelle Z. Rosaldo, who explained:

> Male dominance, though apparently universal, does not in actual behavioral terms assume a universal content, or a universal shape. On the contrary, women typically have power and influence in political and economic life. . . . For in every case in which we see women confined, by powerful men or by the responsibilities of child care and the home, one can cite others which display female capacities to fight back, to speak out in public, perform physically demanding tasks, and even to subordinate the needs of infant children (in their homes or on their backs) to their desires for travel, labor, politics, love or trade. . . . Male dominance . . . does not inhere in any isolated and measurable set of facts. Rather, it seems to be an aspect of the organization of collective life, a pattern of expectations and beliefs which gives rise to imbalance in ways people interpret, evaluate, and respond to particular forms of male and female action.[109]

Clearly, for Jaggar, a more useful approach to an analysis of patriarchy is an account of specific instances of female oppression in place x at time y, while keeping the broader scope of patriarchy's pervasiveness in the background.

Jaggar's reservations about radical feminist theory led her to be equally cautious about the social change strategies that emerge from this body of thought. According to many radical feminists, there is only one possibility for real women's liberation and that is the creation of "womanspaces"—places such as women's cooperatives, clinics, clubs, and shelters that emphasize decision by consensus, the tapping of spiritual resources, and the giving of mutual aid. Jaggar said that these alternative institutions have helped fragment the hegemony of male-dominated culture because in them each woman is encouraged to use her powers as she sees fit. But even though womanculture is an incredibly supportive environment for women, Jaggar did not believe that it is either the only or necessarily the best means to women's liberation.[110]

When womanculture is identified with the kind of lesbian community
Mary Daly envisions, then total separation from men—or, certainly, a
refusal to have anything to do with the institution of heterosexuality—
is identified as the only or best way for a woman to exercise power-to,
especially the power-to control her own body. Jaggar conceded that if
a woman has intimate relationships only with other women, she can
avoid the exploitation of her reproductive capacities as well as the
oppression inherent in traditional male-female relationships. Nevertheless,
Jaggar pointed out that when a woman has the ability to say "no" to
a man, she is only partially in control of her body. The other part is
the ability to say "yes"—to engage in a nonexploitative relationship with
a man. It concerned Jaggar that some radical feminists hold out no hope
whatsoever for truly consensual heterosexual relations on the grounds
that men are, by nature, incapable of being anything other than exploitative.

Another criticism Jaggar directed against womanculture is that it tends
to overestimate its power, as when it announces that its nonpatriarchal
economic institutions will prove too much for capitalism to withstand.
Economic institutions that favor democratic participation over competition
will, she predicted, probably be less productive than profit-minded,
patriarchal economic institutions. This is not to say that nonpatriarchal
economic institutions will be unsuccessful in the ways that really matter
to the women who enter them; but it is to say that their financial success
will be difficult to achieve and that they are thus unlikely to pose a
serious threat to capitalism.

Jaggar also expressed concern that the radical feminist womanculture
movement pays scant attention to issues of race and class and may simply
be a place for white, relatively privileged women to celebrate themselves.
Separation from men is not, she wrote, what all oppressed women either
need or want. Although some radical feminists have claimed that racism
and classism stem from sexism and, as the creations of men, will be
eradicated in a womanculture,[111] not all radical feminists have been
particularly attentive to the concerns of women of color or poverty.
Womanculture cannot liberate all women unless it is expansive enough
to include those women who believe that, at least for them, racism or
classism are more oppressive than sexism.

Woman's Emotions: Are They the Root of Her "Goodness"?

In "Some Critical Reflections on Radical Feminism," Joan Cocks
pointed out the failings as well as the successes of contemporary radical
feminism, focusing on the ways in which it presents itself as a counterculture. Radical feminism, she said, prides itself on existing in opposition to patriarchy, on affirming the very things "the fathers" devalue

and degrade. In vociferously affirming the subordinated aspects of patriarchal dualities—such as man/woman, dominance/nurturance, culture/nature, reason/emotion—radical feminists are, said Cocks, undeniably engaged in revolutionary activity, in gainsaying the patriarchy, in constituting a very real alternative to the dominant, or hegemonic, culture. As Cocks commented, feminist counterculture is "living reassurance against the fear that the hegemony is totalitarian in its ability to forestall, control, or co-opt its adversaries."[112] Nevertheless, for all of her praise of it, Cocks was profoundly worried by radical feminism because, in its existence as a counterculture, it defines itself in opposition to male culture, thereby defining that culture as the norm from which to deviate.

Although the radical feminists' rebellious reversal of patriarchal dualities has been useful in women's progression toward liberation, Cocks faulted radical feminism for dooming itself forever to rebellion, for glorifying woman's otherness. When a radical feminist places women exactly where men have—in the same space with passion, fertility, irrationality, sexuality, disease, and reproduction—she may be dooming women to a perpetual rebellion and separation that ultimately serves not women but men.

> What both feminists and phallocentrists see as a hegemony based on masculine precepts of domination, performance, hierarchy, abstraction, and rationality, finds its antipode in a women's community proclaiming itself as naturally nurturant, receptive, cooperative, intimate, and exulting in the emotions . . . [feminists] assume that such principles exist and that they have been fixed and dichotomous since the dawn of patriarchal history. Thus it is that the dominant culture and the counterculture engage in a curious collusion, in which . . . a rebellious feminism takes up its assigned position at the negative pole.[113]

Cocks developed the example of one duality, that of reason/emotion, to demonstrate how the radical feminist use of duality may be more enslaving than liberating. Although Cocks recognized that the split between reason and emotion "features as a central ideological constituent of the sex/gender system," with its role being to "confine women within a small circle of thought and action," she did *not* think that this split is the direct result of the sex/gender system.[114]

Unlike radical feminists who equate male/female with reason/emotion and make of the conglomerate duality an historical universal, Cocks traced the development of these two dualities separately.[115] She concluded that "male" did not always mean "rational," and that "female" did not always mean "emotional": "While Western culture has always . . . incorporated some idea of a male Self and a female Other, it has not always linked the Self to reason and the Other to emotion. More striking,

it has not always treated reason and emotion . . . as exclusive categories."[116]
According to Cocks, the ancients did not split reason off from emotion
as the moderns do; rather, they emphasized the ways in which reason
and emotion work together in the lives of fully human persons. Thus,
even if the ancients made the mistake of presuming that only men could
be fully human persons, they did not make the further mistake of
describing the fully human person as either exclusively rational or
exclusively emotional.

Cocks argued that three historical developments caused the moderns
to compound the ancients' original gender-biased mistake by first severing
reason from emotion and then associating reason with full personhood—
that is, with *manhood*. The first of these developments was the rise of
positive science. The moderns broke from the ancients as explanations
of natural events came to refer less to some controlling immaterial force
or supernatural deity and to depend more on observable causes and
functions. As a function of a newly found "objectivity" and "materialism,"
the emerging empirical sciences sought to separate the elements of
reason—logic, fact, lack of bias—from those of emotion—interest, motive,
value.

The second development was the rise of capitalism. With the advent
of an economy whose dynamic was the maximization of profit, the
humanizing, or moral, aspects of work were deemphasized. Craftsmanship,
community, and the sense of working with nature gave way to the new
values of productivity, competition, and exploitation. Being rational means
to be efficient—that is, to segment and to specialize the work process
so that the most goods can be produced for the least cost. Being
nonrational means to be inefficient—that is, to waste time debating the
eternal verities. Reason for the moderns has nothing to do with determining the ends of morality and everything to do with enabling people
to secure whatever they want, no matter how evil.

> According to its rules of procedure in scientific discourse, and to the way it
> has developed as a practical concept in economic life, reason cannot comment
> on the validity of moral ends. It can help an industrial order achieve a
> functional efficiency and can praise it for churning out an increased number
> of goods with the same investment of time, energy, and capital. But it can
> have nothing to say about their right distribution, the justice of the conditions
> under which they were made, or the virtue in their infinite multiplication.
> With such moral silence comes emotional silence: competing calculations
> about the efficiency of means to an end have no resonance in the heart.[117]

The third development was the rise of the technocratic state. In this
kind of state, technics displaces not only ethics but also politics. People

do not talk about the good, true, and beautiful or even about power. Rather, they talk about facts. Cost-benefit analyses, statistics, and the bottom line push aside negotiations, compromises, and trade-offs. In this type of state, there is no room for the blood, sweat, and tears of people; there is only room for emotionless, rational numbers.

Cocks's historical account of the process by which reason was split from emotion suggested that there is nothing inherently male about reason. Thus, Cocks worried that the radical feminist tendency to reject domination, men, and reason as a single package and to embrace instead nurturing, women, and emotion, also as a single package, is leading radical feminists to retreat even further into a private garden of womanly delights where manly concerns are not permitted to intrude. The "grappling with the personal as political" is, she insisted, degenerating "into an absorption with the personal as personal."[118] Cocks pointed out that radical feminists are increasingly calling themselves "cultural" or "spiritual" feminists. In Cocks's estimation, the fascination with the personal, the psychological, and the sexual threatens to render radical feminism apolitical and therefore irrelevant to most women—particularly those women who (must) deal with their oppression in other than personal, psychological, and sexual terms.

The divide between reason and emotion, as with other gender-identified dualities, must be bridged, said Cocks, with a recognition of the interplay between the two. Cocks did not believe that reason and emotion have to be conceived as polar opposites because emotion has rational aspects and reason has emotional aspects. Women's "intuition," for instance, is not a sixth sense, an exclusively emotional capacity peculiar to women; rather, it is a set of reasonable predictions arising from "careful attention to the nuances of personal relationships, from an intelligence trained on the minutely perceptible exterior signs in people around them of loneliness, pride, disappointment, and changes of heart."[119] Conversely, men's "objectivity" is not a strictly rational capacity peculiar to men; rather, it is a mode of justifying and even of excusing behavior that is guided by personal feelings as well as by impersonal logic.

As Cocks saw it, by identifying rationality with maleness, radical feminists are forfeiting a weapon in their struggle against patriarchy. Unless they renounce the idea that male reason is separate from and hostile to female emotion, Cocks predicted that radical feminists will continue to feel out of control, even crazed. Rather than purposefully suppressing their ability to give *reasons* for their actions and deliberately hiding their capacity to challenge opponents, including feminist ones, radical feminists should, said Cocks, use their powers of logical and spirited argumentation not only to take back the night for women but also to give them a very large place in the sun. Cocks believed that

radical feminists must begin again to see themselves not as people who
live in a "magical web outside of history and society," but as people
who live very much *in* history and *in* conflict, even with themselves.[120]

In many ways, Cocks yearned for the *political* radical feminism of the
1960s, which emphasized campaigns, causes, and commitments. The
radical feminism of the 1980s struck Cocks as perhaps too self-indulgent
and narcissistic. Talk of womanculture, goddesses, and female spirituality
bothered her—and, admittedly, if the retreat inward does not eventually
lead outward, the majority of women may be deprived of the kind of
political leadership needed to achieve full liberation. Nevertheless, as a
final caveat to Cocks's critique, it is important to reaffirm at least the
symbolic significance, if not also the very practical reality, of the radical
feminist women's community. To add to and subtract from the patriarch's
calculations, or to start counting anew, that is the eternal feminist
question.[121] As Ti-Grace Atkinson noted years ago, "The feminist dilemma
is that we have the most to do, and the least to do it with. We must
create, as no other group in history has been forced to do, from the
very beginning."[122] That women's space has grown large enough for
some radical feminists to become lost in it may in and of itself signal
a tremendous feminist achievement.

Woman's Goodness: Does It Exist?

According to Jean Elshtain, radical feminism's mistake is to suggest
that males and females are, on the ontological level, two kinds of creature—
the men corrupt and the women innocent. Such an ontology denies the
individuality and the history of all men and women. It implies that what
is important and real about us is some a priori essence that is as
predetermined as our genetic makeup. Elshtain asserted that explanations
for male attitudes and actions that begin and end with the excuse that
it is "just the way they [men] are" provide no real enlightenment at all
as to the way individual men think, act, and simply are. Among the
radical feminists Elshtain singled out for particular criticism was Susan
Brownmiller, author of a major book on rape. For Brownmiller, "the
male ideology of rape (is a) conscious process of intimidation by which
all men keep *all* women in a state of fear."[123] As Elshtain read Brownmiller,
she hears her saying that men who have not *yet* raped a woman or who
actively protest rape are bearing false witness to their real identity. To
be a man means to reaffirm consciously one's identity by oppressing,
repressing, and suppressing women. Furthermore, it is not only that men
are socialized into this role (although it is this, too); this power over
women actually defines men. It is the essence of manhood. Whereas
Marxists would say that the male ideology of rape is a historical con-

sequence of capitalism that can only be eradicated with the demise of the capitalist system, radical feminist Brownmiller suggested that rape is an abiding feature of patriarchy that will never end as long as women live in a world of men. This pessimism disturbed Elshtain, who insisted that unless an analysis offers some potential for change, it is empty.

Falling into the trap of essentialism—the conviction that men are men and women are women and that there is no way to change either's nature—is an analytic deadend as well as a political danger. Essentialist claims about what makes certain groups of people the way they are (for example, women, blacks, Jews) are the political-philosophical constructs of conservatism. The history of essentialist arguments is one of oppressors telling the oppressed to accept their lot in life because "that's just the way it is." Essentialist arguments were used to justify slavery, to resist the Nineteenth Amendment (which gave women the vote), and to sustain colonialism by arguing "altruistically" that "the natives are unable to run their own governments." By agreeing that women are a priori nurturing and life giving, and that men are a priori corrupt and obsessed with death, many radical feminists are buying into the male-dictated dichotomies they are trying to avoid. As Joan Cocks pointed out, a standard radical feminist strategy is to retain the categories that have historically defined each gender, but to revalue them so that the female traits are the positive ones and the male traits the negative ones.

Elshtain believed that we must overthrow the categories that entrap us in rigid roles, even if some of those roles are ones we value. Roles, she said, are simplistic definitions that make every man a conscious exploiter and oppressor and every woman an exploited and oppressed victim. But, she emphasized, the fact of the matter is that not every woman is a victim and not every man is a victimizer. Elshtain cited Mary Beard's *Women as a Force in History* (a liberal-feminist text that charted women's role in shaping preindustrial culture)[124] and Sheila Rowbotham's *Women, Resistance, and Revolution* (a Marxist-feminist text that detailed women's involvement in twentieth-century revolutions)[125] to show that women have played strong and active roles in social history. Elshtain also pointed to examples of men who have supported women in their liberatory struggles. A denial that such men exist confuses the women who do not want to live in isolation from these men. "Told she will fail to take her place in the world as it is presently organized unless she becomes a grim militant or a 'woman-identified-woman,' told relations of mutuality between men and women are not only difficult but impossible, she can only wonder whose interests and needs are being served through such distortions."[126] According to Elshtain, essentialism in any form has no place in the complex world we live in.

Also at issue in Elshtain's critique of radical feminism was the inevitability and universality of patriarchy. Because power-over is, according to radical feminists, the essence of all men, patriarchy is the sociopolitical expression of that essence. All societies in which men and women live together are, by definition, patriarchal and misogynistic. In order to prove this, Mary Daly interprets as forms of woman hating Hindu suttee, Chinese footbinding, African female circumcision, and Western gynecology. This cross-cultural comparison of the institutionalized mutilation of female bodies is supposed to reveal the universal nature of patriarchy. Elshtain pointed out, however, that "comparing the way of life of Mbuti Pygmies [sic] with that of a complex, technological modern society like our own, for example, and labeling both patriarchical is rather like trying to derive an elephant from an earthworm."[127] Elshtain said that in making such comparisons, Daly overlooks the rich diversity of different societies. This is a problem for any theory that tries to define all situations with a single monocausal model. Furthermore, as a Western feminist searching for non-Western forms of patriarchy, Daly is sometimes unaware of her own cultural baggage. As an outsider, she is not always privy to the contextual meaning "patriarchal" rituals have for their female participants. African female circumcision is a case in point. For Daly, it means patriarchy because this is her explanation for such phenomena; for the woman circumcised, it may mean something different—for example, a rite of passage into a much-coveted womanhood or a means of rebelling against civilized, Christian, colonial powers. Of course, Daly would argue that this woman is blind to what is being done to her and why. But there is at least a chance that it is Daly's vision, not the woman's, that is somewhat clouded. As Audre Lorde has written, Daly's failure to acknowledge the possibility that African and Asian rituals may have positive, non-Western meanings suggests a certain ethnocentrism on her part.[128]

Still, in evaluating the term *patriarchy* as used by most radical feminists, Elshtain was willing to attribute to it a metaphorical rather than an historical meaning. As such, it is a term that carries a certain emotional force and lends direction to women searching for a point of attack. Yet even in its metaphorical capacity, the concept of patriarchy is troubling. Elshtain acknowledged that patriarchy is a useful analytical tool for those women who are just beginning to rethink their political and personal experiences. But beyond this, patriarchy becomes a blunt instrument. If chanted incessantly, the formula "men *over* women; women *for* men" becomes monotonous and ultimately even meaningless. The refusal of many radical feminists to move beyond their initial understandings of the nature and function of patriarchy can contribute to the "broken record effect" that some women experience while reading certain radical feminist texts.[129] Elshtain speculated that this intractibility is rooted in some radical feminists' fear that they may have certain things—even ugly things—in common with the patriarchs. Elshtain's speculation was based on her belief that we are all "inescapably male and female," and just as some men cannot tolerate their "feminine" qualities, some radical feminists are unable to accept their own "masculine" qualities. Thus, they project these qualities onto men, exaggerating these qualities' awfulness in order to shield themselves from this part of their own personalities.

This defensiveness can lead a radical feminist toward a utopian vision of an all-women community. Man encompasses evil; woman encompasses good. Because the essence of womanhood is power-to, a world of women will be warm, supportive, nurturing, and full of creativity. It will be a return to the womb. Only men are holding women back. Elshtain believed that if her critique was on target, then many radical feminists may be in for a disappointment if and when men stop holding women back, and women leave the private realm for the public realm, only to discover that women, like men, can fail morally. Elshtain asked us to reconsider the concept of "pure voice"—that is, the idea that the victim, in her status as victim, speaks in a pure voice—"I suffer, therefore I have moral purity."[130] This belief about women's moral purity is exactly what Victorian men used to keep women on high pedestals, away from the world of politics and economics, and Elshtain was distressed that radical feminists have not expanded beyond this nineteenth-century male notion. □

CONCLUSION

Although radical feminism is by no means a flawless feminist perspective, feminists owe much to it. The insight that sexuality is the root cause of women's oppression is vital to any woman seeking to understand her personal and political position in society. To realize that women's oppression *as* women is very likely to continue in a liberal state where women have exactly the same formal rights as men and even in a Marxist state where invidious class distinctions have been eradicated is to realize something extremely important. Even if a feminist is not willing to remove herself from the institution of heterosexuality, she is probably more than willing to identify the ways in which male dominance and female submission are playing themselves out in her life and to stop engaging in practices that make of her a passive victim. Similarly, even if a feminist is not ready, willing, and/or able to live in an exclusively female community, she will certainly want to share her strength, power, and joy with other women in mutually reinforcing thought, word, and deed.

All movements need radicals, and the women's movement is no exception. Were it not for radical feminists, we would have been even slower to understand the connections among not only pornography, prostitution, sexual harassment, rape, and woman battering, but also among contraception, sterilization, abortion, artificial insemination by donor, in vitro fertilization, and contracted motherhood. Radical feminists have repeatedly shown us how women's bodies can be used by men against women and how they can be used by women for women. Radical feminists have also taught us how to celebrate women's nature. Even if there is no such thing as an essential female nature—a supremely nurturant, wise, and benign nature—it is empowering to think that it is good—indeed extremely good—to be a woman. What feminists owe to radical feminism is the conviction that what women share is their sexuality and that even if this sexuality has been a source of danger for women in the past, it can become a locus of pleasure and power for each and every woman in the future.

CHAPTER FIVE

———————— ■ ————————

Psychoanalytic Feminism

ALTHOUGH SIGMUND FREUD has been castigated by many feminists
for apparently basing his notion of penis envy, or "the girl's perception
of herself and all those like her as inferior castrates," on an assumption
of male superiority, it is not clear that his work on female sexuality
should be dismissed with a mere wave of the hand.[1] Given that psychoanalytic feminists have found within Freud liberating as well as
oppressive streams of thought, it is worth our effort to understand
precisely what Freud said about female sexuality. Only then will we be
able to appreciate what is groundbreaking about feminist revisions and
reinterpretations of Freudian psychoanalysis. □

THE ROOTS OF PSYCHOANALYTIC FEMINISM

Freud's theories concerning sexuality generated considerable controversy
among his contemporaries. The intensity of this controversy was not due
merely to Freud's having publicly addressed formerly taboo topics:
homosexuality, sadism, masochism, oral, and anal sex. Nor was the
intensity due solely to the fact that many of his theories struck his readers
as counterintuitive. Rather the intensity of the controversy was due largely
to Freud's suggestion that all sexual "aberrations," "variations," and
"perversions" can be and usually are stages in the development of what
he identified as *normal* human sexuality.[2]

According to Freud, children go through distinct psychosexual development stages, and the temperament of any given adult is the product
of how he/she deals with these stages. Gender, in other words, is the
product of sexual maturation. Because they experience their sexuality
differently (as a result of biology), girls and boys ultimately end up with
contrasting gender roles. If men adjust to their sexual maturation normally
(that is, typically), they will end up displaying expected masculine traits;
if women develop normally, they will end up displaying expected feminine

traits. Although Freud admitted that to some extent we are all androgynous, he wanted to say that, by virtue of anatomy, women should
develop feminine traits and men masculine ones.[3]

The basis for these conclusions is to be found in *Three Contributions
to the Theory of Sexuality*. In the second essay, "Infantile Sexuality,"
Freud discussed the sexual stages of infancy. Because adults in Freud's
time equated sexual activity with reproductive genital sexuality—that
is, heterosexual intercourse—adults thought that children were sexless.
Freud's argument, however, was that children's sexuality is "polymorphous
perverse"—that insofar as the infant is concerned, its entire body, and
especially its orifices and appendages, is sexual terrain. The infant moves
from this type of "perverse" sexuality to "normal" heterosexual genital
sexuality by passing through several stages. During the *oral* stage, the
infant receives pleasure from suckling his/her mother's breast and also
the next best thing, his/her thumb. During the *anal* stage, the two- or
three-year-old child particularly enjoys the sensations associated with
controlling the expulsion of his/her feces. During the *phallic* stage, the
three- or four-year-old child discovers the pleasure potential of the genitals
and either resolves or fails to resolve the so-called Oedipus and castration
complexes. At around age six, the child ceases to display overt sexuality
and begins a period of *latency* that ends around puberty, at which time
the young person enters the *genital* stage characterized by a resurgence
of sexual impulses. If all goes according to plan, the libido (defined by
Freud as undifferentiated sexual energy) will be directed outward, away
from autoerotic and homoerotic stimulation, and toward a member of
the opposite sex.

As explained in Freud's third essay, "The Transformation of Puberty,"
the critical juncture of the preceding psychosexual drama is the child's
resolution of the Oedipus and castration complexes. According to psychoanalytic doctrine, the fact that boys have penises while girls do not
fundamentally affects the way in which boys and girls go about resolving
the complexes of the phallic stage. The boy's Oedipus complex stems
from his natural attachment to his mother, for it is she who nurtures
him. Because of this, he wants to possess her—to have sexual intercourse
with her—and to kill his father, the rival for his attentions. Freud believed,
however, that this desire is short-lived because the boy has good reason
to fear his father. Having seen either his mother or some other female
naked, the boy speculates that these creatures without penises must have
been castrated, by his father no less. Shaken by this thought, the boy
fears that his father will castrate him should he dare to act upon his
desires for mother. This fear causes the boy to squelch his mother love,
a painful process during which he begins to develop what Freud called
a superego.[4]

To the degree that the superego is the internalization by the son of the father's values, it is a patriarchal, social conscience. Boys who successfully resolve the Oedipus and castration complexes develop a particularly strong superego because in the process of giving up mother love (albeit out of fear of castration), they learn how to submit themselves to the authority of the fathers. Were it not for the trauma of the Oedipus and castration complexes, then, boys would never grow up to be men who are willing to tow the party line and keep civilization marching along by becoming one of the fathers.

Significantly, the female experience of the Oedipus and castration complexes is drastically different from that of the male. Like the boy, the girl's first love object is her mother. But unlike the typical boy whose love object will remain a woman throughout his life, the typical girl has to switch from desiring a woman to desiring a man—at first her father and later on men who take the place of father. According to Freud, this transition from a female to a male love object begins when the girl realizes that she does not have a penis, that she is castrated. "They [girls] notice the penis of a brother or playmate, strikingly visible and of large proportions, at once recognize it as the superior counterpart of their own small and inconspicuous organ (the clitoris), and from that time forward they fall a victim to envy for the penis."[5]

Obsessed by her lack, the girl become increasingly envious of, say, her brother's penis and comes to blame her mother for having inadequately equipped her. In her resentment she turns away from her mother and makes her father her love object. But, said Freud, if a person loses a love object (in this case, mother), one way to handle this loss is to become, in some way or other, the abandoned love object. Thus, the girl identifies herself with her mother, trying to take her mother's place with father. As a result, the girl comes to hate her mother not only because her mother deprived her of a penis but also because her mother is a rival for the father's affections. At first, the girl desires to have her father's penis, but gradually she begins to desire something even more precious— a baby, which, for her, is the ultimate penis substitute.[6]

Not all girls turn into women who want babies, however. Some girls come to despise the inferior female clitoris so much that they turn away from sex altogether. Later in life, these girls will be labeled neurotic, especially if they experience frigidity (the inability to achieve orgasm). In contrast to these girls, there are those who refuse to accept the fact of their castration and to stop masturbating. These girls develop what Freud termed a "masculinity complex," imitating masculine traits in their modus vivendi and, in "extreme" cases, becoming lesbians.[7]

Freud admitted that in his scheme it is much more difficult for girls than for boys to achieve normal adult sexuality. The boy's first love object is a woman, his mother. If all goes as usual, his love objects will continue to be women, and the primary source of his boyhood sexual gratification—the penis—will continue to be the primary source of his adult sexual gratification. Like the boy, the girl's first love object is also a woman, her mother. But if all goes as usual in her case, the girl will make a transfer from having a *woman* as a love object to having a *man* as a love object. Moreover, if she wishes to be classified as a "normal" adult woman, the girl will have to change her erotogenic zone from the masculine clitoris to the feminine vagina.[8]

According to Freud, before the phallic stage, the girl has active sexual aims. Like the boy, she wants to take sexual possession of her mother with her clitoris. If the girl goes through the phallic stage successfully, however, she will enter the stage of latency without this desire; and when genital sensitivity reappears at puberty, the pubescent girl will no longer long to use her clitoris actively. Instead, she will use it passively—for autoerotic masturbation or as part of foreplay preparatory to heterosexual intercourse. But because the clitoris is not easy to desensitize, there is always the possibility that the pubescent girl will either regress back into the active clitoral stage or, exhausted from suppressing her clitoris, give up on sexuality altogether.

Significantly, the long-term consequences of penis envy and rejection of the mother go beyond possible frigidity. The girl's passage through the Oedipus and castration complexes supposedly scars her with several undesirable gender traits as she grows toward womanhood. First, she becomes *narcissistic* as she switches from active to passive sexual aims. Girls, said Freud, seek not so much to love as to be loved; and the more beautiful a girl is, the more she expects and demands to be loved. Second, girls become *vain*. As a compensation for her original lack (the penis), a girl comes to overvalue the rest of her physical experience, as if what she has could make up for what she does not have. Finally, girls become victims of an exaggerated sense of *shame*. It is, said Freud, not uncommon for a girl to be so embarrassed by the sight of her own body that, for example, she insists on dressing and undressing under her bedsheet.[9]

Girls fall victim, however, to more than just narcissism, vanity, and shame. Freud suggested that there are yet more deleterious consequences of the fact that the relation between the Oedipus complex and the castration complex for females is the exact reverse of what it is for males. The threat of castration in boys, we will recall, brings the Oedipus complex to an end. In girls, however, the lack of a penis is what drives them into their Oedipus complex and keeps them there indeterminately. "Whereas in boys the Oedipus complex succumbs to the castration complex, in girls it is made possible and led up to by the castration complex."[10] As Freud saw it, it is a mixed blessing that the girl is spared the equivalent of the boy's traumatic resolution of his Oedipal complex under threat of castration; for it is only undergoing a sexual trauma of these proportions—by being pushed, albeit out of fear, to internalize the father's values—that an individual can develop a strong superego, which gives rise to the traits that mark civilized people. Compared to men, women are not conscientious enough, not moral enough, and not civilized enough.

> I cannot escape the notion . . . that for women the level of what is ethically normal is different from what it is in men. Their super-ego is never so inexorable, so impersonal, so independent of its emotional origins as we require it to be in men. Character traits which critics of every epoch have brought up against women—that they show less sense of justice than men, that they are less ready to submit to the great necessities of life, that they are more influenced in their judgments by feelings of affection or hostility— all these would be amply accounted for by the modification of their super-ego which we have already inferred.[11]

In other words, female moral inferiority is due to the fact that girls lack a penis. Girls, because they do not have to worry about being castrated, are not nearly so motivated as boys are to become obedient rule fol- lowers. □

STANDARD FEMINIST CRITIQUES OF FREUD

Because penis envy and everything that flows from it paint such an unflattering portrait of women, many feminists were, and still are, angered by traditional Freudian theory. In the 1970s, feminists with otherwise widely different agendas—in this instance Betty Friedan, Shu- lamith Firestone, and Kate Millett—made Freud a common target. They argued that women's social position and powerlessness relative to men had little to do with female biology and much to do with the social construction of femininity.

According to Betty Friedan, Freud's ideas were shaped by his culture, which she described as Victorian even though Freud wrote many of his most influential essays about female sexuality in the 1920s and 1930s. Psychoanalysis is, for Friedan, another social science whose theorists and practitioners simply see what their culture wants them to see. When social scientists claim that they have identified a universal characteristic of essential human nature, said Friedan, we can be fairly confident that all they have really identified is some trait common to many people in their own culture. What most disturbed Friedan about Freud, however, was his supposed biological determinism. As she interpreted it, Freud's aphorism "Anatomy is destiny"[12] means that a woman's reproductive role, gender identity, and sexual preference are determined by her lack of a penis and that any woman who does not follow the course nature has set for her is in some way "abnormal."[13]

Not only did Friedan reject Freud's methodology; she also rejected his inquiry's subject matter: sexuality. We will recall that in *The Feminine Mystique,* Friedan identified an overemphasis on sex as one of the forces that keep women out of the public world of politics, economics, and culture. What women need is not sexual freedom but the freedom to grow more generally as persons. By encouraging women to think that female discontent and dissatisfaction have their roots in women's lack of the penis per se, rather than in the privileged socioeconomic and cultural status it confers on its possessors, traditional Freudian theory leads women to believe, falsely, that women are defective. Moreover, reasoned Friedan, whenever a woman believes that in lieu of possessing the penis, her fulfillment rests in having a baby, she is a victim of the "feminine mystique." Thus, insisted Friedan, even though Freud helped us confront our sexuality openly, we must criticize him for making sex—especially procreative sex—the be-all and end-all of women's existence.[14]

What Shulamith Firestone liked about Freud is precisely what Betty Friedan disliked about him—his emphasis on sexuality. Nevertheless, Firestone did fault him for his apolitical interpretation of female sexuality. She was bothered that Freud viewed the penis, for example, as the object of women's desire rather than the symbol of the power girls and women lack. She was even more distressed by Freud's insensitivity to the "hierarchy of power" in the family and by his failure to recognize what every child knows—"that in every way, physically, economically, emotionally, he [or she] is completely dependent on, thus at the mercy of" his or her parents, especially the father.[15]

Firestone believed that Freud's failure to focus on power accounts for the essential conservatism of today's neo-Freudian establishment. Non-Freudians, said Firestone, emphasize adjustment to the pathological power relations embodied in the nuclear family. Rather than looking for ways to alter these relations—to free women and children from the tyranny of the husband/father—neo-Freudians advance a psychology that is "reactionary to its core, its potential as a serious discipline undermined by its usefulness to those in power."[16] All too often, therapy is characterized by the determination to reconcile women to both the ideology of femininity and the structures of (capitalist) patriarchy. The invisibility of power in neo-Freudian theory, concluded Firestone, allows power to go unchallenged in its use.[17]

Had Freud recognized the pathological power relationships in the family, said Firestone, he would have reasoned that "if early sexual repression is the basic mechanism by which character structures supporting political, ideological, and economic serfdom are produced, an end to the incest taboo [the root cause of the Oedipus complex], through abolition of the family, would have profound effects: sexuality would be released from its straight jacket to eroticize our whole culture, changing its very definition."[18] As Firestone saw it, the oppression of children and women by men will continue until the Oedipus complex, which demands that children distinguish between bad, *sexual* feelings for their parents, and good, *loving* feelings for their parents, is exploded. If children are permitted to combine their sexual and loving feelings for their parents, especially their mothers, then the power dynamic between parents and children, men and women, will be so altered that society as we know it will be radically transformed.

Like Friedan and Firestone, Millett also focused on the biological determinism of Freud and especially of the neo-Freudians (disciples, it seems, frequently display greater fervor than the master). She was particularly bothered by the neo-Freudian belief that male sexual aggression is rooted in the "biological . . . necessity for overcoming the resistance of the sexual object."[19] Out of commitment to this belief, some of Freud's disciples went to ridiculous extremes in their attempt to prove it. Not content to study aggressive behavior among primates, they looked for male aggression everywhere, including in the most unlikely species: for example, the prehistoric cichlid fish. Supposedly, the males of this species were able to impregnate the females of their species only because the latter responded to their advances with "awe." Millett picked out this "fishy" example deliberately to show, as Friedan might, that there is little *real* evidence for the theory that nature has determined that women play second fiddle to men.[20]

Not only was Millett decidedly resistant to biological determinism in any way, shape, or form, she found the concept of penis envy a transparent instance of male egocentrism. Instead of celebrating woman's power to give birth, neo-Freudians interpret it as a pathetic attempt to possess a substitute penis. "Freudian logic has succeeded in converting childbirth, an impressive female accomplishment . . . into nothing more than a hunt for a male organ."[21] Had Freud not made the penis the centerpiece of his theory of sexuality, he would have been able to better hear what his patients were identifying as the real causes of their neuroses.

A case in point is that of Dora, an eighteen-year-old woman whom Freud treated for a typical case of "hysteria." A bright and intelligent woman, Dora was a member of a typical Viennese middle-class family: father, mother, son, daughter. It was also, from Freud's point of view, a typical Oedipal family with father and daughter aligned against mother and son. This "wholesome," all-Viennese family, however, was involved in some heavy sexual hanky-panky. Dora's father was having an affair with a longtime family friend, Frau K., whose husband Herr K. had sexual designs on Dora from the time she was fourteen. Although Dora had a close relationship with Frau K.—she had found in Frau K. the affectionate "mother" her own mother had never been—she broke this relationship off as soon as she realized what was going on and demanded that her father end his extramarital affair. Her father denied the affair, attributing to his daughter's "hysterical" state not only this "fantasy" but also the "fantasy" in which Herr K. played the role of a lecherous seducer. To his credit, Freud believed Dora's account of Herr K.'s advances but provided her with an explanation for her hysteria according to which her *real* problems were her sexual jealousy of Frau K. and her inability to be sexually excited by Herr K.'s advances. Apparently unimpressed by Freud's diagnosis, Dora terminated treatment with him after three months. Freud interpreted her abrupt termination of treatment as an instance of transference, that Dora had transferred her negative as well as positive feelings toward her father and Herr K. to Freud himself. She would wreak revenge on Freud by deserting him and through him all men. Freud read her to be saying, "Men are all so detestable that I would rather not marry."[22]

Following Millett's train of thought, we, unlike Freud, might regard Dora's reasons for not wishing to get married as quite rational given the emotional wringer through which she had been squeezed. At the very least, we would be sympathetic toward Dora, a teen-aged girl who, although she told Freud that she was often "overcome by the idea that she had been handed over to Herr K. as the price of his tolerating the relationship between her father and his wife," did not receive all the support an adolescent victim of sexual abuse needs.[23] Oddly, despite his belief that Herr K. and Dora's father were in "cahoots," and despite his realization that Dora's father was paying him to convince Dora that she had an overly active imagination, Freud did not make complete use of this information in his treatment of Dora. So we must wonder whether, had Freud made greater use of the information he held, Dora might have received better therapy. □

PURSUING PSYCHOANALYSIS
IN FEMINIST DIRECTIONS

Despite the general feminist critique against Freud, feminists who have used him productively argue that most of Friedan's, Firestone's, and Millett's critiques are best leveled against Freud's disciples—theorists such as Helene Deutsch[24] and Erik Erikson[25]—rather than against Freud himself. During the last two decades or so, at least four varieties of psychoanalytic feminism have evolved, each developing the Freudian corpus in feminist directions. A first variety attempts to cleanse Freudianism of any and all traces of biological determinism; a second pays scant attention to the overly discussed Oedipus complex, analyzing instead the pre-Oedipal stage during which the mother-infant relationship is most intense; a third focuses on the strengths rather than the much-discussed weaknesses of woman's morality; and a fourth reinterprets the Oedipus complex, giving it nonpatriarchal meanings. Together these four varieties of psychoanalytic feminism have shown that Freudian thought may have liberating as well as enslaving potential for women.

The Feminist Rejection
of Freud's Biological Determinism

Given that Freud's claims about woman's nature are those that most enrage feminists, it is not surprising that the first group of psychoanalytic feminists to emerge all rejected biological determinism, emphasizing instead the experiential and cultural influences that shape woman's gender identity and behavior. Alfred Adler, Karen Horney, and Clara Thompson all offered views that contended in some way that women's (and men's) experience of sexuality has been socially constructed. Thus, the theorists empowered women by insisting that biology is not destiny.

Alfred Adler

Adler admitted of only one important biological fact in human development: the helplessness of the infant. This infantile experience of powerlessness, or "inferiority," directs our lifelong struggle against feelings of overwhelming impotence. In striving for "superiority"—the experience of powerfulness—nothing is absolutely determined. A person's biological contours and/or experience does not lead logically and inevitably to certain psychological traits or future experiences. Each of us has, said Adler, a "creative self" that actively mediates the givens of biology and finds in them goals for the future. We are, according to Adler, a species shaped more by our visions of the future than by our roots in the past.[26]

Given his philosophical assumptions about human nature—which were far more optimistic than those of Freud, who viewed us as creatures driven by rather dark forces—Adler was able to provide, for example, new interpretations for why so-called neurotic women suffer from a sense of inferiority, for why they are plagued by "masculinity complexes." Neurotic women, said Adler, have been thwarted in their striving for "superiority," the achievement of power by the "creative self," and as a consequence have developed neuroses as manifestations of their dissatisfaction. Neurotic women are actually protesting their situation under patriarchy, a situation that Adler recognized: "All our institutions, our traditional attitudes, our laws, our morals, our customs, give evidence of the fact that they [women] are determined and maintained by privileged males for the glory of male domination."[27] Simply by acknowledging that the cards are stacked against women in patriarchy, Adler provided "neurotic women" with the raw material for their cure.

Karen Horney

Like Adler, Karen Horney emphasized the role a person's environment plays in his or her growth as persons. A medical school student in turn-of-the-century Berlin, Horney experienced firsthand the ways in which society constricts women's creative development. She made the point that women's feelings of inferiority originate not in recognition of their "castration" but in realization of their social subordination. Although Horney conceded that women are symbolically castrated, in that they have been denied the power the penis represents, she refused to accept that ordinary women are radically defective beings simply because they lack penises. She argued instead that patriarchal culture creates women as feminine (passive, masochistic, narcissistic), and then convinces them that "femininity"—actually a defensive adaptation to male domination—characterizes their true selves. In this light, "masculinity complexes" appear perfectly reasonable; any woman who, understandably, undertakes what Horney called the "flight from womanhood" will reach for what has been considered valuable and privileged—masculinity.[28] Women do not want to be men because they are enamored of the penis; they want to be men because men are in control of society.[29]

Clara Thompson

Clara Thompson sided with Adler and Horney in portraying development as a process of growth away from one's biology and toward mastery of one's environment. Human development refers, she claimed, to the task of self-formation. In the tradition of interpersonal psychology—which views our relationships with others as crucial to our development and well-being—Thompson explained female passivity as the product of a set of asymmetrical male-female relationships in which constant deferral to male authority causes women to have weaker egos than men do. Female and male identities do not emanate from unchanging female and male biologies. Rather, they emerge from ever-changing social ideas about what it means to be male or female. Along with Adler and Horney, Thompson believed that women's guilt, inferiority, and self-hatred are grounded in culture and the cultural use of biology, not in biology itself. Thus, the transformation of the legal, political, economic, and social structures that contain culture is a necessary step in the transformation of women's psychology.[30]

In the process of reinterpreting Freud's observations, Adler, Horney, and Thompson effectively broke from him. First, they spoke of masculine bias and male dominance and offered a political as well as psychoanalytic analysis of women's situation, something Freud did not do. Second, they offered a unitary theory of human development, not dualistic theories of male and female development. Adler, Horney, and Thompson advanced creativity, activity, and growth that are gender blind, thus leaving no room for the kind of fatalism about women's situation that expresses itself through ideas of women's unchanging nature. Last, and perhaps most interestingly, all three conceived of the self as something that develops uniquely and individually in each person and grows out of the interface between nature and culture. For Adler, Horney, and Thompson, there is not *one* universally healthy, normal, and natural male self for men and *another* universally healthy, normal, and natural female self for women. Rather, there are as many selves as there are people.[31]

The Feminist Case for and Against Dual Parenting

Both Dorothy Dinnerstein and Nancy Chodorow focus on the pre-Oedipal stage of psychosexual development, when the infant is still symbiotically attached to its mother, as the key to understanding how sexuality and gender are constructed and why their mode of construction nearly always results in male dominance. Much of what is wrong with men and women as individuals (and us as a society), according to Dinnerstein and Chodorow, is traceable to the fact that women do all the mothering. Were men to mother just as much as women do, speculate Dinnerstein and Chodorow, boys and girls would grow up realizing that fathers as well as mothers have both weaknesses and strengths and that neither men nor women are to blame for the human condition (for the fact that we have material bodies and are destined to die).

Dorothy Dinnerstein on the Mermaid and the Minotaur

According to Dinnerstein, our culture's gender arrangements have influenced how men and women conceive of themselves and each other, and the resulting portrait is not pretty. In it, women are "mermaids" and men are "minotaurs." "The treacherous mermaid, seductive and impenetrable female representative of the dark and magic underwater world from which our life comes and in which we cannot live, lures voyagers to their doom. The fearsome minotaur, gigantic and eternally infantile offspring of a mother's unnatural lust, male representative of mindless, greedy power, insatiably devours live human flesh."[32]

Because Dinnerstein found this portrait so ugly, she sought to explain why we continue, albeit in different hues, to paint it over and over again. The answer to our pathological need to make monsters of ourselves is buried, she discovered, deep in our psychosexual development, in the pre-Oedipal stage. The infant's relationship with her or his mother is profoundly symbiotic because the infant is initially incapable of distinguishing between self and mother. Given that the maternal body is the infant's first encounter with the material or physical universe, the infant experiences it as a symbol of an unreliable and unpredictable universe. Mother is the source of pleasure and pain for the infant, who is never certain whether his or her physical and psychological needs will be met. As a result, the infant grows up feeling very ambivalent toward mother figures (women) and what they represent (the material/physical universe, or nature). Not wanting to reexperience utter dependence on an all-powerful force, men seek to control both women and nature, to exert power over them. Concomitantly, fearing the power of the mother within themselves, women seek to be controlled by men. Tragically, men's need to control women and women's need to be controlled by men leads, said Dinnerstein, to a *mis*shapen set of six gender arrangements, which serve as a paradigm for destructive human relations in general.

As the first characteristic of current gender relationships, Dinnerstein pointed to the fact that men are more sexually possessive than women. Because men need to feel in control, they hope to overcome the fact that they were once absolutely dependent on their mothers by totally possessing their wives and lovers now. In this situation, when a woman is unfaithful to a man, the man feels again his initial despair upon realizing that his mother had a self separate from his own, a self intent on getting her own way rather than his. This re-felt sense of despair explains, said Dinnerstein, men's violent reactions to their wives' and/or lovers' infidelities, which can range from extramarital affairs to action that suggests a less than perfectly loving, self-sacrificing woman.

Curiously, although many women accept men's sexual possessiveness as some sort of right, they do not generally claim the same right for themselves. Dinnerstein explained this asymmetry as follows: Because a woman fears the power of the mother within herself, she is always in search of a man who needs her—that is, a man who can control her. The more a man says he needs her, the more she wants to be with him. But because a man does not represent the mother to her in the way that she represents the mother to him, she lacks part of his drive toward possessiveness of "the mother." After all, no matter how deep the symbiosis she achieves with him, it will not equal the kind of symbiosis that can be achieved with a woman/mother. Consequently, if a man leaves a woman, she will not feel the same intensity of grief she felt when her mother originally left her.[33]

The second mark of current gender arrangement is, according to Dinnerstein, the muting of female erotic impulsivity. A muted female eroticism is one oriented exclusively toward male pleasure. Through sexual intercourse, the woman seeks to satisfy the man, and whatever pleasure she experiences is experienced vicariously as delight in his satisfaction. Her own sexual wants and needs must go unattended; for were she to insist on their fulfillment, she and the man would recall the shock they both felt as infants when they first recognized their mothers as "I's" who had lives and interests of their own. Moreover, were she to let her partner satisfy her, the woman would feel enormous guilt for having abandoned her primary love object (mother and women) for a secondary love object (father and men). Better to deprive herself of sexual pleasure, she senses, than suffer the pangs of conscience.[34]

This guilt on the part of women contributes to the third feature of what Dinnerstein identified as present gender relations—the idea that sexual excitement and personal sentiment must be tied together for women but not for men. Because of the guilt she feels about abandoning her mother, a woman refuses to allow herself even vicarious pleasure in sex unless the relationship is infused with the same type of all-encompassing love that existed between her and her mother. In order to feel good about a sexual encounter, a woman must believe that the relationship underlying it is like the one she initially had with her mother: deep, binding, and strong. Only such a relationship can possibly justify her rejection of her mother. To abandon mother for a "one-night stand," for example, would be to settle for a superficial intimacy that can only approximate the deep intimacy of mother-child symbiosis.

In contrast to women, men are notorious for their ability to separate sex from intense emotional commitment. This ability is also rooted in the mother-infant relationship, especially in the loss of the illusion of infant omnipotence. In the male-female sexual relationship, the man feels especially vulnerable because a woman "can reinvoke in him the unqualified, boundless, helpless passion of infancy."[35] Depending on how hard a man has worked to be in charge of his destiny, he will be threatened by the overwhelming powers of sexual passion. He will fear being once again overwhelmed by a woman able to shatter his ego by withdrawing herself from him. Thus, he will seek to remain in control of the sexual act, distancing himself from the woman with whom he is having intercourse.

The fourth hallmark of gender arrangements today is, claimed Dinnerstein, that women are denied personhood and are viewed as "Its" as opposed to men who are seen as "I's." Because we encounter woman before we are able to distinguish I's from Its (that is, centers of sentience from impersonal forces of nature), Dinnerstein speculated that we initially perceive mother not as a person but as an awesome, all-enveloping object. In contrast, because we usually encounter father as a major role-player in our lives after we have successfully made the traumatic I-It distinction, we have less difficulty recognizing that the man who wants to take us skating or out for ice cream is indeed an I just as we are I's. Dinnerstein believed that if we can appreciate the difference between (1) experiencing mother as an object, as an It, before we have made a self-other distinction and (2) experiencing father as a subject, as an I, after we have made this distinction, then we can also fathom why female power—be it in the private or public realm—is profoundly threatening to both men and women. We can also understand why men have such a need to control women and why women have such a need to be controlled by men.[36]

The fifth characteristic of both traditional and contemporary gender arrangements is, claimed Dinnerstein, rooted in our general ambivalence toward the flesh. We hate it because it limits our control and because we know it will ultimately die; yet we love it because it gives us pleasure. Our general ambivalence toward the body is, however, intensified in the case of woman. On the one hand, woman's body is powerful because it represents the forces of life; on the other hand, woman's body is disgusting because it bleeds and oozes. Because men's bodies do not carry culture's symbolic baggage, men can imagine their bodies to be largely free of the impurities and problems associated with women's bodies. Rather unfairly, men get over any remaining ambivalence they may have about the male body by displacing all their fears of the flesh onto the female body. The denigration of the female body as dirty, foul, and sinful causes woman to deny her bodily core of self-respect, which deprives her of the ability to reject confidently all the negative feelings being projected onto her body. As a result, woman comes to hate the body and to punish it in many and sundry ways.[37]

Dinnerstein observed that the final characteristic of gender arrangements is the tacit agreement between men and women that men should go out into the public world and that women should stay behind, within the private sphere. Women funnel their energies into symbiosis, into relationships, eschewing enterprise for fear of putting power back into the hands of women; and men funnel their passions into enterprise, eschewing symbiosis, or relationships, for fear of losing control. Regrettably, the terms of this bargain permit both men and women to remain children, who are so busy playing roles that they fail to confront the human condition and themselves as they actually are and might potentially be were they to take responsibility for themselves and their world.

As Dinnerstein saw it, all six destructive gender arrangements are due to women's control over childrearing and to our subsequent tendency to blame mother/woman for everything wrong with the human condition, especially the fact that we are limited beings destined to fail and ultimately to die. We blame mother/woman for our limitations, speculated Dinnerstein, because it is mother/woman who presides when we first skin our knee, when we are forced to take the blame for losing our gloves, when we get the flu, and when our sand castle is demolished by a merciless wave. Dinnerstein was convinced that unless we all learn to stop blaming mother/woman for the human condition, we cannot hope to overcome our destructive gender arrangements, a set of relationships symptomatic of our increasing inability to deal with each other and our world. Interestingly, Dinnerstein's solution to the scapegoating of women was to institutionalize dual parenting. Only when men share equally with women the task of nurturing infants—only when the blame and anger that traditionally went exclusively to women is distributed equally to both genders—can we possibly realize that no one, male or female, is to blame for the human condition. It simply is, and we have to help each other deal with it.

Nancy Chodorow on the Reproduction of Mothering

To the degree that Dinnerstein was mystified about why human beings want to preserve a destructive set of gender arrangements, Chodorow wondered why women *want* to mother. Although puzzled by the fact that so many contemporary women *see* themselves primarily as mothers or potential mothers, Chodorow rejected the two standard explanations of this phenomenon: that women are destined to be mothers by nature and that women are conditioned to be mothers by society.

Chodorow easily dismissed the idea that women's mothering is innate or instinctive, a lasting, genetic consequence of the human species' evolution from its formative period as hunters and gatherers. Even if it made sense in primitive times for pregnant women and nursing mothers to gather food close to the home site, and for men to hunt farther afield, this is no longer the case. Today both men and women can do all their hunting and gathering at the local grocery store, and there is no compelling reason why women should forage for the asparagus while men attack the meat counter.

In addition to finding "nature" theories of motherhood uncompelling, Chodorow found "nurture" theories of motherhood equally unconvincing. According to Chodorow, any theory of mothering based on the notion that women embrace, as their own, a set of socially constructed and validated feminine gender roles is flawed because it relies on the idea that gender roles *can* be freely chosen. By the time a person is old enough to make choices about anything—let alone something as fundamental as gender roles—he or she has *already* been engendered. In other words, femininity is not a way of being that a girl deliberately decides to assume; rather, it is a slow, gradual process that seizes the psyche of a girl before she is self-consciously aware of herself as a girl.

As Chodorow saw it, the desire to mother, like the desire to be feminine, is implanted in girls before they become women. Thus, mothering has little to do with conscious choice and much to do with an unconscious desire to mother. So deep is this desire that most women find the question, *why* do you want to mother? puzzling if not unanswerable.

Chodorow's point was a subtle one. The skills needed for *adequate* mothering cannot be learned simply by imitation (by watching how mother does it). Nor can they be learned by an act of the will (by deciding that "now I am going to start mothering"). Nor can they be imposed on women by men; for unless a woman, "*to some degree* and *on some unconscious or conscious level,*" views herself as "maternal," she cannot mother adequately no matter how hard she tries.[38]

In order to explain why so many women are in fact able to mother adequately—that is, to empathize with children—Chodorow analyzed the pre-Oedipal stage. She pointed to the different "object-relational" experiences that boys and girls have as infants with their mothers and fathers. According to Chodorow, the pre-Oedipal stage is sexually charged for boys in a way that it is not for girls. Feeling a sexual current between himself and his mother, the son senses that his mother's body is not like his body. As he enters the Oedipal stage, the son realizes how much of a problem his mother's otherness is. He cannot remain attached to her (overwhelmingly in love with her) without risking his father's wrath. Not willing to take this risk, the son separates from his mother. What makes this process of separation less painful for the son is his dawning realization that power and prestige are to be had through identification with men—in this case, the father. Apparently, social contempt for women helps the boy define himself in opposition to the female sex his mother represents.[39]

In contrast to the mother-son pre-Oedipal relationship, the mother-daughter pre-Oedipal relationship is characterized by what Chodorow termed "prolonged symbiosis" and "narcissistic over-identification." Because both the daughter and mother are female, the daughter's sense of gender and self is continuous with that of her mother. Although the symbiosis between mother and daughter is weakened during this Oedipal stage, it is never really broken. What prompts a girl to distance herself from the mother is what her father symbolizes: the autonomy and independence that characterizes a subjectivity, or I, on the one hand and the ability to sexually satisfy a woman—in this case, her mother—on the other. Thus, as Chodorow interpreted it, penis envy arises for the girl both because the penis symbolizes male power *and* because it is the sexual organ that apparently satisfies her mother. "Every step of the way . . . a girl develops her relationship to her father while looking back at her mother—to see if her mother is envious, to make sure she is in fact separate, to see if she is really independent. Her turn to her father is both an attack on her mother and an expression of love for her."[40]

Although most girls do finally transfer their primary love from a female to a male object, Chodorow suggested that this transfer of love is never completed. Whether a girl develops into a heterosexual woman or not, she will tend to find her strongest emotional connections with other women; and although Chodorow did not stress the point in her analysis, the pre-Oedipal mother-daughter relationship provides a reference point for lesbian relationships.[41]

The psychosexual development of boys and girls is, said Chodorow, not without social implications. The boy's separateness from his mother is the source of his inability to relate deeply to others, an inability that prepares him for work in the public sphere, which values single-minded efficiency, a down-to-business attitude, and competitiveness. Similarly, the girl's oneness with her mother is the source of her capacity for relatedness, a capacity that is necessary for her role as nurturant wife and mother in the private sphere. Ironically, the better a woman "mothers," the more she will be faulted. We expect mothers to be perfect, to strike a golden mean between too little mothering on the one hand and too much mothering on the other hand; and we attribute all manner and fashion of evils to imperfect mothers who mother too little or too much. Too little mothering, said Dinnerstein, has the same effect on both boys and girls: It makes them psychotic. In contrast, too much mothering has different effects on boys and girls. Whereas it makes girls overly dependent on their mothers and less than fully autonomous, it makes boys resentful and defensive toward women, impels their search for nonthreatening and undemanding sexual partners, and leads them to reject their own needs for emotional intimacy and to scorn those of their sexual partners.

Chodorow explained the phenomena of too little mothering and of too much mothering in both psychoanalytic and sociological terms. If a woman mothers too little, it is probably because her own mother was inadequate. Lacking a nurturant role model, the underloved girl's capacity for relatedness, for connecting empathetically with people, goes undeveloped. If a woman mothers too much, it is probably because her own needs for intimacy are not being met by her husband. Not feeling related enough, she may cast her daughter as a substitute mother, recreating her first mother-daughter intimacy; or she may cast her son as a substitute father, fantasizing about her son as the powerful "doctor" or "lawyer," someone whose shadow can conceal her. Under these conditions, a woman expects from her children what only an adult should be expected to give her; and a man, feeling out of place in the nursery, loses the opportunity to develop his capacity for relatedness.[42]

Given her analysis of what she perceived as the problem—that woman's capacity for relatedness is overdeveloped and man's underdeveloped—Chodorow, like Dinnerstein, predictably proposed dual parenting as the solution to it. Chodorow believed that dual parenting is a structural adjustment that would permit women and men to develop those parts of their psyches that are currently underdeveloped and, therefore, to raise male and female children equally capable of adequately mothering the next generation of children. Specifically, dual parenting would have at least three specific results. First, Chodorow suggested, the equal presence of the father as well as the mother would diffuse the intensity of the mother-child relationship. Second, a mother who has a meaningful life outside the home is not so likely to view her child as her raison d'être. Third, a boy raised partly by a father would not develop fears of maternal power or "expectations of women's unique self-sacrificing qualities."[43] Girls and boys would grow up expecting men as well as women to be loving and women as well as men to be autonomous. Boys would no longer have to reject feminine feelings of nurturance as unworthy of a real man.

Comparison and Contrast of Dinnerstein and Chodorow

What is common to both Chodorow and Dinnerstein is their conviction that the oppression of *women* originates in the female monopoly on mothering. Explanations of female subordination that focus on differences in physical strength, on the workings of capital, or on the laws of society miss this crucial point. Despite this major agreement, however, differences of substance as well as style characterize Dinnerstein's and Chodorow's respective analyses.

Dinnerstein drew a stark picture of gender relations that accentuates some of the sadder moments in our self-development. Because our experience of being mothered has been so overwhelming, even terrifying, Dinnerstein described our transition from infancy to adulthood as the slow and painful process of rejecting the mother, of devaluing women and all things female. On account of his sexual *dissimilarity* to his mother, a boy can make this break completely, thereby realizing his desire for independence, for omnipotence. On account of her sexual *similarity* to her mother, however, a girl can never really break from her mother. A woman, precisely because she *is* a woman, will remain less than autonomous so long as the experience of self-definition is understood largely as the process of maternal—hence female—rejection.

In contrast, Chodorow's picture of mothering was less stark, less preoccupied with the omnipotent mother who must be controlled, if not by domination, then by rejection. As Chodorow saw it, the infant's connection with its mother is not exactly shattered, with all of the rage and vindictiveness that such a sharp break entails; instead the connection is gradually eroded, especially for girls. For Chodorow, the mother-child relationship is less intense than it is for Dinnerstein, and Chodorow described mothering's consequences for society as being something less corrupt and invidious than "malaise." This more temperate approach indicates that for Chodorow the measure of difference between males and females is how connected they are to mother, not how much they seek to control mother. Chodorow spoke of the current gender arrangement in terms of ego boundaries and parenting capacities, not in terms of perversion or neurosis. In the main, this is a difference in style from Dinnerstein, but it also reflects a difference in substance. Dinnerstein focused on the unappeased anger of both men and women over their infantile experience with capricious female power; Chodorow emphasized the unconscious need of both men and women to reproduce, as adults, the infantile experience of symbiosis. Dinnerstein saw female mothering largely as a source of fear and rage; Chodorow viewed it primarily as a seductive locus of connectedness and intimacy.[44]

Despite their differences, Dinnerstein and Chodorow did agree that dual parenting is the solution to the problems associated with female mothering. Mothering must become parenting if women are to cease being the scapegoats of wailing infants and raging men. Men must become equal parents with women in order to free women from *sole* responsibility for the human condition. Dual parenting will, in the estimation of Dinnerstein and Chodorow, break down the sexual division completely. Only when both sexes raise children will men and women feel truly free to develop themselves as autonomous, nurturant people who are equally comfortable in both the private and the public domain.

Critiques of Dinnerstein and Chodorow in General and of Dual Parenting in Particular

Despite their general interest in the writings of Dinnerstein and Chodorow, critics have leveled three specific charges against both theorists. The first is simply that Dinnerstein and Chodorow focused too much on the inner dynamics of the psyche and not enough on the external permutations of society as the primary source of women's oppression. The second is that Dinnerstein and Chodorow wrongly used one kind of family—the capitalist, middle-class, white, heterosexual, nuclear family— as the paradigm for all kinds of family. The third is that far from ending women's oppression, dual parenting may actually exacerbate it.

When critics complain that Dinnerstein and Chodorow stressed psychic dynamics over social structures, they wish to object to the thesis that the family determines society—that the formation of masculine and feminine gender identities and behavior patterns within the family unit

causes the construction of certain kinds of social structures.[45] As Dinnerstein and Chodorow saw it, legal, political, economic, and cultural
systems would be dramatically different if most women did not think
of themselves as mothers. Women are not mothers *because* law, politics,
economics, or culture has made them mothers. As the critics see it,
Dinnerstein and Chodorow were putting the cart before the horse. Society
determines the family, not the reverse.[46]

The second criticism leveled against Dinnerstein and Chodorow is
that they failed to appreciate the diverse forms the family takes inter-
culturally as well as intraculturally. When Dinnerstein and Chodorow
explained the pre-Oedipal and Oedipal stages, they had in mind the two-
parent, heterosexual family. But even if children in these kinds of family
experience the Oedipus and castration complexes, it is not clear that
children in a single-parent family, or children raised by a lesbian or
homosexual couple, undergo them. Nor is it clear that children raised
in an extended family undergo them. Like many psychoanalytic thinkers,
notes the critic, Chodorow and Dinnerstein often conflated the families
they knew best (their own families, for example) with The Family, a
universal construct that never has or will exist.

The third and most serious critique of Dinnerstein and Chodorow
faults them for selecting the wrong cure for women's oppression. Jean
Bethke Elshtain has singled out Dinnerstein for particularly strong words.
Dinnerstein, said Elshtain, believed that women have less of a need to
control things and people than men have. As a result of their special
symbiotic relationships to their mothers, daughters grow up to be
nurturant, affectionate, and caring persons, who are "less avid than men
as hunters and killers, as penetrators of Mother Nature's secrets, plunderers
of her treasure, outwitters of her constraints."[47] We must wonder, then,
exclaimed Elshtain, what will happen to all of women's positive qualities,
as well as men's negative qualities, when children are no longer intensely
and exclusively mothered by women. Will men become better for spending
more time in the nursery and women worse for spending less?

Dinnerstein's answer to this kind of query was optimistic. Dual
parenting will have positive effects on both boys and girls. No longer
overwhelmed by the omnipotent mother, boys will grow up needing
neither to control women nor to curb the feminine voice within themselves.
As a result, men will be able to forge intense relationships with women
without feeling threatened and to develop their latent, nurturant capacities.
Girls will remain caring, compassionate, and considerate "even as they
gain public roles, authority, power."[48]

But even if Dinnerstein's answer might have satisfied some critics'
doubts about dual parenting, it did not satisfy Elshtain's. Elshtain asked
why it is that men pick up all of the wondrous feminine qualities

previously denied to them, whereas women do not pick up any of the horrendous male qualities previously spared them. If men will become more nurturant by taking care of their babies, then perhaps women will become more aggressive by doing battle in the nation's boardrooms, courtrooms, and hospitals. In sum, according to Elshtain, Dinnerstein failed to ask herself what will be lost as well as gained through the process of dual parenting.

If Elshtain has singled out Dinnerstein for criticism on the point of dual parenting, Alice Rossi has targeted Chodorow. Rossi argued that Chodorow failed to take seriously the possibility that certain biological necessities may rule out dual parenting; allowing people other than women to care for infants may prove disastrous.[49] Women have been found, said Rossi, to be more inherently sensitive to and perceptive of infants' needs, and the traditional caricature of the bumbling father pinning the diaper on his baby may have some basis in fact.[50] Rossi also evidenced a certain pessimism as to whether sons and daughters will ever separate equidistantly from their mothers, even if their mothers co-parent them with their fathers. Women's psychology, said Rossi, as well as women's biology, including menstruation and pregnancy, may mean that daughters will always identify more with their mothers than sons will. A son will always be at a remove from his mother simply because of the differences in their biology. Even if men as well as women mothered, this would still be the case, which suggests that differentiated gender roles and their supposed negative consequences might coexist with dual parenting. Dual parenting, said Rossi, might be merely a rearrangement of our problems, not an answer to them. Still, she conceded, entrusting babies to men—giving dual parenting a try—is preferable to handing babies over to institutionalized child care, where their biological roots would be cut.[51]

Yet another critic, Janice Raymond, formulated a critique of dual parenting that applied equally well to Dinnerstein and Chodorow. Upon hearing either Dinnerstein's or Chodorow's defense of dual parenting for the first time, observed Raymond, *heterosexuals* are likely to consider it a reasonable solution to distorted gender relations. After all, if "male absence from child rearing" is leading the world to nuclear war, among other disasters, then, by all means, let father spend at least as much time in the nursery as mother, especially if his being there will cause future generations of men and women to be less misogynistic. But, warned Raymond, to insist that dual parenting is the solution to the human malaise is to elevate men once again to the status of "saviors." This solution gives men even more power than they now have—emotional power within the family as well as political and economic power outside the family. In addition, to advocate dual parenting is once again to thwart "gyn-affection," or woman-to-woman attraction and interaction.[52]

As Raymond saw it, the fact that women mainly mother is not *the* problem or even *a* problem. Rather, the problem, as Adrienne Rich suggested in *Of Woman Born,* is that women mother when, where, and how *men* want them to. The purpose of the Oedipus complex, suggested Raymond, is to teach girls how to direct their love away from women and toward men, and what motivates a girl to submit to this pain is that she sees her mother loving her father in a special way—so special that she surmises that men must be worthy of a love that women are not. Raymond speculated that were the girl to see her mother loving other women in a special way, the girl would grow up with extremely positive feelings about herself and other women. Despite their mutual claim that female bonds are stronger and deeper than male bonds, neither Dinnerstein nor Chodorow considered the possibility that women are powerful and strong enough to join together in communities of care— communities supportive enough to give women as well as children the kind of love they would not otherwise find.[53]

Janice Raymond's critique was a powerful one—so powerful, in fact, that it may lead us to agree that dual parenting is a misguided response to women's oppression. But, as Hester Eisenstein has pointed out, this would be to discount all the positive, feminist reasons for dual parenting, which Dinnerstein predicted will have at least four good consequences.[54]

First, dual parenting will, Dinnerstein believed, enable us to stop projecting all of our ambivalence about carnality and mortality unto one parent, the female. Because both parents will be involved in the parenting process from the infant's birth onward, we will no longer associate our bodily limitations with the female parent only. It will not even occur to us to link our carnality and mortality with the deliberate intentions of either parent. Thus, we will be forced to deal with the human condition as a given that has nothing to do with gender. No longer will we feel compelled to blame Eve for tempting Adam with the apple.

Second, dual parenting will, in Dinnerstein's estimation, enable us to overcome our ambivalence about growing up. We remain childish because we approach life as if it were a drama in which women are assigned one role to play and men another. Women play the nurturant mother-goddess role, while men play the mighty world-builder role. Yet both sexes not only doubt whether they can perform these roles satisfactorily; they also wish to break free of them. With the institution of dual parenting, these roles will no longer be split along gender lines. As a result, women will no longer feel totally responsible for nurturing, and men will no longer feel totally responsible for making the world go round. Once men as well as women engage in mothering, and once women as well as men engage in enterprise, the roles of mother goddess and of world builder will be divested of their destructive mystique.

Third, Dinnerstein was convinced that dual parenting will also help us overcome our ambivalence toward the existence of other separate beings. In the present situation, we do not fully acknowledge each other as autonomous agents. We tend to view other people as means toward an end—the end of making ourselves feel better about ourselves—rather than as separate beings, each of whom is an end unto himself or herself. With the inception of dual parenting, we will not require others to validate our existence. In other words, once we are free to choose whatever combination of nurturing and enterprising activities we prefer, we will no longer need as much confirmation and reinforcement from others that our actions are valuable and necessary.

Finally, Dinnerstein believed that dual parenting will help us overcome our ambivalence about enterprise. All people, but especially men, tend to use world building as a defense against death. Indeed, the wonders of civilization can be read as the tragic testimony of a species that strives to achieve the good, the true, and the beautiful, knowing full well that everyone and everything are doomed to disintegration. Given his traditional role as world builder, man has not been permitted to express reservations about the ultimate worth of his worldly projects. But woman, given her traditional role as mother goddess—the wise one who is not easily deceived by the pomp and circumstance of civilization—has been permitted to articulate her misgivings about civilization. Indeed, said Dinnerstein, women have played the part of court jesters, poking fun at the games men play; and women's irreverence has served to release the tension that ripples through the world of enterprise. As a result, things have never seemed bad enough for us to change the course of history. Dual parenting will enable us to see just how bad the world situation is. Because men and women will have an equal role in world building as well as in childbearing, women will no longer be able to play court jesters. With nowhere to hide, not even in laughter, both sexes will be required to put aside their games in order to reshape what is, fundamentally, a misshapen world.

The Feminist Case for and Against Woman's Morality

Carol Gilligan on the Advantages
of a Different Voice for Women

Carol Gilligan challenged the Freudian notion that men have a well-developed sense of justice—a sense of morality—whereas women do not. She argued instead that men and women have different conceptions of morality, each equally coherent and developed and equally valid. Unlike

Chodorow and Dinnerstein, Gilligan was not especially concerned with the origins of these differing moralities, although she did suggest that the importance of separation and autonomy in men's lives often leads them to focus the discussion of morality around issues of justice, fairness, rules, and rights, whereas the importance of family and friends in women's lives leads them to emphasize people's wants, needs, interests, and aspirations. Instead, Gilligan was preoccupied with the systematic bias of traditional philosophical and psychological literature on moral development. This bias has hindered recognition of women's conception of morality as a valid one and has instead found it—and women—to be deficient.[55]

Gilligan's main target was her former teacher, Harvard's Lawrence Kohlberg. Despite her admiration for much of Kohlberg's work on the psychology of moral development, Gilligan accused him of advancing *male* notions of justice as the norm for *human* moral development and of regarding women who fail to live up to these norms as somehow morally underdeveloped. As Gilligan saw it, the failure of women to fit into the Procrustean bed of male morality argues for redesigning the bed, not for reconstituting women. Male norms may simply be too narrow to accommodate anything other than the male point of view. Thus, if psychologists want to accurately assess women's moral development, they must rethink their criteria for moral development and attend to women's as well as to men's mode of expression.[56]

In the process of listening to what each of twenty-nine women had to say about her decision to abort or not to abort her fetus, what Gilligan discovered was that no matter their age, social class, marital status, or ethnic background, all of these women had a conception of the self different from that of the typical man. Whereas men tend to see the self as an autonomous, separate being, women tend to view it as an interdependent being whose identity depends on others. These different views of the self, said Gilligan, account for at least four empathetic differences between the way in which men and women make moral decisions.

First, women tend to stress the moral agent's continuing relationships to others, whereas men tend to stress the agent's formal, abstract rights. Thus, the typical woman is prepared to forsake some of her rights if she can thereby cement a faltering, but extremely meaningful, human relationship. Second, when making a moral decision, women espouse a somewhat more consequentialist point of view, calculating the effects of the moral agent's action on all who will be touched by it, whereas men espouse a somewhat more nonconsequentialist point of view, according to which principles must be upheld even if some people get hurt in the process. Third, women are usually more willing to accept excuses for a moral agent's behavior, whereas men generally label behavior as morally inexcusable just because it is morally unjustifiable. (To excuse an act is to point to extenuating circumstances that mitigate its *wrongness;* to justify an act is to articulate reasons for its *rightness.*) Finally, women usually interpret a moral choice within the context of the historical circumstances that produced it, whereas men usually abstract that choice from its particularities and analyze it as if it represented some universal type of moral choice.

The last of these differences was one about which Gilligan had some strong opinions. As she saw it, to the degree that moral educators encourage their students to discuss hypothetical agents rather than actual agents, their students will be taught a faulty pattern of moral reasoning.

> Hypothetical dilemmas, in the abstraction of their presentation, divest moral actors from the history and psychology of their individual lives and separate the moral problems from the social contingencies of its possible occurrence. . . . Only when substance is given to the skeletal lives of hypothetical people is it possible to reconsider the social injustice that their moral problems may reflect and to imagine the individual suffering their occurrence may signify or their resolution engender.[57]

Here Gilligan implied that this test is not just limited, but downright flawed. Morality based on abstract scenarios has little to do with the morality of day-to-day life.

Gilligan best illustrated this point when discussing male and female responses to Kohlberg's famous example of a moral dilemma in which Heinz cannot afford the drug his dying wife desperately needs in order to survive. Should he steal the drug or not? When presented with this problem, said Gilligan, boys approach it analytically as if they were solving a math problem. An eleven-year-old boy named Jake, for example, solves Heinz's dilemma by weighing the rights of the pharmacist to receive payment for his property against the rights of the wife to life: "A human life is worth more than money, and if the druggist only makes $1,000, he is still going to live, but if Heinz doesn't steal the drug, his wife is going to die."[58] In contrast, Gilligan claimed, women presented with this same problem approach it synthetically, as if they were resolving a human relations problem. As a result, they are apt to concretize or personalize Kohlberg's hypothetical moral dilemma. Rather than accept the terms of Heinz's moral dilemma, which are forcing him to choose between two wrongs, women will modify them. Gilligan gave the example of a woman, Amy, who finds the puzzle in Heinz's dilemma to lie with the druggist. Amy reasons that if the druggist knew that Heinz's wife will otherwise die, he would willingly give the drug to Heinz.[59] Gilligan's point in comparing responses like those of Jake and Amy was not to devalue Jake's way of handling Heinz's dilemma; rather it was to show that although Amy handles Heinz's dilemma differently than Jake does, her mode of moral reasoning is just as valid.

Because Gilligan believed that women's style of moral reasoning diverges in several important ways from that of men, she rejected Kohlberg's scale of moral development as a universal standard upon which to evaluate both men's and women's moral progress. Kohlberg's scale consists of six stages through which a person must pass if he or she is to become a fully functioning moral agent. Stage one is "the punishment and obedience orientation." To avoid the "stick" of punishment and/or receive the "carrot" of a reward, the child does as he or she is told. Stage two is "the instrumental relativist orientation." Based on a limited principle of reciprocity—"you scratch my back and I'll scratch yours"—the child does what satisfies his or her own needs and occasionally the needs of others. Stage three is "the interpersonal concordance or 'good boy–nice girl' orientation." The adolescent conforms to prevailing mores because he or she seeks the approbation of other people. Stage four is "the 'law and order' orientation." The adolescent begins to do his or her duty, show respect for authority, and maintain the given social order for its own sake. Stage five is "the social-contract legalistic orientation." The adult adopts an essentially utilitarian moral point of view according to which individuals are permitted to do as they please, provided that they refrain from harming people in the process. Stage Six is "the universal ethical principle orientation." The adult adopts an essentially Kantian moral point of view that provides a moral perspective "universal" enough to serve as a critique of any conventional morality, including that of the United States. The adult is no longer ruled by self-interest, the opinion of others, or the force of legal convention, but by self-legislated and self-imposed universal principles, such as those of justice, reciprocity, and respect for the dignity of human beings as individual persons.[60]

Gilligan took exception to Kohlberg's sixfold scale not because it reflects an immoral or amoral position, but because girls and women tested on it rarely get past stage three. She feared that people would interpret this curious result as somehow confirming Freud's sense that women are less moral than men, but it also occurred to Gilligan that women's low scores on Kohlberg's test had little to do with any deficiency in women's ability to reason morally and much to do with the construction of Kohlberg's scale.

Gilligan's reflections ultimately led her to develop an alternative to Kohlberg's scale that, in her opinion, more adequately represents women's approach to moral reasoning. For Kohlberg, the moral self is an individual legislating absolute laws for everyone without exception. In contrast, for

Gilligan, the moral self is an individual working with other individuals to identify mutually agreeable solutions to thorny human relations problems. Whereas Gilligan described Kohlberg's "male" moral point of view as an ethics of justice, she described her "female" moral point of view as an ethics of care. Gilligan believed that woman's moral development takes her from an egocentric, or selfish, position to an overly altruistic, or self-sacrificial, position and, finally, to a self-with-others position in which her interests count as much as anyone else's.

At level one, the least-developed level of moral sensibility, a woman's care is directed completely inward. She feels scared and vulnerable, in need of affection and approval. For example, the women in Gilligan's abortion study who felt alone in the world, helpless, and uncared for saw a baby as someone who would care for them, who would give them some love. However, as they struggled through their abortion decisions, many came to describe as "selfish" the decision to bring a child into the world without having the material and psychological resources to care for him or her. In Gilligan's estimation, for a woman to come to this kind of conclusion is to reach level two of moral development.

At level two, a woman shifts from self-centeredness to other-directedness. She becomes the stereotypical nurturant woman, who subjugates her wants and needs to those of other people's and who claims that all she wants to do is what the other person wants. This is the kind of woman who, in Gilligan's study, would have her lover, husband, parents, or church tell her whether to have an abortion. According to Gilligan, a woman can suppress her wants and needs in the interest of sustaining a relationship only so long before she starts feeling resentful. Thus, to develop as a moral person, a woman must take steps to avoid this destructive boiling point. She must, insisted Gilligan, push beyond level two to level three of moral development, where she will learn how to care for herself as well as others.

At level three, the decision to abort, for example, becomes a complex choice the woman must make about how best to care for the fetus, herself, and anyone likely to be affected by her decision. One of the women in Gilligan's study explained her decision to have an abortion as just such a choice: "I would not be doing myself or the child or the world any kind of favor having this child. I don't need to pay off my imaginary debts to the world through this child, and I don't think that it is right to bring a child into the world and use it for that purpose."[61] Thus, in Gilligan's view, a woman attains full moral stature when she stops vacillating between egoism and altruism, recognizing instead the falseness of this polarity and the depth of her connection to others and of their connection to her.

The Limits of Gilligan's Analysis

We will recall that Gilligan introduced her work by stating that she was merely putting empirical evidence into order so that everyone will recognize women as moral agents. Beyond this, Gilligan insisted, she was making no sex-based generalizations to the effect, for example, that all and only men espouse an ethics of justice or that all and only women espouse an ethics of care.

> The different voice I describe is characterized not by gender but theme. Its association with women is an empirical observation, and it is primarily through women's voices that I trace its development. But this association is not absolute, and the contrasts between male and female voices are presented here to highlight a distinction between two modes of thought and to focus a problem of interpretation rather than to represent a generalization about either sex.[62]

But even if it was not Gilligan's *intention* to make generalizations about the possibly distinct moralities of men and women, critics complain that her literary examples and research data lead readers to generalize that *men* focus on rights, claims, self-interested demands, strict duties and obligations, burdens, and limits on autonomy and that *women* focus on responsibilities to respond empathetically, to show concern in close relations, and to nurture and give aid. Thus, Gilligan must take some responsibility for the passionate debates occasioned by the publication of *In a Different Voice*.[63]

The first of these debates has to do with Gilligan's methodology. Critics fault Gilligan for not raising enough of the right issues. Because the women in her abortion study were from a variety of ethnic backgrounds and social classes, ranged in age from fifteen to thirty-three, differed in marital status and educational background, Gilligan should have been more attentive to racial, class, and individual differences as well as to gender differences.[64] Obvious questions were left unasked—questions about men's attitudes toward abortion (in this case, the lovers, husbands, fathers, and friends of the women in Gilligan's sample) and how they differ from women's, and questions about who speaks the language of care/justice, under what *historical* circumstances, and why. The fact that Gilligan did not ask these questions is, in the critics' estimation, a sign that despite her disclaimers, Gilligan was in fact preoccupied with proving that *man's* moral reasoning is different from *woman's*. Not wanting to "complicate" her analysis with facts that would weaken her hypothesis, she chose at some level to oversimplify it.

The second debate occasioned by Gilligan's work has to do with the negative consequences of associating women with an ethics of care. In

"The Liberation of Caring," William Puka cautioned Gilligan that in a patriarchal society, caring is often woman's strategy for survival and not a proud celebration of feminine character. He also contended that all three levels of moral development articulated by Gilligan[65] are problematic; indeed, Gilligan's entire ethic of care is a moral scheme more likely to oppress a woman than to liberate her.

Within patriarchy, wrote Puka, level one is a coping mechanism used by a woman intent on avoiding rejection or domination. "I'm out for myself" is a statement likely to be uttered by a woman who feels that she has to put herself in front of other people because other people, especially men, are not likely to concern themselves about her personal needs and interests.[66]

Level two, which often develops out of level one, is a resumption of the "conventional slavish approach" that women usually adopt in a patriarchal society. Although level two is frequently described as altruistic, as if a woman always freely chooses to put other people's needs and interests ahead of her own, in reality level two is another coping mechanism. The other-directedness of level two development is meant to reward women or at least minimize their punishment at the hands of men.[67]

Level three, continued Puka, is a much more complicated coping mechanism that involves elements of self-protection and slavish servitude. "Here a woman learns where she can exercise her strengths, interests, and commitments (within the male power structure) and where she would do better to comply (with that structure). A delicate contextual balance must be struck to be effective here."[68]

Although in Puka's mind level three represents a high degree of "cognitive liberation" for a woman, insofar as she is rationally calculating her chances of surviving and possibly even thriving within patriarchy, it fails to signify a *personal* liberation for her. As Puka saw it, women and men cannot be truly interdependent as things stand, and women cannot strike a perfect and abiding balance between egoism and altruism. Within a patriarchy, because of men's power over women, male-female relationships are inevitably imbalanced, as is the relationship between egoism and altruism in a woman's life. Any ethics for women that overemphasizes relationships and underemphasizes rights risks valorizing an ethics that may reinforce women's subordination to men.

Clearly, this last debate between Puka and Gilligan is not easy to resolve. It reminds us once again, that within patriarchy, women are always meeting the tip of the two-edged sword. It is one thing to strive for the mean between egoism and altruism under ideal conditions and quite another to strive for this balance point under conditions very less than ideal. Thus, we are faced with a paradox: Women must, temporarily, care less so that men can learn to care more. The problem is not *caring—*

concern and compassion are qualities essential to the truly moral person. The problem is *women* caring too much and, sometimes, for the wrong reasons.

Toward a Feminist Reinterpretation of the Oedipus Complex

Juliet Mitchell on Psychoanalysis and Feminism

Like Dinnerstein, Chodorow, and Gilligan, Juliet Mitchell accepted psychoanalysis as being more than convenient for feminist analysis. Mitchell was aware of the apparent failings of Freud's more traditional followers, a fact that explains her determination to distinguish between neo-Freudian texts (for which she had little use) on the one hand and Freud's original writings and feminist psychoanalysis (for which she had much use) on the other.[69]

Freud's theory, as Mitchell understood it, is not a simple-minded enunciation of the slogan "biology is destiny." On the contrary, his is a theory that demonstrates how social beings emerge from merely biological ones. Psychosexual development is a process of the "social interpretation" of biology, *not* the inexorable manifestation of biological destiny. Because Freud was not always careful to emphasize that he was studying psychosexual development among a specific group of people, his analysis can be read as a general or universal claim—that is, as a claim that if we understand the way sexuality was constructed in nineteenth-century Vienna among the petite bourgeoisie, we also understand the way in which sexuality is constructed anywhere, anytime. Mitchell insisted that the particular emphases of Freud's analysis, its incidental features, must be separated from the general parameters, its essence. The nuclear family, a relatively recent social construction, is simply a current embodiment of what is indeed a universal principle—the pattern that Freud names the Oedipal situation.[70]

When Mitchell agreed with Freud that the Oedipal situation is universal, she meant that without a prohibition on incest, human society is an impossibility. According to anthropologist Claude Lévi-Strauss, upon whose work Mitchell relied, if sexual relations are permitted, indeed encouraged, within the biological family, there is no impetus for that family to expand beyond its narrow confines—to form reproductive alliances between itself and other biological families, thereby creating the expanded network we call "society."[71]

As Lévi-Strauss explained it, the incest taboo is the impetus that, by forbidding sexual relations within the family, forces people to form other, larger, social organizations. Of course, a mere ban on sexual intercourse within families is not enough. There must also be some way to facilitate

sexual intercourse among families. Lévi-Strauss claimed that this facili-
tation takes the form of an exchange system among biological families—
specifically, the exchange of women among men. If a woman is forbidden
by the incest taboo from marrying her brother or father, she will be
pushed to marry some man outside of her biological family. If women
were not exchanged (married off), the biological family unit would keep
reproducing itself in simple form, and society, as we know it, would
never take shape. So, it is not because "there is anything biologically
'wrong' with incest" that there is an incest taboo; it is just that "the
command to exchange exogamously forbids the cul-de-sac of endogamy."[72]
The exchange of women among men, according to Lévi-Strauss, constitutes
humans' "decisive break" with the beasts, and, added Mitchell, the fact
that men exchange women rather than vice versa accounts for the patriarchal
character of human society.[73]

The laws for the exchange of women are, said Mitchell, anchored deep
in the unconscious, surfacing during the individual's painful resolution
of the Oedipus complex. But because men no longer need to exchange
women in order to create society, Mitchell suspected that the Oedipus
complex is otiose.

> In economically advanced societies, though the kinship-exchange system still
> operates in a residual way, other forms of exchange—i.e., commodity ex-
> change—dominate and class, not kinship structures, prevail. It would seem
> that it is against a background of the *remoteness* of a kinship system that the
> ideology of the biological family comes into its own. In other words, the
> relationship between two parents and their children assumes a dominant role
> when the complexity of a class society forces the kinship system to recede.[74]

Because men do not have to exchange *women* in order to link biological
families one to the other, the incest taboo is unnecessary; and because
the incest taboo is no longer necessary, the ban on it renders the Oedipus
complex all the more traumatic. The only positive feature of this lamentable
state of affairs, said Mitchell, is that it makes clear the "social non-
necessity" of patriarchy because the construction of society no longer
depends on men exchanging women.[75]

The Limits of Mitchell's Analysis

Mitchell's critics find much of her analysis useful, but they remain
unconvinced by it. What is lacking in her discussion of psychoanalysis
and patriarchy, they say, is an adequate explanation for why *women* are
exchanged and why the *father* has power over the family. Mitchell sought
the answers to these questions in Freud's *Totem and Taboo*, in which
Freud described a primal murder of an original mythical father. The
totem is the symbol of the father, and associated with it are two taboos,

one against destruction of the totem and one against incest. In the myth, a group of brothers bands together in order to kill the feared and envied father: feared because of his power, envied because of his harem. Following their act of patricide, the brothers, feeling very guilty and not knowing quite what to substitute for the law of the father, collectively reestablish his two taboos. Freud commented that whereas the brothers' reinscription of the *totem* taboo is "founded wholly on emotional motives," their reinscription of the *incest* taboo is founded on a "practical" as well as an emotional basis.

> Sexual desires do not unite men but divide them. Though the brothers had banded together in order to overcome their father, they were all one anothers' rivals in regard to the women. Each of them would have wished, like his father, to have all the women to himself. The new organization would have collapsed in a struggle of all against all, for none of them was of such over-mastering strength as to be able to take on his father's part with success. Thus the brothers had no alternative, if they were to live together, but—not, perhaps, until they had passed through many dangerous crises—to institute the law against incest, by which they all alike renounced the women whom they desired and who had been their chief motive for dispatching their father.[76]

In sum, the brothers **must** refrain from incest; only then can patriarchy, in which they have a vested interest, thrive.

Although Mitchell's critics tend to dismiss the myth of the primal crime as, after all, *only a myth,* many do concede this myth's power. What the father symbolizes may indeed be universal in human society—namely, the desire to be transcendent, to assert one's will triumphantly, to be, in some sense of the term, "the boss." The father—and here Mitchell was borrowing from Jacques Lacan—is "he who is ultimately capable of saying 'I am who I am.'" The father represents success in the "Symbolic Order"; he is disentangled from confusions and struggles. He is clear thinking, farseeing, and powerful. Because he can say "I am who I am," he can name things for what they are.[77]

But as seductive as the image of the transcendent father, the omnipotent patriarch, may be, that image is also oppressive, asserted Mitchell. Insofar as the Oedipus complex is the vehicle of patriarchy, it represents what must be destroyed if women are to be liberated. But given that the Oedipus complex is patriarchy's expression of the individual's entry into culture, if it is destroyed, nonpatriarchal society must find a substitute for it or deteriorate into disordered, unlawed chaos.[78]

Sherry Ortner, a noted feminist anthropologist and theorist, disagreed with Mitchell that the Oedipus complex must be destroyed. As Ortner saw it, what is wrong with the Oedipal structure is not the structure per se but the "male and female valences" that society has attached to it. Because these valences are historical accretions, they can be eliminated, said Ortner; and with their elimination, the Oedipal process can be freed from its current patriarchal agenda.[79] In developing her argument, Ortner insisted that labeling authority, autonomy, and universalism as male and love, dependence, and particularism as female is not essential to the Oedipus complex. Gender valences are simply the consequences of a child's actual experience with men and women. So long as children experience only women in the role of mothering, the Oedipus complex will continue to function as the expression of the father's power, of patriarchy. Thus, the best way to change the gender valences of the Oedipus complex is, according to Ortner, to inaugurate a system of dual parenting. Were both men and women to parent and to engage in enterprise, children would not grow up with the impression that men are made to rule and women to nurture. In sum, the key to destroying patriarchy is not exploding the Oedipus complex but changing our system of childrearing.

> The Oedipus complex is part of a theory of the development of the person. It is a powerful, and significantly, an eminently dialectical theory: the person evolves through a process of struggle with and ultimate supersession . . . of symbolic figures of love, desire, and authority. As a general structure . . . (without gender valences attached to the particular figures), there seems no need to dispose of (and . . . probably no possibility of disposing of) this process.[80]

Although Ortner's strategy for destroying patriarchy without also destroying society sounds eminently reasonable, Ortner may have underestimated the strength of the traditional gender valences. The force of Mitchell's work is her conviction that the original attribution of social and symbolic roles on the basis of gender is buried *very* deep in our psyches. Changing our system of parenting may in the end be no more than a surface change. Our psyches may be too set in their ways for a reformist measure to jolt them into a new state of being. We may, as Mitchell suggested, have to risk revolution against the entire Oedipal process. □

CONCLUSION

What is enormously appealing about Dinnerstein's, Chodorow's, Gilligan's, and Mitchell's works is that they mesh with many of our ordinary intuitions about sexual behavior, mothering, and moral conduct. Although critics correctly point out all the exceptions to the rules enumerated by psychoanalytic feminists, many a woman has found in *The Mermaid and the Minotaur, The Reproduction of Mothering, In a Different Voice,* and *Psychoanalysis and Feminism* persuasive explanations for her need to love and be loved; for her willingness to give up a high-powered career for an intimate family life; and for her willingness to forgive and to forget male abuse and/or neglect.

To be sure, psychoanalytic explanations for women's oppression do not provide a total explanation for female subordination. Legal, political, and economic institutions and structures must also be taken into account. Nevertheless, to free herself from what is holding her back, a woman must do more than fight for her rights as a citizen; she must also probe the depths of her psyche in order to exorcise the original primal father from it. Only then will she have the space to think herself anew and become who she has the power to be.

CHAPTER SIX

—————————— ■ ——————————

Socialist Feminism

ALTHOUGH IT MAY SEEM ODD that this chapter on socialist feminism did not directly follow and continue upon the chapter on Marxist feminism, in point of fact the socialist feminist project can be understood as nothing less than the confluence of Marxist, radical and, more arguably, psychoanalytic streams of feminist thought.[1] Socialist feminism is largely the result of Marxist feminists' dissatisfaction with the essentially gender-blind character of Marxist thought—that is, with the tendency of Marxist patriarchs to dismiss women's oppression as not nearly as important as workers' oppression. Supposedly, what women suffer at the hands of men is slight compared to what the proletariat suffers at the hands of the bourgeoisie.

While some Marxist feminists have waited for women's turn, some have been more impatient. Clara Zetkin, one of Lenin's co-revolutionaries, was a case in point. In fact, Lenin is unfavorably remembered by feminists because he berated Zetkin for encouraging women members of the Communist party to discuss sexual issues.

> The record of your sins, Clara, is even worse. I have been told that at the evenings arranged for reading and discussion with working women, sex and marriage problems come first. They are said to be the main objects of interest in your political instruction and educational work. I could not believe my ears when I heard that. The first state of proletarian dictatorship is battling with the counter-revolutionaries of the whole world. The situation in Germany itself calls for the greatest unity of all proletarian revolutionary forces, so that they can repel the counter-revolution which is pushing on. But active Communist women are busy discussing sex problems and the forms of marriage— "past, present and future." They consider it their most important task to enlighten working women on these questions.[2]

From Lenin's point of view, Zetkin was discussing trivial matters and catering to women's self-indulgent tendencies, when she should have been fostering their revolutionary consciousness. But, as Zetkin saw it, there was a real need for women to understand the forms that oppression took in the "private" as well as "public" domain.

Following Zetkin's lead, many contemporary socialist feminists have become convinced that living in a class society is not the only, or even primary, cause of women's oppression *as* women. Although women in socialist countries such as Cuba, mainland China, the USSR, and the Eastern bloc have entered the labor force and are largely economically independent of men, socialist as well as capitalist women remain in the grip of patriarchy. As socialist feminists see it, traditional Marxist feminists are able to explain how capitalism caused the separation of the workplace from the homestead and why homestead activities were gradually devalued; but they are unable to explain adequately why capitalism assigned *women* to the homestead and *men* to the workplace.[3] The categories of Marxist analysis, observed socialist feminist Heidi Hartmann, "give no clues about why particular people fill particular places. They give no clues about why *women* are subordinate to *men* inside and outside the family and why it is not the other way around. *Marxist categories, like capital itself, are sex-blind.* The categories of Marxism cannot tell us who will fill the empty places."[4]

In contrast to traditional Marxist feminists, radical feminists do provide a full gender analysis of who will fill which places under patriarchy. So long as every avenue of power—business, medicine, law, politics, academics—is in male hands, women will either be confined to the home or relegated to the least prestigious and most poorly paid lines of work. A problem with radical feminist analysis, however, is that even though it usefully identifies, as Catharine MacKinnon and Mary Daly have, a material base for women's oppression in pornography, prostitution, sexual harassment, rape, woman battering, purdah, suttee, foot binding, and clitoridectomy, it tends to view patriarchy as a universal phenomenon. This gravitation toward the universal causes some radical feminists to condemn, for example, clitoridectomy in the same breath with rape, without first entertaining the possibility, that, unlike rape, clitoridectomy may have a different meaning in Kenya than in the United States.[5]

Like radical feminists, psychoanalytic feminists also give a full gender analysis of why it is that men fill the slots in the public world, while women fill the slots in the private world. But psychoanalytic feminists attribute this slotting to the ways in which men's and women's gender identities and behavioral repertoires are constructed deep in the unconscious, which is little affected by revolutionary activity in the economic and political sphere. As useful as the psychoanalytic feminist analysis is, it suffers from two limitations: (1) like radical feminism, it often makes universalist claims—in this instance about the pre-Oedipal and Oedipal stages—forgetting that these stages best explain the psychosexual drama as it is staged not in all times and places but in modern times and in Western places; and (2) unlike radical feminism, it fails to articulate a *material* base for women's oppression, pointing instead to *psychic* structures that critics dismiss as imaginary.[6]

To overcome the limits of traditional Marxist feminism on the one hand, and of radical and psychoanalytic feminism on the other, socialist feminists have developed two different approaches—dual-systems theory and unified-systems theory. These approaches both aim to provide a complete explanation of women's oppression, but they do so in very different ways.[7]

Dual-systems theorists maintain that patriarchy and capitalism are distinct forms of social relation and distinct sets of interest, which, when they intersect, oppress women in particularly egregious ways.[8] For women's oppression to be fully understood, both patriarchy and capitalism must be analyzed first as separate phenomena and then as phenomena that dialectically relate to each other. What makes dual-systems theory exceptionally complex is the fact that although all dual-systems theorists describe capitalism as a material structure or historically rooted mode of *production,* only some describe patriarchy as a material structure or historically rooted mode of *reproduction/sexuality.* Others describe patriarchy as a nonmaterial structure—that is, a largely ideological and/or psychoanalytic structure that transcends the contingencies of space and time.

In contrast to dual-systems theorists, unified-systems theorists attempt to analyze capitalism and patriarchy together through the use of one concept. According to these theorists, capitalism is no more separate from patriarchy than the mind is from the body. This is an even more ambitious form of socialist feminism than is the dual-systems approach, for if there is *one* conceptual lens through which all of the dimensions of women's oppression can be filtered, then it may be possible to unite *all* of the feminist perspectives that we have so far discussed. □

DUAL-SYSTEMS THEORY

A Nonmaterialist Account of Patriarchy
plus a Materialist Account of Capitalism

Iris Young claimed that Juliet Mitchell was an example of a dual-system theorist who coupled a nonmaterialist account of patriarchy with a materialist account of capitalism.[9] Mitchell's account of patriarchy was nonmaterial because her analysis of the family was largely nonmaterial. Mitchell believed that some aspects of women's life within the family are economic—the result of changes made in the mode of production across space and through time; that others are biosocial—the result of the interplay between female biology and the social environment; and that still others are ideological—the result of the ideas society has about the way in which women should relate to men. No matter how much the mode of production changes, these biosocial and ideological aspects will remain essentially the same. Thus, even under socialism, women will remain somewhat oppressed unless the defeat of capitalism is accompanied by the defeat of patriarchy. But even though the economic aspects of patriarchy can be altered by *material* means—through a change in the mode of production—its biosocial and ideological aspects can be altered only by *nonmaterial* means—through a rewriting of the psychosexual drama that has been producing men and women as we know them for a very long time. Thus, the Marxist revolutionary must link arms with the Freudian psychoanalyst in order to effect women's full and final liberation.[10]

Juliet Mitchell on Woman's Estate

Mitchell's dual-systems theory has its origins in her first major book, *Woman's Estate*. In this work, Mitchell abandoned the traditional Marxist-feminist position according to which woman's condition is simply a function of her relation to capital, of whether or not she is part of the productive work force. In place of this monocausal explanation for woman's oppression, Mitchell suggested that woman's status and function are *jointly* determined by her role in production *and* in reproduction, the socialization of children, and sexuality.

> The error of the old Marxist was to see the other three elements as reducible to the economic; hence the call for the entry into production was accompanied by the purely abstract slogan of the abolition of the family. Economic demands are still primary, but must be accompanied by coherent policies for the other three elements (reproduction, sexuality and socialization), policies which at particular junctures may take over the primary role in immediate action.[11]

In the course of her 1971 attempt to determine which of these elements most oppress contemporary women, Mitchell came to the disturbing conclusion that women are making progress only in the area of sexuality—a progress that is sometimes more apparent than real.[12] Taken to extremes, sexual liberation becomes a disguised form of sexual oppression. In the past, women were condemned for being whores; today women are condemned for being virgins. Too much of any good thing, suggested Mitchell, is as bad as too little of it. If the production-and-work, sex-for-procreation-only ethos spawned by contemporary capitalism is bad for people, a mandatory consumption-and-fun, sex-for-sex's-sake ethos could be even worse.[13]

But even if women's progress in the area of sexuality is punctuated by moments of retrogression as well as progression, there is movement in a somewhat positive direction. In contrast, women's progress in the areas of production, reproduction, and the socialization of children has, said Mitchell, ground to a near halt. Insofar as production is concerned, women are still lagging behind men, even though women are just as physically and psychologically qualified for high-paying and/or prestigious jobs as men are.[14] Likewise, insofar as reproduction is concerned, women are still bound by the causal chain, "maturity—family—absence from production and public life—sexual inequality," even though safe, effective, and inexpensive reproduction-controlling technologies are increasingly being made available to the general public. Finally, insofar as the socialization of children is concerned, women are still making mothering a full-time job, even though fewer women are having more than one or two children.[15]

Mitchell speculated that the reason progress toward women's liberation is so slow is that the family—which she associated with reproduction, sexuality, and the socialization of children—serves ideological and biosocial as well as economic functions. Even if a socialist mode of production requires the end of the family as an economic unit, it cannot end the family as an ideological and biosocial unit. Because of the way in which our psyches have been constituted, women's oppression as women will persist unless our psyches have a revolution equivalent to the economic one that effects the transition from capitalism to socialism.

Juliet Mitchell on Psychoanalysis and Feminism

Although Mitchell did not develop her thoughts on psychoanalysis in *Woman's Estate,* she did develop them in *Psychoanalysis and Feminism.* As I noted in Chapter 5, Mitchell believed that the psychology of women produced by the castration and Oedipus complexes is essentially constant within patriarchal society, which, as she interpreted it, is the *only* kind of human society there is. No matter when and where a woman lives, no matter how rich or poor, or black or white, or beautiful or ugly she is, "in relation to the law of the father," one woman will have approximately the same status and function as any other woman.[16]

Because Mitchell was convinced that the causes of women's oppression are buried very deep in the human psyche, she rejected the claim of some liberal feminists that social reforms aimed at giving women a more equal place in society could really do so. Women's suffrage, co-educational studies, and affirmative action policies might change the "expression of femininity," but they cannot, in her view, significantly change the position of women. Likewise, Mitchell rejected the claim of some radical feminists that reproductive technology is the key to women's liberation because, as she saw it, a biological solution cannot resolve a psychological problem. Finally, Mitchell rejected the claim of traditional Marxist feminists that an economic revolution aimed at overthrowing the capitalist order will make men and women full partners in action and friends in virtue.[17] Just because women enter the productive work force to labor side by side with men does not mean that women will return home in the evening arm in arm with men. Mitchell observed that none other than Mao Tse-tung admitted that "despite collective work, egalitarian legislation, social care of children, etc., it was too soon for the Chinese really deeply and irrevocably to have changed their *attitudes* towards women."[18] As Mitchell saw it, attitudes toward women will never really change so long as female and male psychology are dominated by the phallic symbol. Thus, patriarchy as well as capitalism must be overthrown; and because, for Mitchell, patriarchy is human society, its overthrow equals the overthrow of human society as we have known it.

In the concluding chapter of *Psychoanalysis and Feminism,* Mitchell revealed the degree of her dualism. She agreed that the universal forms of patriarchal ideology do intersect with the particular structures of a society's reigning economic system, thereby constituting complex phenomena such as the extended family of feudalism or the nuclear family of capitalism. But she did not believe that we can transform either the ideological or the economic situation by focusing exclusively on the points of their *interpenetration.* Given that, in Mitchell's estimation, the ideological mode of patriarchy and the economic mode of capitalism are two separate spheres, we should use Marxist strategies to overthrow capitalism and psychoanalytic strategies to overthrow patriarchy. Not only must we replace capitalism with socialism, we must replace patriarchy with . . . what? Here, Mitchell hesitated. Before the institution of private property, socialist societies did presumably exist. But, said Mitchell, "no society has yet existed—or existed for a sufficient length of time—for the 'eternal' unconscious to have shed its immortal nature. While matrilineages are certainly to be found, it seems as though matriarchies can be ruled out."[19]

It is probably a mistake to infer from this passage that Mitchell wished to substitute socialist matriarchies for capitalist patriarchies, but we must wonder just what the alternative to patriarchy is. Indeed, were it not for those radical feminists who write science fiction or utopian novels, treatises such as Mitchell's would leave us unsure of the contours of a nonpatriarchal society. We will recall, for example, that in *Woman on the Edge of Time,* Marge Piercy described a world in which children are gestated ex utero and reared by three co-mothers (two men and one woman or two women and one man). These trios share their parental obligations and pleasures with so-termed kidbinders who direct communal child care centers where young boys and girls learn what it means to be a person. Indeed, so person centered is Piercy's utopia that the personal pronouns "he," "his," "she," and "her" have been dropped in favor of an all-purpose, neuter pronoun, "per."[20] Perhaps the Oedipus complex is still operative, minus its pernicious "gender valences," in Piercy's utopia; then again, perhaps the Oedipus complex has been totally dissolved as the result of women giving up the power to give birth—a form of power that, for Piercy, is the paradigm for all forms of power.[21] In either event, if Mitchell was serious about a cultural revolution aimed at transforming the unconscious, she must provide us with the weapons to fight what may be the most dangerous battle ever fought in history. At stake is nothing less than culture, the thin line separating humans from all other animals.

A Materialist Account of Patriarchy
plus a Materialist Account of Capitalism

Heidi Hartmann, like Juliet Mitchell, is a dual-systems theorist, but one who exemplifies the second kind of dual-systems theorist in Young's scheme. Whereas Mitchell views patriarchy as the ideological form of women's oppression, represented in each person's unconscious by the Oedipus complex, Hartmann views it as a structure of relations in society that has a very *material* base in men's historical control over women's labor power.

Hartmann's materialist analysis of patriarchy had its origin in her dissatisfaction with the traditional Marxist tendency to interpret women's oppression primarily or exclusively in terms of how women stand in relation to production. This tendency largely explains the desire of Marxist feminists to focus their studies on working-class women and/or to understand gender oppression in terms of class oppression. Hartmann pointed out that it is difficult to establish that all women—including housewives, retired women, unemployed women, and women going to school full time—are actual workers. She noted that Marxist feminists such as Mariarosa Dalla Costa and Selma James, for example, have tried every means to prove that housewives are performing genuine productive work for capital.

But by focusing all their intellectual energies on subsuming women's relation to men under workers' relation to capital, said Hartmann, Marxist feminists are slighting the real object of feminist analysis: male-female relations. Hartmann maintained that although the categories of Marxist analysis—for example, class, reserve army of labor, wage laborer—help explain the generation of a particular occupational structure, they leave unexplained "why *women* are subordinate to *men* inside and outside the family and why it is not the other way around."[22] Therefore, if we are to understand women's relation to men as well as workers' relation to capital, a Marxist analysis of capitalism needs to be complemented with a feminist analysis of patriarchy.

As Hartmann's materialist account of capitalism is the standard one of traditional Marxism, we need focus here only on Hartmann's materialist account of patriarchy. Hartmann defined patriarchy as "a set of social relations between men which have a material base, and which, though hierarchical, establish or create interdependence and solidarity among men that enable them to dominate women."[23] This material base rests in men's control over women's labor power; this control is constituted by restricting women's access to important economic resources and by disallowing women any control over female sexuality and especially female reproductive capacities. Men's control over women's labor power varies from society to society and across time. Among whites in Western capitalist countries, this control is exercised primarily through the institution of monogamous heterosexual marriage, female childbearing and childrearing, female domestic work, women's economic dependence on men, the state, and numerous institutions based on male bonding. All of these elements explain why it is that men control women rather than vice versa. Thus, Mitchell's understanding of patriarchy as ideology was, in Hartmann's estimate, misguided. Patriarchy operates mostly in the material realm, not the psychological realm. Male control assumes very concrete forms. It appears, for example, in the shape of a woman's need to please her husband or lover so that he does not leave her and their children; or in the shape of a woman's need to please her boss so that he does not fire her.[24]

Although a strong partnership currently exists between capital and patriarchy in Western capitalist countries, this partnership was hard won because man's interests in woman are not necessarily the same as capital's. In the nineteenth century, for example, the vast majority of men (patriarchs each in their own small, proletarian right) wanted "their women at home to personally service them." A smaller number of men (the capitalists) wanted most women (excluding their own, of course) to work in the wage labor market.[25] Only if some way could be discovered to enable all men to have their way with women could a partnership be achieved between patriarchy and capitalism.

Whereas a Marxist analysis predicts that patriarchy "will wither away in the face of capitalism's need to proletarianize everyone," a feminist analysis predicts that capitalism and patriarchy will reach some sort of compromise on the woman question.[26] With history on her side, Hartmann exclaimed that, in this instance at least, feminist analysis is correct.

Although capital initially relied on the labor power of women and children as well as of men, it eventually capitulated to proletarian men's demand that their children and women be sent home. Proletarian men were more often than not against women working, for two reasons. First, because women were willing to work for less, they constituted "cheap competition" for men. Second, because no one, not even a woman, can serve two masters, "the household of the workingman suffers whenever his wife must help to earn the daily bread."[27] Although proletarian men could have solved the first problem by pressing for equal wages for men, women, and children, they chose instead to lobby for a "family wage" large enough to permit women and children to stay at home. Realizing "that housewives [produce] and [maintain] healthier workers than wage-working wives and that educated children become better workers than non-educated ones,"[28] and also realizing that women and children could always be persuaded to reenter the work force for low wages at a later date, capitalists consented to give proletarian men a family wage.

For decades, the family wage served as the primary patriarchal rationale for keeping women and children out of the workplace. This rationale is, however, of less significance today than it was yesterday. Capitalistic forces are pushing an increasing number of women into the workplace, as families discover that two incomes are necessary for the "good life" in the United States. But this move of women into the realm of work has not fundamentally diminished men's power over women. Through the sexual division of labor, patriarchy maintains the subordinate status of women both in the workplace and in the home. In a workplace that is divided into high-paying, male-dominated jobs and low-paying, female-dominated jobs,[29] men earn $1.00 for every $.64 women earn.[30] In the home, working women, but not working men, experience the stresses and strains of the double day. Study after study shows that the husbands of working women do not do much more work around the house than the husbands of stay-at-home housewives.[31]

Reflecting on the present sexual division of labor, which results in the underpayment and overwork of *women,* Hartmann concluded that men's desire to control women is at least as strong as capital's desire to control workers.[32] Capitalism and patriarchy, she insisted, are not two heads of the same beast. They are two different beasts, each of which must be fought with different weapons. □

CRITIQUES OF DUAL-SYSTEMS THEORIES

Critics have faulted dual-systems theorists for a variety of reasons, raising slightly different objections against dual-systems theories with an ideological component than against those with no such component. As

critic Iris Young saw it, ideological accounts of patriarchy are based on
a conception of men's rule over women as universal, impervious to
historical change. In Young's view, the problem with this view of patriarchy
is twofold. First, it can engender not only a sense of hopelessness among
women, but also "serious cultural, ethnic, racial, and class biases in the
account of the allegedly common structures of patriarchy."[33] The wife
of a Carrington ("Dynasty") does not experience patriarchy in the same
way as an Edith Bunker ("All in the Family") or a Claire Huxtable
("The Bill Cosby Show"). Second, this view may lead to the false
impression that because patriarchy exists primarily "in the head" as an
idea, it is not as oppressive to women as are the knitty-gritty facts of
capitalist life. "The theory of patriarchy supplies the *form* of women's
oppression, but traditional Marxist theory supplies its content, specificity,
and motors of change. Thus this version of the dual systems theory fails
to challenge traditional Marxism because it cedes to that Marxism
theoretical hegemony over historically material social relations."[34] What
Young's comment suggests, then, is that mixed dual-systems theories
(accounts that couple an ideological analysis of patriarchy with a materialist
analysis of capitalism) ultimately reduce to a single-system theory, Marxism, in which capitalism is the *primary* cause of women's oppression.[35]

Although unmixed dual-systems theories (accounts that give materialist
analyses of both patriarchy and capitalism) avoid the problems of mixed
ones, they are, said Young, nonetheless flawed. In identifying the family
as crucial to patriarchy, thoroughly materialist dual-systems theorists lean
toward a separate-spheres model. In this model, the sphere of home and
family is where one kind of production—usually women's—occurs, and
the sphere outside the home and family is where a second kind of
production—usually men's—occurs. Thus, patriarchy develops in the
first sphere and capitalism in the second.[36]

The separate-spheres model of capitalism and patriarchy is, claimed
Young, problematic in several ways. First, capitalism is, in Young's opinion,
largely responsible for the split between the family and economy. Because
the categories of "in" and "outside" the family came into being with
capitalism, dual-systems theorists incorrectly speak of the development
of patriarchy *in* the family and of capitalism *outside* the family. There
was no "inside" to the family until capitalism created an "outside" for
it. Second, accepting a distinction that is so central to bourgeois ideology
is not exactly a progressive thing to do. Liberal philosophy maintains
the political status quo by drawing a firm line between the public and
private realms. This boundary prevents comparisons and contrasts between
the life of a family member and of a worker—the kind of ideational
reflection that facilitates the development of revolutionary consciousness.
Third, a separate-spheres model fails to specify the character of women's

oppression outside the family. If working women are oppressed not simply as workers or as women but as women workers, then, said Young, dual-systems theory is particularly unhelpful. Working women's oppression is sui generis. To merely add an analysis of women's oppression to that of workers' oppression is not to explain working women's oppression.[37]

In order to remedy what she perceived as the weaknesses of dual-systems theory, Young sketched out an alternative unified-systems theory. Her goal was to move gender differentiation from the periphery of Marxism into its core. Young reasoned that if traditional Marxism is lacking something so fundamental as a gender analysis, then socialist feminists should not waste their time trying to plug its gaps with a scattering of feminist observations. Rather, socialist feminists should substitute for traditional Marxism a "thoroughly *feminist historical materialism.*"[38] What feminists need, contended Young, is not a *gender-blind* Marxist theory in which maleness or femaleness has nothing to do with whether we are oppressed, but a profoundly *gendered* Marxist theory in which our maleness or femaleness has everything to do with whether we are oppressed. Whether Young provided such a gendered theory is a question to which we now proceed. □

TOWARD A UNIFIED-SYSTEMS THEORY

Gender Division of Labor as a Unifying Concept

As I have noted, traditional Marxism takes class as its central category of analysis. Dual-systems theorists have, in Young's view, rightly claimed that because class is a gender-blind category, it is not adequate for the analysis of women's specific oppression or even its identification. Consequently, Young believed that feminists who wish to avoid the pitfalls of the dual-systems approach to capitalist patriarchy need to develop a new core concept for Marxist theory. She suggested that the gendered category "division of labor" has the conceptual power to transform Marxist feminist theory into socialist feminist theory, which is powerful enough to accommodate the insights of Marxist, radical, and psychoanalytic feminists in a unitary framework.

According to Young, a division-of-labor analysis has the advantage of being more specific than a class analysis. Whereas class analysis aims to scan the system of production as a whole, focusing on the means and relations of production in the most general terms possible, a division-of-labor analysis pays attention to the individual people who do the producing in society. In other words, a class analysis calls for only the most abstract discussion of the respective roles of the bourgeoisie and the proletariat, whereas a division-of-labor analysis requires a detailed, very concrete discussion of, for example, who gives the orders and who takes them, who does the stimulating work and who does the drudge work, who works the desirable shift and who works the undesirable shift, and who gets paid more and who gets paid less. Clearly, then, division-of-labor analysis can better explain why *women* usually take the orders, do the drudge work, work the undesirable shift, and get paid less, while *men* usually give the orders, do the stimulating work, work the desirable shift, and get paid more.

But even if a division-of-labor analysis stirs up issues (of gender as well as race and ethnicity) that a strict class analysis cannot, this does not mean that capitalism and patriarchy are necessarily linked. All this analysis really suggests is that a Marxist class analysis can be supplemented by a feminist division-of-labor analysis (almost any dual-systems theorist would be glad to follow this suggestion). As someone working toward a unified system, however, Young insisted that a division-of-labor analysis is a substitute, not a supplement, for class analysis. We do not need one theory, Marxism, to explain *gender-neutral capitalism* and another theory—be it "radical" or "psychoanalytic"—to explain *gender-biased patriarchy*. Rather, we need a theory—a socialist feminist theory—that can explain to us *gender-biased capitalism*. Capitalism is, was, and always will be essentially and fundamentally a patriarchy. *"My thesis,"* wrote Young, *"is that marginalization of women and thereby our functioning as a secondary labor force is an essential and fundamental characteristic of capitalism."*[39]

Young's thesis was a controversial one, a major departure from the more traditional Marxist view according to which workers, be they male or female, are interchangeable.[40] As Young saw it, capitalism is very much aware of its workers' gender and, I may add, race and ethnicity. Because a large reserve of unemployed workers is necessary to keep wages low and to meet unanticipated demands for increased supplies of goods and services, capitalism has both implicit and explicit criteria for determining who shall constitute its primary, employed work force and who shall act as its secondary, unemployed work force. For a variety of reasons, not the least being a well-entrenched gender division of labor, capitalism's criteria identified men as "primary" work force material and women as "secondary" work force material. Because women were needed at home in a way that men were not—or so patriarchy concluded—men were more free to work outside the home than women were.

If Young's observation was correct, we must ask her why, if patriarchy antedates capitalism, it is not also, as the dual-systems theorists believe, essentially and fundamentally separate from it. Young's response was a long one. She reminded us that class structure, a phenomenon that characterizes capitalism, did not come into existence together with it. In feudal times, for example, there were class constructions such as serfdom and lordship that dictated a person's place in the social structure. As the system of free enterprise developed, these old class constructions were disassembled and replaced by new ones. Thus, although the proletariat and bourgeois classes are specific to the capitalist system, the concept of class is a legacy from precapitalist arrangements. Nevertheless, Young argued, just because the phenomenon of class society preceded capitalism, it is not *independent* of capitalism.[41] Rather, class society is in a process of gradual historical transformation, and the shape it takes depends on the contours of the reigning economic system. Likewise, although patriarchy, or male domination, certainly existed in precapitalist times, it, too, is in a process of gradual historical transformation, and its shape also depends on the contours of the reigning economic system.

Under capitalism as it exists today, women experience patriarchy as unequal wages for work equal to that of men; sexual harassment on the job; uncompensated domestic work; and the pernicious dynamics of the public-private split. Earlier generations of women also experienced patriarchy, but they lived it differently depending on the dynamics of the reigning economic system. As with class society, reasoned Young, patriarchy should not be considered a system *separate* from capitalism just because it existed *first*. In fact, class and gender structures are so intertwined that neither one actually precedes the other. A feudal system of gender relations accompanied a feudal system of class arrangements, and the social relations of class and gender grew together and evolved over time into the forms we now know (for example, the capitalist nuclear family). To say that gender relations are independent of class relations is to ignore how history works.

A look at the formation of our particular system of capitalist patriarchy or patriarchal capitalism will help us appreciate Young's insistence that capitalism and patriarchy are Siamese twins. In her essay "Beyond the Unhappy Marriage: A Critique of the Dual Systems Theory," Young provided a historical analysis of the gender division of labor. She traced the decline in women's relative status as they moved from a precapitalist economy into a capitalist one.

In precapitalist times marriage was, said Young, an "economic partnership"; wives did not expect to be supported by their husbands. They generally retained their own property, labored side by side with their husbands in home-based businesses, and even participated in craft guilds on equal terms with their spouses. The advent of capitalism, however, dissolved the economic partnership between husbands and wives. A new deal was struck for men and women when the forces of capitalism drove a wedge between the workplace and the home, sending men, as a primary work force, out into the former, and confining women, as a secondary work force, to the latter. Women became that reserve army of labor to which I have already made reference. Thus, when new industries opened, such as the New England textile mills, women were usually recruited to fill the initial need; and, when wars had to be fought by the men, women quickly took over the factory jobs only to be sent packing when "Johnny" came marching home. Young cited examples such as these to support her thesis that the "marginalization of women" is essential to capitalism. She also invoked the work of Esther Boserup, who showed how, with their nations' transformation into capitalist economies, Third World women rapidly move from the primary to the secondary work force.[42] So convinced was Young of her analysis that she challenged her readers to find a single advanced capitalist society in which women's labor is not, at root, marginalized. Only if such an instance is discovered, wrote Young, are we warranted in regarding the marginalization of women's labor as peripheral to capitalism.[43]

Alienation as a Unifying Concept

Like Young, Alison Jaggar is working toward a unified-systems theory, and like Young she advanced a concept other than class as the quintessential Marxist concept. In her book *Feminist Politics and Human Nature*, Jaggar identified "alienation" as the concept that will provide us with a theoretical framework powerful enough to accommodate the main insights of Marxist, radical, psychoanalytic, and even liberal feminist thought.

> Contemporary feminists are united in their opposition to women's oppression, but they differ not only in their views of how to combat that oppression, but even in their conception of what constitutes women's oppression in contemporary society. Liberal feminists . . . believe that women are oppressed insofar as they suffer unjust discrimination; traditional Marxists believe that women are oppressed in their exclusion from public production; radical feminists see women's oppression as consisting primarily in the universal male control of women's sexual and procreative capacities; while socialist feminists characterize women's oppression in terms of a revised version of the Marxist theory of alienation.[44]

Jaggar began her analysis by reminding us that for Marx, work is the humanizing activity par excellence; it is meant to connect us to the products of our minds and bodies, nature, and other people. Under capitalism, however, work becomes a dehumanizing activity. Labor is organized in ways that put us at odds with everything and everyone, including ourselves. Jaggar also reminded us that traditional Marxists insist that a person has to participate directly in the capitalist relations of production in order to be considered truly alienated. This technical interpretation of alienation forces us to conclude, counterintuitively in

Jaggar's estimation, that non-wage-earning women are not alienated and that wage-earning women experience alienation in precisely the same ways that wage-earning men do. But, said Jaggar, if we are more concerned about the spirit than the letter of Marxist thought, we can provide an interpretation of alienation according to which each and every woman is, in *special gender-specific ways,* separated from all those processes and people she needs to achieve wholeness as a person.[45]

Jaggar organized her discussion of woman's alienation, her fragmentation and splintering, under the rubrics of sexuality, motherhood, and intellectuality. In the same way that a wage worker is alienated, or separated, from the product(s) upon which he works, a woman is alienated from the product upon which she works: her body. A woman may say that she diets, exercises, and dresses for herself, but in reality she is probably shaping and adorning her flesh for men. A woman has little or no say about when, where, how, or by whom her body will be used because it can be appropriated from her through acts as various as raping on the one hand and "standing on the corner, watching all the girls go by," on the other. Likewise, to the same degree that a wage worker is gradually alienated from himself, in the sense that his body begins to feel like a thing, a mere machine from which labor power is extracted, a woman is gradually alienated from herself. As she works away on her body—plucking this eyebrow and shaving that underarm, slimming this thigh and augmenting that breast, painting this nail and corseting that torso—her body becomes an object for men and for herself. Finally, just as a wage worker is in competition with other wage workers for "top dollar," a woman is in competition with other women for the "male gaze": for male approbation and approval. Female friendship is often so strong among lesbian women, suggested Jaggar, because lesbian women are not each other's rivals for male attention.[46]

Motherhood, like sexuality, is also an alienating experience for women. A woman, contended Jaggar, is alienated from the *product* of her reproductive labor when not she, but someone else, decides how many children she ought to bear. In some societies, where children's labor power is used nearly as much as adults' labor, a woman is pressured into bearing as many children as physically possible. In other societies, where children are viewed as an economic burden, a woman is discouraged from having as many children as she wishes. Many a woman has been pressured into an unwanted abortion or sterilization.[47]

Similarly, continued Jaggar, women are alienated from the *process* of their reproductive labor. Obstetricians manage women's deliveries with the most sophisticated technological instruments available; worse, for little or even no good cause, obstetricians take total control of the birthing process, sometimes performing medically unnecessary Caesarian sections and/or anesthetizing a woman against her wishes. In the future, as the new reproductive technologies develop, women are likely to be further alienated from the product and process of childbirth. In vitro fertilization makes possible so-called full surrogacy, in which a woman can have one or more of her eggs surgically removed, fertilized in vitro with her husband's sperm, and then transferred into the womb of another woman for gestation. Likewise, artificial insemination by donor makes possible so-called partial surrogacy, in which a woman agrees to gestate a child to which she is genetically related so that the genetic father of the child and his wife will have the pleasure of rearing the child to adulthood. Although it may be argued that a woman's decision to contract a surrogate or to serve as a surrogate represents a free choice on her part, her choice may well be no more voluntary than some of the sterilizations, abortions, and/or unwanted pregnancies into which women have been bullied.[48]

Childrearing, like childbearing, is an alienating experience when scientific experts (most of whom are male), not women, take charge of it. As Jaggar saw it, the pressures on mothers are enormous because, with virtually no assistance, they are supposed to execute every edict of the experts. Isolated in her suburban home, each mother labors longer days and even longer nights in order to raise her children the experts' way rather than her way.

Echoing the words of Adrienne Rich in *Of Woman Born* (see Chapter 3), Jaggar explained that contemporary childrearing practices ultimately alienate, or estrange, mothers from their children.

> The extreme mutual dependence of mother and child encourages the mother to define the child primarily with reference to her own needs for meaning, love and social recognition. She sees the child as her product, as something that should improve her life and that often instead stands against her, as something of supreme value, that is held cheap by society. The social relations of contemporary motherhood make it impossible for her to see the child as a whole person, part of a larger community to which both mother and child belong.[49]

One of the most distressing features of a mother's alienation from her children is that her inability to see her children as persons is equaled only by their inability to see her as a person. Here, Jaggar alluded to Dorothy Dinnerstein and some of the other psychoanalytic feminists discussed in Chapter 5, all of whom described the ways in which children gradually turn on their mothers by viewing them not as persons, but as objects who are guilty of doing either too little or too much for them. In addition to separating mothers from their children, the conditions of contemporary motherhood drive wedges between mothers and fathers. All too many arguments begin with a demanding father "laying down the law" for the household and a resentful mother executing its terms. So restricting is this law, that the standards governing "proper" mothering impede the growth of friendships between women, as mothers compete with each other to produce and to process the perfect child:[50] what I would describe as the well-mannered, multitalented, physically fit, achievement-oriented boy or girl who wins all the class awards and whose photograph appears on every other page of the yearbook.

Finally, said Jaggar, not only are many women alienated from their own sexuality and from the product and process of motherhood; they are also alienated from their intellectual capacities. A woman is made to feel so unsure of herself that she hesitates to express her ideas in public, for fear that her thoughts are not worth expressing; and she scurries up and down the hallowed halls of academe frequently fearing that she will be exposed as a pretender, not possessor, of knowledge. To the extent that men set the terms of thought and discourse, suggested Jaggar, women are never at ease.[51]

To the same degree that Young was convinced that a gender division of labor is essential to capitalism, Jaggar believed that "use of the theoretical framework of alienation identifies women's contemporary oppression as a phenomenon peculiar to the capitalist form of male dominance."[52] Under capitalism, woman's oppression takes the form of her alienation from everything and everyone, especially herself, that could be a source of integration for her.[53] According to Jaggar, a proper understanding of women's oppression is a necessary first step toward eliminating that oppression. But even if knowledge or awareness of women's oppression is necessary for women's liberation, it is not sufficient. Even though oppression can distort a woman's perceptions, it exists not just in the mind; it lurks in social institutions and cultural structures. Unless its external manifestations can be squashed, all that consciousness raising will do is increase, to excruciatingly painful levels, a woman's awareness of her alienation. □

CRITIQUES OF UNIFIED-SYSTEMS THEORIES

Catharine MacKinnon has, on two grounds, faulted most attempts at a synthetic socialist feminism. First, such syntheses merely incorporate central feminist issues such as reproduction, sexuality, and the socialization of children into "an essentially unchanged Marxian analysis." Second, such syntheses invariably reduce "the woman question" to "the worker question."[54] But Young and Jaggar cannot be faulted on either of these grounds. Not only did Young change Marxian analysis by moving it from a class analysis to a division of labor analysis; she also insisted that the marginalization of women in capitalism is the most important phenomenon for socialist feminists to study. In a similar vein, Jaggar focused on the concept of alienation, arguing that women's oppression must be understood in terms of alienation rather than class. Thus, if Young's and Jaggar's unified-systems theories are flawed, they will have to be flawed either because any methodology that calls itself Marxist has to make *class* analysis its priority, or because they do not permit women to ask and answer nagging questions about reproduction, sexuality, and the socialization of children.

The Limits of Gender Division of Labor as a Unifying Concept

In defense of her substitution of division-of-labor analysis for class analysis, Young argued persuasively not only that division of labor is "a category both more concrete in its level of analysis and broader in extension than the category of class," but also that it is a category that appears as frequently in Marx's own work as does the category of class.[55] If Young was correct, then, it seems that the most effective way to overthrow capitalist patriarchy is to move women from the secondary work force into the primary work force. Although Young made no such suggestion, there may be something to such a strategy if, for example, we view the comparable worth struggle (see Chapter 2) as a program of action aimed not only at making women the economic and social equals of men but also at tearing down the walls of capitalist patriarchy.

Socialist feminists participate in the comparable worth movement because they are looking for ways to break down what is an increasingly scandalous hierarchy of wages, providing some people with seven-figure salaries and others with a pittance. The justification generally given for this state of affairs is that the market rewards the people who do the most valuable work with the highest salary. But as socialist feminists see it, it is doubtful that, objectively speaking, the market is rewarding the most deserving people. What is more, continue socialist feminists, it is not clear that anyone's work is worth so *much* more than anyone else's. The comparable worth debate is an opportunity, therefore, to flatten the hierarchy of wages by establishing that most female-dominated occupations require as much knowledge, skills, mental acuity, and accountability as do most male-dominated occupations. It is also an opportunity to argue the point that the relative value of a person's occupation should not affect his/her right to a decent wage, one that allows him/her to thrive as a human person. Thus, from a socialist feminist point of view, a benefit of the comparable worth movement would be for working women to receive the kind of wage working men receive; but an even greater benefit would be a shift from a dual-labor market, in which some people (mostly women and minorities) are paid half as much as other people (mostly white men) to a unified-labor market committed to approximately equal wages for everyone. Comparable worth, then, is one specific way to demarginalize women's work that weakens class structures and gender structures simultaneously.

Assuming that Young was correct—that the shift of women from the margins to the center of the workplace will erode or even destroy capitalist patriarchy—we must wonder whether the state of affairs subsequent to capitalist patriarchy will represent a major improvement in women's estate. Young suggested that if the situation was better for women in precapitalist times, then perhaps it will also be better for them in postcapitalist times. But does history, especially the history of ideas, establish that women in precapitalist times were men's psychological as well as economic equals? Even if it does establish this, is it really possible to replace the oppression of capitalist patriarchy with anything better than the lesser oppression of socialist patriarchy, a system that reforms without revolutionizing women's estate? If patriarchy is the constant term in a changing series of compound phrases—precapitalist patriarchy, capitalist patriarchy, postcapitalist patriarchy—does this not at least suggest that patriarchy may, after all, be eternal and universal unless the very natures of men and women are changed?

Finally, Young claimed that a gender-based division-of-labor analysis can address not only issues related to women's role in reproduction and the socialization of children but also issues related to women's sexuality. As Young saw it, on a practical level, to struggle against the sexual abuse of women is to struggle against capitalism and patriarchy at one and the same time. Being sexually harassed in the workplace, for example, keeps women from forgetting that in a capitalist patriarchy, women's bodies can be exploited and exposed "as symbols of pleasure, luxury, and convenience."[56] Indeed, in a recent case of sexual harassment, female coal miners were, from the moment they appeared on the scene, scrutinized by male eyes. Although the tension between the female and male coal miners was considerable, it was bearable until a rash of graffiti, focusing on the women's physical characteristics, appeared on the mine walls. One woman who had small breasts was called "inverted nipples," and another woman who supposedly had protruding lower vaginal lips was called the "low-lip express." Subjected to such offensive social commentary on this and other occasions, the female miners found it increasingly difficult to maintain their sense of self-respect, and their personal and professional lives began to deteriorate. Eventually, these women sued their employers for sexual harassment and won. As a result of their victory, these women reported feelings of empowerment at home as well as at work—a new ability to assert their rights and to articulate their needs. Over this kind of self-confident women patriarchy has little hold.[57]

Although Young cautioned that not all struggles against sexual abuse— she mentioned rape counseling and "take back the night" patrols—are as much struggles against capitalism as against patriarchal structures, it is not clear why she needed to issue this caveat.[58] If capitalist patriarchy is a unitary system, then women's victories in the "public" realm will spill over into the "private" realm, and vice versa. A woman who participates in a "take back the night" patrol will discover that she is not alone. Armed with an expanded sense of self, such a woman will have the power to resist the forces—many of them explicitly capitalist— that would reduce her to an object.

But even if Young's own examples did not undermine her analysis, it may still be that some struggles against sexual abuse will erode only patriarchal structures, and that the bond between socialism and feminism may dissolve at these junctures, once again separating Marxist feminists from their radical and psychoanalytic feminist sisters. For now, however, the bond seems to be holding.

The Limits of Alienation as a Unifying Concept

Like Young's analysis of division-of-labor, Jaggar's analysis of alienation was very persuasive. As Jaggar read Marx, the essential meaning of alienation is "that things or people which in fact are related dialectically to each other come to seem alien, separated from or opposed to each other."[59] Using this understanding of alienation, Jaggar effectively took aim at virtually *all* relations that are oppressive, or characterized by dominance/submission. Not only did Jaggar make specific proposals for social change in the areas of reproductive freedom, wages, and organizational independence for women; she outlined ways to incorporate in our daily lives the socialist feminist values of "equality, cooperation, sharing, political commitment, freedom from sexual stereotyping, and freedom from personal possessiveness."[60] This list stands in contrast to the alienation so many women currently experience.

The only major point that has been raised against Jaggar's analysis is one that she brought up herself: namely, that it is not immediately clear that all women really occupy the same standpoint. Jaggar admitted that socialist feminists have only recently begun to consider seriously the "epistemological consequences" of the differences as well as the similarities among women. Rather than fearing this new development, Jaggar endorsed it. She believed that by working through their racial, ethnic, and individual differences, many kinds of women can together develop "a systematic representation of reality that is not distorted in ways that promote the interests of men above those of women."[61]

The fact that many women have not been willing or even able to take part in this process means, of course, that women are still the captives of a systematic representation of reality that is distorted in ways that promote men's over women's interests. However, Jaggar claimed, the bad news—"we women have only begun to fight"—*is* the good news. Women's standpoint is not an ossified truth that some feminist academicians have chiseled in stone for all women to worship; rather, it is a kaleidoscope of truths, continually shaping and reshaping each other, as more and different women begin to work and think together.[62] The challenge, therefore, for socialist women is to draw on the experiences of all women, never falling prey to the temptation to valorize the experiences of one group of women—for example, the most oppressed group of women— as somehow the paradigm for what it means to be a woman. □

CONCLUSION

Currently, socialist feminists are no longer content with simply fitting capitalism and patriarchy together, whether it be through the use of two concepts or one. As typified here by Alison Jaggar and Iris Young, these theorists seek to encompass not only Marxist but also radical and psychoanalytic insights under one conceptual umbrella. If successful, such a feminist theory would resolve the existing differences among the many currents of feminism. Were this to happen, the voices of feminists as historically and philosophically diverse as Clara Zetkin, Nancy Chodorow, and Mary Daly would ring out in harmony, not discord. The potential of such an overarching theory is obviously great. Imagine the power of the omnipotent mother, a coven of Amazing Amazons, and a fistful of women workers standing in sisterhood.

Just as obviously, however, the difficulties of orchestrating such disparate traditions need to be acknowledged. Any unitary theory—even a theory that relies on a very resilient notion of a standpoint—runs the risk of erasing, or at least eroding, the differences that exist among women. This is a risk that requires great courage, for no feminist wants to achieve unity at the expense of diversity. Still, it is a risk worth taking.

CHAPTER SEVEN

■

Existentialist Feminism

SHORTLY BEFORE SIMONE DE BEAUVOIR died, Margaret A. Simons and Jessica Benjamin interviewed her for the journal *Feminist Studies*. In their background commentary, Simons and Benjamin commented on the significance of de Beauvoir's major theoretical work, *The Second Sex*.

> De Beauvoir's analysis of women's oppression in *The Second Sex* is open to many criticisms: for its idealism—her focus on myths and images and her lack of practical strategies for liberation; for its ethnocentrism and androcentric view—her tendency to generalize from the experience of European bourgeois women, with a resulting emphasis on women's historic ineffectiveness. Still, we have no theoretical source of comparable sweep that stimulates us to analyze and relentlessly question our situation as women in so many domains—literature, religion, politics, work, education, motherhood, and sexuality. As contemporary theorists explore the issues raised in *The Second Sex,* we can see that in a sense all feminist dialogue entails a dialogue with Simon de Beauvoir. And a discussion with her can be a way of locating ourselves within our feminist past, present, and future.[1]

Clearly, *The Second Sex* has within a short thirty-year span achieved the status of a classic in feminist thought. Thus, no introduction to feminist thought would be nearly complete without a discussion of this work, which has helped many feminists understand the full significance of woman's otherness.

As there has been some question about the precise relationship between de Beauvoir's *The Second Sex* and Jean-Paul Sartre's *Being and Nothingness,* some reference to this debate may prove useful. The first and ultimately mistaken view is that de Beauvoir's *The Second Sex* is simply an application of Sartre's *Being and Nothingness* to woman's specific situation. This is a view fed by the popular misconception that Sartre was de Beauvoir's lifelong lover and mentor. In point of fact, he was neither. Although Sartre and de Beauvoir were lovers for many years, by the late 1940s their physical relationship had apparently ended. Similarly, although Sartre was for awhile de Beauvoir's teacher, by the time they both became well-known authors, de Beauvoir was anything but Sartre's student. On the contrary, she was his intellectual companion and, at times, his teacher.[2]

But even if it is misleading to overemphasize the contribution of Sartre's philosophy to that of de Beauvoir's, it is not inappropriate to show some of the ways de Beauvoir used existentialist categories in *The Second Sex*. At times, de Beauvoir simply used Sartrean terms without transforming their meanings; at other times, however, she did effect such a transformation to fit her philosophical and feminist purposes. Although not necessary, an understanding of Sartre may enrich our appreciation of de Beauvoir as an original thinker. □

SARTRE'S *BEING AND NOTHINGNESS:*
A BACKDROP TO *THE SECOND SEX*

Sartre was the populizer of a body of ideas rooted in the philosophies of G.W.F. Hegel, Edmund Husserl, and Martin Heidegger. Chief among these ideas for Sartre was Hegel's description of the psyche as a "self-alienated spirit." Hegel saw consciousness presiding in a divided arena. On the one hand lies the transcendent self, or observing ego, and on the other hand lies the immanent self, or the observed ego.[3] Sartre made this distinction between the observer and the observed by dividing Being into two parts: Being-for-Itself (*pour-soi*) and Being-in-Itself (*en-soi*). Being-in-Itself refers to the constant, material existence that humans share with animals, vegetables, and minerals, whereas Being-for-Itself refers to the moving, conscious existence that humans share only with other humans.[4]

The distinction between Being-in-Itself and Being-for-Itself is useful in an analysis of the human person, particularly if we associate Being-in-Itself with the body. The body has constant and objective being. Because it can be seen, touched, heard, smelled, and/or tasted, the body is the perceived. In contrast, the perceiver—the entity that does the seeing, touching, hearing, smelling, and/or tasting—is not itself a perceptible object but, according to Sartre, still has a certain kind of Being: Being-for-Itself. To appreciate what Being-for-Itself is all about, picture for a moment someone momentarily conscious of the fingers on her hand. Her "I" is identified with her fingers because they are after all *her* fingers, not anyone else's. However, her "I" is also distinct from her fingers because she is at the same time more than, or other than, her fingers. According to Sartre, what separates one's "I"—one's consciousness or one's mind—from one's body is, paradoxically, nothing (literally *no-thing,* or nothingness).

To the first two forms of being, Sartre added a third, Being-for-Others. Although Sartre sometimes described this mode of being as a *Mit-sein,* as a communal being-with, he more frequently described it negatively, as involving "a perpetual conflict as each For-itself seeks to recover its own Being by directly or indirectly making an object out of the other."[5] The social relations constituted by the action of consciousness within a society are inherently in conflict because each Being-for-Itself establishes itself as a subject, as a self, precisely by defining other beings as objects, as Others. This suggests that the process of self-definition is one of seeking power over other beings. "While I attempt to free myself from the hold of the Other, the Other is trying to free himself from mine; while I seek to enslave the Other, the Other seeks to enslave me. . . . Descriptions of concrete behavior must be seen within the perspective of *conflict.*"[6] In establishing all other beings as Others, each self describes and prescribes roles for the Other to conform to. Moreover, each subject conceives of itself as transcendent and free and views the Other as immanent and enslaved.

But even if freedom is the distinguishing characteristic of a self, it is paradoxically a curse, not a blessing. It is a curse because so long as a person is conscious, there is no relief from the freedom to choose and affirm. There are no answers in life, just questions. Worse, there is no such thing as *human nature,* an essence common to all human persons, that determines what a person ought to be. Rather, there is only a *human condition,* into which all persons are cast, equally, without self-definition. Existence, said Sartre, precedes essence. In other words, we exist only as amorphous, living organisms until we create separate and essential identities for ourselves through conscious action—that is, through making choices, coming to decisions, reaffirming old purposes and projects, or affirming new ones.

Sartre saw an intimate connection between his conception of freedom— so different from that of either the liberal or the Marxists—and his conception of nothingness.[7] He insisted that because nothing compels us to act in any one way, we are absolutely free. Our futures are totally open; none of the blanks has been filled in for us. But as we start filling in these blanks, we are overcome with a sense not so much of finding ourselves as of losing ourselves. When we elect one possibility for ourselves, we simultaneously annihilate all the others. We buy the future at the cost of our past, a cost that burdens our psyches. If we argue that we do not experience any of the psychic burdens—dread, anguish, nausea— that he described, Sartre will accuse us of "bad faith," a state of being akin to self-deception, false consciousness, or delusion.

Sartre analyzed several types of bad faith, the most typical being such a complete absorption into a role that one seems to oneself to have no choices left. A cafe waiter was one of Sartre's favorite examples of role-playing taken to its extreme.[8] Anyone who has ever been to a four-star French restaurant has probably met the character Sartre had in mind. Everything about the quintessential French waiter is highly stylized: He will present the wine list with the requisite flourish; he will grimace if the diner selects the wrong combination of courses; and he will behave in an overly solicitous manner should the diner's soup arrive lukewarm. The waiter acts in these ways not so much because his job depends on it as because his role-playing helps him to avoid the fundamental uncertainties and ambiguities of human existence. As we have seen, all conscious beings, Beings-for-Themselves, are without essence or definition. They must define themselves through the mutually related processes of decisionmaking and action-taking. In contrast, all nonconscious beings, Beings-in-Themselves, are *massif.* That is, they are what they are. Conscious beings supposedly yearn for the safe, uncomplicated state of nonconscious beings. The questions that afflict conscious beings, the possibilities that haunt them, are, said Sartre, their awful freedom, which will not leave them alone, but instead summons them to be or not to be. Thus, the aim of bad faith is to escape this unpleasant freedom. The waiter avoids varying his role and instead pretends that there is only one kind of waiter he can ever be.

Another mode of bad faith occurs when we pretend that we are thing-like, that we are just a body, another object in the world to which we can observe things happening—things that have, in a way, nothing to do with us. Sartre's example here was of a young woman who is dating a man with designs on her body. To preserve the particular excitement of the occasion—such as "I have been noticed by this man . . . how interesting I must be"—the woman wards off her dawning realization that she has a decision to make (presumably, whether to sleep with him). Each time her companion makes a leading statement—for example, "I find you so attractive"—she attempts to "disarm" the phrase of its sexual implications. She is controlling the situation quite well, but then the man takes her hand. The moment of decision appears to have come. To leave the hand there is to "engage herself" in the flirtation; to withdraw the hand is to ruin what has so far been a pleasant time together. But then bad faith comes to the woman's rescue. She leaves her hand in the man's hands, but "she does not notice that she is leaving it."[9] She achieves this state of nonconsciousness, of blissful oblivion, of thing-hood by engaging her companion in lofty intellectual and spiritual conversation, achieving thereby the separation of her soul from her body. "The hand," said Sartre, "rests inert between the warm hands of her companion—neither consenting nor resisting—a thing."[10] By divorcing herself from her hand, the woman masks from herself that she is a free subject, not a determined object.

The problem with trying to live in bad faith is twofold. First, no matter how hard the conscious subject tries to live in bad faith, in the final analysis complete bad faith is an ontological impossibility. *Pour-soi,* the conscious subject, cannot be *en-soi,* the nonconscious object. Only death, the foreclosure of all possibilities, permits the conscious subject to escape, once and for all, from freedom. Second, no matter how we try to excuse or justify it, bad faith is an ethical horror. If freedom has any meaning, it is in taking responsibility for one's actions, in realizing that there is always room for some sort of choice, no matter how constricted one's circumstances.

Sartre had no patience with Freudians who would destroy the ethical project by permitting people to hide from their responsibility in the so-called unconscious. For Sartre, not only our decisions and actions but also our feelings are conscious. We use our emotions to work magic tricks. When our lives get too difficult to handle, we consciously work ourselves up into a rage, or down into a depression. We then use these emotional extremes as excuses for our unreadiness and unwillingness to cope with life. Similarly, said Sartre, if manic-depressives or obsessive-compulsives cannot explain their afflictions, it is because they are repressing these explanations. Whereas Freud spoke of unconscious wishes unconsciously repressed, Sartre spoke of falsehoods, of people refusing to admit what they know are ultimately the reasons/explanations for their actions.[11]

Of all Sartre's categories, Being-for-Others is probably the most suited for a feminist analysis. According to Sartre, human relations are variations on two basic themes of conflict between rival consciousnesses—between self and Others. First, there is love, which is essentially masochistic. Second, there are indifference, desire, and hate, which are essentially sadistic.[12]

Fools that we are, most of us start out with very grand ideas about love, about harmonizing the self and the Other. The quest for love, we believe, is our attempt to be one with the Other; an attempt akin to the Christian mystic's effort to become one-with-God without, of course, forsaking his or her unique personal identity. Mystical union, we believe, is a very mysterious state. The mystic is at one and the same time himself or herself *and* God. It is this mysterious state, however, that we wish to create for ourselves. At the physical level, such union without absorption would mean that my lover, for example, would live my body as he simultaneously lives his own. My lover would know my body in such a way that he would erase all separation between us without depriving either of us of our quality of otherness. Similarly, at the psychological level, such union without absorption would mean that my lover would know my psychic states, would know me and be me, and still not rob me of my identity or lose his own.

Such union without absorption is, said Sartre, an impossible dream. We live in a very nonmystical world. There is no possibility of harmony, or union, between the self and the Other; the self's need for total freedom is too absolute to be shared. Our attempts at love—at union without absorption—will always deteriorate to mutual possession—to mutual objectification. Exhausted by the struggle to maintain our subjectivity, our freedom, but still desiring a relationship (albeit one that is literally self-destructive) with the Other, we may be led to masochism, the prospect of losing our subjectivity altogether in that of the Other, who is now invited to treat us as a mere object.

Masochism is, for Sartre, not the perversion of love but its essential consequence. Through pain and humiliation, we hope to erase our subjectivity, to actually become the object that the Other, the torturer, perceives as us. Our suffering may seem to testify that we have no choice in the matter; however, Sartre explained, this is a delusion, for in order to be masochists we must *choose* to apprehend ourselves as objects. Thus, as a flight from subjectivity, masochism is a dead end. The more we try to reduce ourselves to mere objects, the more we are aware of ourselves as the subjectivities who are attempting this reduction.[13]

Defeated in our attempt to exist either as lovers or as failed lovers (masochists), we may be driven to indifference-desire, or sadism-hate, the attempt to defy the freedom of the Other. Our defiance begins quietly with indifference, a form of what Sartre called "blindness," or a non-recognition of the subjectivity of Others. Blind, we make no attempt to apprehend the Other as anything but an object: "I scarcely notice [others]; I act as if I were alone in the world."[14] This solipsism is ego building, for it allows us to overlook the fact that we are determined by Others, shaped by the look of those Others among whom we strut as if we were the sole subject in the world. When we are indifferent to Others, we pretend that they do not exist, that they cannot define us or pigeonhole us. Nevertheless, what occurs unacknowledged by us still in fact occurs: There *are* Others in whose eyes we are objects. What we refuse to recognize, then, may at any moment intrude upon us. The Other may at any moment direct at us an altogether human look and we may receive it. "Brief and terrifying flashes of illumination," said Sartre, may rip through the shroud of our indifference, forcing us to recognize the subjectivity, the freedom of the other.[15]

Should we receive such a look, our attempt at total indifference will fail and we will instead experience desire—specifically, sexual desire. To desire the Other sexually is to want the Other as mere flesh, as total object. But no sooner do we appropriate the desired body as mere flesh than we discover that it was not the Other's flesh that we desired.

> To be sure, I can grasp the Other, grab hold of him, knock him down. I can, providing I have the power, compel him to perform this or that act, to say certain words. But everything happens as if I wished to get hold of a man who runs away and leaves only his coat in my hands. It is the coat, it is the outer shell which I possess. I shall never get hold of more than a body, a psychic object in the midst of the world.[16]

Disappointed by what we have received from the Other through the caress, we may now resolve to use humiliation and cruelty (sadism) to squeeze more out of him or her. Sadism is our attempt to reduce the Other to a mere body, a thing, an obscenity. However, just when we think we are about to triumph over the Other—that is, just when the Other's consciousness seems ready to yield to the demands of his or her tortured body—the Other may look us in the eye and refuse, after all, to submit to our will. By reestablishing the Other as a subject, insisted Sartre, this look, like all looks, will frustrate our attempt at sadism.

Unable to eliminate the threat of the Other even through sadism, our only recourse is hate: the wish for the death of the Other, a wish that is explained by the fact that we want to wipe out forever that self who has, by looking at us as objects, threatened our freedom. If we feel that we have been ridiculous or evil or cowardly objects in the Other's consciousness, we may wish to wipe out that embarrassment by destroying that consciousness. Sartre pointed out that hatred of a particular Other is, in reality, hatred of all Others. If we wish not to be a self-for-Others, logically we should have to annihilate all Others. But hate is also futile, for even if all Others ceased to exist, the memory of their looks would live on forever in our consciousness, inseparable from whatever ideas we might try to form about ourselves. So, even our last resource does not suffice. "Hate does not enable us to get out of the circle. It simply represents the final attempt, the attempt of despair. After the failure of this attempt nothing remains for the for-itself except to re-enter the circle and allow itself to be infinitely tossed."[17] □

SIMONE DE BEAUVOIR: EXISTENTIALISM FOR WOMEN

In making it clear that she had adopted the ontological and ethical claims of existentialism, de Beauvoir announced that, from the beginning, man has named himself the Self and woman the Other.[18] According to Dorothy Kaufmann McCall, de Beauvoir's development of the Sartrean thesis—man as Self, woman as Other—in *The Second Sex* was "completely her own."[19] If the Other is a threat to the Self, then woman is a threat to man; and if man wishes to remain free, he must subordinate woman to him. To be sure, woman is not the only Other who knows oppression; blacks know what it is to be oppressed by whites, and the poor know what it is to be oppressed by the rich. Nonetheless, insisted Kaufmann McCall, woman's oppression by man is unique for two reasons: "First, unlike the oppression of race and class, the oppression of woman is not a contingent historical fact, an event in time which has sometimes been contested or reversed. Woman has always been subordinate to man. Second, women have internalized the alien point of view that man is the essential, woman the inessential."[20]

Destiny and History of Woman

A good way to test de Beauvoir's characterization of woman's oppression as "unique" is to ponder her analysis of how woman became the Other, not only different and separate from man but also inferior to him. She advanced this analysis in the first three chapters of *The Second Sex,* which she respectively entitled, "The Data of Biology," "The Psychoanalytic Point of View," and "The Point of View of Historical Materialism." Although biologists, psychoanalysts (Freudians), and Marxists have important things to say about the causes and reasons for woman's condition, as de Beauvoir saw it none of them truly explains why woman, not man, is the Other.

De Beauvoir argued that biology sets forth facts that society will interpret to suit its ends. Biology identifies the basic difference between male and female as one rooted in the reproductive roles of males and females.

> The sperm, through which the life of the male is transcended in another, at the same instant becomes a stranger to him and separates from his body, so that the male recovers his individuality intact at the moment when he transcends it. The egg, on the contrary begins to separate from the female body when, fully matured, it emerges from the follicle and falls into the oviduct; but if fertilized by a gamete from outside, it becomes attached again through implantation in the uterus. First violated, the female is then alienated—she becomes, in part, another than herself.[21]

These reproductive "facts" suggested to de Beauvoir why it may be harder for a woman to become and remain a self, especially if she has a child; however, these facts did not also suggest to de Beauvoir that women's capacity for selfhood is less than men's. Her general point was that although biological and physiological facts about woman—such as her primary role in reproduction relative to man's secondary role, her physical weakness relative to man's physical strength, and her inactive role in heterosexual intercourse relative to man's active role—may be real enough, how much value we attach to these facts is up to us as social beings.

> The enslavement of the female to the species and the limitations of her various powers are extremely important facts; the body of woman is one of the essential elements in her situation in the world. But that body is not enough to define her as woman; there is no true living reality except as manifested by the conscious individual through activities and in the bosom of a society. Biology is not enough to give an answer to the question that is before us: why is woman the Other?[22]

In other words, woman is more than her body. She is not to be reduced to Being-in-Itself because she is also Being-for-Itself. Thus, we must look for causes and reasons beyond those suggested by female biology and physiology to account for why woman has been selected by society to play the role of the Other.

When de Beauvoir looked beyond biology to psychology, especially psychoanalysis, for a better explanation of woman's Otherness, she was disappointed. According to de Beauvoir, traditional Freudians all tell essentially the same story about woman: that she is a creature who must struggle between her "viriloid" and her "feminine" tendencies, the first expressed through clitoral eroticism, the second through vaginal eroticism. To win this battle—to become normal—woman must overcome her "viriloid" tendencies; that is, she must transfer her love from a woman to a man. Although de Beauvoir conceded Freud's genius, which, for her, consisted in his having forwarded the bold idea that sexuality is the ultimate explanation for why things are the way they are, she nevertheless rejected it as simplistic.

> There is no need of taking sexuality as an irreducible datum, for there is in the existent a more original "quest of being," of which sexuality is only one of the aspects. The psychoanalysts hold that the primary truth regarding man is his relation with his own body and with the bodies of his fellows in the group; but man has a primordial interest in the substance of the natural world which surrounds him and which he tries to discover in work, in play, and in all the experiences of the "dynamic imagination." Man aspires to be at one concretely with the whole world apprehended in all possible ways. To work the earth, to dig a hole, are activities as original as the embrace, as coition, and they deceive themselves who see here no more than sexual symbols.[23]

In other words, civilization cannot be explained merely as the product of repressed and/or sublimated sexual impulses. Civilization is more complicated than this, and so are the relations between men and women.

In particular, de Beauvoir found Freud's explanation for the Otherness of woman to be lacking. Freud's theory of women's castration complex is, in her estimation, a poor psychological explanation for their inferior and subservient social status. Freudians, she lamented, believe that woman's low social status relative to man is unavoidable because she lacks the organ that symbolizes superiority and authority. Anticipating by decades a central position in the U.S. woman's movement, de Beauvoir refused to concede that it is woman's mere lack of a penis that consigns her to second-class personhood and citizenship. The reason women suffer from so-called penis envy is not that they want a penis per se, but that they desire the material and psychological privileges that society has accorded to men. The privileges of men, observed de Beauvoir, are not to be traced to certain features of the male anatomy; rather, the "prestige of the penis" is to be explained "by the sovereignty of the father." Thus, women are the Other not because they lack penises but because they lack power.[24]

Finally, de Beauvoir considered Marx's explanation for why woman is the Other and found it nearly as unsatisfying as Freud's. Marx contended that women are oppressed because of the forms their lives have had to take in class society, in which the masses of men and women have been oppressed by a small ruling class. For Marxists, the material conditions of life are ultimately the fundamental facts of human history. Oppression is rooted in the social organization through which one class (owners of the productive means) exploits the labor of another (those who must work to live); and until capitalism is overthrown and the means of production are owned by all, no oppression—whether by class, nation, race, or sex—will be eradicated from society.

But as de Beauvoir saw it, the relations between men and women will not automatically change even if we move from capitalism to socialism. Women are just as likely to remain the Other in a socialist society as in a capitalist society. Engels erred in tracing men's will to power to the institution of private property, and he erred in tracing women's oppression to the beginnings of capitalism. According to de Beauvoir, "If the human consciousness had not included . . . an original aspiration to dominate the Other, the invention of the bronze tool could not have caused the oppression of woman."[25] Engels's presentation, she said, failed to convince her the oppression of women is a necessary consequence of the institution of private property.

Unsatisfied by the traditional biological, psychological, and economic explanations of women's oppression, de Beauvoir sought an ontological explanation based on woman's *being*. She looked at woman and recognized a self that man has defined as Other. In determining the reasons for this definition, de Beauvoir observed that as soon as we assert ourselves "as subject and free being, the idea of the Other arises. From that day the relation with the Other is dramatic: the existence of the other is a threat, a danger."[26] Due to a variety of factors, most of them related to their freedom from reproductive burdens, men probably had the time and energy to use air, wind, fire, and water to create new instruments, to invent, to shape the future. Perceiving themselves as subjects capable of risking their lives in combat, for example, men perceived women as objects, capable only of giving life: "It is not in giving life but in risking life that man is raised above the animal; that is why superiority has been accorded in humanity not to the sex that brings forth but to that which kills."[27] Because of this alleged difference, women were decisively relegated by men to the sphere of Otherness—the realm of immanence, of the body.

Myths About Woman

As civilization developed, men discovered that one of the best ways to control woman is to construct myths about her—myths meant to explain the unexplainable, to simplify the complex, to rationalize the irrational. Throughout her analysis of man's myths about woman, de Beauvoir stressed two points: First, what man wants from women is everything that man lacks; and second, woman is a chameleon whose being is as mutable as nature.

In a chapter summarizing the writings of five male authors about women, de Beauvoir demonstrated the ways in which each of these authors, depending on his own specific self-image, had constructed for himself an ideal woman. "Montherlant, the solar spirit, seeks pure animality in her; Lawrence, the phallicist, asks her to sum up the feminine sex in general; Claudel defines her as a soul-sister; Breton cherishes Mélusine, rooted in nature, pinning his hope on the woman-child; Stendhal wants his mistress intelligent, cultivated, free in spirit and behavior: an equal."[28]

What is common to these distinctively different ideals of women is that in each case the ideal woman is urged to forget, deny, or in some way negate herself. Henry Montherlant's woman exists in order to make her man feel virile. D. H. Lawrence's woman gives up being what she wants to be so that her man can be what he wants to be. Paul Claudel's woman is the handmaid not only of God but also of man. André Breton's woman is burdened with a heavy guilt trip—provided that her love is deep enough, she can effect for her man the equivalent of salvation;

otherwise, he will be damned. Stendhal's woman risks life and limb in a passionate attempt to save her lover from ruin, prison, death. What makes these ideals of woman especially problematic, wrote de Beauvoir, is that in most of them woman has a *duty* to sacrifice herself for man.[29]

In addition to idealizing/idolizing the self-sacrificial woman, man's myths about woman betray a fundamental ambivalence about her nature. In words that anticipate those of psychoanalytic feminist Dorothy Dinnerstein and radical feminist Susan Griffin, de Beauvoir described the ways in which men connect nature to women. Like nature, woman reminds men of both life and death. At one and the same time, woman is innocent angel and guilty demon. Because her natural body reminds man that he is subject to disease, disintegration, death, and decay, man delights in her artificial body. Feathered and furred, powdered and perfumed, the "animal crudity" of woman (her "odor") is hidden from man in his flight from carnality and the mortality to which her body points.[30]

If woman could simply scoff at the image of her "ideal," then the situation would not be so perilous for her. But woman is unable to do so because man has the power to control her—to use her for his own purposes no matter the cost she has to pay. Honoré de Balzac, said de Beauvoir, summarized man's attitude toward woman when he wrote, "Pay no attention to her murmurs, her cries, her pains; *nature has made her for our use* and for bearing everything: children, sorrows, blows and pains inflicted by man. Do not accuse yourself of hardness. In all the codes of so-called civilized nations, man has written the laws that ranged woman's destiny under this bloody epigraph: '*Vae victis!* Woe to the weak!'"[31] Finally, what makes the myth of woman so horrific is that many women come to internalize it as an accurate reflection of what it means to be woman.

Woman's Life Today

Unlike Sartre, de Beauvoir specified social roles as the primary mechanisms the self, or subject, uses to control the Other, or the object. She labeled woman's tragic acceptance of her own Otherness the feminine "mystery," which continues from generation to generation through the painful socialization of woman into passive, or feminine, roles. Speaking from her own experience—that of a bourgeois French girl growing up between the two world wars—de Beauvoir insisted that from the beginning, girls recognize that their bodies are different from those of boys. The dolls they are given signal the "brutal and prescribed drama" they will some day play on behalf of the human species.[32] With puberty, with the swelling of their breasts, and with the beginning of their menstrual flows, girls are compelled to accept and internalize as shameful and inferior their Otherness, which is ossified, said de Beauvoir, in the institutions of marriage and motherhood.

As de Beauvoir saw it, the role of wife blocks women's freedom. Although de Beauvoir believed that men and women are able to love each other deeply, she also believed that the institution of marriage destroys spontaneity between lovers by transforming freely given feelings into mandatory duties and shrilly asserted rights. What is more, marriage enslaves women. What a woman (especially a bourgeois woman) gains from marriage is "gilded mediocrity lacking ambition and passion, aimless days indefinitely repeated, life that slips away gently toward death without questioning its purpose."[33] Women pay for their "happiness" with their freedom. De Beauvoir insisted that this price is too high for anyone because the kind of contentment, tranquility, and security that marriage offers woman drains her soul of its capacity for greatness.

> It is not without some regret that she shuts behind her the doors of her new home; when she was a girl, the whole countryside was her homeland; the forests were hers. Now she is confined to a restricted space; Nature is reduced to the dimensions of a potted geranium; walls cut off the horizon. But she is going to set about overcoming these limitations. In the form of more or less expensive bric-a-brac she has exotic countries and past time; she has her husband representing human society, and she has her child, who gives her the entire future in portable future.[34]

If the role of wife limits woman's self-development, the role of mother does so even more.[35] Although de Beauvoir conceded that the task of *rearing* a child to adulthood can be an active engagement, she underscored the fact that *bearing* a child is not an activity but rather a natural function. Not one to mince words, de Beauvoir stressed the ways in which pregnancy alienates a woman from herself, making it difficult for her to chart, unencumbered, the course of her destiny. Like radical feminist Shulamith Firestone, de Beauvoir was skeptical about the supposed joys of pregnancy, observing that even women who want to have children seem to have a tough time of it. Also like Firestone, de Beauvoir was worried about the way in which the mother-child relationship is so easily distorted. At first the child seems to liberate the mother from her object status because she "obtains in her child what man seeks in woman: an other, coming nature and mind, who is to be both prey and *double*."[36] But as time goes on, the child becomes a demanding tyrant—a toddler, an adolescent, an adult, a conscious subject that, by looking at mother, can turn her into an object, into a machine for cooking, cleaning, caring, giving, and especially sacrificing. Reduced to an object, the mother, not unexpectedly, begins to view and to use her child as an object, as something that can make up for her deep sense of frustration.

Clearly, "wifing" and "mothering" are, in de Beauvoir's estimation, two feminine roles that block woman's bid for freedom. We would think, then, that women could escape the trap of femininity by assuming the role of the career, or professional, woman, whose happiness does not depend on her ability to please a specific man and/or his children. It turns out, however, that a career woman can no more escape the cage of femininity than a wife and mother can. Indeed, in some ways, the career woman has it worse than the stay-at-home wife and mother because she is at all times and places expected to be and act like a woman. In other words, a career woman is expected to add to her professional duties those "duties" implied in her femininity, whereby femininity is meant a certain sort of pleasing appearance. As a result, she develops an internal conflict between her professional and feminine interests. To the degree that she develops her professional interests, the career woman will feel that she is falling woefully short of the epitome of femininity: the long-nailed, perfectly coiffed, well-dressed woman who spends her days at the beauty salon and dress fitter's. However, to the degree that she pays attention to her appearance, the career woman will find herself playing "second fiddle" to the career man who, unlike her, is not required to cultivate narcissism as a virtue.[37]

Wives, mothers, and career women, observed de Beauvoir, agree to play their feminine roles for a variety of reasons. Sometimes women play these roles not so much because they want to, as because they have to in order to survive economically and/or psychologically. Although virtually all women engage in feminine role-playing, three kinds of woman play the role of "woman" to the hilt. They are, said de Beauvoir, the prostitute, the narcissist, and the mystic.

De Beauvoir's analysis of the prostitute was complex. On the one hand, the prostitute is a paradigm for woman as Other, as object, as the exploited one. On the other hand, the prostitute, like the man who purchases her services, is an exploiter. She prostitutes herself, suggested de Beauvoir, not simply for the money but for the homage men pay to her otherness.

Continuing her controversial interpretation of prostitution, de Beauvoir argued that, as compared to wives and girlfriends, prostitutes get something for yielding their bodies to men's dreams: "wealth and fame."[38] Conceding to her readers that the ordinary streetwalker often sells her body because it is the only thing she has to sell, de Beavoir nonetheless insisted that the *hetaira*, the exceptional "call girl" who regards not only her body but her entire personality as capital, usually has the upper hand in any relationship.[39] Men need her even more than she needs them. De Beauvoir's point seemed to be that even if the *hetaira*, like the wife and the mother, cannot escape being the Other, at least she is able to use her Otherness to her own personal advantage. (As disturbing as I find de Beauvoir's account, and as much as I want to resist it, I am reminded of a former colleague of mine—a brilliant and beautiful Third World woman who captured the imagination of many of my male colleagues. At one point she said to me, "So, they want me to be the Other. Well, I *will* be the Other for them. But they will have to pay." And they did, for she had a way of trivializing and humiliating them both as men and as intellectuals.)

A feminine role even more problematic than that of prostitute is that of narcissist. De Beauvoir claimed that narcissism in woman follows from her Otherness. Woman is frustrated as a subject because she is not allowed to engage in self-defining activity and because her feminine activities are not fulfilling. "Not being able to fulfill herself through projects and objectives, [woman] is forced to find her reality in the immanence of her person. . . . She gives herself supreme importance because no object of importance is accessible to her."[40]

Woman then becomes her own object. Believing herself to be an object—a belief confirmed by most everyone around her—she is fascinated by, and perhaps even fixated on, her own image: face, body, clothes. The sense of being both subject and object at once is illusory because the synthesis of Being-for-Itself and Being-in-Itself is wholly impossible, yet the narcissist is defined by just that sense of supposedly transcended duality. De Beauvoir quoted a Mme. Mejerowsky as a narcissist par excellence: "I love myself, I am my God!" Much of this fascination with the object of herself arises as the woman creates her object double in the effort to assert a unique personality. Narcissism is at first helpful for woman because as an adolescent, she "can draw from the worship of her ego the courage to face the disquieting future," but the end result is that woman is enchained by the need to please man and by the "tyranny of public opinion."[41] The narcissist's self-worth comes not from the activities of being feminine per se but from society's reaction to her femininity.

Probably the most problematic feminine role is that of the mystic who seeks to be the supreme object of a supreme subject. The mystic, wrote de Beauvoir, confuses God with man and man with God. She speaks of divine beings as if they were human beings, and she speaks of men as if they were gods. What the mystic seeks in divine love, said de Beauvoir, is "first of all what the *amoureuse* seeks in that of man: the exaltation of her narcissism: this sovereign gaze fixed attentively, amorously, upon her is a miraculous godsend."[42] The mystic does not pursue transcendence through God. Instead, she seeks to be possessed supremely by a God who would have no other woman before Him. What the mystic wants from God is the exaltation of her objecthood.

In reflecting back upon her descriptions of the wife, the mother, the career woman, the prostitute, the narcissist, and the mystic, de Beauvoir came to the conclusion that the tragedy of these roles is that they are not fundamentally of woman's own making. Not a maker herself, woman has been offered up to the masculine world of productive society for approval. She has, said de Beauvoir, been constructed by man, by his structures and institutions. But because woman, like man, has no essence, she need not continue to be what man has made her to be. Woman can be a subject, can engage in positive action in society, and can redefine or abolish her roles as wife, mother, career woman, prostitute, narcissist, and mystic. Woman can create her own self because there is no essence of eternal femininity that prescribes a readymade identity for her. All that is holding woman back from self-creation is society—a patriarchy that is, in de Beauvoir's estimation, reaching its end: "What is certain is that hitherto woman's possibilities have been suppressed and lost to humanity, and that it is high time she be permitted to take her chances in her own interest and in the interest of all."[43] Woman, like man, is a subject rather than an object; she is no more Being-in-Itself than man is. She, like man, is Being-for-Itself, and it is high time for man to recognize this fact.

There are, of course, no easy ways for woman to escape what de Beauvoir repeatedly described as woman's immanence—the limits, definitions, and roles that society, propriety, and men have imposed on her. Nevertheless, if woman wants to stop being the second sex, the Other, then she must overcome the forces of circumstance; she must have her say and her way as much as man does. On the way to transcendence, there are, said de Beauvoir, three strategies that women can employ.

First, women must go to work. Although de Beauvoir admitted that work in a capitalist world is oppressive and exploitative and recognized that the woman who works outside the home is likely to be working inside the home also, de Beauvoir discounted these negativities. In words reminiscent of Harriett Taylor, de Beauvoir insisted that if work can be monotonous and deadening for men, then women should share that experience in the same environment—that is, at work and not in the home. No matter how menial a woman's job is, de Beauvoir believed that it will open up possibilities for that woman. In work, woman "regains her transcendence"; she "concretely affirms her status as subject," as someone who is actively charting the course of her destiny.[44]

Second, women can become intellectuals, members of the vanguard of change for women. Intellectual activity, after all, is the activity of one who thinks, looks, and defines, not the nonactivity of one who is thought about, looked at, and defined. De Beauvoir encouraged women to study writers such as Emily Brontë, Virginia Woolf, and Katherine Mansfield who have been able to take themselves seriously enough as writers to probe death, life, and suffering respectively.[45]

Third, and finally, women can work toward a socialist transformation of society. Like Sartre, de Beauvoir held out hope for an end to the subject/object, self/other conflict among human beings in general and between men and women in particular. In *Being and Nothingness,* Sartre added a footnote to his conclusion that all attempts at love—at the triumph over the subject-object dichotomy—are bound to lapse into either masochism or sadism. His "considerations," said Sartre, "do not exclude the possibility of an ethics of deliverance and salvation. But this can be achieved only after a radical conversion which we cannot discuss here."[46] The radical conversion that Sartre had in mind is a Marxist revolution. The struggle between one human being and another, which in *Being and Nothingness* arose from a psychological necessity derived from the nature of consciousness itself, became, in Sartre's *The Critique of Dialectical Reason,* a struggle between workers and capitalists caused not by psychological but by economic necessity. Only when all people have adequate food, clothing, and shelter can they even begin to think about overcoming the psychological barriers that separate them.

Like Sartre, de Beauvoir also believed that one of the keys to women's liberation is economic, a point that she emphasized in her discussion of the independent woman. De Beauvoir reminded her readers that even though we can create ourselves, our efforts to shape ourselves into what we want to be will always be limited by the kind of existence that has been given us. Just as a sculptor's creativity is limited by the marble block at hand, our freedom is limited by our society. If we want to be all that we can possibly be as individuals, we must first clear the social space for this project. □

CRITIQUES OF EXISTENTIALIST FEMINISM

A Communitarian Critique of Existentialist Feminism

Jean Bethke Elshtain made three major points in her critique of Simone de Beauvoir's *The Second Sex.* The first is that the book was not accessible to the majority of women. "Immanence" and "transcendence," "essence" and "existence," "Being-for-Itself" and "Being-in-Itself" are ideas that do not arise directly out of woman's lived experience. These ideas are abstractions that arise from the philosopher's armchair speculations. De Beauvoir's technical words, said Elshtain, are more likely to "pummel" less formally educated women into agreeing with her than to persuade them that they are indeed the second sex.[47]

The second major point in Elshtain's critique concerned her objections to the ways in which de Beauvoir treated the female body in particular. In *The Second Sex,* woman's body often appears negative: unfortunate, insignificant, dirty, shameful, burdensome, inherently alienating. Elshtain suggested that de Beauvoir's profound distrust of the body was rooted in an existentialist distress about the carnality and mortality of the flesh and in a feminist concern about the ways in which the female body imposes special burdens upon woman—burdens that are both quantitatively and qualitatively more onerous than those the male body imposes upon men. The body is a problem within the existentialist framework insofar as it is a stubborn and unavoidable object limiting the freedom of each conscious subject. De Beauvoir recorded in her memoirs her own war against the flesh: her squashed sexual urges; her attempts to do without sleep; her sense of horror as she relentlessly aged.[48] Because the slow disintegration of the body signals the coming of death—the end of consciousness, of freedom, of subjectivity—existentialists such as de Beauvoir have little desire to celebrate a body that represents to them the forces of death.

De Beauvoir's general distrust of the body, suggested Elshtain, became a very specific mistrust of the female body. As de Beauvoir saw it, a woman's individuality, or personhood, is won at the cost of rejecting her reproductive capacities. In contrast, a man's individuality does not require such a price. After sexual intercourse, the man remains exactly as he was before sexual intercourse. But if fertilization takes place after sexual intercourse, a woman is no longer the same person, or even a person: "Ensnared by nature, the pregnant woman is plant and animal, a stock-pile of colloids, an incubator, an egg; she scares children proud of their young, straight bodies and makes young people titter contemptuously because she is a human being, a conscious and free individual, who has become life's passing instrument."[49]

In focusing on this harsh passage and others like it, Elshtain claimed that de Beauvoir's apparent horror of the body, particularly the female body, led her to attack the institutions of marriage and motherhood as thoroughly oppressive ways of existing that women must reject. As a choice of strategy, this attack is likely to be off-putting to a woman who is only beginning to feel the latent possibilities within herself; certainly it is likely to alienate any woman who associates the body with life as well as death and who regards pregnancy, childbirth, and breastfeeding as rewarding experiences. In sum, according to Elshtain, de Beauvoir's intellectualized approach to the body is likely to alienate the woman who refuses to privilege the mind over the body and who does not believe that Being-in-Itself is an inherently defective mode of being.[50]

Lastly, Elshtain criticized de Beauvoir for accepting and perhaps celebrating largely male norms. All of de Beauvoir's complaints about woman's body and character, insisted Elshtain, translate into a valorization of man's body and character: active, virile, dominant, transcendent. The denigration of woman's body arises from the elevation of the ideal of man's body. The deploring of woman's association with nature contrasts with the admiration of man's construction of culture. Thus, de Beauvoir's prescription for women's oppression was that women achieve freedom in and through the ways men have traditionally achieved freedom. As Elshtain saw it, de Beauvoir's diagnosis of women's condition and her prescription for its cure were both severely flawed. To ask women to give up their female identities, without considering the ramifications of trading in sisterhood for the universal brotherhood of mankind, is irresponsible.[51]

A Philosophical Critique of Existentialist Feminism

In *Man of Reason,* a book about the construction of gender in Western philosophy, Genevieve Lloyd argued that de Beauvoir's philosophical categories were at odds with some fundamental feminist needs. Transcendence, Lloyd said, is a male ideal by definition. To accept the ideal of transcendence as somehow liberating places the feminist in a paradox. The origin of the paradox lies in the opposition that Sartre and de Beauvoir said exists between the looker and the looked-at, between self and Other. One is either looking, acting, transcending or one is being looked at, passive, immanent. There is no in between. What this means for woman is that she must, by refusing to be complicit in her Otherness, leap from immanence into transcendence. But Lloyd thought there is a problem here peculiar to women. Even if immanence, or "the kingdom of life," is not women's natural domain but a domain men have created in order to imprison women therein, it is, nonetheless, the space in which many women currently abide. Likewise, even if women are by nature no more Being-in-Itself than men are, women are still conceptually linked with Being-in-Itself in the same way that men are. Thus, "'transcendence' in its origins, is a transcendence *of* the feminine."[52] A woman, said Lloyd, will necessarily be alienated from herself by any attempt at transcendence: "Male transcendence . . . is different from what female transcendence would have to be. It is breaking away from a zone which for the male, remains intact—from what is for him the realm of particularity and merely natural feelings. For the female, in contrast, there is no such realm which she can both leave and leave intact."[53] Small wonder, then, that Lloyd faulted de Beauvoir's philosophy for seeming to ask women to self-destruct. □

CONCLUSION

The criticisms that have been brought against de Beauvoir should be taken seriously. But they should also be carefully scrutinized. What is going on here is, in part, a profound debate about whether it is more liberating to think of women simply as the product of a complex cultural construction or to think of woman primarily as the expression of a female way of being that represents all that is best about being human. What is also going on here is a debate we have heard several times now: Will the female body keep woman oppressed, or will it set woman free?

Despite the force of Elshtain's and Lloyd's critiques, much can and has been said in defense of de Beauvoir's profound feminism. That de Beauvoir's vocabulary was philosophical is indisputable; that her book was long (nearly one thousand pages) and her literary style challenging are also indisputable. But the fact that she spoke in her own voice— that of an educated, bourgeois French woman—does not mean that her words do not resonate in wide circles of women. The publication of *The Second Sex* was met with a furor. De Beauvoir was shocked that some of her supposedly enlightened friends—for example, existentialist Albert Camus—had no use for the book, regarding it as an assault upon masculinity.[54] She was also disheartened by the chilly response of the local Communist party, which regarded *The Second Sex* as yet another trivial catalogue of female complaints intended to distract people from genuine class struggle.[55] To be sure, de Beauvoir also had her supporters; her book sold 22,000 copies in the first week of its publication. But what pleased Simone de Beauvoir the most, according to one of her biographers, were the letters she received from grateful women of every social class whose lives had changed in positive directions after reading *The Second Sex*. Whatever difficulties de Beauvoir's prose may have presented to some of her readership, they obviously heard a liberating message in it.[56]

The charge that de Beauvoir was hostile to the body, especially to the female body, is one for which ample textual evidence exists in *The Second Sex* and many of de Beauvoir's novels. When de Beauvoir observed that women have within their bodies a "hostile element"—namely, "the species gnawing at their vitals," her words evoked feelings of fear, weakness, and disgust.[57] Nevertheless, despite her suspicion of the body and her valorization of the mind, de Beauvoir's mind-body dualism was never so thorough as that of Sartre. Certainly her attitude toward the emotions commonly associated with the body was never as negative as his. Indeed, de Beauvoir cautioned Sartre that his attitude toward the body and the emotions was *too* inflexible: "I criticized Sartre for regarding his body as a mere bundle of striated muscles, and for having cut it out of his emotional world. If you gave way to tears or nerves or seasickness, he said, you were simply being weak. I, on the other hand, claimed that stomach and tear ducts, indeed the head itself, were all subject to irresistible forces on occasion."[58]

The fact that de Beauvoir permitted herself and others to give in to their bodies and emotions from time to time is not a sign that de Beauvoir was willing to renegotiate her view on the body in general and on the female body in particular. In recent years, de Beauvoir openly conceded that "it's good to demand that a woman should not be made to feel degraded by, let's say, her monthly periods; that a woman refuse to be made to feel ridiculous because of her pregnancy; that a woman be able to be proud of her body, and her feminine sexuality."[59] But even though de Beauvoir made this important concession, she remained resistant to any all-out celebration of the female body. When informed by Simons and Benjamin that, like many French feminists, many U.S. feminists were making woman's body the centerpiece of their feminism, de Beauvoir replied that she was opposed to this privileging of a special female way of being.

> There is no reason at all to fall into some wild narcissism, and build, on the basis of these givens, a system which would be the culture and the life of women. I don't think that women should repress their givens. She has the perfect right to be proud of being a woman, just as man is also proud of his sex. After all, he has the right to be proud of it, under the condition, however, that he does not deprive others of the right to a similar pride. Everyone can be happy with her or his body. But one should not make this body the center of the universe.[60]

As de Beauvoir saw it, the problem with making woman's body the linchpin of her liberation is that it mistakes a biological fact for a social fact. Woman's body—as wonderful as it is—should not prescribe, or mandate, a definite mode of existence for her. Within the limits that constrain any human person, each and every woman can shape her own existence.

This last point—that whatever her circumstances, each woman is still able to shape the course of her own destiny—must be carefully understood. De Beauvoir recognized the legal, political, economic, social, and cultural circumstances that restrain and constrain woman. She also recognized the ways in which woman has let herself be restrained and constrained by these circumstances. But this complicity is not *merely* complicity, for woman lives beyond as well as in her complicity with man. She is both determined by and free of patriarchy. "People," wrote Carol Ascher, "make decisions to break out of or remain within varying degrees of constraint, at times no positive decision may be possible. Yet the decision is made, and the individual is responsible for it."[61] Thus, when de Beauvoir asked woman to transcend the limits of her immanence, de Beauvoir was not asking woman to negate herself but rather to cast off those weights that are impeding her progress toward authentic selfhood. To be sure, some of these weights are too heavy for any individual to cast off; but others can be disposed of through small and large acts of empowerment. What is now does not always have to be. No one or no thing can hold women back forever.

CHAPTER EIGHT

■

Postmodern Feminism

MORE THAN ANY OTHER TYPE OF FEMINIST thought—liberal, Marxist, radical, psychoanalytic, socialist, and existentialist—postmodern feminism has an uneasy relationship to feminism. Postmodern feminists worry that because feminism purports to be an explanatory theory, it, too, is in danger of trying to provide *the* explanation for why woman is oppressed or *the* ten steps all women must take in order to achieve true liberation. Because postmodern feminists reject traditional assumptions about truth and reality, they wish to avoid in their writings any and all reinstantiations of phallologocentric thought, which is thought ordered around an absolute word (*logos*) that is "male" in style (hence, the *phallus*). Hélène Cixous has publicly stated that terms such as *feminist* and *lesbian* are parasitic upon phallologocentric thought because they connote "deviation from a norm instead of a free sexual option or a place of solidarity with women."[1] Better for women seeking liberation to avoid such terms, which suggest a unity that blocks difference.

Although postmodern feminists' refusal to construct one explanatory theory may threaten the unity of the feminist movement, and pose theoretical problems for those feminists hoping to provide us with an overarching explanation and solution for women's oppression, this refusal adds fuel to the feminist fires of plurality, multiplicity, and difference. What postmodern feminists as diverse in thinking as Hélène Cixous, Luce Irigaray, and Julia Kristeva offer to each woman who reads them is an opportunity to become herself. □

SOME MAJOR INFLUENCES
ON POSTMODERN FEMINIST THOUGHT

Until recently, postmodern feminism was referred to as "French feminism." As many of the women articulating this thought were either French nationals or women living in France (especially Paris), Anglo-

217

America labeled all of them "French."[2] The term *postmodern feminism* gained credence as U.S. audiences realized that what such writers as Cixous, Irigaray, and Kristeva had in common was not so much their "Frenchness" as their philosophical perspective, which was shared by postmodern philosophers such as Jacques Derrida and Jacques Lacan. Like Derrida, Cixous, Irigaray, and Kristeva are deconstructionists in the sense that they delight in illuminating the "internal contradictions in seemingly perfectly coherent systems of thought," which serves to attack "ordinary notions of authorship, identity and selfhood."[3] Like Lacan, Cixous, Irigaray, and Kristeva are very much interested in reinterpreting traditional Freudian psychoanalytic theory and practice.

But to say that these three feminists share a philosophical perspective with Derrida and Lacan is not to say that they are dedicated Derrideans or Lacanians or that they share either man's politics.[4] In fact, enormous political differences exist among these, as well as other less well-known, postmodern feminists. Some postmodern feminists write simply to spin theory as an art form; others write primarily to motivate women to change their ways of being and doing in the real world.

Significantly, U.S. audiences still have a somewhat skewed view of postmodern feminism because initial translations of postmodern feminist writings were few and selective. An organization called Psychoanalyze et politique (Psych et po), with which Hélène Cixous is closely associated, served for many years as a gatekeeper for what Anglo-American audiences regard as "postmodern feminist" texts. If a writer did not share Psych et po's interest in semiotics and psychoanalysis, and if a writer was judged too "feminist" (too concerned about women's *actual* lot),[5] then that writer's work was usually rejected for publication. Although writers with different philosophical perspectives and political sensitivities than those of Psych et po are now finding other publishers to market their books, problems remain. The mere use of a single label (postmodern feminism) does not erase the differences among thinkers who find themselves tied together by an external perception that does not always do justice to the internal reality of who they think they are as individual theorists.

Nevertheless, even if it is misguided to make any substantive gener-alizations about postmodern feminists, it is not unhelpful to see the ways in which their writings are related to deconstructionist, psychoan-alytic, and existentialist streams of thought. One of our tasks, therefore, is to approximate the degree to which at least three postmodern feminists (Cixous, Irigaray, and Kristeva) have accepted and/or rejected aspects of Derridean, Lacanian, and de Beauvorian thought on their separate ways to writing something about women that has not been written before.

Postmodern Feminism and Existential Feminism

Many of the roots of postmodern feminism are found in the work of Simone de Beauvoir, who, we will recall, phrased the essential question of feminist theory as, Why is woman the *second sex*? Or, as the question may be rephrased in postmodern terms, Why is woman the Other? Why does woman remain earthbound, in immanence and determinism, as she watches man fly off into the realm of transcendence, the zone of freedom? De Beauvoir's answers may or may not have satisfied us, but no reader of *The Second Sex* can turn to its last page without concluding that to be "second," or "Other" is not the best way to be.

Postmodern feminists take de Beauvoir's understanding of Otherness and turn it on its head. Woman is still the Other, but rather than interpreting this condition as something to be transcended, postmodern feminists proclaim its advantages. The condition of Otherness enables women to stand back and criticize the norms, values, and practices that the dominant culture (patriarchy) seeks to impose on everyone, including those who live on its periphery—in this case, women. Thus, Otherness, for all of its associations with oppression and inferiority, is much more than an oppressed, inferior condition. Rather, it is a way of being, thinking, and speaking that allows for openness, plurality, diversity, and difference.

Postmodern Feminism and Deconstruction

Emphasis on the positive side of Otherness—of being excluded, shunned, "frozen out," disadvantaged, unprivileged, rejected, unwanted, abandoned, dislocated, marginalized—is a major theme in deconstruction. The deconstructist approach takes a critical attitude toward everything, including particular ideas or social injustices as well as the structures upon which they are based, the language in which they are thought, and the systems in which they are safeguarded. Deconstruction is antiessentialist not only in viewing the search for universal definitions as useless, but also in actively challenging the traditional boundaries between oppositions such as reason/emotion, beautiful/ugly, and self/other as well as between disciplines such as art, science, psychology, and biology.

So total is the antiessentialism of the deconstructionist, that he or she questions two of the assumptions that almost everyone holds: that there is an essential unity of self through time and space termed *self-identity* and that there is an essential relationship between language and reality termed *truth*. The notion of a unified, or integrated, self is challenged by reference to the idea that the self is fundamentally split between its conscious and unconscious dimensions. In turn, the notion of truth is challenged by reference to the idea that language and reality are variable and shifting, missing each other in a Heraclitean flux. Words do not stand for things, for pieces of reality. Rather, reality eludes language, and language refuses to be pinned down or limited by reality. Clearly, these ideas are philosophically unsettling.

The notion that there is neither self-identity nor truth—that the order within our lives and our language is an imposed, inessential structure—caught the attention of writers/theorists such as Cixous, Irigaray, and Kristeva. But it was not the only deconstructionist idea that interested them. Several deconstructionists, Jacques Lacan and Jacques Derrida in particular, have noted the ways in which our language excludes the "feminine" from it. Even though Lacan and Derrida have made a number of distressing statements about women's sexuality, their differing presentations of the excluded "feminine" have served postmodern feminism well.

Jacques Lacan

Building upon anthropologist Claude Lévi-Strauss's contention that every society is regulated by a series of interrelated signs, roles, and rituals, Lacan termed this series "the Symbolic Order."[6] For a child to function adequately within society, he or she must internalize the Symbolic Order through language; and the more a child submits to the linguistic rules of society, the more those rules will be inscribed in his or her unconscious. In other words, the Symbolic Order regulates society through the regulation of individuals; so long as individuals speak the language of the Symbolic Order—internalizing its gender roles and class roles—society will reproduce itself in fairly constant form.[7]

Given his emphasis on our unconscious acceptance and internalization of the Symbolic Order, it is not surprising that, for Lacan, the Symbolic Order *is* society, that system of relationships that antedates us and into which we must fit. Reinterpreting Sigmund Freud's theory to suit his own purposes, Lacan stated that the unconscious is structured like a language—specifically, that of the Symbolic Order. If we are to fit into this order, said Lacan, we must go through several stages, slowly submitting to the "Law of the Father."

In the first, or pre-Oedipal, phase—called the Imaginary phase, which is the antithesis of the Symbolic Order—a child is completely unaware of his own ego boundaries. He has no sense of where his body begins and that of his mother ends.[8]

In the second, or mirror, phase (also part of the Imaginary) the child recognizes himself as a self. Held in front of a mirror by an adult, the child initially confuses his image both with his real self and with the image of the adult holding him. Gradually the child figures out that the image in the mirror is not a real person but an image of himself. For

Lacan, the mirror stage is very significant, for it instructs us that the child must become two in order to become one. The self comes to see[9] itself as a real self only by first appearing to itself as a mirror image of its real self. Lacan believed that this initial process of self-constitution serves as a paradigm for all subsequent relations; the self is always finding itself through reflections in the Other.

The third, or Oedipal, phase follows a period of growing estrangement between mother and child. No longer does the child view himself and his mother as a unity; rather he regards his mother as the Other— someone to whom he must communicate his wishes and, therefore, someone who, due to the limitations of language, can never truly fulfill them. During the Oedipal phase proper, the already weakened mother-child relationship is broken by the intervention of the father.[10] Fearing symbolic castration (the loss of the phallic signifier for all that is gratifying), the child separates from his mother in return for a medium, language, through which he can maintain some connection with the mother—the original, never-to-be-had-again source of total gratification.[11]

Boys experience the process of splitting from the mother differently than girls do. In the Oedipal phase, the male child rejects identification with his mother, with the undifferentiated and silent state of the womb, and identifies instead with his anatomically similar father, who represents the Symbolic Order, the word. Through identification with his father, the male child not only enters into subjecthood and individuality but also internalizes the dominant order, the value-laden roles of society. In sum, the male child is born again—this time into language.

On account of their anatomy, girls cannot wholly identify with their fathers in the psychosexual drama. As a result, girls cannot fully accept and internalize the Symbolic Order. From this we can make one or two conclusions. On the one hand, we can conclude that women are *excluded* from the Symbolic Order, confined to its margins, left out in the cold, so to speak. This seemed to be Freud's point when he claimed that because girls do not undergo the castration complex in the same way that boys do, their moral sense is not as developed. On the other hand, we can conclude that women are *repressed* within the Symbolic Order, forced into it unwillingly. Because women are largely unable to internalize the "law of the fathers," this law must be imposed from the outside. Femininity is squelched, silenced, and straightjacketed because the only words that women are given are masculine words. The loss here is profound because the only language in which women can think and speak cannot in any way express what they feel.

Like Freud, Lacan had a hard time finding a place for women within his framework. Because females cannot completely resolve the Oedipal complex, the feminine does not and cannot exist within the Symbolic

Order.[12] Women are, for Lacan, permanent outsiders, which is a disturbing and, arguably, antifeminist assumption.[13] Lacan did speculate that were we to try to do the impossible—to know women—we would have to begin our inquiry at the level of feminine sexual pleasure (*jouissance*), which cannot be known because it cannot be expressed in the phallic language of the fathers. But, continued Lacan, so long as the Oedipus complex reigns (so long as individuals keep submitting to the authority of society), *jouissance* can only be glimpsed. Thus, feminine sexual pleasure, as that which experiences a totally repressed existence at the core of the Symbolic Order, exists at the level of potentiality. Were *jouissance* to be thought and spoken, the Symbolic Order would be shattered and splintered.

Jacques Derrida

In his attempt to free himself from the dreary singularity of thought in the Symbolic Order, Derrida found an alternative in the plurality and difference of the feminine. Although some postmodern feminists have criticized Derrida for mystifying and romanticizing woman from a decidedly male point of view, they have generally found his overall critique of the Symbolic Order useful for some of their own purposes.[14]

Derrida criticized three aspects of the Symbolic Order: (1) logocentrism, the primacy of the spoken word, which is less subject to interpretation than the written word; (2) phallocentrism, the primacy of the phallus, which connotes a unitary drive toward a single, ostensibly reachable goal; and (3) dualism, the manner in which everything is explained in terms of binary oppositions. Derrida traced these "isms" to traditional philosophy's search for meaning, a search he rejected as pointless because meaning does not exist. Language does not, said Derrida, provide us with the meanings or essences of objects, concepts, or persons somehow located outside of it. Rather language creates meaning, the only meaning to which it can refer. Because there is no being (presence) to be grasped, there is, continued Derrida, no nothingness (absence) with which to contrast it. Were we able to liberate thought from the binary opposition, being-nothingness, we would no longer be compelled to neatly oppose our thoughts, one against the other (male-female, nature-culture, speech-writing). Rather, we would find ourselves free to think new and different thoughts.

What Derrida wanted to do, then, was to liberate thinking from the assumption of singularity—that one single truth or essence, a "transcendental signified," exists, in and of itself, as a giver of meaning. Because the only language he had available was the logocentric, phallocentric, binary language that constricted his thought, Derrida was ultimately pessimistic about winning the revolution he was fomenting.

Nevertheless, he believed that the Symbolic Order can be resisted by showing how traditional interpretations of texts (for Derrida, anything communicated through language is a text) have suppressed alternative interpretations of them.[15] Derrida's use of *différance*—the inevitable, meaning-creative gap between the object of perception and our perception of it—has encouraged many postmodern feminists to make their own uses of this phenomenon. As we shall see, regardless of whatever differences of content and style distinguish postmodern feminists one from the other, in general they believe that woman, the Other, the feminine, has been left, unthematized and silent, in the gap that continually blocks union between language and reality. □

POSTMODERN FEMINISM: THREE PERSPECTIVES

If deconstructionists have anything in common, it is their critique of dominant, totalizing structures such as language and knowledge and their celebration of the Otherness that preoccupied Simone de Beauvoir in *The Second Sex*. Postmodern feminists similarly attempt to criticize the dominant order, particularly its patriarchal aspects, and to valorize the feminine, woman, the Other. Like Lacan and Derrida, postmodern feminists admit that it is extremely difficult to challenge the Symbolic Order when the only words available to do so are words that have been issued by this order. The danger, in other words, is that by insisting that all is plural, multiple, and different, postmodern feminists will, in effect, either assert a traditional metaphysical position or make a standard truth claim. It is this danger that prompts some postmodern feminists to reject any label that ends in "ism," including feminism. Labels, they fear, always carry with them the "phallologocentric drive to stabilize, organize and rationalize our conceptual universe."[16] Nonetheless, despite some of their own disclaimers, it is difficult not to classify as "feminist" Hélène Cixous and Julia Kristeva as well as Luce Irigaray, who has less qualms about the label "feminist."[17] The writings of all three are profoundly feminist in the sense that they offer to women the most fundamental liberation of all—freedom from oppressive *thought*. To be sure, what is largely at stake here is our understanding of the term *feminist;* but even if this is not the time to decide, once and for all, what feminism is, it is probably the time to consider the possibility that its meanings are ever changing.

Hélène Cixous

Hélène Cixous is primarily a novelist experimenting with literary style. In applying Derrida's notion of *différance* to writing, she contrasted feminine writing (*l'écriture féminine*) with masculine writing (*literatur*). Understood psychoanalytically, masculine writing is rooted in a man's genital and libidinal economy, which is emblemized by the phallus. For a variety of sociocultural reasons, masculine writing has reigned supreme over feminine writing. In the words of Ann Rosalind Jones, man (white, European, and ruling class) has claimed, "I am the unified, self-controlled center of the universe. The rest of the world, which I define as the Other, has meaning only in relation to me, as man/father, possessor of the phallus."[18]

Cixous has objected to masculine writing and thinking because they are cast in binary oppositions. Man has unnecessarily segmented reality by coupling concepts and terms in pairs of polar opposites, one of which is always privileged over the other. In her essay "Sorties," Cixous listed some of these dichotomous pairs:

> Activity/Passivity
> Sun/Moon
> Culture/Nature
> Day/Night
> Thought has always worked through opposition.
> Speaking/Writing
> Parole/Ecriture
> High/Low
> Through dual, hierarchical oppositions.[19]

In Cixous's view, all these dichotomies find their inspiration in the fundamental dichotomous couple, man/woman, in which man is associated with all that is active, cultural, light, high, or generally positive and woman with all that is passive, natural, dark, low, or generally negative. Moreover, the first term of man/woman is the term from which the second departs or deviates. Man is the self; woman is his Other. Thus, woman exists in man's world on his terms. She is either the Other for man, or she is unthought. After man is done thinking about woman, "what is left of her is unthinkable, unthought."[20]

Cixous challenged women to write themselves out of the world men have constructed from them by putting into words the unthinkable/unthought. The kind of writing that Cixous identified as woman's own—marking, scratching, scribbling, jotting down—connotes movements that bring to mind Heraclitus's ever-changing river. In contrast, the kind of writing Cixous associated with man comprises the bulk of the accumulated wisdom of humankind. Because these thoughts have been stamped with the official seal of approval, they are no longer permitted to move or change. Thus, for Cixous, feminine writing is not merely a new style of writing; it is "the very possibility of change, the space that can serve as a springboard for subversive thought, the precursory movement of a transformation of social and cultural standards."[21]

By developing a way of writing that is not limited by the rules that currently govern language, women will change the way the Western world thinks and writes and with it women's place in that world. But Cixous cautioned women that any attempt "to break up, to destroy" the Symbolic Order (language) is risky business. Trying to write the nonexistent into existence, "to foresee the unforeseeable," may, after all, be too much of a strain for women writers to sustain.[22]

In the process of further distinguishing woman's writing from man's, Cixous drew many connections between male sexuality and masculine writing on the one hand and female sexuality and feminine writing on the other. Male sexuality, which centers on what Cixous called the "big dick," is ultimately boring in its pointedness and singularity.[23] Like male sexuality, masculine writing, usually termed *phallocentric* writing by Cixous, is also ultimately boring. Men write the same old things with their "little pocket signifier"—the trio of penis/phallus/pen.[24] Fearing the multiplicity and chaos that exist outside their Symbolic Order, men always write in black ink, carefully containing their thoughts in a sharply defined and rigidly imposed structure.

In contrast, female sexuality is, for Cixous, anything but boring.

> Almost everything is yet to be written by women about femininity: about their sexuality, that is, its infinite and mobile complexity; about their eroticization, sudden turn-ons of a certain miniscule-immense area of their bodies; not about destiny, but about the adventure of such and such a drive, about trips, crossings, trudges, abrupt and gradual awakenings, discoveries of a zone at one time timorous and soon to be forthright.[25]

Like female sexuality, feminine writing is open and multiple, varied and rhythmic, full of pleasures and, perhaps more importantly, of possibilities. "Her writing can only keep going, without ever inscribing or discerning contours. . . . She lets the other language speak—the language of 1,000 tongues which knows neither enclosure nor death. . . . Her language does not contain, it carries; it does not hold back, it makes possible."[26] When a woman writes, said Cixous, she writes in "white ink,"[27] letting her words flow freely where she wishes them to go.

Running through Cixous's writing are an optimism and joy that are lacking in both Derrida, for whom logocentrism is inevitable, and in Lacan, for whom the phallus will always dominate. Cixous believes that we can escape the dichotomous conceptual order within which we have been enclosed and that women have the capacity to lead this revolt. If woman explores her body, "with its thousand and one thresholds of order," said Cixous, she "will make the old single-grooved mother tongue reverberate with more than one language."[28] The id, implied Cixous, is the source of *all* desires. "Oral drive, anal drive, vocal drive—all these drives are our strengths, and among them is the gestation drive—just like the desire to write: a desire to live self from within, a desire for the swollen body, for language, for blood."[29] For Cixous, desire, not reason, is the means to escape the limiting concepts of traditional Western thought.

Luce Irigaray

Although Luce Irigaray agrees with Cixous that feminine sexuality and the female body are sources of feminine writing, there are substantial differences between Cixous and Irigaray. Unlike Cixous, Irigaray is first and foremost a psychoanalyst seeking to liberate the feminine from male philosophical thought, including the thought of Derrida and Lacan.[30]

We will recall that, in Lacan, the Imaginary is the pre-Oedipal domain of prelinguistic, specular identifications in which the child mistakes itself for its own mirror image and then gradually comes to the realization that its image is not his or her real self. With this realization, the child enters the Symbolic Order prepared to assume the "I" in language— that is, to assert his or herself as a distinct subjectivity, separate from other subjectivities, or I's. Like Lacan, Irigaray is interested in the contrasts between the Imaginary and the Symbolic. However, her understanding of the Imaginary differs from that of Lacan in several ways, not the least being that, for Irigaray, there is a difference between a male imaginary and a female imaginary.[31]

For Lacan, the Imaginary is a kind of prison because the self is the captive of illusory images. After successfully completing the Oedipal phase, boys will be liberated from the Imaginary and enter the Symbolic Order—the realm of language and selfhood. Girls, however, because they never completely resolve the Oedipal phase, remain behind in the Imaginary. Rather than viewing this entrapment as sheer negativity, Irigaray suggested that there may be untapped possibilities for women in the Imaginary. What we know about the Imaginary and what we know about woman, including her sexual desire, has been told to us from a male point of view. The only woman we know is the "masculine feminine," the phallic feminine, woman as man sees her. Irigaray suggested that there may be another perspective both on the Imaginary and on woman, including her sexual desire. There may, Irigaray said, not only be a "feminine feminine," a nonphallic feminine, but also a way to bring woman to selfhood and language that does not have to be mediated in any way through men.[32]

The purpose of conceiving the "feminine feminine" is not, however, to define it. Any statement that definitively asserts what the real, or true, feminine *is,* said Irigaray, will recreate the "phallic" feminine: "To claim that the feminine can be expressed in the form of a concept is to allow oneself to be caught up again in a system of 'masculine' representations, in which women are trapped in a system or meaning which serves the auto-affection of the (masculine) subject."[33] What obstructs the progression of women's thoughts out of the Imaginary is the concept of Sameness, the ideational result of masculine narcissism and singularity.

Irigaray used the word *speculum* (a concave mirroring medical instrument often used in vaginal examinations) to capture the nature and function of the idea of Sameness in Western philosophy and psychoanalysis. "Specularization," commented Toril Moi, "suggests not only the mirror-image that comes from the visual penetration of the speculum inside the vagina," but also "the necessity of postulating a subject that is capable of *reflecting* on its own being."[34] Because of narcissistic philosophical "specularization"—which is epitomized in the medievals' description of God as thought thinking thought—masculine discourse has never been able to understand woman, or the feminine, as anything other than a reflection of man, or the masculine. Thus, it is impossible to think the "feminine feminine" within the structures of patriarchal thought. When men look at women, they see not women but reflections, or images and likenesses, of men.

In her study of Western philosophy and psychoanalysis, Irigaray found Sameness everywhere: in thinkers as various as Plato, René Descartes, G.W.F. Hegel, Friedrich Nietzsche, Sigmund Freud, and Jacques Lacan. Her analysis of Sameness in Freud's theory was particularly important because she used it to criticize his theory of female sexuality. Freud saw the little girl not as feminine in any positive sense but only in her negativity; as a "little man" without a penis. He suppressed the notion of difference, characterizing the feminine instead as a lack. Woman is a reflection of man, the Same as a man, except in her sexuality. Female sexuality, because it does not mirror the male's, is an absence, or lack, of the male's. Where woman does not reflect man, *she does not exist* and, suggested Irigaray, will never exist until the Oedipus complex is exploded and the "feminine feminine" released from its repression.[35]

In realizing that Western culture is loathe to abandon the Freudian, and, for that matter, Lacanian accounts of how the self—that is, the *male* self—is constituted, Irigaray suggested three strategies aimed at enabling woman to experience herself as something other than "waste" or "excess" in the little structured margins of a dominant ideology.[36] First, women need to pay attention to the nature of language. Although it concerns her that our words are so obviously "male," Irigaray is very much opposed to the idea of trying to create a gender-neutral voice. Not only is the search for "neutrality" pointless (because no one is really neutral about anything), it is also an excuse to use the passive voice, which distances subject from object and hides the identity of the speaker from the reader/listener. Stressing the fact that women will not find liberation in abstract personhood, Irigaray pointed out that "neither *I* nor *you,* nor *we* appears in the language of science."[37] Science forbids the "subjective," often because it wishes to mask the identities of its agents. The unwillingness of science—and, for that matter, traditional philosophy and psychoanalysis—to take responsibility for its own words and deeds profoundly distresses Irigaray. Thus, she urged women to join together in order to find the courage to speak in the active voice, avoiding at all costs the false security, and ultimate inauthenticity, of the passive voice.

The second strategy for liberation that Irigaray advocated is related to female sexuality. Like Cixous, she was much taken with the multiplicity that the female sexual organs imply. She suggested that multiplicity begins at the level of woman's anatomy. "So woman does not have a sex organ? She has at least two of them, but they are not identifiable as ones. Indeed, she has many more. Her sexuality always at least double, goes even further: it is plural."[38]

Irigaray did not simply contrast the plural, circular, and aimless vaginal/clitoral libidinal economy of women with the singular, linear, and teleological phallic libidinal economy of men; she also argued that the expression of these libidinal economies is not restricted to sexuality, but instead extends to all forms of human expression, including social structures. Patriarchy is thus the manifestation of masculine libidinal economy and will remain the order of the day until the repressed "feminine feminine" is set free. One way adult women can unshackle this potentiality—this power—is to engage in lesbian and autoerotic practice, for by virtue of exploring the multifaceted terrain of the female body, women will learn to speak words and think thoughts that will blow the phallus over.

The third strategy women can use in their battle against patriarchy, said Irigaray, is to mime the mimes men have imposed on women. If women exist only in men's eyes, as images, women should take those images and reflect them back to men in magnified proportions: "Through her acceptance of what is in any case an ineluctable mimicry, Irigaray doubles it back on itself, thus raising the parasitism to the second power. . . . Miming the miming imposed on woman, Irigaray's subtle specular move (her mimicry *mirrors* that of all women) intends to *undo* the effects of phallocentric discourse simply by *overdoing* them."[39]

To be sure, conceded Irigaray, mimicking is not without its perils. The distinction between mimicking the patriarchal definition of woman in order to subvert it and merely fulfilling this definition is not clear. In her attempts to overdo this definition, woman may be drawn back into it. Nevertheless, despite this risk, no woman should lose the opportunity to break out of the male imaginary and into a female one.

Throughout Irigaray's work, there is a tension between her conviction that we must finally end the process of labeling and categorizing and her competing conviction that we cannot help but to engage in this process.[40] Because Irigaray has dared to express both of these convictions, sometimes in the same breath, her critics describe her as self-contradictory. Rather than feeling embarrassed by the ambiguities and ambivalences in her writing, she delights in them. For Irigaray, self-contradiction is a form of rebellion against the logical consistency required by phallo-centrism.

> "She" is indefinitely other in herself. This is doubtless why she is said to be whimsical, incomprehensible, agitated, capricious . . . not to mention her language, in which "she" sets off in all directions leaving "him" unable to discern the coherence of any meaning. Hers are contradictory words, somewhat mad from the standpoint of reason, inaudible for whoever listens to them with ready-made grids, with a fully elaborated code in hand.[41]

In refusing to be pinned down even by her own theory, Irigaray not only resists dominant phallocentrism but also says something about a life whose multiple meanings can never be totally frozen or ossified by the phallocentric concepts that would squeeze its differences into an ultimately boring Sameness.

Julia Kristeva

Kristeva differs from Cixous and Irigaray in several respects. Whereas Cixous and Irigaray tend to identify the "feminine" with biological women, and the "masculine" with biological men, Kristeva resists any such identification. If a child has the choice, upon entry into the Symbolic Order, of identifying with either the mother or the father, and if the extent of the child's masculinity or femininity depends on the extent of this identification, then children of both sexes have the same choices open to them. Boys can identify with their mothers, and girls can identify with their fathers. Moreover, boys can exist and write in a "feminine" mode, and girls can exist and write in a "masculine" mode. To collapse language into biology—to insist that simply because of their anatomy, women write differently than men—is, says Kristeva, to force men and women, once again, into patriarchy's straightjacket. Many men—particularly those with an ambiguous relation between their biological sex and their linguistic self-expression—are capable of writing in a "feminine" style.

A second respect in which Kristeva differs from Cixous and Irigaray is in her radical adherence to the notion that, even *if* the feminine can be expressed, it must not be. "*Woman as such* does not exist," proclaimed Kristeva.[42] Such concepts as "woman" and "the feminine" are rooted in metaphysics, the essentialist philosophy that deconstruction seeks to deconstruct. Woman is a viable concept politically, but not philosophically. Kristeva clarified this position in an interview with Psych et po.

> The belief that "one is a woman" is almost as absurd and obscurantist as the belief that "one is a man." I say "almost" because there are still many goals which women can achieve: freedom of abortion and contraception, day-care centers for children, equality on the job, etc. Therefore, we must use "we are women" as an advertisement or slogan for our demands. On a deeper level, however, a woman cannot "be"; it is something which does not even belong in the order of *being*.[43]

The fact that woman cannot *be* on this deeper level—that she is always becoming and never being—allies her with other groups excluded from the dominant: homosexuals, Jews, racial and ethnic minorities, and other assorted "misfits." More than Cixous and Irigaray, Kristeva linked social revolution to poetic revolution, insisting that "the historical and political experiences of the twentieth century have demonstrated that one cannot be transformed without the other."[44] What preoccupied Kristeva is the idea that the scapegoating of certain groups—for example, the Jews during the German Third Reich—is grounded in the "abject," or an irrational sense of disgust traceable to the infant's pre-Oedipal experiences with its own body and that of its mother (excrement, blood, mucous). Originally, this repulsion is not a rejection of the "feminine." Because the infant is symbiotically attached to the mother, the infant has no sense of sexual difference. Only with the castration complex does this sense come and with it a linkage of the "feminine" with the "abject."[45] Thus, society's fundamental problem is with the abject, the "feminine" being but one specification of it.

Kristeva wanted society to come to terms with the abject (with what has been marginalized or repressed by culture). The marginalized discourses found in madness, the irrational, the maternal, and the sexual must release their revolutionary powers into language. Using Lacan's framework, Kristeva drew a contrast between the "semiotic," or pre-Oedipal stage, and the "Symbolic," or post-Oedipal stage.[46] As she saw it, phallologocentric thought is founded on a repression of the semiotic and therefore, of the sexually unidentified pre-Oedipal maternal body. This maternal *space* is characterized by a *time* very different from the time that characterizes the Symbolic Order. Whereas time in the semiotic is cyclical (repetitive) and monumental (eternal), time in the Symbolic Order is the time of history—linear or sequential time pointed toward a goal.[47] Thus, the kind of writing that is linear, rational, or objective and has normal syntax is repressed, whereas the kind of writing that emphasizes rhythm, sound, and color and that permits breaks in syntax and grammar is fundamentally unrepressed because it has room for whatever disgusts and/or horrifies us. Kristeva believed that a liberated person is someone able to acknowledge "the play of semiotic and Symbolic"—the continual vacillation between disorder and order.[48] □

CRITIQUE OF POSTMODERN FEMINISM

Readers of Cixous, Irigaray, and Kristeva sometimes complain that these postmodern feminists apparently delight in their opacity, viewing clarity as one of the seven deadly sins of the phallologocentric order. Admittedly, this complaint is not unjustified insofar as it is very difficult to distinguish between "phallocentrism" and "logocentrism," between difference and *différance,* between multiplicity and plurality, between the semiotic and the Symbolic. What may be unjustified, however, is the point to which this complaint often leads: namely, to the rejection of postmodern feminism as "feminism for academicians."

For some critics this rejection of postmodern feminism is based on a hasty and stereotypical dismissal of academicians as people who live in ivory towers separated from the real world; as "minds" who live in a realm of ideas devoid of bleeding, sweating, crying bodies. For other critics, however, this rejection of postmodern feminism is an expression of a desire not to engage in elitist thinking—that is, the kind of thinking that bars all but the privileged few from a discussion. These critics view postmodern feminists as contemporary Epicureans who withdraw from real revolutionary struggle—marches, campaigns, boycotts, protests—into a garden of intellectual delights. Surrounded by friends, by people who share their philosophical perspective, postmodern feminists "use language and ideas in such a specific way that no one else can understand what they are doing."[49] Rarely do they leave their blissful surroundings, and as time passes, what they have to say becomes increasingly irrelevant to the majority of women.

Other critics are not particularly disturbed by the opacity of postmodern feminist texts. What they are worried about is the content of these texts, particularly what strikes them as some sort of biological essentialism that preaches woman's salvation through woman's actual flesh-and-blood body. Although some of these criticisms may be accurate, many are the result of problems in translation. Most postmodern feminist texts maintain a distinction between "(1) women as biological and social entities and (2) the 'female,' 'feminine' or 'other,' where 'female' stands metaphorically for the genuinely other in a relation of *difference* (as in the system consciousness/unconsciousness) rather than opposition."[50] To be sure, this distinction is sometimes blurred, as in some of Cixous's writings, but, for the most part, these blurs take place in readers' minds.

Still other critics fault postmodern feminists for valorizing the female over the male, the feminine over the masculine. What is instructive about this critique is that it reminds us once again that postmodern feminists do not profess any common theory. In fact, Kristeva has criticized Irigaray and Cixous for trying to create a feminine language and female society outside masculine language and male society. As Kristeva saw it, any such move is dangerous because it breaks off communication between the semiotic and the Symbolic, a rupture that leads in one of two directions: fascistic patriarchy or fascistic matriarchy.[51] Whether Kristeva's critique of Irigaray and Cixous is warranted is not really the issue here. The issue is that, like many other feminists, postmodern feminists are struggling to discern the relationship between women's oppression and oppression in general. Should feminists work for woman's liberation or for all oppressed people's liberation? Should feminism be subsumed into humanism? Should women passionately and pridefully preserve all that is female, or should women work to go beyond the categories "man" and "woman" to a pluralistic society unconstructed by gender? The questions, and the challenges they pose, are not ones for postmodern feminists alone.

A final criticism that has been raised against postmodern feminism is that its philosophical assumptions will lead us toward chaos. As much delight as we may take in the postmodern feminist assault on unitary answers, it is not clear, say the critics, that we can sustain any sort of community, including feminist community, in the midst of total multiplicity, diversity, and profusion.

> The reality of a world that is provisional in meanings, where logic is denigrated as a mode of thought, where all interpretations are valid and values are upset but not replaced, would be impossible. Reminding us that the world we live in and the codes we live by are neither natural nor innocent is one thing . . . but can hardly provide us with a new world that can grow out of this one . . . [or with an imagining of] how new conceptual frameworks could be developed, how values and priorities decided and how boundaries set: for all these things must exist, if differently.[52]

The issue here is profoundly philosophical, political, and personal. Whether difference is a threat or an opportunity is probably a matter for each of us to decide. Postmodern feminists may have thematized "the Many" in particularly vivid ways. But the real world problem of creating community is as much ours as theirs. Difference will not disappear simply because postmodern feminists stop reminding us about it. □

CONCLUSION

Despite all the criticisms that have been raised against postmodern feminism, it is one of the most exciting developments in contemporary feminist thought. Although Cixous, Irigaray, and Kristeva have distinctively different agendas, they share certain tendencies such as an appreciation for the possibilities latent in nothingness, absence, the marginal, the peripheral, the repressed. Moreover, they share what seems a common desire to think nonbinary, nonoppositional thoughts, the kind that may have existed before Adam was given the power to name the animals; to determine the beginnings and ends of things: "And out of the ground the LORD God formed every beast of the field, and every fowl of the air; and brought *them* unto Adam to see what he would call them— and whatsoever Adam called every living creature, that was the name thereof."[53] We can imagine this original state prior to Adam's intrusion either as a Taoist undifferentiated "uncarved block,"[54] as a Lacanian Imaginary, as a Kristevan abject, or as any number of disordered conditions—the point being that there was, in the beginning, *no word,* but only myriad voices that could have been interpreted in any number of ways.

Whether women can, by breaking silence, by speaking and writing, help overcome binary opposition, phallocentrism, and logocentrism, I do not know. All that I do know is that we humans could do with a new conceptual start. In our desire to achieve unity, we have excluded, ostracized, and alienated so-called abnormal, deviant, and marginal people. As a result of this policy of exclusion, we have impoverished the human community. We have, it seems, very little to lose and much to gain by joining a variety of postmodern feminists in their celebration of multiplicity. For even if we cannot all be One, we can all be Many. There may yet be a way to achieve unity in diversity.

■

Conclusion:
Standpoints and Differences

THE PRIMARY PURPOSE OF THIS BOOK has simply been to highlight some of the main perspectives in feminist thought, yet readers may expect a conclusion that provides reasons for preferring one feminist perspective to another. I do not think that I can provide readers with these kinds of reason. I do know, however, that I am very much attracted both to the postmodern feminist description of where women currently are—at the margins and on the periphery—and to the socialist feminist description of where women could be—in the center. It is enormously appealing to be an outsider—to be uncorrupted by the system, to see and feel what other people do not see and feel, to be free of tight constraints and unnecessary restraints. But it is equally appealing to be an insider—to be a valued member of the team, to share a common vision, to have, as Aristotle said, "partners in virtue and friends in action."[1]

In rereading the concluding chapter of Alison Jaggar's book, *Feminist Politics and Human Nature,* I was once again persuaded that she has in fact shown that as a theory, socialist feminism is difficult to improve upon. It has all the desiderata of a theory: It is objective and neutral, and it has evidential and explanatory power.[2]

"Objectivity" and "neutrality" meant something different for Jaggar than they do for many theorists. Jaggar rejected both the traditional definition of objectivity, according to which the objective person makes a judgment based purely on the facts without any reference to values, and the traditional definition of impartiality, according to which the impartial person listens with equal dispassion to the arguments of Attila the Hun and Mother Teresa of Calcutta. As Jaggar saw it, truly objective and neutral persons are neither oblivious to values nor incapable of taking a stand. Rather, lacking a vested interest in the status quo, they are the kind of people who are able to understand the world clearly and to communicate that understanding honestly. With nothing either to lose or gain, truly objective and neutral persons simply speak their mind,

235

show their hand, and say it like it is. Among the people who share these abilities, said Jaggar, are socialist feminists: women who are able to see very clearly and to communicate very honestly precisely because the status quo has no real hold on their thoughts, words, and actions.

Because socialist feminists are objective and neutral, they make, in Jaggar's estimation, excellent scientists and philosophers. Although many socialist feminist arguments about women qua women are speculative and require actual investigation into the daily lives of real women, this investigation is, according to Jaggar, already under way. The initial results are promising. Jaggar pointed to several psychological, psychoanalytic, sociological, anthropological, and educational studies, each of which showed, specifically, that woman's way of knowing, of developing from childhood to adulthood, of reasoning through a moral problem, and of perceiving the world differs from that of man.

Encouraged by these findings, socialist feminists have used them successfully in their effort to provide a comprehensive, or nearly complete, account of women's oppression. More than any other feminist perspective, socialist feminism's fundamental attitude is synthetic—eager to explain each and every aspect of woman's oppression as a part of a large and systematic whole. As Jaggar saw it, traditional Marxist feminism glosses over patriarchy, whereas radical feminism glosses over capitalism. Likewise, psychoanalytic feminism pays too little attention to the construction of sexuality and gender within the psyche. Finally, existentialist feminism is able to show only why Marxist, radical, and psychoanalytic accounts do not satisfactorily explain women's Otherness. Socialist feminism, in contrast, refuses to stop until it has explained the nature and function of women's oppression in toto.

Paradoxically, the fact that socialist feminism comes so close to explaining women's oppression in toto and to providing women with a standpoint from which they can effect their liberation is a matter of concern for me. With postmodern feminists, I do wonder sometimes whether woman's standpoint may be yet another instantiation of the phallus or logos. As bad as it is for a woman to be bullied into submission by a patriarch's unitary truth, it is even worse for her to be judged not a real feminist by a matriarch's unitary truth. I know that I do not like to be accused of "false consciousness" or to be branded a "pseudo feminist," and I suspect that no feminist likes to be told that her explanation of women's oppression is benighted and befuddled.

So, here I am: stretched between the One and the Many, as if I had been reassigned to Philosophy 101, "Introduction to Philosophy." But even as I lie down on the rack, I realize that no one is waiting to torture me. My agonizing is largely of my own doing because socialist feminism—

at least the kind Jaggar advances—is not incompatible with postmodern feminism—at least the kind Kristeva advances.

What inspires me to a hope for a dynamic convergence between Anglo-American and Continental feminism is that Jaggar apparently agrees with Kristeva that "the time has perhaps come to emphasize the multiplicity of female expressions and preoccupations so that from the intersection of these differences there might arise, more precisely, less commercially, and more truthfully, the real fundamental difference between the two sexes."[3] This agenda is familiar to any feminist theorist who wants to discover/create a standpoint for woman but who does not want to collapse the differences among women into the "Universal Woman."[4] Of course, any such program of action will not get very far unless the differences among women are fully explored. Thus, there is a great need for women of color and working-class women as well as white and middle-class women to speak their own minds and to express their own feelings. Feminist theory is at its best when it reflects the lived experience of women, when it bridges the gap between mind and body, reason and emotion, thinking and feeling.

As I see it, attention to difference is precisely what will help women achieve unity. Audre Lorde, whose very person is a celebration of difference—Black, lesbian, feminist, disfigured by breast cancer—and whose poetry is a voice against the duality of mind/body, wrote that as we come to know, accept, and explore our feelings, they will "become sanctuaries and fortresses and spawning grounds for the most radical and daring of ideas—the house of difference so necessary to change and the conceptualization of any meaningful action."[5] Feelings lead to ideas and ideas lead to action, said Lorde.

There was a time when I viewed my white, middle-class, heterosexual self as a permanent obstacle or wall isolating me from women of color, from working-class and upper-class women, from lesbian women. But then I realized that difference does not necessarily mean ultimate separation. I think here of the kaleidoscope I used to play with as a child, and the delight I took in bringing together hundreds of chips of colored rock into a single beautiful pattern—only to break that pattern and bring together an even more beautiful one. As I grew older, I no longer played with my kaleidoscope. The ephemerality of its patterns increasingly distressed me as I learned about the good, the true, and the beautiful. But today I no longer view ephemerality as a problem because I am no longer in quest of the meaning of life. Rather, I understand that change and growth are necessary to life and that what makes feminist thought liberating is its vitality, its refusal to stop changing, to stop growing.

As I look back over the pages of this book, I take vicarious pleasure and pride in the different thoughts women have conceived in order to liberate themselves from oppression. To be sure, some of these thoughts have sent women stumbling down cul-de-sacs; but most of them have brought women at least a few steps closer to liberation. Because feminist thought is kaleidoscopic, the reader's preliminary impression may be one of chaos and confusion, of dissension and disagreement, of fragmentation and splintering. But a closer inspection will always reveal new visions, new structures, new relationships for personal and political life, all of which will be different tomorrow than today. What I most treasure about feminist thought, then, is that although it has a beginning, it has no end, and because it has no predetermined end, feminist thought permits each woman to think her own thoughts. Apparently, not the truth but the truths are setting women free.

■

Notes

INTRODUCTION

1. This is a common objection raised against feminist thought. See, for example, Catharine A. MacKinnon, "Feminism, Marxism, Method, and the State: An Agenda for Theory," *Signs: Journal of Women in Culture and Society* 7, no. 3 (Spring 1982): 528.

2. Mary Wollstonecraft, *A Vindication of the Rights of Woman,* Carol H. Poston, ed. (New York: W. W. Norton, 1975).

3. John Stuart Mill, "The Subjection of Women," in John Stuart Mill and Harriet Taylor Mill, *Essays on Sex Equality,* Alice S. Rossi, ed. (Chicago: University of Chicago Press, 1970), pp. 184–185.

4. Friedrich Engels, *The Origin of the Family, Private Property and the State* (New York: International Publishers, 1972), p. 103.

5. See George Gilder, *Sexual Suicide* (New York: Quadrangle Books, 1973); Lionel Tiger, *Men in Groups* (New York: Random House, 1969).

6. See Mary Vetterling-Braggin, ed., *"Feminity," "Masculinity," and "Androgyny"* (Totowa, N.J.: Rowman & Littlefield, 1982), p. 6.

7. Although radical feminists often locate the root cause of male power in men's biology—more precisely, in the penis as a natural instrument of aggression, mastery, and violence—radical feminists have not seriously proposed the elimination of this biological organ as an alternate way to eliminate women's oppression.

8. Shulamith Firestone, *The Dialectic of Sex* (New York: Bantam Books, 1970).

9. Mary O'Brien, *The Politics of Reproduction* (Boston: Routledge & Kegan Paul, 1981).

10. See, for example, Genea Corea, *The Mother Machine: Reproduction Technologies from Artificial Insemination to Artificial Wombs* (New York: Harper & Row, 1985).

11. Adrienne Rich, *Of Woman Born* (New York: W. W. Norton, 1976); Sara Ruddick, "Maternal Thinking," in *Mothering: Essays in Feminist Theory,* Joyce Trebilcot, ed. (Totowa, N.J.: Rowman & Allanheld, 1984).

12. Catharine MacKinnon elaborated upon the sex/gender system in MacKinnon, "Feminism, Marxism, Method, and the State," pp. 515–516.

13. At times, feminists, including some radical feminists who generally espouse a nurture theory, have conceded that perhaps men and women differ with respect to verbal ability, quantitative ability, creativity, cognitive style, spatial ability, and certain physical abilities. However, this concession has been less than wholesale because it is qualified with the point that effective socialization tends to minimize most of these differences. See Eleanor Emmons MacCoby and Carol Nagy Jacklin, *The Psychology of Sex Differences* (Stanford, Calif.: Stanford University Press, 1974).

14. Margaret Mead, *Sex and Temperament* (New York: William Morrow, 1935).

15. Ellen Willis, "The Conservatism of *Ms.*" in *Feminist Revolution*, Redstockings, ed. (New York: Random House, 1975), p. 170.

16. See, for example, Janice Raymond, *The Transsexual Empire* (Boston: Beacon Press, 1979), pp. 158–159.

17. Rosemarie Tong, *Women, Sex and the Law* (Totowa, N.J.: Rowman & Littlefield, 1984).

18. Mary Daly, *Gyn/Ecology: The Metaethics of Radical Feminism* (Boston: Beacon Press, 1978).

19. Charlotte Bunch, "Lesbians in Revolt," in *Women and Values*, Marilyn Pearsall, ed. (Belmont, Calif.: Wadsworth, 1986), pp. 128–132.

20. Carol S. Vance, ed., *Pleasure and Danger: Exploring Female Sexuality* (Boston: Routledge & Kegan Paul, 1984).

21. MacKinnon, "Feminism, Marxism, Method, and the State," p. 15.

22. Dorothy Dinnerstein, *The Mermaid and the Minotaur: Sexual Arrangements and Human Malaise* (New York: Harper Colophon Books, 1977), p. 161.

23. Juliet Mitchell, *Psychoanalysis and Feminism* (New York: Vintage Books, 1974), p. 415.

24. Sherry B. Ortner, "Oedipal Father, Mother's Brother, and the Penis: A Review of Juliet Mitchell's *Psychoanalysis and Feminism,*" *Feminist Studies* 2, nos. 2-3 (1975): 179.

25. Nancy Chodorow, *The Reproduction of Mothering* (Berkeley: University of California Press, 1978).

26. Simone de Beauvoir, *The Second Sex*, H. M. Parshley, trans. and ed. (New York: Vintage Books, 1974).

27. Juliet Mitchell, *Woman's Estate* (New York: Pantheon Books, 1971).

28. Juliet Mitchell, *Psychoanalysis and Feminism* (New York: Vintage Books, 1974), pp. 414–416.

29. Alison M. Jaggar, *Feminist Politics and Human Nature* (Totowa, N.J.: Rowman & Allanheld, 1983), pp. 316–317.

30. See Sandra Harding, *The Science Question in Feminism* (Ithaca, N.Y.: Cornell University Press, 1986); and Nancy C.M. Hartsock, "The Feminist Standpoint: Developing the Ground for a Specifically Feminist Historical Materialism," in *Feminism and Methodology*, Sandra Harding, ed. (Bloomington: Indiana University Press, 1987).

31. Harding, *The Science Question in Feminism*, p. 28.

CHAPTER ONE

1. Douglas MacLean and Claudia Mills, eds., *Liberalism Reconsidered* (Totowa, N.J.: Rowman & Allanheld, 1983).

2. Susan Wendell, "A (Qualified) Defense of Liberal Feminism," *Hypatia* 2, no. 2 (Summer 1987): 65–94.

3. Alison M. Jaggar, *Feminist Politics and Human Nature* (Totowa, N.J.: Rowman & Allanheld, 1983).

4. Ibid., p. 33.

5. Michael J. Sandel, ed., *Liberalism and Its Critics* (New York: New York University Press, 1984), p. 4. I owe this reference to Michael Weber, who also clarified for me the distinction between the "right" and the "good."

6. Jaggar, *Feminist Politics and Human Nature*, p. 31.

7. According to Carole Pateman, the private world is one "of particularism, of subjection, inequality, nature, emotion, love and partiality" (Carole Pateman, *The Problem of Political Obligation: A Critique of Liberal Theory* [Berkeley: University of California Press, 1979], p. 190).

8. According to Carole Pateman, the public world is one "of the individual, or universalism, of impartial rules and laws, of freedom, equality, rights, property, contract, self-interest, justice—and political obligation" (ibid., p. 198).

9. Michael Sandel employed this terminology in *Liberalism and Its Critics*, p. 4.

10. Wendell, "A (Qualified) Defense of Liberal Feminism," p. 66.

11. See Zillah Eisenstein, *The Radical Future of Liberal Feminism* (Boston: Northeastern University Press, 1986), p. 175. Eisenstein's critique of Friedan may have been unduly harsh, for some of Friedan's suggestions for political action in *The Second Stage* make considerable sense.

12. Wendell, "A (Qualified) Defense of Liberal Feminism," p. 90.

13. Eisenstein, *The Radical Future of Liberal Feminism*, pp. 96–99.

14. Mary Wollstonecraft, *A Vindication of the Rights of Woman*, Carol H. Poston, ed. (New York: W. W. Norton, 1975).

15. Ibid., p. 56.

16. Ibid., p. 23.

17. Jean-Jacques Rousseau, *Emile*, Allan Bloom, trans. (New York: Basic Books, 1979).

18. Recently, Allan Bloom advanced a contemporary argument in support of sexual dimorphism. See Allan Bloom, *The Closing of the American Mind* (New York: Simon & Schuster, 1987), pp. 97–137.

19. Wollstonecraft, *A Vindication of the Rights of Woman*, p. 61.

20. Ibid.

21. Ibid., p. 152.

22. Immanuel Kant, *Groundwork of the Metaphysic of Morals*, H. J. Paton, trans. (New York: Harper Torchbooks, 1958).

23. Jane Roland Martin, *Reclaiming a Conversation: The Ideal of the Educated Woman* (New Haven, Conn.: Yale University Press, 1985), p. 76.

24. Wollstonecraft, *A Vindication of the Rights of Woman*, p. 152.

25. Judith A. Sabrosky, *From Rationality to Liberation* (Westport, Conn.: Greenwood Press, 1979), p. 31.

26. Wollstonecraft, *A Vindication of the Rights of Woman*, p. 147.

27. Ironically, Wollstonecraft's personal life was driven by emotions. According to Zillah Eisenstein, "Within her private, personal life, she [Wollstonecraft] tried unsuccessfully to live the life of independence. She tried to commit suicide twice as a result of an intense and long love affair with Imlay, rejected the notion of marriage for herself until late in life, had a child out of wedlock by choice, supported her two sisters for most of their lives, and died in childbirth" (*The Radical Future of Liberal Feminism*, p. 106).

28. Wollstonecraft, *A Vindication of the Rights of Woman*, p. 34.

29. Kant, *Groundwork of the Metaphysic of Morals*, pp. 63–64, 79, 95–98.

30. Alice S. Rossi, "Sentiment and Intellect: The Story of John Stuart Mill and Harriet Taylor Mill," in John Stuart Mill and Harriet Taylor Mill, *Essays on Sex Equality*, Alice S. Rossi, ed. (Chicago: University of Chicago Press, 1970), p. 28.

31. John Stuart Mill and Harriet Taylor, "Early Essays on Marriage and Divorce," in ibid., pp. 75, 81, and 86.

32. Ibid., p. 75.

33. Harriet Taylor Mill, "Enfranchisement of Women," in ibid., p. 95.

34. Ibid., p. 104 (emphasis added).

35. Ibid., p. 105.

36. Mill and Taylor, "*Early Essays on Marriage and Divorce*," pp. 74–75.

37. Taylor Mill, "Enfranchisement of Women," p. 105.

38. Eisenstein, *The Radical Future of Liberal Feminism*, p. 131.

39. Richard Krouse, "Mill and Marx on Marriage, Divorce, and the Family," *Social Concept* 1, no. 2 (September 1983): 48.

40. John Stuart Mill, "The Subjection of Women," in *Essays on Sex Equality*, Rossi, ed., p. 221.

41. Susan Moller Okin, *Women in Western Political Thought* (Princeton, N.J.: Princeton University Press, 1979), pp. 197–232.

42. Wollstonecraft, *A Vindication of the Rights of Woman*, p. 77.

43. Mill, "The Subjection of Women," p. 186.

44. Ibid., p. 154.

45. Ibid., p. 213.

46. John Stuart Mill, "Periodical Literature 'Edinburgh Review,'" *Westminster Review* 1, no. 2 (April 1824): 526.

47. Wollstonecraft, *A Vindication of the Rights of Woman*, p. 39.

48. See Mill's description of Harriet Taylor in John Stuart Mill, *Autobiography* (London: Oxford University Press, 1924), pp. 156–160.

49. Mill, "The Subjection of Women," p. 177.

50. Betty Friedan, *The Feminine Mystique* (New York: Dell, 1974).

51. Eisenstein, *The Radical Future of Liberal Feminism*, p. 179.

52. Friedan, *The Feminine Mystique*, pp. 69–70.

53. Ibid., pp. 22–27.

54. Ibid., p. 380.

55. Ibid., p. 330.

56. Betty Friedan, *The Second Stage* (New York: Summit Books, 1981).

57. Ibid., p. 27.

58. Ibid., pp. 20–21.

59. Eisenstein, *The Radical Future of Liberal Feminism*, p. 190.

60. Ibid.

61. Friedan, *The Second Stage*, p. 112.

62. Ibid., p. 148.

63. According to Judith Stacey, Friedan believed that beta lifestyles—nontraditional models that emphasize "fluidity, flexibility and interpersonal sensitivity"—were overtaking alpha lifestyles—traditional Western male models that emphasize "hierarchical, authoritarian, strictly task-oriented leadership based on instrumental, technological rationality." See Judith Stacey, "The New Conservative Feminism," *Feminist Studies* 9, no. 3 (Fall 1983): 562.

64. For an analysis that supports that of Friedan, see Lenore J. Weitzman, *The Divorce Revolution: The Unexpected Social and Economic Consequences for Women and Children in America* (New York: Free Press, 1981).

65. Quoted in John Leo, "Are Women 'Male Clones'?" *Time*, August 18, 1986, p. 63.

66. Quoted in ibid., p. 64.

67. Betty Friedan, "How to Get the Women's Movement Moving Again," *New York Times Magazine*, November 3, 1985, p. 108.

68. Eisenstein, *The Radical Future of Liberal Feminism*, p. 176.

69. For a detailed discussion of the distinction between sex and gender, see Ethel Spector Person, "Sexuality as the Mainstay of Identity: Psychoanalytic Perspectives," *Signs: Journal of Women in Culture and Society* 5, no. 4 (Summer 1980): 606.

70. Cited in Hunter College Women's Studies Collective, *Women's Realities, Women's Choices: An Introduction to Women's Studies* (New York: Oxford University Press, 1983), p. 521.

71. Liberal feminists do not all agree that women and minority male candidates should be viewed as equally disadvantaged. The more *liberal* a liberal feminist is, the more likely she is to view gender and race/ethnic disadvantages as on a par. The more *feminist* a liberal feminist is, the more likely she is to focus her attention exclusively on women.

72. Jane English, "Sex Roles and Gender: Introduction," in *Feminism and Philosophy,* Mary Vetterling-Braggin, Frederick A. Elliston, and Jane English, eds. (Totowa, N.J.: Rowman & Littlefield, 1977), p. 39.

73. There is much debate about how factors such as race, class, and ethnicity affect the social construction of gender. See Carol Stack, *All Our Kin* (New York: Harper & Row, 1974).

74. By no means has the interest in androgyny been confined to liberal feminists. Radical feminists have also explored this notion, expressing, however, more reservations about it.

75. Carolyn G. Heilbrun, *Toward the Promise of Androgyny* (New York: Alfred A. Knopf, 1973), pp. x–xi.

76. Sandra L. Bem, "Probing the Promise of Androgyny," in *Beyond Sex-Role Stereotypes: Readings Toward a Psychology of Androgyny,* Alexandra G. Kaplan and Joan P. Bean, eds. (Boston: Little, Brown, 1976), p. 51ff.

77. Although not a liberal feminist, Joyce Trebilcot has forwarded an analysis of androgyny that liberal feminists have found useful. See Joyce Trebilcot, "Two Forms of Androgynism," in *"Femininity," "Masculinity," and "Androgyny,"* Mary Vetterling-Braggin, ed. (Totowa, N.J.: Rowman & Littlefield, 1982), pp. 161–170.

78. In her *Feminist Politics and Human Nature,* Alison Jaggar reminded us that gender neutrality can go to ridiculous extremes. In 1976, the Supreme Court ruled that exclusion of pregnancy-related disabilities from an employer's disability plan is no more sex discriminatory than is exclusion of diabetes-, hepatitis-, or bronchitis-related disabilities. The Court counted as irrelevant the fact that whereas diabetes, hepatitis, and bronchitis are diseases that befall both women and men, only women are subject to pregnancy-related disabilities (*General Electric Co.* v. *Gilbert et al.,* 1976 *United States Reports* 42, n, pp. 161–170). Jaggar commented that "the accidental biological fact of sex does have political relevance and, in so doing, it challenges the liberal feminist ideal of the 'sex-blind' androgynous society" (p. 47).

79. Jean Bethke Elshtain, *Meditations on Modern Political Thought: Masculine/Feminine Themes from Luther to Arendt* (New York: Praeger, 1986).

80. Jean Bethke Elshtain, "Feminism, Family and Community," *Dissent* 29 (Fall 1982): 442.

81. Jean Bethke Elshtain, *Public Man, Private Woman* (Princeton, N.J.: Princeton University Press, 1981), p. 252.

82. In the nineteenth century, many of the Suffragists waxed eloquently about women's moral superiority. See *History of Woman Suffrage,* Ida Husted Harper, ed. (New York: National American Woman Suffrage Association, 1922), vol. 5, p. 126. See, for example, the section on feminist ethics in *Women and Values,* Marilyn Pearsall, ed. (Belmont, Calif.: Wadsworth, 1986), pp. 266–364.

83. Elshtain, *Public Man, Private Woman,* p. 253.

84. Ibid., p. 243.

85. Ibid., p. 251.

86. Ibid., p. 336.

87. Ibid., p. 237.

88. Jaggar, *Feminist Politics and Human Nature*, p. 28.

89. For someone who disputes the contention that only members of the human species can be persons, see Peter Singer, *Practical Ethics* (New York: Cambridge University Press, 1979).

90. Jaggar, *Feminist Politics and Human Nature*, pp. 40–42.

91. Ibid., p. 41.

92. Naomi Scheman, "Individualism and the Objects of Psychology," in *Discovering Reality: Feminist Perspectives on Epistemology, Metaphysics, Methodology, and the Philosophy of Science,* Sandra Harding and Merrill B. Hintikka, eds. (Dordrecht, The Netherlands: D. Reidel, 1983), pp. 225–244.

93. Ibid., p. 232.

94. Mary Gibson, "Rationality," *Philosophy and Public Affairs* 6, no. 3 (Spring 1977): 193–225.

95. Susan Wendell recently argued that Jaggar was wrong to attribute to liberal feminism the same philosophical assumptions she attributes to liberalism in general. Wendell argued that liberal feminists are committed neither to separating the rational from the emotional nor to valuing the former over the latter. In Wendell's experience, liberal feminists are not dualists—metaphysical or normative—but are, rather, fully aware that reason/mind and emotion/body are integrated in all human personalities and activities and "equally necessary to human survival and the richness of human experience." She suggested that this awareness accounts for the liberal feminist position on gender roles. Because they are committed to a view that celebrates the *whole* human person, most liberal feminists are just as eager to see their sons develop their emotional repertoires and domestic skills as they are to see their daughters develop their rational capacities and professional talents. Complete human beings are *both* rational and emotional. Thus, Wendell urged all feminists to read liberal feminist texts sympathetically—that is, as "a philosophically better kind of liberalism" (Wendell, "A [Qualified] Defense of Liberal Feminism," p. 66).

96. Ellen Willis, "The Conservatism of *Ms.,*" in *Feminist Revolution*, Redstockings, ed. (New York: Random House, 1975), pp. 170–171.

97. According to Jean Grimshaw, one of these exceptions is Janet Radcliffe Richards. In *The Skeptical Feminist* (London: Routledge & Kegan Paul, 1980), Radcliffe Richards saw her task as extricating what she called "feminism" from nonessential commitments—commitments expressed in arguably "vague proposition(s)" such as the statement "that the structure of society really does work against women" (p. 99). Sexual discrimination at the workplace, argued Radcliffe Richards, does not consist in an abstract and amorphous structural conspiracy against women in general; rather it consists in concrete and identifiable actions such as that of Mr. John Doe's refusal to hire Ms. Jane Smith simply because she is a woman.

98. Willis, "The Conservatism of *Ms.,*" p. 170.

99. Wendell, "A (Qualified) Defense of Liberal Feminism," p. 86.

CHAPTER TWO

1. Richard Schmitt, *Introduction to Marx and Engels* (Boulder, Colo.: Westview Press, 1987), pp. 7–8.

2. Ibid., p. 14.

3. Karl Marx, *A Contribution to the Critique of Political Economy* (New York: International Publishers, 1972), pp. 20-21.

4. Nancy Holmstrom, "A Marxist Theory of Women's Nature," *Ethics* 94, no. 1 (April 1984): 464.

5. Robert L. Heilbroner, *Marxism: For and Against* (New York: W. W. Norton, 1980), p. 107.

6. Henry Burrows Acton, *What Marx Really Said* (London: MacDonald, 1967), p. 41.

7. Ernest Mandel, *An Introduction to Marxist Economic Theory* (New York: Pathfinder Press, 1970), p. 25.

8. Marx's discussion of surplus value and exploitation are found in his three-volume work *Capital*, particularly volumes one and two. For a more detailed introduction to these concepts, see Wallis Arthur Suchting, *Marx: An Introduction* (New York: New York University Press, 1983).

9. Schmitt, *Introduction to Marx and Engels*, pp. 96-97.

10. For an elaboration of these points, see Mandel, *An Introduction to Marxist Economic Theory.*

11. Karl Marx, *The 18th Brumaire of Louis Bonaparte* (New York: International Publishers, 1968), p. 608.

12. Here the term *class* is being used in a sense that falls short of the technical Marxist sense. As we shall see, it is very debatable that women form a true class.

13. Allen W. Wood, *Karl Marx* (London: Routledge & Kegan Paul, 1981), p. 8.

14. Heilbroner, *Marxism: For and Against*, p. 72.

15. Karl Marx, "Economic and Philosophic Manuscripts," in *Early Writings*, T. B. Bottomore, ed. (New York: McGraw-Hill, 1964), p. 122. I owe this reference as well as several good analyses of alienation to Michael Weber.

16. Ann Foreman, *Femininity as Alienation: Women and the Family in Marxism and Psychoanalysis* (London: Pluto Press, 1977), p. 65.

17. Ibid., pp. 101-102.

18. Quoted in David McLellan, *Karl Marx* (New York: Penguin Books, 1975), p. 33.

19. Karl Marx and Friedrich Engels, "The German Ideology," in *The Marx-Engels Reader*, Robert C. Tucker, ed. (New York: W. W. Norton, 1978), p. 199.

20. Schmitt, *Introduction to Marx and Engels*, p. 202.

21. Michèle Barrett, *Women's Oppression Today* (London: Verso, 1980), p. 9.

22. Friedrich Engels, *The Origin of the Family, Private Property and the State* (New York: International Publishers, 1972), p. 103.

23. Ibid.

24. Notions of hunting and gathering as popularized from anthropological work are often oversimplified. We should be aware, therefore, of the danger of attributing a rigid sexual division of labor to "hunting and gathering" societies, past and present. Women and children may contribute meat to the diet, just as men may contribute root or grain foods. Noticing Engels's dependence on stereotypical ideas of women's and men's work should lead readers to view Engels's account as less than accurate history. (I owe this reminder to Antje Haussen Lewis.)

25. Engels quoted approvingly the controversial thesis of a now largely discredited anthropologist that women in pairing societies wielded considerable political as well as economic power. "The women were the great power among the clans, [gentes], as everywhere else. They did not hesitate, when occasion required 'to knock off the

horns,' as it was technically called, from the head of a chief, and send him back to the ranks of the warriors" (*The Origin of the Family, Private Property and the State*, p. 113). Apparently, it did not strike Engels as odd that a powerful matriarch would let herself be forcibly seized as a wife by a man whose "horns" she could have had "knocked off."

26. Ibid.

27. Lise Vogel, *Marxism and the Oppression of Women: Towards a Unitary Theory* (New Brunswick, N.J.: Rutgers University Press, 1983), p. 82.

28. Engels, *The Origin of the Family, Private Property and the State*, p. 117.

29. Jane Flax asked *why* a group of matriarchs would have let men control the tribe's animals and/or use the fact of their control to gain power over women (Jane Flax, "Do Feminists Need Marxism?" in *Building Feminist Theory: Essays from "Quest," A Feminist Quarterly* [New York: Longman, 1981], p. 176).

30. Engels, *The Origin of the Family, Private Property and the State*, p. 117.

31. Karl Marx and Friedrich Engels, *The German Ideology* (New York: International Publishers, 1970), p. 51.

32. Engels, *The Origin of the Family, Private Property and the State*, pp. 118–119.

33. Ibid., p. 120.

34. Ibid., p. 121.

35. Ibid., p. 137.

36. Ibid., p. 128.

37. Ibid., pp. 137–139.

38. Ibid., p. 79.

39. Barrett, *Women's Oppression Today*, p. 49.

40. Engels, *The Origin of the Family, Private Property and the State*, p. 72.

41. Flax, "Do Feminists Need Marxism?" p. 176.

42. Marx and Engels, *The German Ideology*, p. 51.

43. Alison M. Jaggar, *Feminist Politics and Human Nature* (Totowa, N.J.: Rowman & Allanheld, 1983), p. 69.

44. Flax, "Do Feminists Need Marxism?" p. 176.

45. Heidi I. Hartmann, "The Family as the Locus of Gender, Class, and Political Struggle: The Example of Housework," *Signs: Journal of Women in Culture and Society* 6, no. 3 (1981): 371.

46. Engels, *The Origin of the Family, Private Property and the State*, pp. 71–72.

47. Hilda Scott, *Working Your Way to the Bottom* (London: Pandora Press, 1984), p. 142.

48. Ellen Malos, "Introduction," in *The Politics of Housework*, Ellen Malos, ed. (London: Allison & Busby, 1980), p. 17.

49. Ibid., p. 20.

50. Margaret Benston, "The Political Economy of Women's Liberation," *Monthly Review* 21, no. 4 (September 1969), p. 16.

51. Ibid., p. 21.

52. Mariarosa Dalla Costa and Selma James, "Women and the Subversion of the Community," in Mariarosa Dalla Costa and Selma James, *The Power of Women and the Subversion of Community* (Bristol, England: Falling Wall Press, 1972), p. 34.

53. In the final analysis, Dalla Costa and James viewed men as the dupes of capital rather than as the wily oppressors of women. Men, they said, appear to be the sole recipients of domestic services, but, in fact, "the figure of the boss is concealed behind that of the husband" (ibid., pp. 35–36).

54. Wendy Edmond and Suzie Fleming expressed the same conviction in even more forceful terms: "Housewives keep their families in the cheapest way; they nurse

the children under the worst circumstances and all the toiling of thousands of housewives enables the possessing classes to increase their riches, and to get the labour-power of men and children in the most profitable way" (Wendy Edmond and Suzie Fleming, "If Women Were Paid for All They Do," in *All Work and No Pay*, Wendy Edmond and Suzie Fleming, eds. [London: Power of Women Collective and Falling Wall Press, 1975], p. 8).

55. Ibid., p. 9.

56. In 1972, the Chase Manhattan Bank estimated that for her average 100-hour work week, the housewife should be paid $257.53. In that same year, white males in the work force had average incomes of $172 a week; white females had average incomes of $108 a week. See A. C. Scott, "The Value of Housework for Love or Money?" *Ms.* (June 1972): 56–58.

57. Unless a woman's salary is quite high, it may cost more for her to work outside the home than simply to work within the home. Many women report that their paycheck goes to child care expenses, commuter expenses, and new wardrobes. See Barbara Bergmann, *The Economic Emergence of Women* (New York: Basic Books, 1986), p. 212.

58. Carol Lopate, "Pay for Housework?" *Social Policy* 5, no. 3 (September-October 1974): 28.

59. Ibid., pp. 29–31.

60. Holmstrom, "'Women's Work,' the Family and Capitalism," *Science and Society* 45, no. 1 (Spring 1981): 208.

61. There is an argument to make against this assertion: namely, that work expands to fill time.

62. Johanna Brenner and Nancy Holmstrom, "Women's Self-Organization: Theory and Strategy," *Monthly Review* 34, no. 11 (April 1983): 40.

63. Johanna Brenner and Maria Ramas, "Rethinking Women's Oppression," *New Left Review* 144 (March-April 1984): 71.

64. Ibid., pp. 49–53.

65. Roslyn L. Feldberg, "Comparable Worth: Toward Theory and Practice in the United States," *Signs: Journal of Women in Culture and Society* 10, no. 2 (Winter 1984), 311–313.

66. "Paying Women What They're Worth," *QQ Report from the Center for Philosophy and Public Policy* 3, no. 2 (Spring 1983): 1.

67. Helen Remick, "Major Issues in *a Priori* Applications," in *Comparable Worth and Wage Discrimination: Technical Possibilities and Political Realities*, Helen Remick, ed. (Philadelphia: Temple University Press, 1984), p. 102.

68. Ibid., p. 103.

69. Jake Lamar, "A Worthy But Knotty Question," *Time*, February 6, 1984, p. 30.

70. Teresa Amott and Julie Matthaei, "Comparable Worth, Incomparable Pay," *Radical America* 18, no. 5 (September-October 1984): 25.

71. Ibid.

72. Ibid., pp. 26–27.

73. Paradoxically, Elshtain discovered precisely these sentiments in the work of Marxist feminist Sheila Rowbotham. See Sheila Rowbotham, *Woman's Consciousness, Man's World* (Baltimore, Md.: Penguin Books, 1973).

74. Jean Bethke Elshtain, *Public Man, Private Woman* (Princeton, N.J.: Princeton University Press, 1981), pp. 254–286.

75. Ibid.

76. Engels, *The Origin of the Family, Private Property, and the State*, p. 145.

77. Antje Haussen Lewis pointed out to me the "conservatism" of many Marxist feminists when it comes to the future of the family.

78. Jaggar, *Feminist Politics and Human Nature*, p. 221.

79. Engels, *The Origin of the Family, Private Property, and the State*, p. 63.

80. Alison Jaggar, "Prostitution," in *Women and Values*, Marilyn Pearsall, ed. (Belmont, Calif.: Wadsworth, 1986), p. 112.

81. Karl Marx, *Economic and Philosophical Manuscripts of 1844* (New York: International Publishers, 1964), p. 133.

82. In point of fact many of the men who use prostitutes are members of the working class. In fact, some Marxists argue that the more alienated and exploited a man is, the more likely he is to seek out the services of a prostitute.

83. Elshtain, *Public Man, Private Woman*, p. 265.

84. Roberta Hamilton, *The Liberation of Women: A Study of Patriarchy and Capitalism* (London: George Allen & Unwin, 1978), pp. 93–94.

85. Eli Zaretsky, "Socialism and Feminism I: Capitalism, the Family, and Personal Life, Part I," *Socialist Revolution* 3, nos. 1/2 (January-April 1973): 83.

86. Eli Zaretsky, "Socialism and Feminism III: Socialist Politics and the Family," *Socialist Revolution* 4, no. 1 (January-March 1974): 93.

87. Heidi Hartmann, "The Unhappy Marriage of Marxism and Feminism: Towards a More Progressive Union," in *Women and Revolution: A Discussion of the Unhappy Marriage of Marxism and Feminism*, Lydia Sargent, ed. (Boston: South End Press, 1981), p. 7.

88. Zaretsky, "Socialism and Feminism III," p. 87.

89. Hartmann, "The Unhappy Marriage of Marxism and Feminism," p. 6.

90. Brenner and Holmstrom, "Women's Self-Organization," p. 45.

91. Foreman, *Femininity as Alienation*, p. 36.

92. Brenner and Holmstrom, "Women's Self-Organization," p. 44.

CHAPTER THREE

1. Alison M. Jaggar and Paula S. Rothenberg, eds., *Feminist Frameworks* (New York: McGraw-Hill, 1984), p. 186.

2. Shulamith Firestone, *The Dialectic of Sex* (New York: Bantam Books, 1970), pp. 1–12.

3. Friedrich Engels, *Socialism: Utopian or Scientific*, quoted in ibid., p. 4.

4. Firestone, *The Dialectic of Sex*, p. 12.

5. Engels, *Socialism: Utopian or Scientific*, quoted in ibid., p. 4.

6. Because the claim that biology is the cause of women's oppression sounds similar to the claim that women's biology is their destiny, it is important to stress the difference between these two claims. Whereas conservatives believe that the constraints of nature exist necessarily, radical feminists insist that it is within women's power to overcome them.

For some conservative views, see George Gilder, *Sexual Suicide* (New York: Quadrangle Books, 1973); and Lionel Tiger, *Men in Groups* (New York: Random House, 1969).

For some feminist views, see Mary Vetterling-Braggin, ed., *"Femininity," "Masculinity," and "Androgyny"* (Totowa, N.J.: Rowman and Littlefield, 1982).

7. Firestone, *The Dialectic of Sex*, p. 12.

8. Alan Soble, *Pornography: Marxism, Feminism, and the Future of Sexuality* (New Haven, Conn.: Yale University Press, 1986), pp. 10–37.

9. Firestone, *The Dialectic of Sex*, p. 242.

10. Ibid., p. 1.

11. Ibid.

12. Ibid., pp. 198–199.

13. Marge Piercy, *Woman on the Edge of Time* (New York: Fawcett Crest Books, 1976).

14. Ibid., p. 102.

15. Ibid., pp. 105–106.

16. Ibid., p. 183.

17. I owe this last point to Antje Haussen Lewis.

18. Anne Donchin, "The Future of Mothering: Reproductive Technology and Feminist Theory," *Hypatia* 1, no. 2 (Fall 1986): 131.

19. Azizah al-Hibri, *Research in Philosophy and Technology*, Paul T. Durbin, ed. (London: JAL Press, 1984), vol. 7, p. 266.

20. Piercy, *Woman on the Edge of Time*, p. 105.

21. Mary O'Brien, *The Politics of Reproduction* (Boston: Routledge & Kegan Paul, 1981), p. 8.

22. Ibid., p. 29ff.

23. Ibid., pp. 35–36.

24. Ketchum observed that this may change if better tests for paternity are developed. Sara Ann Ketchum, "New Reproductive Technologies and the Definition of Parenthood: A Feminist Perspective" (unpublished paper, June 18, 1987), p. 52.

25. Ibid., pp. 54–55. I owe some of the interpretations of Ketchum in this paragraph to Nancy Gannon.

26. O'Brien, *The Politics of Reproduction*, pp. 58–60.

27. Adrienne Rich, *Of Woman Born* (New York: W. W. Norton, 1979), p. 11.

28. Rich cited the following Persian myth recorded by Frieda Fromm-Reichmann in "On the Denial of Woman's Sexual Pleasure": "There is a Persian myth of the creation of the World which precedes the biblical one. In that myth a woman creates the world, and she creates it by the act of natural creativity which is hers and which cannot be duplicated by men. She gives birth to a great number of sons. The sons, greatly puzzled by this act which they cannot duplicate, become frightened. They think 'Who can tell us, that if she can *give* life, she cannot also *take life*.' And so, because of their fear of this mysterious ability of women, and of its reversible possibility, they kill her" (ibid., p. 111).

29. Ibid., p. 112.

30. Ibid., pp. 38–39.

31. Firestone, *The Dialectic of Sex*, p. 199.

32. Andrea Dworkin, *Right-wing Women* (New York: Coward-McCann, 1983), pp. 174, 184.

33. Dworkin made the point that no one *misses* prostitutes. What she means is that people do not ask themselves what a prostitute could have been had she not been a prostitute (ibid., p. 179).

34. Dworkin, *Right-wing Women*, p. 184.

35. Ibid., p. 186.

36. Ibid., pp. 187–188.

37. Margaret Atwood, *The Handmaid's Tale* (New York: Fawcett Crest Books, 1985).

38. Although we are never certain, it seems that most citizens of Gilead are infertile because of environmental causes: toxic waste, air pollutants, nuclear fallout.

39. Atwood, *The Handmaid's Tale*, p. 164.

40. Genea Corea, *The Mother Machine: Reproduction Technologies from Artificial Insemination to Artificial Wombs* (New York: Harper & Row, 1985), pp. 107–119.

41. Genea Corea, "Egg Snatchers," in *Test-Tube Women: What Future for Motherhood?* Rita Arditti, Renate Duelli Klein, and Shelley Minden, eds. (London: Pandora Press, 1984), p. 45.

42. Robyn Rowland, "Reproductive Technologies: The Final Solution to the Woman Question," in ibid., pp. 365–366.

43. Ibid., p. 368.

44. Alison M. Jaggar, *Feminist Politics and Human Nature* (Totowa, N.J.: Rowman & Allanheld, 1983), p. 256.

45. Ann Oakley, *Woman's Work: The Housewife, Past and Present* (New York: Pantheon Books, 1974), p. 186.

46. Ibid., pp. 187, 199.

47. Ibid., p. 201.

48. Ibid., pp. 201–202.

49. Ibid., pp. 202–203.

50. Ibid., p. 203.

51. The claim that adopted children fare just as well as biological children is more controversial than Oakley believed. See, for example, Betty Reid Mendell, *Where Are the Children? A Close Analysis of Foster Care and Adoption* (Lexington, Mass.: Lexington Books, 1973).

52. The claim that any nurturant adult is as good a caretaker as a biological mother is more controversial than Oakley believed. See, for example, Alice S. Rossi, "A Biosocial Perspective on Parenting," *Daedalus* 106, no. 2 (Spring 1977): 1–32.

53. The kibbutzim have come under fire recently. See, for example, "The Pathogenic Commune," *Science News* 122, no. 76 (July 3, 1982): 76.

54. Firestone, *The Dialectic of Sex*, p. 229.

55. Ibid., pp. 228–230.

56. Rich, *Of Woman Born*, p. 174.

57. Ibid., p. 13.

58. Ibid., p. 57.

59. Ibid., p. 13.

60. I owe this point to Antje Haussen Lewis.

61. Rich, *Of Woman Born*, p. 57.

62. Ibid., pp. 31–32.

63. Jeffner Allen, "Motherhood: The Annihilation of Women," in *Woman and Values*, Marilyn Pearsall, ed. (Belmont, Calif.: Wadsworth, 1986), pp. 99–100.

64. Rich, *Of Woman Born*, pp. 211–212.

65. Because the term *surrogate mother* suggests that such a woman is not a *real* mother, but a substitute mother, many feminists prefer the term *contracted mother*.

66. Mary Ruth Mellown, "An Incomplete Picture: The Debate About Surrogate Motherhood," *Harvard Women's Law Journal* 8 (Spring 1985): 233.

67. Corea, *The Mother Machine*, p. 230.

68. Robert H. Miller, "Surrogate Parenting: An Infant Industry Presents Society with Legal, Ethical Questions," *Ob-Gyn Review* 18 (1983): 3.

69. Corea, *The Mother Machine*, p. 214.

70. Lee Flourney, a district attorney with the Berkshire County Office, Pittsfield, Massachusetts, recounted this case to me. The name of the defendant and some details of the case were altered.

71. Corea, *The Mother Machine*, p. 231.

72. Patricia A. Avery, "'Surrogate Mothers' Center of a New Storm," *U.S. News & World Report*, June 6, 1983, p. 76.

73. Corea, *The Mother Machine*, pp. 213–249.

74. "A Surrogate's Story of Loving and Losing," *U.S. News & World Report*, June 6, 1983, p. 77.

75. *Boston Globe*, October 2, 1987, p. 1.

76. The expression was favored by lawyer John A. Robertson, "Embryos, Families, and Procreative Liberty: The Legal Structure of the New Reproduction," *Southern California Law Review* 59, no. 5 (July 1986): 1001.

77. This statement would have to be adjusted for cases of so-called full surrogacy where the surrogate, or contracted, mother is gestating an embryo to which she is not genetically related.

78. Phyllis Chesler, *Sacred Bond: The Legacy of Baby M* (New York: Times Books, 1988).

79. *In the Matter of Baby M*, 525A.2d 1128 (New Jersey Superior Court 1987).

80. Elizabeth Kolbert, "New York State Senators Introduce Bill to Uphold Surrogate Contracts," *New York Times*, (February 4, 1987), p. B2.

81. Peter Singer and Deane Wells, *Making Babies: The New Science and Ethics of Conception* (New York: Charles Scribner's Sons, 1984), p. 111.

82. Barbara Katz Rothman, "Case Studies: When a Pregnant Woman Endangers Her Fetus—Commentary," *Hastings Center Report* 16 (February 1986): 25.

83. Claudino Escoffier-Lambiotte, "The Fetal Medicine Debate: The Controversy over 'Pre-Birth' Intervention," *World Press Review*, September 30, 1983, pp. 34–36.

84. Note, "Surrogate Motherhood: Contractual Issues and Remedies Under Legislative Proposals," *Washburn Law Journal* 23 (1983–1984): 622.

85. Note, "Rumpelstiltskin Revisited: The Inalienable Rights of Surrogate Mothers," *Harvard Law Review* 79 (1986): 1953–1954.

CHAPTER FOUR

1. Joan Cocks, "Wordless Emotions: Some Critical Reflections on Radical Feminism," *Politics and Society* 13, no. 1 (1984): 29.

2. Kate Millett, *Sexual Politics* (Garden City, N.Y.: Doubleday, 1970), p. 25.

3. Ibid., pp. 43–46.

4. Ibid., pp. 176–177.

5. Josephine Donovan, *Feminist Theory: The Intellectual Traditions of American Feminism* (New York: Frederick Ungar, 1985), p. 145.

6. Henry Miller, *Sexus* (New York: Grove Press, 1965), pp. 181–182.

7. Millett, *Sexual Politics*, p. 178.

8. Herbert Barry III, Margaret K. Bacon, and Irwin L. Child, "A Cross-Cultural Survey of Some Sex Differences in Socialization," in *Selected Studies in Marriage and the Family*, Robert F. Winch, Robert McGinnis, and Herbert R. Barringer, eds., 2nd ed. (New York: Holt, Rinehart and Winston, 1962), p. 267.

9. In the 1970s, Millett asserted that what society needs is a single standard of "sex freedom" for boys and girls, and a single standard of parental responsibility for fathers and mothers. Without such unitary standards for sexual and parental behavior, equality between men and women will remain ephemeral (Millett, *Sexual Politics*, p. 62).

10. Ibid.

11. Marilyn French, *Beyond Power: On Women, Men and Morals* (New York: Summit Books, 1985), p. 72.

12. To be sure, assuming that early humans lived in harmony with nature stands in contrast to "man-the-hunter" theories, according to which a social group values men more than women because men hunt for the meat that is supposedly necessary for the group's survival.

13. French, *Beyond Power*, pp. 25–66.

14. Ibid., p. 67.

15. Ibid., p. 69.

16. Susan Griffin, *Woman and Nature: The Roaring Inside Her* (New York: Harper & Row, 1978).

17. Ibid., p. 68.

18. Ibid., p. 443.

19. Joyce Trebilcot, "Conceiving Wisdom: Notes on the Logic of Feminism," *Sinister Wisdom* (Fall 1979): 46.

20. Alison M. Jaggar, *Feminist Politics and Human Nature* (Totowa, N.J.: Rowman and Allanheld, 1983), p. 252.

21. French, *Beyond Power*, pp. 495–500.

22. Ibid., pp. 487–488.

23. Dorothy Dinnerstein, *The Mermaid and the Minotaur: Sexual Arrangements and Human Malaise* (New York: Harper Colophon Books, 1977), p. 5.

24. French, *Beyond Power*, p. 538.

25. Ibid., p. 505.

26. I owe several of the thoughts in this paragraph to Antje Haussen Lewis, Elaine Freedman, and Michael Weber.

27. Mary Daly, *Beyond God the Father: Toward a Philosophy of Women's Liberation* (Boston: Beacon Press, 1973).

28. If we use French's terms here, we can say that immanent Be-ing infuses women with the power-to grow into their own image and likeness rather than be molded into the image and likeness of a transcendent God interested only in expressing his power-over others.

29. Alice Rossi, "Sex Equality: The Beginning of Ideology," in *Masculine/Feminine*, Betty Roszak and Theodore Roszak, eds. (New York: Harper & Row, 1969), pp. 173–186.

30. Daly, *Beyond God the Father*, p. 105.

31. Mary Daly, *Gyn/Ecology: The Metaethics of Radical Feminism* (Boston: Beacon Press, 1978), p. 59.

32. Ibid., pp. 107–312.

33. Ibid., p. xi.

34. Ibid., p. 68.

35. See Ann-Janine Morey-Gaines, "Metaphor and Radical Feminism: Some Cautionary Comments on Mary Daly's *Gyn/Ecology*," *Soundings* 65, no. 3 (Fall 1982): 347–348.

36. Daly, *Gyn/Ecology*, p. 334.

37. Ibid., p. 336.

38. Ibid., p. 337.

39. Friedrich Wilhelm Nietzsche, *On the Genealogy of Morals*, Walter Kaufmann and R. Hollingdale, trans. (New York: Vintage Books, 1969), p. 44.

40. This paragraph is the better for my conversations with Michael Weber.

41. Daly, *Gyn/Ecology*, pp. 14–15.

42. Mary Daly, *Pure Lust: Elemental Feminist Philosophy* (Boston: Beacon Press, 1984), p. 203.

43. Ibid., p. 2.

44. Ibid., pp. 2–3.

45. Ibid., p. 35.

46. I owe this last incantation to Antje Haussen Lewis.

47. Daly, *Pure Lust*, pp. 317–318.

48. Ibid., p. 204.

49. Betty Friedan, *The Feminine Mystique* (New York: Dell, 1974).

50. Daly, *Pure Lust*, p. 206.

51. Lal Coveney, Margaret Jackson, Sheila Jeffreys, Leslie Kay, and Pat Mahoney, eds., *The Sexuality Papers: Male Sexuality and the Social Control of Women* (London: Hutchinson, 1984), p. 9.

52. Catharine A. MacKinnon, "Feminism, Marxism, Method, and the State: An Agenda for Theory," *Signs: Journal of Women in Culture and Society* 7, no. 3 (Spring 1982): 533.

53. Ibid., p. 570.

54. Ibid., p. 533.

55. Carolyn M. Shafer and Marilyn Frye, "Rape and Respect," in *Women and Values*, Marilyn Pearsall, ed. (Belmont, Calif.: Wadsworth, 1986), p. 195.

56. MacKinnon, "Feminism, Marxism, Method, and the State," pp. 532–534.

57. According to the principle of legal moralism, a person's liberty may be restricted to protect other specific individuals, but especially society as a whole from immoral behavior, where the word *immoral* means neither "harmful" nor "offensive" but something like "against the rule of a higher authority" (God) or "against a societal taboo." For more about this principle, see Joel Feinberg, *Social Philosophy* (Englewood Cliffs, N.J.: Prentice-Hall, 1973), pp. 36–41.

58. According to the principle of legal paternalism, a person's liberty may be restricted to protect himself or herself from self-inflicted harm, or, in its extreme version, to guide that person, whether he or she likes it or not, toward his or her own good. For more about this principle, see ibid., pp. 45–52.

59. According to the harm principle, a person's liberty may be restricted to prevent physical or psychological injury to other specific individuals; likewise, a person's liberty may be restricted to prevent impairment or destruction of institutional practices and regulating systems that are in the public interest. For more about this principle, see ibid., pp. 25–31.

60. According to the offense principle, a person's liberty may be restricted to prevent offense to other specific individuals, where "offense" is interpreted as behavior that causes feelings of embarrassment, shame, outrage, or disgust in those against whom it is directed. For more about this principle, see ibid., pp. 41–45.

61. Rosemarie Tong, "Feminism, Pornography, and Censorship," *Social Theory and Practice* 8, no. 1 (Spring 1982), 1–17.

62. Laura Lederer, ed., *Take Back the Night: Women on Pornography* (New York: William Morrow, 1980).

63. U.S. Commission on Obscenity and Pornography, *Report of the Commission on Obscenity and Pornography* (Washington, D.C.: U.S. Government Printing Office, 1970), p. 27.

64. Aric Press and Ann McDaniel, "Hard-Core Proposals," *Newsweek*, April 28, 1986, p. 39, citing the Attorney General's Commission on Pornography's preliminary report.

65. Donald Mosher, "Sex Differences, Sex Guilt, and Explicitly Sexual Films," *The Journal of Social Issues* 29, no. 3 (March 1973): 95–112.

66. See Sarah J. McCarthy, "Pornography, Rape, and the Cult of Macho," *The Humanist* 40, no. 5 (September-October 1980): 19.

67. E. Donnerstein and L. Berkowitz, "Victim Reactions in Aggressive-Erotic Films as a Factor in Violence Against Women," *Journal of Personality and Social Psychology* 41 (1981): 410–424.

68. Deirdre English, "The Politics of Porn: Can Feminists Walk the Line?" *Mother Jones* (April 1980): 44.

69. David Reisman, "Democracy and Defamations: Control of Group Libel," *Columbia Law Review* 42 (May 1942): 770.

70. Catharine A. MacKinnon, "Francis Biddle's Sister: Pornography, Civil Rights, and Speech," in Catharine A. MacKinnon, *Feminism Unmodified: Disclosures on Life and Law* (Cambridge, Mass.: Harvard University Press, 1987), p. 176.

71. Appendix I, Minneapolis, Minn., Code of Ordinances, Title 7, Ch. 139, 1 amending 39.10.

72. Stuart Taylor, Jr., "Pornography Foes Lose New Weapon in Supreme Court," *New York Times*, February 25, 1986, p. 1.

73. Nan D. Hunter and Sylvia A. Law, Brief Amici Curiae of Feminist Anti-Censorship Task Force et al. to U.S. Court of Appeals for the Seventh Circuit, *American Booksellers Association, Inc. et al.* v. *William H. Hudnut III et al.* (April 18, 1985): 9–18.

74. Ibid., p. 11.

75. Catharine A. MacKinnon, "On Collaboration," in MacKinnon, *Feminism Unmodified*, pp. 198–205.

76. Daniel Linz, Charles W. Turner, Bradford W. Hesse, and Steven D. Penrod, "Bases of Liability for Injuries Produced by Media Portrayals of Violent Pornography," in *Pornography and Sexual Aggression*, Neil M. Malamuth and Edward Donnerstein, eds. (New York: Academic Press, 1984), pp. 277–282.

77. Catharine A. MacKinnon, "Pornography, Civil Rights, and Speech," *Harvard Civil Rights-Civil Liberties Law Review* 20, no. 1 (1985): 39–41.

78. *New York* v. *Ferber*, 458 U.S. 747 (1982).

79. Catharine A. MacKinnon, "The Art of the Impossible," in MacKinnon, *Feminism Unmodified*, pp. 10–14.

80. Quoted in Appendix I, Minneapolis, Minn., Code of Ordinances, Title 7, Ch. 139, 139.10 adding (m) *Coercion into Pornographic Performances*.

81. Appendix I, Minneapolis, Minn., Code of Ordinances, Title 7, Ch. 139, 139.10 adding (l) *Discrimination by Trafficking in Pornography*.

82. MacKinnon, "Francis Biddle's Sister," pp. 191–195.

83. There is another way to interpret MacKinnon and Dworkin's claim about the centrality of pornography—an interpretation that strengthens their claim. If, for example, pornography does not refer simply to the women-hating depictions that litter books, magazines, and films, but rather to the way in which male-female relationships have been constructed under the institution of compulsory heterosexuality—an institution that, according to radical feminists, forces women to live not for themselves but exclusively for the emotional gratification and sexual satisfaction of men—then pornography may indeed be the sine qua non of women's oppression.

84. Ibid., p. 533.

85. Samois is probably the largest and most vocal lesbian S&M organization. It gained visibility through its publication *What Color Is Your Handkerchief? A Lesbian S/M Sexuality Reader*, Samois, ed. (Berkeley, Calif.: Samois, 1979).

86. Bat-Ami Bar On, "Feminism and Sadomasochism: Self-Critical Notes," in *Against Sadomasochism: A Radical Feminist Analysis*, Robin Ruth Linden, Darlene R. Pagano, Diana E.H. Russell, and Susan Leigh Star, eds. (East Palo Alto, Calif.: Frog in the Well, 1982), p. 74.

87. In a public letter, Marissa Javel, for instance, explained that for her and many other lesbians, S&M is a learning, not a cathartic, experience. See Marissa Javel, "Letter from a Former Masochist," in ibid., pp. 16–22.

88. Audre Lorde and Susan Leigh Star, "Interview with Audre Lorde," in ibid., p. 69.

89. Hilde Hein, "Sadomasochism and the Liberal Tradition," in ibid., p. 87.

90. Carol Vance, ed., *Pleasure and Danger: Exploring Female Sexuality* (Boston: Routledge & Kegan Paul, 1984).

91. Gayle Rubin, "Thinking Sex: Notes for a Radical Theory of the Politics of Sexuality," in ibid., pp. 267–319.

92. Charlotte Bunch, "Lesbians in Revolt," in *Women and Values*, Marilyn Pearsall, ed. (Belmont, Calif.: Wadsworth, 1986), p. 131.

93. Ibid., p. 129.

94. Ibid., p. 130.

95. I owe this last point to Antje Haussen Lewis.

96. Gerre Goodman, George Lakey, Judy Lashof, and Erika Thorne, *No Turning Back: Lesbian and Gay Liberation for the '80s* (Philadelphia: New Society Publishers, 1983), pp. 73–74.

97. Marilyn Frye, "Some Reflections on Separatism and Power," in *The Politics of Reality* (Trumansburg, N.Y.: The Crossing Press, 1983), p. 96.

98. Ibid., p. 103.

99. Jill Johnston, *Lesbian Nation: The Feminist Solution* (New York: Simon & Schuster, 1974), p. 149.

100. Adrienne Rich, "It Is the Lesbian in Us . . . , " in Adrienne Rich, *On Lies, Secrets, and Silence: Selected Prose, 1966–1978* (New York: W. W. Norton, 1979), p. 201.

101. Adrienne Rich, "Compulsory Heterosexuality and Lesbian Existence," *Signs: Journal of Women in Culture and Society* 5, no. 4 (Summer 1980): 648–649.

102. Daly, *Pure Lust*, p. 366.

103. Ibid., pp. 371–372.

104. Daly, *Gyn/Ecology*, p. 381.

105. Goodman et al., *No Turning Back*, p. 83.

106. Ibid.

107. Jaggar, *Feminist Politics and Human Nature*, p. 109.

108. I owe this last point to Elaine Freedman.

109. M. Z. Rosaldo, "The Use and Abuse of Anthropology: Reflections on Feminism and Cross-Cultural Understanding," *Signs: Journal of Women in Culture and Society* 5, no. 3 (1980): 394.

110. Jaggar, *Feminist Politics and Human Nature*, p. 286.

111. Bunch, "Lesbians in Revolt," p. 233.

112. Cocks, "Wordless Emotions," p. 33.

113. Ibid., pp. 33–34.

114. Ibid., p. 35.

115. What Cocks was arguing here is very debatable. For another point of view, see Genevieve Lloyd, *The Man of Reason: "Male" and "Female" in Western Philosophy* (Minneapolis: University of Minnesota Press, 1984).

116. Cocks, "Wordless Emotions," p. 38.

117. Ibid., p. 44.

118. Ibid., pp. 44, 50.

119. Ibid., p. 48.

120. Ibid.

121. I owe this "eternal feminist question" to Antje Haussen Lewis.

122. Ti-Grace Atkinson, "Radical Feminism: A Declaration of War," in *Women and Values*, Marilyn Pearsall, ed. (Belmont, Calif.: Wadsworth, 1986), p. 125.

123. Susan Brownmiller, *Against Our Will: Men, Women and Rape* (New York: Simon & Schuster, 1975), pp. 14–15.

124. Mary R. Beard, *Woman as Force in History* (New York: Collier Books, 1972).

125. Sheila Rowbotham, *Women, Resistance and Revolution* (New York: Vintage Books, 1972).

126. Jean Bethke Elshtain, *Public Man, Private Woman* (Princeton, N.J.: Princeton University Press, 1981), p. 228.

127. Ibid., p. 213.

128. Audre Lorde, "An Open Letter to Mary Daly," in *This Bridge Called My Back*, Cherríe Moraga and Gloria Anzaldúa, eds. (Watertown, Mass.: Persephone Press, 1981), pp. 94–97.

129. Elshtain, *Public Man, Private Woman*, p. 226.

130. Ibid., p. 225.

CHAPTER FIVE

1. Juanita H. Williams, *Psychology of Women* (New York: W. W. Norton, 1977), p. 27.

2. Sigmund Freud, *Sexuality and the Psychology of Love* (New York: Collier Books, 1968).

3. I owe this point to Michael Weber.

4. Sigmund Freud, "Some Psychical Consequences of the Anatomical Distinction Between the Sexes," in Freud, *Sexuality and the Psychology of Love*, p. 192.

5. Ibid., pp. 187–188.

6. Sigmund Freud, "Femininity," in Sigmund Freud, *The Complete Introductory Lectures on Psychoanalysis*, James Strachey, trans. and ed. (New York: W. W. Norton, 1966), p. 542.

7. Ibid., pp. 593–594.

8. Many students of Freud have noted that some of Freud's arguments run counter to the case for a shift in female erotogenic zones. Freud noted that male and female sexual organs develop out of the same embryonic structures and that vestiges of the male reproductive structures are found in the female and vice versa. Thus, human anatomy is bisexual. Moreover, Freud commented that although "femininity" is ordinarily associated with "passivity," and "masculinity" with "activity," this association is misleading because women can be active, and men passive, in some directions. It is more precise to say that although feminine persons prefer passive aims, and masculine persons active aims, considerable activity is required to achieve any aim whatsoever. When it comes to a sexual aim—switching one's erotogenic zone from the clitoris to the vagina, for example—it takes incredible sexual energy or activity (libido) to accomplish the transition. See ibid., p. 580.

9. Ibid., p. 596.

10. Sigmund Freud, "Some Psychical Consequences of the Anatomical Distinction Between the Sexes," p. 191.

11. Ibid., p. 193.

12. Sigmund Freud, "The Passing of the Oedipus Complex," in Freud, *Sexuality and the Psychology of Love*, p. 181.

13. Betty Friedan, *The Feminine Mystique* (New York: Dell, 1974), pp. 93-94.

14. Ibid., p. 95.

15. Shulamith Firestone, *The Dialectic of Sex* (New York: Bantam Books, 1970), pp. 48-49.

16. Ibid., p. 69.

17. Ibid., pp. 68-69.

18. Ibid., p. 47.

19. Viola Klein, *The Feminine Character* (London: Routledge & Kegan Paul, 1971), p. 77.

20. Kate Millett, *Sexual Politics* (Garden City, N.Y.: Doubleday, 1970) p. 109.

21. Ibid., p. 185.

22. Sigmund Freud, *Dora: An Analysis of a Case of Hysteria*, Philip Rieff, ed. (New York: Collier Books, 1963), p. 142.

23. Ibid., p. 50.

24. Helene Deutsch, *The Psychology of Women: A Psychoanalytic Interpretation* (New York: Grune & Stratton, 1944), vol. 1, p. 327. For Deutsch, the feminine character has three components: passivity, masochism, and narcissism. Passivity is central and is modeled on women's role in sexual intercourse and on their "attitude of receptive waiting and expectancy." This passivity is closely linked with women's masochism, which Deutsch defined not as the enjoyment of pain but as an attraction to experiences, such as sexual intercourse and childbirth, that mix pain and pleasure. Both of these characteristics are contrasted with narcissism, which in women can exceed its own bounds and thereby become an immature and unhealthy (but not unfeminine) demand for attention in order to make up for feelings of insecurity and inferiority.

The normal woman, then, is stretched atop a tightrope, balancing her passive, masochistic existence for others with her narcissistic concern for herself. If she is too assertive, too aggressive, or too intellectual, she must be resisting her feminine role, and Deutsch claimed that this is harmful and unnatural, creating "inner conflict." Should a woman lose her balance by erring in the direction of narcissism, she will be plunged into another abyss of abnormality.

Deutsch claimed that the best way for the normal woman to maintain her feminine balance is to weigh herself down with a biological child who will discipline her selfish desires. For Deutsch, women's sexuality is "continuous with its natural consequences, pregnancy and childbirth," and any demand for recreational sex will compromise the procreative function of women's biology. Deutsch's notion was thus based on the idea that women are made, always and essentially, to be mothers, and, therefore, the normal woman orients herself and her sexuality toward men and procreation. The normal woman is feminine, and she is a mother—and she is happy and healthy that way.

For more on Deutsch, see Williams, *Psychology of Women*, pp. 36-49.

25. Erik Erikson, "The Inner and the Outer Space: Reflections on Womanhood," *Daedalus* 93, no. 2 (1964): 582-606. For Erik Erikson, not the psychology of women in particular but the ego formation of everyone in general is of central concern. Although Erikson paid close attention to the way in which environment shapes our biology, his emphasis on nurture failed to disabuse him of the idea that there are innate psychological differences between men and women that originate in the "ground-plan of the body." In a study of children's play constructions, he found that girls created stable interior scenes with an occasional male intruder, whereas boys created

towers and buildings decorated with protrusions and subject to destruction. Erikson believed that these differences in spatial organization were analogous to the differences in male and female anatomies and that because of their biology, women are concerned with inner space and with procreation. Pregnancy, then, means fulfillment, whereas childlessness means emptiness and despair. In Erikson's eyes, because the penis is so apparently present, the vagina and womb must by contrast be absent, representing some essential lack in women. In light of his discussion of inner and outer space, Erikson's protestations that social training matters tremendously, and that he does not mean to "doom" every woman to "perpetual motherhood," fade considerably. In the final analysis, Erikson, like Deutsch, thought that women are unable to escape their female biological destiny, "since woman is never not-a-woman."

For more on Erik Erikson, see Williams, *Psychology of Women*, pp. 48–62.

26. Alfred Adler, *Understanding Human Nature* (New York: Greenberg, 1927).

27. Ibid., p. 123.

28. Karen Horney, "The Flight from Womanhood," in Karen Horney, *Feminine Psychology* (New York: W. W. Norton, 1973), pp. 54–70.

29. Recently, there has been much debate among feminists in regard to the theories of Karen Horney. In the past, feminists have felt that she began her examination of woman within the structure of Freudian theories of the superior moral character of man and that as her theories progressed, she moved to an examination of the character of the "whole person" rather than to a focus on women. However, recent analyses have penetrated deeper into Horney's ideas and have shown them to have some very positive contributions to feminism. Very simply, Horney's theory of character development revolves around the idea that there is a deep, true self within everyone. To allow that inner self free expression involves a resolution between three different pulls in character formation, which she calls the self-effacing, the expansive, and the resigned. When this triangle is not balanced, when too much weight is given to one need and not enough to the others, then the inner self is covered up and muffled by false, neurotic, or idealized conceptions of self. However, if a balance is achieved among the three, the inner self is allowed to be expressed. Many feminists now see that this kind of inner liberation from unnatural, unhealthy pulls of any one of the three characteristics is a necessary step to any kind of further, external liberation for women within a society. See Susan Rudnick Jacobsohn, "An Ambiguous Legacy," *Women's Review of Books* 5, no. 4 (January 1988): 22.

30. Clara Thompson, "Problems of Womanhood," in *Interpersonal Psychoanalysis: The Selected Papers of Clara Thompson*, M. P. Green, ed. (New York: Basic Books, 1964).

31. For a more complete discussion of Adler, Horney, and Thompson, see Williams, *Psychology of Women*, pp. 65–73.

32. Dorothy Dinnerstein, *The Mermaid and the Minotaur: Sexual Arrangements and Human Malaise* (New York: Harper Colophon Books, 1977), p. 5.

33. Ibid., pp. 40–54.

34. Ibid., pp. 59–66.

35. Ibid., p. 66.

36. Given that a man cannot enter a symbiotic relationship with a woman without reinvoking painful memories of his total helplessness before the infinite power of the mother, Dinnerstein theorized that he will use his power to fulfill his basic needs for security, love, and self-esteem. This bid for omnipotence extends to control over both nature and women, two forces that must be kept in check lest their presumably uncontrollable powers be unleashed. In contrast to a man, a woman can safely seek symbiosis with a man as a means to attain the ends of security, love, and self-esteem.

She can do this because, for her, symbiosis with a man does not conjure up the specter of the omnipotent mother. However, the *idea* of herself being/becoming an omnipotent mother does terrify her; and this specter may explain woman's discomfort with female power (ibid., p. 61).

37. Ibid., pp. 124–134.

38. Nancy Chodorow, *The Reproduction of Mothering* (Berkeley: University of California Press, 1978), p. 32.

39. Ibid., p. 107.

40. Ibid., p. 126.

41. Ibid., p. 200.

42. Ibid., pp. 135, 187.

43. Ibid., p. 218.

44. Michael Weber was very helpful in formulating this paragraph.

45. Judith Lorber, "On *The Reproduction of Mothering:* A Methodological Debate," *Signs: Journal of Women in Culture and Society* 6, no. 3 (Spring 1981): 482–486.

46. After a while, this whole debate becomes very frustrating. In Chodorow's defense, it must be pointed out that she espoused less of a one-way causality thesis (family->society) and more of an interactive thesis (family<->society) than many of her critics admitted.

47. Jean Bethke Elshtain, *Public Man, Private Woman* (Princeton, N.J.: Princeton University Press, 1981), p. 288.

48. Ibid., p. 290.

49. Alice Rossi, "On *The Reproduction of Mothering:* A Methodological Debate," *Signs: Journal of Women in Culture and Society* 6, no. 3 (Spring 1981): 497–500.

50. Of course, this is a *traditional* caricature. Currently, films and television series are celebrating a new kind of father who has an initially difficult time taking care of his infant or child, but soon becomes better at the job than his wife or lover—or ex-wife or ex-lover.

51. Interestingly, critics of Chodorow who did not share Rossi's *biological* concerns argued that although dual parenting is an improvement over women's monopoly on mothering, "parenting . . . not just by biological parents but by communities of interested adults" is to be preferred to dual parenting. These critics insist that although men and women have much to gain by engaging equally in parenting, everyone— particularly children—will be better off if we stop viewing children as the possessions and responsibilities of their biological parents and start viewing them instead as people for whom society as a whole is responsible. (Judith Lorber, "On *The Reproduction of Mothering:* A Methodological Debate," *Signs: Journal of Women in Culture and Society* 6, no. 3 [Spring 1981]: 486).

52. Janice Raymond, "Female Friendship: Contra Chodorow and Dinnerstein," *Hypatia* 1, no. 2 (Fall 1986): 44–45.

53. Ibid., p. 37.

54. Hester Eisenstein, *Contemporary Feminist Thought* (Boston: G. K. Hall, 1983), pp. 84–86.

55. In "Some Psychical Consequences of the Anatomical Distinction Between the Sexes," p. 193, Freud said of women that "their super-ego is, never so inexorable, so impersonal, so independent of its emotional origins as we require it to be in men."

56. Carol Gilligan, *In a Different Voice* (Cambridge, Mass.: Harvard University Press, 1982), pp. 2–23.

57. Ibid., p. 100.

58. Ibid., p. 26.

59. Ibid., pp. 28–29.

60. Lawrence Kohlberg, "FROM IS TO OUGHT: How to Commit the Naturalistic Fallacy and Get Away with It in the Study of Moral Development," in *Cognitive Development and Epistemology*, T. Mischel, ed. (New York: Academic Press, 1971), pp. 164–165.

61. Gilligan, *In a Different Voice*, p. 92.

62. Ibid., p. 2.

63. One related debate draws attention to the fact that Gilligan's readers are frequently left with the impression that a female ethic of care is *better* than a male ethic of justice. Many radical feminists would gladly applaud Gilligan were she indeed arguing that women's moral values are not only different from men's but also better. But Gilligan insisted that she was claiming only a difference, not a superiority. Her aim, she stressed, was to ensure that woman's moral voice be taken as seriously as man's. But if Gilligan was not making any superiority claims, then her book may not be normative enough. Critics probe: "So which is it better to be: just or caring? Should we be like Abraham, who was willing to sacrifice his beloved son Isaac so as to fulfill God's will? Or should we be like the mother whose baby Solomon threatens to cut in half?" (We will recall that in this biblical story, two women claim to be the same child's mother. To be fair to both, Solomon, in his ultimate wisdom, decides to divide the baby in two, causing the true mother to forsake her claim in order to secure the child's survival.) Gilligan resisted answering these questions, although she certainly led many of her readers to view Abraham as a religious fanatic and to view the real mother in the Solomon story as a person who has her values properly ordered.

As Gilligan saw it, the question of which is better—an ethics of care or an ethics of justice—is an apples-or-oranges question. Like apples and oranges, an ethics of care and an ethics of justice are both good. But to insist that one kind of morality is the best is to manifest a nearly pathological need for a unitary, absolute, and universal moral standard that can erase our very real moral tensions as with a magic wand. If we are to achieve moral maturity, Gilligan implied, we must be willing to vacillate between an ethics of care and an ethics of justice. But even if her critics were willing to concede that ethical vacillation is indeed morally acceptable, they are not willing to let Gilligan simply describe an ethics of care on the one hand and an ethics of justice on the other without at least attempting to translate between these two systems. Such attempts at translation would, believe her critics, do much to reinforce Gilligan's later claim that the ethics of care and of justice are ultimately compatible.

For more details, see ibid., pp. 151–174.

64. In a study of northern blacks migrating back to the rural South, sociologist Carol Stack discovered that the men and women in her study valued equally the ethic of care. Stack inferred from her data that "under conditions of economic deprivation there is a convergence between women and men in their construction of themselves in relationship to others" and that "these conditions produce a convergence also in women's and men's vocabulary of rights, morality, and the social good." Carol Stack, "The Culture of Gender: Women and Men of Color," *Signs: Journal of Women in Culture and Society* 11, no. 2 (Winter 1986): 322–323.

65. Gilligan, *In a Different Voice*, pp. 74–95.

66. William Puka, "The Liberation of Caring (A Different Voice for Gilligan's "Different Voice") (unpublished manuscript), p. 5.

67. Ibid., pp. 5–7.

68. Ibid., p. 7.

69. Juliet Mitchell, *Women's Estate* (New York: Pantheon Books, 1971), pp. 164–165.

70. Ibid., p. 170.

71. Juliet Mitchell, *Psychoanalysis and Feminism* (New York: Vintage Books, 1974), p. 370.

72. Ibid., p. 373.

73. Ibid., p. 375.

74. Ibid., p. 378.

75. Ibid., pp. 409–414.

76. Sigmund Freud, "Totem and Taboo," in *The Standard Edition of the Complete Psychological Works of Sigmund Freud*, James Strachey, trans. and ed. (New York: W. W. Norton, 1966), p. 144.

77. Jacques Lacan, *The Language of the Self* (Baltimore, Md.: Johns Hopkins University Press, 1968), p. 271.

78. Mitchell, *Psychoanalysis and Feminism*, p. 415.

79. Sherry B. Ortner, "Oedipal Father, Mother's Brother, and the Penis: A Review of Juliet Mitchell's *Psychoanalysis and Feminism*," *Feminist Studies* 2, nos. 2-3 (1975): 179.

80. Ibid.

CHAPTER SIX

1. According to many thinkers—Ann Foreman for one—Marx and Freud are ultimately incompatible. As Foreman saw it, Wilhelm Reich's, Herbert Marcuse's, Erich Fromm's, and Juliet Mitchell's separate attempts to fuse together Marxism and psychoanalysis all failed. "To accept Freud's theory of the unconscious and the instincts would in effect require abandoning the Marxist theory of revolutionary change. For Marxism's central premise was that a development in consciousness not simply at an individual level, but at the level of a whole class, the working class, was possible; and the concept of socialism took its meaning from the idea of collective and conscious control. In short, to synthesize Marxism and psychoanalysis was an impossible task." See Ann Foreman, *Femininity as Alienation: Women and the Family in Marxism and Psychoanalysis* (London: Pluto Press, 1977), pp. 42–63.

2. Vladimir Ilich Lenin, *The Emancipation of Women: From the Writings of V. I. Lenin* (New York: International Publishers, 1934), p. 101.

3. The line between contemporary Marxist feminists and socialist feminists is most difficult to draw. Despite my best efforts to assign thinkers to their correct category, I know that not everyone would agree with my classifications. Readers should be aware of this problem.

4. Heidi Hartmann, "The Unhappy Marriage of Marxism and Feminism: Towards a More Progressive Union," in *Women and Revolution: A Discussion of the Unhappy Marriage of Marxism and Feminism*, Lydia Sargent, ed. (Boston: South End Press, 1981), pp. 1–41.

5. Clitoridectomy, or female circumcision, is probably a practice that harms women. The health hazards of the practice are enough to constitute an argument against it. Nevertheless, the practice has been invested with weighty cultural baggage having to do with the passage from girlhood to womanhood and/or having to do with the integrity of native customs against the force of colonial powers' morality. Thus, any wholesale condemnation of clitoridectomy is problematic.

6. I owe several of the points in this paragraph and the one preceding it to Antje Haussen Lewis and Michael Weber.

7. Although working simultaneously with Marxist and radical feminism is challenging, working simultaneously with Marxist and psychoanalytic feminism presents an even greater challenge. Marx and Freud had quite different views of the relation between nonmaterial and material life, between psychology and society. Material life is what mattered to Marx, whereas psychic life is what mattered to Freud. That these men have paid attention only to fragments—albeit important fragments—of human life may make their theories peculiarly blind to, and perhaps ultimately incompatible with, each other. Psychoanalysis may in fact be no more compatible with Marxism than liberalism is. Moreover, the attempt to put psychoanalysis and Marxism under one feminist roof, along with radical feminism, may not even be desirable. After all, overarching theories have been known to leave little room for criticism, internal dialogue, or change.

8. In order not to complicate matters here in the introduction, I have not attempted to explain the ways in which dual-systems theorists attempt to link their twofold analysis of patriarchy and capitalism with Marx and Engels's twofold analysis of reproduction and production. In order to justify the attention they pay to gender as well as to class, socialist feminists frequently quote the following lines from *The German Ideology:* "According to the materialistic conception, the determining factor in history is, in the final instance, the production and reproduction of immediate life. This, again, is of a two-fold character: on the one side, the production of the means of existence, of food, clothing and shelter and the tools necessary for that production; on the other side, the production of human beings themselves, the propagation of the species. The social organization under which the people of a particular historical epoch and a particular country live is determined by both kinds of production; by the stage of development on the one hand and of the family on the other" (Karl Marx and Friedrich Engels, *The German Ideology* [New York: International Publishers, 1970], p. 49).

9. Iris Young, "Socialist Feminism and the Limits of Dual Systems Theory," *Socialist Review* 10, nos. 2-3 (March-June 1980): 174.

10. Juliet Mitchell, *Psychoanalysis and Feminism* (New York: Vintage Books, 1974), p. 412.

11. Juliet Mitchell, *Woman's Estate* (New York: Pantheon Books, 1971), pp. 100–101.

12. There is a datedness about Mitchell's analysis. Nevertheless, her caveat to us is well taken. Women's progress is frequently punctuated by regressions and suspended on plateaus. Women have not come as long a way as they should have by now.

13. Mitchell, *Woman's Estate*, pp. 114–115.

14. Mitchell was convinced that women's limited role in production cannot be explained solely or even primarily by her supposed physical weakness. In the first place, men have forced women to do "women's" work, and "women's" work in all its varieties requires much physical strength. Second, even if women are not as physically strong as men, and even if their original, limited role in production can be attributed to their gap in strength, this same gap cannot explain women's current, limited role in production (ibid., p. 104).

15. Ibid., p. 107.

16. Mitchell, *Psychoanalysis and Feminism*, p. 408.

17. Ibid., pp. 415–416.

18. Ibid., p. 412.

19. Ibid., p. 415.

20. Marge Piercy, *Woman on the Edge of Time* (New York: Fawcett Crest Books, 1976), p. 124.

21. Ibid., p. 105.
22. Hartmann, "The Unhappy Marriage of Marxism and Feminism," p. 10.
23. Ibid., p. 14.
24. Ibid., pp. 15–19.
25. Ibid., p. 19.
26. Ibid., p. 23.
27. Ibid., p. 20.
28. Ibid., p. 22.
29. Bureau of Labor Statistics, March 1982, cited in "Paying Women What They're Worth," *QQ Report from the Center for Philosophy and Public Policy* 3, no. 2 (Spring 1983): 2.
30. Ibid., p. 1.
31. Barbara Bergmann, *The Economic Emergence of Women* (New York: Basic Books, 1986), pp. 266–269.
32. Hartmann also provided examples of how patriarchy adjusts to capitalism. "While the family wage shows that capitalism adjusts to patriarchy, the changing status of children shows that patriarchy adjusts to capital. Children, like women, came to be excluded from wage labor. As children's ability to earn money declined, their legal relationship to their parents changed. At the beginning of the industrial era in the United States, fulfilling children's need for their fathers was thought to be crucial, even primary, to their happy development; fathers had legal priority in cases of contested custody. As children's ability to contribute to the economic well-being of the family declined, mothers came increasingly to be viewed as crucial to the happy development of their children and gained legal priority in cases of contested custody. Here patriarchy adapted to the changing economic role of children: when children were productive, men claimed them; as children became unproductive, they were given to women" (Hartmann, "The Unhappy Marriage of Marxism and Feminism," p. 23).
33. Young, "Socialist Feminism and the Limits of Dual Systems Theory," p. 176.
34. Ibid.
35. Young's comment seems a more appropriate challenge to *Woman's Estate* than to *Psychoanalysis and Feminism*, however. It is in *Woman's Estate*, after all, that Mitchell was careful to state that although reproduction, sexuality, and the socialization of children are each "independent sector[s]" with their "own autonomous realit[ies]," each of these independent sectors is nevertheless "ultimately . . . determined by the economic factor" (Mitchell, *Woman's Estate*, p. 101). Mitchell made no such concession to capitalism in *Psychoanalysis and Feminism*. If anything, we get the sense that however important the economic factors are, they are ultimately determined by ideological factors. History, it seems, dances to the music of the Oedipal beat.
36. Rosalind Petchesky, "Dissolving the Hyphen: A Report on Marxist-Feminist Groups 1-5," in *Capitalist Patriarchy and the Case for Socialist Feminism*, Zillah Eisenstein, ed. (New York: Monthly Review Press, 1979).
37. So preoccupied is dual-systems theory with women's oppression in "women's sphere" (the family) that it views women's oppression in "men's sphere" (the workplace) merely as the reflection of the former. Such an approach, said Young, underemphasizes the specific oppression of women beyond the family by giving inordinate emphasis to family dynamics as the cause of corresponding workplace dynamics. To attribute such causal importance to the family ignores the fact that the operation of workplace sex/gender oppression proceeds along *impersonal* lines, whereas the operation of family sex/gender oppression proceeds along *personal* lines. See Young, "Socialist Feminism and the Limits of Dual Systems Theory," pp. 179–180.

38. Ibid., p. 181.

39. Iris Young, "Beyond the Unhappy Marriage: A Critique of the Dual Systems Theory," in *Women and Revolution*, Sargent, ed., p. 58.

40. Heidi Hartmann, "Capitalism, Patriarchy and Job Segregation by Sex," in *Capitalist Patriarchy and the Case for Socialist Feminism*, Eisenstein, ed., p. 207.

41. Young, "Beyond the Unhappy Marriage," p. 58.

42. Esther Boserup, *Women's Role in Economic Development* (London: George Allen and Unwin, 1970).

43. Young, "Beyond the Unhappy Marriage," pp. 59–61.

44. Alison M. Jaggar, *Feminist Politics and Human Nature* (Totowa, N.J.: Rowman & Allanheld, 1983), p. 353.

45. Ibid., p. 308.

46. Ibid., pp. 309–310.

47. Ibid., pp. 310–311.

48. Although Jaggar did not make specific points about in vitro fertilization, the points I raise here seem to fit her analysis.

49. Jaggar, *Feminist Politics and Human Nature*, p. 315.

50. Ibid.

51. Ibid., p. 316.

52. Ibid., p. 317.

53. Ann Foreman has argued that femininity is itself alienating and, by parity of reasoning, so too is masculinity. Feminine women and masculine men are permitted to develop only certain aspects of their respective persons. As a result, they become caricatures of themselves. Worse, the more exclusively feminine women become and the more exclusively masculine men become, the less men and women have in common. Any points of resonance between the sexes are muted, as men struggle to maintain their power over women and as women struggle to elude patriarchal oppression (Foreman, *Femininity as Alienation*, pp. 150–152).

54. Catharine MacKinnon, "Feminism, Marxism, Method and the State: An Agenda for Theory," *Signs: Journal of Women in Culture and in Society* 7, no. 3 (1982): 524–527.

55. Young, "Beyond the Unhappy Marriage," p. 51.

56. Ibid., p. 64.

57. Raymond M. Lane, "A Man's World: An Update on Sexual Harassment," *The Village Voice*, December 16, 1981, p. 20.

58. Young, "Beyond the Unhappy Marriage," p. 63.

59. Jaggar, *Feminist Politics and Human Nature*, p. 308.

60. Ibid., p. 337.

61. Ibid., p. 371.

62. When interpreting the feminist standpoint theory of Sandra Harding, Jaggar stated the following: "Harding suggests, however, that the difference in women's experience need not be a source of division and weakness. If we learn how to use them, she claims, these differences can be a scientific and political resource for feminism. Her idea is not that feminist theory should only reflect the experience of a single group of women, presumably of the most oppressed; for instance, feminist theory does not have to be grounded only on the experience of physically challenged Jewish lesbians of color. Women's oppression is constantly changing in form and these forms cannot be ranked. Consequently, we cannot identify the standpoint of women with the standpoint of physically challenged women, or of lesbian women, or of women of color or of colonized or immigrant women. For each of these overlapping groups of women, some aspects of reality may be clearly visible and others may be

blurred. A representation of reality from the standpoint of women must drawn on the variety of all women's experience" (ibid., p. 386).

CHAPTER SEVEN

1. Margaret A. Simons and Jessica Benjamin, "Simone de Beauvoir: An Interview," *Feminist Studies* 5, no. 2 (Summer 1979): 336.

2. Terry Keefe, *Simone de Beauvoir* (Totowa, N.J.: Barnes & Noble, 1983).

3. G.W.F. Hegel, *The Phenomenology of Mind*, J. B. Baille, trans. (New York: Harper & Row, 1967).

4. Jean-Paul Sartre, *Being and Nothingness*, Hazel E. Barnes, trans. (New York: Philosophical Library, 1956).

5. Jean-Paul Sartre, *Existentialism*, Bernard Frechtman, trans. (New York: Philosophical Library, 1947), p. 115.

6. Sartre, *Being and Nothingness*, p. 364.

7. I owe this reminder to Michael Weber.

8. Sartre, *Being and Nothingness*, pp. 59–60.

9. Ibid., pp. 55–56.

10. Ibid., p. 56.

11. Jean-Paul Sartre, *The Emotions: Outline of a Theory* (New York: Philosophical Library, 1948).

12. Sartre, *Being and Nothingness*, pp. 252–302.

13. Ibid., pp. 378–379.

14. Ibid., p. 380.

15. Ibid., p. 381.

16. Ibid., p. 393.

17. Ibid., p. 412.

18. "There is no justification for present existence other than its expansion into an indefinitely open future. Every time transcendence falls back into immanence, there is a degradation of existence into the *en-soi*—the brutish life of subjection to given conditions—and of liberty into constraint and contingency. . . . Every individual concerned to justify his existence feels that his existence involves an undefined need to transcend himself, to engage in freely chosen projects" (Simone de Beauvoir, *The Second Sex*, H. M. Parshley, trans. and ed. [New York: Vintage Books, 1974], p. xxxiii).

19. Dorothy Kaufmann McCall, "Simone de Beauvoir, *The Second Sex*, and Jean-Paul Sartre," *Signs: Journal of Women in Culture and Society* 5, no. 2 (1979): 210.

20. Ibid.

21. De Beauvoir, *The Second Sex*, p. 24.

22. Ibid., p. 41.

23. Ibid., p. 51.

24. Ibid., p. 55.

25. Ibid., p. 64.

26. Ibid., pp. 89–90.

27. Ibid., p. 72.

28. Ibid., p. 284.

29. De Beauvoir held out Montherlant and Lawrence for special criticism. Unlike Claudel, Breton, and Stendhal, who believed that the ideal woman freely chooses to sacrifice herself for man not because she is required to do so but because she wants

to, Montherlant and Lawrence made of female self-sacrifice a nearly sacred duty (ibid., pp. 280–285).

30. Ibid., pp. 180–181.

31. Ibid., p. 256n.

32. Ibid., p. 354.

33. Ibid., p. 500.

34. Ibid., pp. 502–503.

35. It is no secret that de Beauvoir was not enamored of motherhood as we know it. The following quote is fairly representative of her view: "As motherhood is today, maternity-slavery, as some feminists call it, does indeed turn today's women into slaves. And I think that motherhood is the most dangerous snare for all those women who want to be free and independent, for those who want to earn their living, for those who want to think for themselves, and for those who want to have a life of their own" (Simons and Benjamin, "Simone de Beauvoir," p. 341).

36. De Beauvoir, *The Second Sex*, p. 571.

37. Ibid., pp. 761–763.

38. Ibid., p. 630.

39. De Beauvoir's view of the prostitute as an exceptional woman who dares to challenge the sexual mores of her society was rooted in several studies, especially those of ancient Greece describing the *hetairae*. In these studies, Athens is delineated as a center for prostitution, where the prostitutes were divided into at least three classes. Lowest on the status ladder were the *pornai*, who were checked over before their services were bought. Of slightly higher status were the *ayletrides*, or players, who entertained guests with their music as well as their bodies. Occupying the highest position were the *hetairae*. In some ways these intellectually gifted as well as physically endowed women were more privileged than were respectable Athenian wives and mothers, who, unlike the *hetairae*, were largely uneducated and somewhat confined to domestic affairs. Indeed, some *hetairae* amassed great wealth and exerted considerable power in the public domain through the men they entertained—this at a time when these men's wives and mothers were without real economic and political power. See Will Durant, *The Life of Greece* (New York: Simon & Schuster, 1939).

Nevertheless, according to several scholars of antiquity, the *hetairae* were not necessarily the most blessed of women. Sarah B. Pomeroy, for example, noted that although the *hetaira* had access to the intellectual life of Athens, and although she had freedom to be with whoever pleased her, her life had definite shortcomings. "That we know of some courtesans who attempted to live as respectable wives, while we know of no citizen wives who wished to be courtesans, should make us reconsider the question of which was the preferable role in Classical Athens—companion or wife" (Sarah B. Pomeroy, *Goddesses, Whores, Wives, and Slaves* [New York: Schocken Books, 1975], p. 92).

In short, the price the *hetaira* paid for sexual freedom and intellectual stimulation was not only status within the Athenian community but some of the less glamorous, although nonetheless meaningful, comforts of home. According to de Beauvoir, however, this may not have been too high a price to pay for the privilege of living in the active rather than the passive voice, thereby achieving a measure of independence from men. See de Beauvoir, *The Second Sex*, pp. 631–636.

40. Ibid., p. 700.

41. Ibid., pp. 710–711.

42. Ibid., p. 748.

43. Ibid., p. 795.

44. Simone de Beauvoir, *The Prime of Life*, Peter Green, trans. (Harmondsworth, England: Penguin Books, 1965), pp. 291–292.

45. De Beauvoir, *The Second Sex*, p. 791.

46. Sartre, *Being and Nothingness*, p. 412n.

47. Jean Bethke Elshtain, *Public Man, Private Woman* (Princeton, N.J.: Princeton University Press, 1981), p. 306.

48. Simone de Beauvoir, *Memoirs of a Dutiful Daughter*, James Kirkup, trans. (Harmondsworth, England: Penguin Books, 1963), p. 131.

49. De Beauvoir, *The Second Sex*, p. 553.

50. Elshtain, *Public Man, Private Woman*, p. 307.

51. For an interesting analysis of de Beauvoir's "linguistic ambivalence," about the terms *brotherhood* and *sisterhood*, see Eléanor Kuykendall, "Linguistic Ambivalence in Simone de Beauvoir's Feminist Theory," in *The Thinking Muse*, Iris Young and Jeffner Allen, eds. (Bloomington: Indiana University Press, 1989).

52. Genevieve Lloyd, *The Man of Reason: "Male" and "Female" in Western Philosophy* (Minneapolis: University of Minnesota Press, 1984), p. 101.

53. Ibid.

54. Anne Whitmarsh, *Simone de Beauvoir and the Limits of Commitment* (Cambridge: Cambridge University Press, 1981), p. 151.

55. Ibid.

56. Ibid.

57. De Beauvoir, *The Second Sex*, p. 34.

58. De Beauvoir, *The Prime of Life*, p. 109.

59. Simons and Benjamin, "Simone de Beauvoir," p. 342.

60. Ibid.

61. Carol Ascher, *Simone de Beauvoir: A Life of Freedom* (Boston: Beacon Press, 1981), p. 146.

CHAPTER EIGHT

1. Cited in Hélène Vivienne Wenzel, "The Text as Body/Politics: An Appreciation of Monique Wittig's Writings in Context," *Feminist Studies* 7, no. 2 (Summer 1981): 270–271.

2. Significantly, directors of women's studies programs in France complain that U.S. academics have a very narrow conception of who counts as a French feminist or as a postmodern feminist. In a review of Claire Duchen's book, *Feminism in France: From May '68 to Mitterrand* (London: Routledge & Kegan Paul, 1986), Elaine Viennot wrote, "To taste the full flavor of these distortions, it is necessary to know that the French feminist movement is, in certain American universities, an object of study (I assure you right away, you would not recognize it . . .), and that this book has every possibility of being bought by every American library; it is also necessary to know that certain of our compatriots (J. Kristeva, J. Derrida . . .) reign over there as masters of the university enclave" (Elaine Viennot, *Etudes Feminists: bulletin national d'information, numéro 1*, Eléanor Kuykendall, trans. [automne 1987], p. 40). Whether the sentiments of this review, published by the Association Pour les Etudes Féministes and the Centre Lyonnais d'Etudes Féministes/Association Femmes, Féminisme et Recherches Rhône Alpes and brought to my attention by Eléanor Kuykendall, are widely shared by French academics is a question for debate. In any event, Viennot's criticisms are not idiosyncratic and merit a careful reading.

3. John Sturrock, "Introduction," in *Structuralism and Since: From Lévi-Strauss to Derrida*, John Sturrock, ed. (New York: Oxford University Press, 1979), p. 14.

4. If any one of these women can be accused of discipleship, it is Kristeva, who usually writes within a Lacanian framework. Nevertheless, her writings depart from Lacan in significant ways.

5. Danièle Steward, "The Women's Movement in France," *Signs: Journal of Women in Culture and Society* 6, no. 2 (Winter 1980): 353.

6. Jacques Lacan, *Écrits: A Selection*, Alan Sheridan, trans. (New York: W. W. Norton, 1977), pp. 64–66.

7. Duchen, *Feminism in France*, p. 78.

8. I use the pronoun "he" here because Lacan often does so.

9. I do not intend a pun here on the phrase "come to see," although I fully realize that this phrase could be interpreted as a linking of a sexual term, "to come," with a perceptual term, "to see."

10. According to Lacan, the original mother-child unity is in some way a metaphor for truth—for an isomorphic relationship between word and object. Ideally, both mother and child, and word and object, would remain united; but society will not stand for such unity. As a result of the castration complex brought on by the arrival of the father, who represents social power symbolized by the phallus, not only mother and child but also word and object must be split.

11. Jacques Lacan, "The Mirror Stage," in *Écrits*, pp. 1–7.

12. Jacques Lacan, "The Meaning of the Phallus," in *Feminine Sexuality*, J. Mitchell and J. Rose, eds. (New York: W. W. Norton, 1982), p. 84.

13. Lacan's and Derrida's "feminism" is a matter of considerable debate. For the most part, critics are suspicious of these two theorists' credentials.

14. I owe this point to Eléanor Kuykendall, who reminded me that sections of Jacques Derrida, *Spurs: Nietzsche's Styles*, Barbara Harlow, trans. (Chicago: University of Chicago Press, 1978); and Jacques Derrida, *The Post Card: From Socrates to Freud and Beyond*, Alan Bass, trans. (Chicago: University of Chicago Press, 1987), are disturbing from a feminist point of view.

15. Jacques Derrida, *Writing and Difference*, Alan Bass, trans. (Chicago: University of Chicago Press, 1978).

16. Toril Moi, *Sexual/Textual Politics: Feminist Literary Theory* (New York: Methuen, 1985), pp. 130–131.

17. Eléanor Kuykendall explained to me Irigaray's tolerance of the label "feminist."

18. Ann Rosalind Jones, "Writing the Body: Toward an Understanding of L'écriture Feminine," *Feminist Studies* 7, no. 1 (Summer 1981): 248.

19. Hélène Cixous and Catherine Clement, "Sorties," in *The Newly Born Woman*, Betsy Wing, trans. (Minneapolis: University of Minnesota Press, 1986), pp. 63, 65.

20. Ibid., p. 65.

21. Hélène Cixous, "The Laugh of the Medusa," in *New French Feminisms*, Elaine Marks and Isabelle de Courtivron, eds. (New York: Schocken Books, 1981), p. 249.

22. Ibid., p. 245.

23. Ibid., p. 262.

24. Elaine Marks and Isabelle de Courtivron, "Introduction III," in *New French Feminisms*, Marks and Courtivron, eds., p. 36.

25. Cixous, "The Laugh of the Medusa," p. 256.

26. Ibid., pp. 259–260.

27. Ibid., p. 251.

28. Ibid., p. 256.

29. Ibid., pp. 259–260.

30. Luce Irigaray has been critical of both Derrida and Lacan. In 1974, she challenged Lacan in her book *Speculum* and was fired from her academic position at l'Université de Paris VIII (Vincennes) because of it. In order to fully appreciate Irigaray's differences from Lacan, readers should refer to Luce Irigaray, *Speculum of the Other Woman*, Gillian C. Gill, trans. (Ithaca, N.Y.: Cornell University Press, 1985).

31. Luce Irigaray, *This Sex Which Is Not One*, Catherine Porter, trans. (Ithaca, N.Y.: Cornell University Press, 1985), p. 28.

32. According to Claire Duchen, Irigaray believes "that before a 'feminine feminine,' a non-phallic feminine, can even be *thought*, women need to examine the male philosophical and psychoanalytical texts which have contributed to the construction of the 'masculine feminine,' the phallic feminine, in order to locate and identify it" (Duchen, *Feminism in France*, pp. 87–88).

33. Irigaray, *This Sex Which Is Not One*, p. 32.

34. Moi, *Sexual/Textual Politics*, p. 132.

35. Irigaray, *This Sex Which Is Not One*, p. 74.

36. Ibid.

37. Luce Irigaray, "Is the Subject of Science Sexed?" Carol Mastrangelo Bové, trans., *Hypatia* 2, no. 3 (Fall 1987): 66.

38. Irigaray, *This Sex Which Is Not One*, p. 32.

39. Moi, *Sexual/Textual Politics*, p. 140.

40. In an interview, Irigaray stated that there is nothing other than masculine discourse. When the interviewer said, "I don't understand what 'masculine discourse' means," Irigaray retorted, "Of course not, since there is no other" (Irigaray, *This Sex Which Is Not One*, p. 140).

41. Irigaray, *This Sex Which Is Not One*, p. 29.

42. Julia Kristeva, *About Chinese Women*, Anita Barrows, trans. (New York: Urizen Books, 1974), p. 16.

43. Julia Kristeva, from an interview with *Tel Quel*, in *New French Feminisms*, Marks and Courtivron, eds., p. 157.

44. Julia Kristeva, *Revolution in Poetic Languages*, Leon Roudiez, trans. (New York: Columbia University Press, 1984).

45. Julia Kristeva, *Powers of Horror*, Leon Roudiez, trans. (New York: Columbia University Press, 1982), pp. 205–206.

46. Julia Kristeva, *Desire in Language*, Leon Roudiez, trans. (New York: Columbia University Press, 1982), pp. 205–206.

47. Julia Kristeva, "Women's Time," Alice Jardine and Harry Blake, trans., *Signs: Journal of Women in Culture and Society* 7, no. 1 (1981): 13–35.

48. Julia Kristeva, "The Novel as Polylogue," in *Desire in Language*, pp. 159–209.

49. Duchen, *Feminism in France*, p. 102.

50. Margaret Whitford, "Luce Irigaray and the Female Imaginary: Speaking as a Woman," *Radical Philosophy* 43 (Summer 1986): 7.

51. Kristeva, "Women's Time," pp. 26–30.

52. Ibid., pp. 102–103.

53. Genesis 2:19.

54. Lao-tzu, "The Tao-te-Ching," in *The Texts of Taoism*, James Legge, ed. (New York: Dover, 1962).

CONCLUSION

1. Aristotle, *Nichomachean Ethics*.

2. Alison M. Jaggar, *Feminist Politics and Human Nature* (Totowa, N.J.: Rowman and Allanheld, 1983), p. 353.

3. Julia Kristeva, "Women's Time," Alice Jardine and Harry Blake, trans., *Signs: Journal of Women in Culture and Society* 7, no. 1 (1981): 13–35.

4. Ibid.

5. Audre Lorde, "Poetry Is Not a Luxury," in *The Future of Difference*, Alice Jardine and Hester Eisenstein, eds. (New Brunswick, N.J.: Rutgers University Press, 1985), p. 126.

---■---

Selected Bibliography

LIBERAL FEMINISM

The Roots of Liberal Feminism

Bentham, Jeremy. *The Principles of Morals and Legislation.* New York: Hafner, 1965.

Berlin, Isaiah. *Two Concepts of Liberty.* Oxford: Clarendon Press, 1961.

Butler, Melissa A. "Early Liberal Roots of Feminism: John Locke and the Attack on Patriarchy." *American Political Science Review* 72(1), 1978, pp. 135–150.

Dworkin, Ronald. "Liberalism." In Stuart Hampshire, ed. *Public and Private Morality,* pp. 113–143. Cambridge: Cambridge University Press, 1978.

———. *Taking Rights Seriously.* Cambridge, Mass.: Harvard University Press, 1977.

Gutmann, Amy. *Liberal Equality.* New York: Cambridge University Press, 1980.

Hobbes, Thomas. *Leviathan.* New York: E. P. Dutton, 1950.

Kant, Immanuel. *Groundwork of the Metaphysic of Morals,* trans. H. J. Paton. New York: Harper Torchbooks, 1958.

Locke, John. *An Essay Concerning Human Understanding,* ed. A. C. Fraser. New York: Dover, 1959.

———. *Two Treatises of Government,* ed. Peter Laslett. New York: Cambridge University Press, 1960.

MacLean, Douglas, and Claudia Mills, eds. *Liberalism Reconsidered.* Totowa, N.J.: Rowman & Allanheld, 1983.

Mill, John Stuart. *Utilitarianism, Liberty, and Representative Government.* New York: E. P. Dutton, 1910.

Rawls, John. *A Theory of Justice.* Cambridge, Mass.: Harvard University Press, 1971.

Sandel, Michael. *Liberalism and Its Critics.* New York: New York University Press, 1984.

———. *Liberalism and the Limits of Justice.* New York: Cambridge University Press, 1982.

Strauss, Leo. *Liberalism: Ancient and Modern.* New York: Basic Books, 1968.

Historical Development of Liberal-Feminist Thought

Berg, Barbara. *The Remembered Gate: Origins of American Feminism.* New York: Oxford University Press, 1979.

Bird, Caroline, and Sara Welles Briller. *Born Female: The High Cost of Keeping Women Down.* New York: Pocket Books, 1969.

Brockett, L. P. *Woman: Her Rights, Wrongs, Privileges, and Responsibilities.* Freeport, N.Y.: Books for Libraries Press, 1970.

DuBois, Ellen Carol, ed. *Elizabeth Cady Stanton, Susan B. Anthony: Correspondence, Writings, Speeches.* New York: Schocken Books, 1981.

Friedan, Betty. "Betty Friedan Critiques Feminism and Calls for New Directions." *New York Times Magazine,* July 5, 1981, pp. 13–15, 32–33, 35.

———. *The Feminine Mystique.* New York: Dell, 1974.

———. "Feminism Takes a New Turn." *New York Times Magazine,* November 18, 1979, pp. 40, 92, 94, 96, 98, 100, 102, 106.

———. "How to Get the Women's Movement Moving Again." *New York Times Magazine,* November 3, 1985, pp. 26, 28, 66–67, 84–85, 89, 98, 106, 108.

———. *The Second Stage.* New York: Summit Books, 1981.

Fuller, Margaret. *Woman in the Nineteenth Century.* New York: W. W. Norton, 1971.

Gilman, Charlotte Perkins. *Women and Economics.* New York: Harper & Row, 1966.

Godwin, William. *Memoirs of Mary Wollstonecraft,* ed. W. Clark Durant. New York: Gordon Press, 1972.

Grimké, Sarah. *Letters on the Equality of the Sexes and the Condition of Woman.* New York: Burt Franklin, 1970.

Kanowitz, Lee. *Women and the Law: The Unfinished Revolution.* Albuquerque: University of New Mexico Press, 1969.

Korsmeyer, Carolyn W. "Reasons and Morals in the Early Feminist Movement: Mary Wollstonecraft." *The Philosophical Forum* 5(1-2), Fall-Winter 1973–1974, pp. 97–111.

Krouse, Richard W. "Mill and Marx on Marriage, Divorce and the Family." *Social Concept* 1(2), September 1983, pp. 36–75.

———. "Patriarchal Liberalism and Beyond: From John Stuart Mill to Harriet Taylor." In Jean Bethke Elshtain, ed. *The Family in Political Thought,* pp. 145–172. Amherst: University of Massachusetts Press, 1981.

Mill, Harriet Taylor. "Enfranchisement of Women." In John Stuart Mill and Harriet Taylor Mill. *Essays on Sex Equality,* ed. Alice S. Rossi, pp. 89–122. Chicago: University of Chicago Press, 1970.

Mill, John Stuart. "The Subjection of Women." In John Stuart Mill and Harriet Taylor Mill. *Essays on Sex Equality,* ed. Alice S. Rossi, pp. 123–242. Chicago: University of Chicago Press, 1970.

Richards, Janet Radcliffe. *The Skeptical Feminist.* London: Routledge & Kegan Paul, 1980.

Rossi, Alice. "Equality Between the Sexes: An Immodest Proposal." *Daedalus* 93(2), 1964, pp. 607–652.

Rossi, Alice, ed. *The Feminist Papers: From Adams to de Beauvoir.* New York: Columbia University Press, 1973.

"Seneca Falls Declaration of Sentiments and Resolutions (1848)." In *Feminism: The Essential Historical Writings,* ed. Miriam Schneir, pp. 76–82. New York: Random House, 1972.

Showalter, Elaine. *Women's Liberation and Literature.* New York: Harcourt Brace Jovanovich, 1971.

Stanton, Anthony Gage. *History of Woman Suffrage.* New York: Arno Press, 1969.

Steinem, Gloria. "Now That It's Reagan." *Ms.,* January 1981, pp. 28–33.

———. *Outrageous Acts and Everyday Rebellions.* New York: Holt, Rinehart & Winston, 1983.

Wollstonecraft, Mary. *A Vindication of the Rights of Woman,* ed. Carol H. Poston. New York: W. W. Norton, 1975.

Wright, Frances. *Life, Letters and Lectures, 1834/44.* New York: Arno Press, 1972.

Critiques of Liberal Feminism

Bolotin, Susan. "Voices from the Post-Feminist Generation." *New York Times Magazine,* October 17, 1982, p. 28.

Brennan, Teresa, and Carole Pateman. "'Mere Auxiliaries to the Commonwealth': Women and the Origins of Liberalism." *Political Studies* 27(2), June 1979, pp. 183–200.

Clark, Lorenne M.G. "Women and Locke: Who Owns the Apples in the Garden of Eden?" In Lorenne M.G. Clark and Lydia Lange, eds. *The Sexism of Social and Political Theory,* pp. 16–40. Toronto: University of Toronto Press, 1979.

Dowling, Colette. *The Cinderella Syndrome: Women's Hidden Fear of Independence.* New York: Summit Books, 1981.

Eisenstein, Zillah. *Feminism and Sexual Equality: Crisis in Liberal America.* New York: Monthly Review Press, 1984.

——. *The Radical Future of Liberal Feminism.* Boston: Northeastern University Press, 1986.

——. "The Sexual Politics of the New Right: Understanding the 'Crisis of Liberalism' for the 1980s." *Signs: Journal of Women in Culture and Society* 7(3), 1982, pp. 567–88.

Elshtain, Jean Bethke. "Feminism, Family, and Community." *Dissent* 29(1), Fall 1982, pp. 441–449. (See also the continuing debate with Barbara Ehrenreich in *Dissent* 30[1], Winter 1983, pp. 103–109.)

——. *Public Man, Private Woman.* Princeton, N.J.: Princeton University Press, 1981.

Evans, Sara. "The Origins of the Women's Liberation Movement." *Radical America* 9(2), 1975, pp. 3–4.

——. "The Politics of Liberal Feminism." *Social Science Quarterly* 64(4), 1983, pp. 880–897.

Ferguson, Kathy E. "Liberalism and Oppression: Emma Goldman and the Anarchist Feminist Alternative." In Michael C.G. McGrath, ed. *Liberalism and the Modern Polity,* pp. 93–118. New York: Marcel Dekker, 1978.

——. *Self, Society and Womankind: The Dialectic of Liberation.* Westport, Conn.: Greenwood Press, 1980.

Flammang, Janet Angela. "Feminist Theory: The Question of Power." *Current Perspectives on Social Theory* 4, 1983, pp. 37–83.

——. "The Political Consciousness of American Women: A Critical Analysis of Liberal Feminism in America." Ph.D. diss., University of California, Los Angeles, 1980.

Gibson, Mary. "Rationality." *Philosophy and Public Affairs* 6(3), Spring 1977, pp. 193–225.

Haack, Susan. "On the Moral Relevance of Sex." *Philosophy* 49, 1974, pp. 90–95.

Hewlett, Sylvia Ann. *A Lesser Life: The Myth of Women's Liberation in America.* New York: William Morrow, 1986.

Jaggar, Alison M. *Feminist Politics and Human Nature.* Totowa, N.J.: Rowman & Allanheld, 1983, pp. 27–50.

——. "On Sexual Equality." In Jane English, ed. *Sex Equality,* pp. 93–107. Englewood Cliffs, N.J.: Prentice-Hall, 1977.

Kirp, David L. *Gender Justice.* Chicago: University of Chicago Press, 1986.

Lakoff, Sanford A. *Equality in Political Philosophy.* Cambridge, Mass.: Harvard University Press, 1964, pp. 129–143.

Leo, John. "Are Women 'Male Clones'?" *Time,* August 18, 1986, p. 63.

McElroy, Wendy. "The True Mothers of Feminism." *Reason* 15(3), 1983, pp. 39–42.

McPherson, C. B. *The Political Theory of Possessive Individualism.* Oxford: Oxford University Press, 1964.

Martin, Jane Roland. *Reclaiming a Conversation: The Ideal of the Educated Woman.* New Haven, Conn.: Yale University Press, 1985.

Nicholson, Linda J. *Gender and History: The Limits of Social Theory in the Age of the Family.* New York: Columbia University Press, 1980.

Okin, Susan Moller. *Women in Western Political Thought.* Princeton, N.J.: Princeton University Press, 1979.

Pateman, Carole. *The Problem of Political Obligation: A Critique of Liberal Theory.* Berkeley: University of California Press, 1979.

Ring, Jennifer. "Mill's 'The Subjection of Women': The Methodological Limits of Liberal Feminism." *Review of Politics* 47(1), January 1985, pp. 27–44.

Sabrosky, Judith A. *From Rationality to Liberation.* Westport, Conn.: Greenwood Press, 1979.

Scheman, Naomi. "Individualism and the Objects of Psychology." In Sandra Harding and Merrill B. Hintikka, eds. *Discovering Reality: Feminist Perspectives on Epistemology, Metaphysics, Methodology, and the Philosophy of Science,* pp. 225–244. Dordrecht, The Netherlands: D. Reidel, 1983.

Shreve, Anita, and John Clemans. "The New Wave of Women Politicians." *New York Times Magazine,* October 19, 1980, p. 28.

Spelman, Elizabeth. "Woman as Body: Ancient and Contemporary Views." *Feminist Studies* 9(3), Fall 1983, pp. 559–583.

Trebilcot, Joyce. "Two Forms of Androgynism." In Mary Vetterling-Braggin, ed. *"Femininity," "Masculinity," and "Androgyny,"* pp. 161–170. Totowa, N.J.: Rowman & Littlefield, 1982.

Wendell, Susan. "A (Qualified) Defense of Liberal Feminism." *Hypatia* 2(2), Summer 1987, pp. 65–94.

Willis, Ellen. "The Conservatism of *Ms.*" In Redstockings, ed. *Feminist Revolution,* pp. 170–171. New York: Random House, 1975.

Wolff, Robert Paul. *The Poverty of Liberalism.* Boston: Beacon Press, 1969.

———. "There's Nobody Here But Us Persons." In Carol Gould and Marx Wartofsky, eds. *Women and Philosophy.* New York: G. P. Putnam, 1976.

Wood, Ellen Meiksins. *Mind and Politics: An Approach to the Meaning of Liberal and Socialist Individualism.* Berkeley: University of California Press, 1972.

MARXIST FEMINISM

Some Marxist Concepts and Theories

Acton, Henry B. *What Marx Really Said.* London: MacDonald, 1967.

Braverman, Harry. *Labor and Monopoly Capital: The Degradation of Work in the Twentieth Century.* New York: Monthly Review Press, 1974.

Buchanan, Allen. *Marx and Justice: The Radical Critique of Liberalism.* Totowa, N.J.: Littlefield, Adams, 1972.

Heilbroner, Robert. *Marxism: For and Against.* New York: W. W. Norton, 1980.

Lenin, Vladimer Ilich. *The Emancipation of Women: From the Writings of V. I. Lenin.* New York: International Press, 1975.

Mandel, Ernest. *An Introduction to Marxist Economic Theory.* New York: Pathfinder Publishers, 1934.

Marx, Karl. *Capital: A Critique of Political Economy.* New York: Vintage Books, 1973.

———. *Early Writings,* trans. and ed. T. B. Bottomore. New York: McGraw-Hill, 1963.

———. *Grundrisse: Foundations of the Critique of Political Economy.* New York: Vintage Books, 1973.

———. *Poverty of Philosophy.* New York: International Publishers, 1963.

Marx, Karl, and Friedrich Engels. *The German Ideology.* New York: International Publishers, 1970.

———. "The Manifesto of the Communist Party." In *The Marx-Engels Reader,* ed. Robert C. Tucker, pp. 331–362. New York: W. W. Norton, 1972.

Schmitt, Richard. *Introduction to Marx and Engels.* Boulder, Colo.: Westview Press, 1987.

Slaughter, Cliff. *Marx and Marxism: An Introduction.* New York: Longman, 1985.

Wood, Allen W. *Karl Marx.* London: Routledge & Kegan Paul, 1981.

Friedrich Engels

Engels, Friedrich. *The Origin of the Family, Private Property, and the State.* New York: International Publishers, 1972.

Flax, Jane. "Do Feminists Need Marxism?" *Building Feminist Theory: Essays from "Quest," A Feminist Quarterly,* pp. 174–185. New York: Longman, 1981.

Lane, Ann J. "Woman in Society: A Critique of Friedrich Engels." In Bernice A. Carroll, ed. *Liberating Women's History,* pp. 4–26. Champaign: University of Illinois Press, 1976.

Contemporary Marxist Feminism

Amott, Teresa, and Julie Matthaei. "Comparable Worth, Incomparable Pay." *Radical America* 18(5), September-October 1984, pp. 21–28.

Barrett, Michèle. *Women's Oppression Today: Problems in Marxist Feminist Analysis.* London: Verso, 1980.

Bebel, August. *Woman Under Socialism.* New York: Schocken Books, 1971.

Beechey, Veronica. "Some Notes on Female Wage Labour in Capitalist Production." *Capital and Class,* Autumn 1977, pp. 45–66.

Benston, Margaret. "The Political Economy of Women's Liberation." *Monthly Review* 21(4), September 1969, pp. 13–27.

Boserup, Esther. *Women's Role in Economic Development.* London: George Allen and Unwin, 1970.

Brenner, Johanna, and Nancy Holmstrom. "Women's Self-Organization: Theory and Strategy." *Monthly Review* 34(11), April 1983, pp. 34–52.

Bridenthal, Renate. "The Dialectics of Production and Reproduction in History." *Radical America* 10(2), March-April 1976, pp. 3–11.

Chao, Paul. *Woman Under Communism: Family in Russia and China.* Bayside, N.Y.: General Hall, 1977.

Coulson, Margaret, Branka Magas, and Hilary Wainwright. "The Housewife and Her Labour Under Capitalism: A Critique." *New Left Review* 89, January-February 1975, pp. 59–71.

Cowan, Ruth Schwartz. "The 'Industrial Revolution' in the Home: Household Technology and Social Change in the Twentieth Century." *Technology and Culture* 17(1), 1976, pp. 1–23.

Dalla Costa, Mariarosa. "A General Strike." In Wendy Edmond and Suzie Fleming, eds. *All Work and No Pay*, pp. 125–127. London: Power of Women Collective and Falling Wall Press, 1975.

Dalla Costa, Mariarosa, and Selma James. *The Power of Women and the Subversion of the Community*. Bristol, England: Falling Wall Press, 1972.

Davin, Delia. *Woman-Work: Women and the Party in Revolutionary China*. Oxford: Clarendon Press, 1976.

Davis, Angela. "The Black Woman's Role in the Community of Slaves." *Black Scholar* 3(4), December 1971, pp. 2–15.

———. *Women, Race, and Class*. New York: Random House, 1981.

Delphy, Christine. *Close to Home: A Materialist Analysis of Women's Oppression*, trans. and ed. Diana Leonard. Amherst: University of Massachusetts Press, 1984.

Donald, M. "Bolshevik Activity Amongst the Working Women of Petrograd in 1917." *International Review of Social History* 27(2), 1982, pp. 129–160.

Dunayevskaya, Raya. *Rosa Luxemburg, Women's Liberation, and Marx's Philosophy of Revolution*. Atlantic Highlands, N.J.: Humanities Press, 1982.

Edmonson, Linda Harriet. *Feminism in Russia, 1900–17*. Stanford, Calif.: Stanford University Press, 1984.

Feldberg, Roslyn L. "Comparable Worth: Toward Theory and Practice in the United States." *Signs: Journal of Women in Culture and Society* 10(2), Winter 1984, pp. 311–328.

Fox, Bonnie, ed. *Hidden in the Household: Women's Domestic Labour Under Capitalism*. Toronto: Women's Educational Press, 1980.

Gardiner, Susan. "Women's Domestic Labour." *New Left Review* 89, January-February 1975, pp. 47–58.

Garson, Barbara. *All the Livelong Day: The Meaning and Demeaning of Routine Work*. New York: Penguin Books, 1975.

Gerstein, Ira. "Domestic Work and Capitalism." *Radical America* 7(4-5), July-October 1973, pp. 101–128. (Special double issue: Women's Labor.)

Glazer-Malbin, Nona. "Housework." *Signs: Journal of Women in Culture and Society* 1(4), 1976, pp. 905–922.

Goldman, Emma. *The Traffic in Women and Other Essays on Feminism*. Albion, Calif.: Times Change Press, 1970.

Gordon, David M., Richard Edwards, and Michael Reich. *Segmented Work, Divided Workers*. New York: Cambridge University Press, 1982.

Guettel, Charnie. *Marxism and Feminism*. Toronto: Women's Educational Press, 1974.

Holmstrom, Nancy. "'Women's Work,' the Family and Capitalism." *Science and Society* 45(2), Summer 1982, pp. 186–211.

Holt, Alix. "Marxism and Women's Oppression: Bolshevik Theory and Practice in the 1920s." In Tova Yedlin, ed. *Women in Eastern Europe and the Soviet Union*, pp. 87–114. New York: Free Press, 1974.

Holt, Alix, ed. *Selected Writings of Alexandra Kollontai*. Westport, Conn.: L. Hill, 1977.

Humphries, Jane. "The Working Class Family, Women's Liberation and Class Struggle: The Case of Nineteenth Century British History." *Review of Radical Political Economics* 9(3), Fall 1977, pp. 25–41.

Kuhn, Annette, and Ann Marie Wolpe, eds. *Feminism and Materialism: Women and Modes of Production*. Boston: Routledge & Kegan Paul, 1978.

Landes, Joan B. "Women, Labor and Family Life: A Theoretical Perspective." *Science and Society* 41(1), Spring 1977, pp. 386–409.

Lopate, Carol. "Pay for Housework." *Social Policy* 5(3), September-October 1974, pp. 27–31.

MacKinnon, Catharine A. "Feminism, Marxism, Method and the State: An Agenda for Theory." *Signs: Journal of Women in Culture and Society* 7(3), Spring 1982, pp. 515–544.

Malos, Ellen, ed. *The Politics of Housework.* London: Allison & Busby, 1980.

Menon, Usha. "Women and Household Labor." *Social Scientists* 10(7), 1982, pp. 30–42.

Meulenbelt, Anja. "On the Political Economy of Domestic Labor." *Quest: A Feminist Quarterly* 4(2), Winter 1978, pp. 18–31.

Molyneux, Maxine. "Beyond the Domestic Labour Debate." *New Left Review* 116, July-August 1979, pp. 3–27.

Mullaney, Marie Marmo. *Revolutionary Women: Gender and the Socialist Revolutionary Role.* New York: Praeger, 1983.

Quick, Paddy. "The Class Nature of Women's Oppression." *Review of Radical Political Economics* 9(3), Winter 1977, pp. 42–53.

Rapp, Rayna. "Gender and Class: An Archaeology of Knowledge Concerning the Origin of the State." *Dialectical Anthropology* 2(4), December 1977, pp. 309–316.

Reed, Evelyn. *Problems of Woman's Liberation.* New York: Pathfinder Press, 1970.

Rosenthal, Bernice Glatzer. "Love on the Tractor: Women in the Russian Revolution and After." In Renate Bridenthal and Claudia Koonz, eds. *Becoming Visible: Women in European History,* pp. 422–444. Boston: Houghton Mifflin, 1977.

Rowbotham, Sheila. *Woman's Consciousness, Man's World.* Baltimore, Md.: Penguin Books, 1973.

Sacks, Karen. "Engels Revisited: Women, the Organization of Production and Private Property." In Rayna R. Reiter, ed. *Toward an Anthropology of Women,* pp. 211–234. New York: Monthly Review Press, 1975.

Saffiote, Heleieth I.B. *Women in Class Society,* trans. Michael Vale. New York: Monthly Review Press, 1978.

Schwartz, Nancy L. "Distinction Between Public and Private Life: Marx on the *Zoon Politikon.*" *Political Theory* 7(2), May 1979, pp. 245–266.

Seccombe, Wally. "The Housewife and Her Labor Under Capitalism." *New Left Review* 83, January-February 1973, pp. 3–24.

Stites, Richard. *The Women's Liberation Movement in Russia: Feminism, Nihilism, and Bolshevism, 1860–1930.* Princeton, N.J.: Princeton University Press, 1978.

Thorne, Barrie, and Marilyn Yalom, eds. *Rethinking the Family: Some Feminist Questions.* New York: Longman, 1982.

Young, Kate, Carol Wolkowitz, and Roslyn McCullagh, eds. *Of Marriage and the Market: Women's Subordination in International Perspective.* London: CSE Books, 1981.

Zaretsky, Eli. "Capitalism, the Family, and Personal Life." *Socialist Revolution* 3(1-2), January-April 1973, pp. 69–125.

——— . "Socialism and Feminism III: Socialist Politics and the Family." *Socialist Revolution* 4(1), January-March 1974, pp. 83–98.

Critiques of Marxist Feminism

Elshtain, Jean Bethke. *Public Man, Private Woman.* Princeton, N.J.: Princeton University Press, 1981, pp. 256–284.

Jaggar, Alison M. *Feminist Politics and Human Nature.* Totowa, N.J.: Rowman & Allanheld, 1983, pp. 51–82.

Sargent, Lydia, ed. *Women and Revolution: A Discussion of the Unhappy Marriage of Marxism and Feminism.* Boston: South End Press, 1981.

Wolf, Margery. *Revolution Postponed: Women in Contemporary China.* Stanford, Calif.: Stanford University Press, 1985.

RADICAL FEMINISM ON
REPRODUCTION AND MOTHERING

Reproduction: Curse or Boon?

Atwood, Margaret. *The Handmaid's Tale.* New York: Fawcett Crest Books, 1985.

Arditti, Rita, Renate Duelli Klein, and Shelley Minden, eds. *Test-Tube Women: What Future for Motherhood?* London: Pandora Press, 1984.

Al-Hibri, Azizah. *Research in Philosophy and Technology,* ed. Paul T. Durbin. London: JAL Press, 1984, vol. 7.

Corea, Genea. *The Mother Machine: Reproductive Technologies from Artificial Insemination to Artificial Wombs.* New York: Harper & Row, 1985.

Donchin, Anne. "The Future of Mothering: Reproductive Technology and Feminist Theory," *Hypatia* 1(2), Fall 1986, pp. 130–138.

Dworkin, Andrea. *Right-wing Women.* New York: Coward-McCann, 1983.

Firestone, Shulamith. *The Dialectic of Sex.* New York: Bantam Books, 1970.

O'Brien, Mary. *The Politics of Reproduction.* Boston: Routledge & Kegan Paul, 1981.

Piercy, Marge. *Woman on the Edge of Time.* New York: Fawcett Crest Books, 1976.

Mothering: Love It or Leave It?

Allen, Jeffner. "Motherhood: The Annihilation of Women." In Marilyn Pearsall, ed. *Women and Values: Readings in Recent Feminist Philosophy,* pp. 91–101. Belmont, Calif.: Wadsworth, 1986.

Alpert, Jane. "Mother Right: A New Feminist Theory." *Ms.,* August 1973.

Cahill, Susan, ed. *Motherhood.* New York: Avon Books, 1982.

Chesler, Phyllis. *Sacred Bond: The Legacy of Baby M.* New York: Times Books, 1988.

Ferguson, Ann. "Motherhood and Sexuality: Some Feminist Questions." *Hypatia* 1(2), Fall 1986, pp. 3–22.

Lázaro, Reyes. "Feminism and Motherhood: O'Brien vs. Beauvoir." *Hypatia* 1(2), Fall 1986, pp. 87–102.

Mellown, Mary Ruth. "An Incomplete Picture: The Debate About Surrogate Motherhood." *Harvard Women's Law Journal* 8, Spring 1985, pp. 231–246.

Oakley, Ann. *Woman's Work: The Housewife, Past and Present.* New York: Pantheon Books, 1974.

Rich, Adrienne. *Of Woman Born: Motherhood as Experience and Institution.* New York: W. W. Norton, 1976.

Rossi, Alice S. "A Biosocial Perspective on Parenting." *Daedalus* 106(2), Spring 1977, pp. 1–32.

Trebilcot, Joyce, ed. *Mothering: Essays in Feminist Theory.* Totowa, N.J.: Rowman & Allanheld, 1984.

RADICAL FEMINISM ON GENDER AND SEXUALITY

Biological Sex and Patriarchal Gender

Christ, Carol P. *Diving Deep and Surfacing: Women Writers on Spiritual Quest*. Boston: Beacon Press, 1980.

―――. "Why Women Need the Goddess: Phenomenological, Psychological, and Political Reflections." In Carol Christ and Judith Plaskow, eds. *Womanspirit Rising*, pp. 273–287. New York: Harper & Row, 1979.

Daly, Mary. *Beyond God the Father: Toward a Philosophy of Women's Liberation*. Boston: Beacon Press, 1973.

―――. *Gyn/Ecology: The Metaethics of Radical Feminism*. Boston: Beacon Press, 1978.

―――. *Pure Lust: Elemental Feminist Philosophy*. Boston: Beacon Press, 1984.

―――. "The Qualitative Leap Beyond Patriarchal Religion." *Quest* 1(4), Spring 1975, pp. 20–40.

French, Marilyn. *Beyond Power: On Women, Men and Morals*. New York: Summit Books, 1985.

Giovanni, Nikki. *My House*. New York: William Morrow, 1972.

Grahn, Judy. *The Work of a Common Woman*. New York: St. Martin's Press, 1979.

Hartsock, Nancy. "Staying Alive." *Quest* 3(3), Winter 1976-1977, pp. 111–122.

Ketchum, Sara Ann. "Female Culture, Womanculture, and Conceptual Change: Toward a Philosophy of Women's Studies." *Social Theory and Practice* 6(2), Summer 1980, pp. 151–162.

Mariechild, Diane. *Mother Wit: A Feminist Guide to Psychic Development*. Trumansburg, N.Y.: Crossing Press, 1986.

Millett, Kate. *Sexual Politics*. Garden City, N.Y.: Doubleday, 1970.

Nietzsche, Friedrich Wilhelm. *On the Genealogy of Morals*. Trans. Walter Kaufmann and R. Hollingdale. New York: Vintage Books, 1969.

Plaskow, Judith. "On Carol Christ on Margaret Atwood: Some Theological Reflections." *Signs: Journal of Women in Culture and Society* 2(2), 1976, pp. 331–339.

Raymond, Janice. "Beyond Male Morality." In Judith Plaskow and Joan Romero, eds. *Women and Religion*, pp. 115–125. Missoula, Mont.: Scholars' Press, 1974.

―――. *A Passion for Friends*. Boston: Beacon Press, 1986.

Rich, Adrienne. *The Fact of a Doorframe: Poems Selected and New, 1950-1984*. New York: W. W. Norton, 1984.

―――. "On Women and Honor: Some Notes on Lying." In Adrienne Rich. *On Lies, Secrets and Silence: Selected Prose, 1966-1978*, pp. 185–194. New York: W. W. Norton, 1979.

Spender, Dale. *Man Made Language*. Boston: Routledge & Kegan Paul, 1980.

Spretnak, Charlene, ed. *The Politics of Women's Spirituality*. New York: Anchor Books, 1982.

Vetterling-Braggin, Mary, ed. *"Femininity," "Masculinity," and "Androgyny."* Totowa, N.J.: Rowman & Littlefield, 1982.

Wakoski, Diane. *The Motorcycle Betrayal Poems*. New York: Simon & Schuster, 1971.

Withorn, Ann. "Helping Ourselves: The Limits and Potential of Self-Help." *Radical America* 14(3), May-June 1980, pp. 25–39.

Feminist Sexuality

Ahrens, Lois. "Battered Women's Refuges: Feminist Cooperatives vs. Social Service Institutions." *Radical America* 14(3), May-June 1980, pp. 41–47.

Barry, Kathleen. *Female Sexual Slavery*. Englewood Cliffs, N.J.: Prentice-Hall, 1979.

Boston Women's Health Book Collective. *Our Bodies, Ourselves*. New York: Simon & Schuster, 1973.

Brownmiller, Susan. *Against Our Will: Men, Women and Rape*. New York: Simon & Schuster, 1975.

Bunch, Charlotte, and Nancy Myron, eds. *Class and Feminism: A Collection of Essays from THE FURIES*. Baltimore, Md.: Diana Press, 1974.

Clark, Lorenne, and Debra Lewis. *Rape: The Price of Coercive Sexuality*. Toronto: Women's Educational Press, 1977.

Coveney, Lal, Margaret Jackson, Sheila Jeffreys, Leslie Kay, and Pat Mahoney, eds. *The Sexuality Papers: Male Sexuality and the Social Control of Women*. London: Hutchinson, 1984.

Dworkin, Andrea. *Our Blood: Prophecies and Discourses on Sexual Politics*. New York: G. P. Putnam, 1981.

————. *Right-wing Women*. New York: Coward-McCann, 1983.

————. *Woman Hating: A Radical Look at Sexuality*. New York: E. P. Dutton, 1974.

Ferguson, Ann. "The Feminist Sexuality Debates." *Signs: Journal of Women in Culture and Society* 10(1) 1984, pp. 106–135.

Frankfort, Ellen. *Vaginal Politics*. New York: Bantam Books, 1973.

Frye, Marilyn. *The Politics of Reality: Essays in Feminist Theory*. Trumansburg, N.Y.: Crossing Press, 1983.

Gordon, Linda. *Woman's Body, Woman's Right: A Social History of Birth Control in America*. New York: Penguin Books, 1977.

Ketchum, Sara Ann, and Christine Pierce. "Separatism and Sexual Relationships." In Sharon Bishop and Marjorie Weinzweig, eds. *Philosophy and Women*, pp. 163–171. Belmont, Calif.: Wadsworth, 1979.

Koedt, Anne, Ellen Levine, and Anita Rapone, eds. *Radical Feminism*. New York: Quadrangle Books, 1973.

Linden, Robin Ruth, Darlene R. Pagano, Diana E.H. Russell, and Susan Leigh Star, eds. *Against Sadomasochism: A Radical Feminist Analysis*. East Palo Alto, Calif.: Frog in the Well Press, 1982.

Martin, Del. *Battered Wives*. New York: Pocket Books, 1976.

Off Our Backs 12(6), June 1982, reporting on Barnard College's Ninth Scholar and the Feminist Conference: Towards a Politics of Sexuality.

Parker, Kathy, and Lisa Leghorn. *Woman's Worth: Sexual Economics and The World of Women*. London: Routledge & Kegan Paul, 1981.

Radical Philosophy, special issue: "Women, Gender, and Philosophy," no. 34, Summer 1983.

Raymond, Janice. *The Transsexual Empire*. Boston: Beacon Press, 1979.

Redstockings, ed. *Feminist Revolution*. New York: Random House, 1978.

Rubin, Gayle. "The Traffic in Women: Notes on the 'Political Economy' of Sex." In Rayna R. Reiter, ed. *Toward an Anthropology of Women*, pp. 157–210. New York: Monthly Review Press, 1975.

Rubin, Gayle, Deirdre English, and Amber Hollibaugh. "Talking Sex." *Socialist Review* 11(4), 1981, pp. 43–62.

Russ, Joanna. *Magic Mommas, Trembling Sisters, Puritans and Perverts*. Trumansburg, N.Y.: Crossing Press, 1985.

Shafer, Carolyn M., and Marilyn Frye. "Rape and Respect." In Marilyn Pearsall, ed. *Women and Values: Readings in Recent Feminist Philosophy*, pp. 188–196. Belmont, Calif.: Wadsworth, 1986.

Schechter, Susan. *Women and Male Violence*. Boston: South End Press, 1982.

Schulman, Alix Kates. "Sex and Power: Sexual Bases of Radical Feminism." *Signs: Journal of Women in Culture and Society* 5(4), 1980, pp. 590–604.

Snitow, Ann, Christine Stansell, and Sharon Thompson, eds. *Powers of Desire: The Politics of Sexuality*. New York: Monthly Review Press, 1983.

Vance, Carole S., ed. *Pleasure and Danger: Exploring Female Sexuality*. Boston: Routledge & Kegan Paul, 1984.

Vida, Ginny, ed. *Our Right to Love*. Englewood Cliffs, N.J.: Prentice-Hall, 1978.

Willis, Ellen. "Towards a Feminist Sexual Revolution." *Social Text* 2(3), Fall 1982, pp. 3–21.

Pornography as Symptom and Symbol of Male-Controlled Female Sexuality

Blakely, Mary Kay. "Is One Woman's Sexuality Another Woman's Pornography?" *Ms.*, April 1985, pp. 37–47.

Dworkin, Andrea. "Pornography's 'Exquisite Volunteers.'" *Ms.*, March 1981, pp. 65–66, 94–96.

——— . *Pornography: Men Possessing Women*. New York: Perigee Books, 1981.

English, Dierdre. "The Politics of Porn: Can Feminists Walk the Line?" *Mother Jones*, April 1980, pp. 20–23, 44–50.

Griffin, Susan. *Pornography and Silence*. New York: Harper & Row, 1981.

——— . *Rape: The Power of Consciousness*. San Francisco: Harper & Row, 1979.

Hunter, Nan D., and Sylvia A. Law. Brief Amici Curiae of Feminist Anti-Censorship Task Force et al. to U.S. Court of Appeals for the Seventh Circuit. *American Booksellers Association, Inc. et al. v. William H. Hudnut III et al.* (April 18, 1985).

Lederer, Laura, ed. *Take Back the Night: Women on Pornography*. New York: William Morrow, 1980.

Linz, Daniel, Charles W. Turner, Bradford W. Hesse, and Steven D. Penrod. "Bases of Liability for Injuries Produced by Media Portrayals of Violent Pornography." In Neil M. Malamuth and Edward Donnerstein, eds. *Pornography and Sexual Aggression*, pp. 277–282. New York: Academic Press, 1984.

MacKinnon, Catharine A. "Feminism, Marxism, Method, and the State: Toward Feminist Jurisprudence." *Signs: Journal of Women in Culture and Society* 8(4), 1983, pp. 635–658.

——— . *Feminism Unmodified: Discourses on Life and the Law*. Cambridge, Mass.: Harvard University Press, 1977.

——— . "Pornography, Civil Rights, and Speech." *Harvard Civil Rights–Civil Liberties Law Review* 20(1), Winter 1985, pp. 39–41.

McCarthy, Sarah J. "Pornography, Rape, and the Cult of Macho." *The Humanist* 40(5), September-October 1980, pp. 11–20.

Minneapolis, Minn. Code of Ordinances, Appendix I; Title 7, Ch. 139, sl, amending s139.10, adding (gg) *Pornography* and (1) *Special Findings on Pornography*. 1983.

Soble, Alan. *Pornography: Marxism, Feminism, and the Future of Sexuality*. New Haven, Conn.: Yale University Press, 1986.

Tong, Rosemarie. "Feminism, Pornography and Censorship." *Social Theory and Practice* 8(1), Spring 1982, pp. 1–17.

U.S. Commission on Obscenity and Pornography. *Report of the Commission on Obscenity and Pornography.* Washington, D.C.: U.S. Government Printing Office, 1970.

Lesbianism as Paradigm for Female-Controlled Female Sexuality

Atkinson, Ti-Grace. *Amazon Odyssey.* New York: Links, 1974.

————. "Lesbianism and Feminism." In Phyllis Birkby, Bertha Harris, Jill Johnston, Esther Newton, and Jane O'Wyatt, eds. *Amazon Expedition: A Lesbian-Feminist Anthology.* Washington, N.J.: Times Change Press, 1973.

————. "Radical Feminism: A Declaration of War." In Marilyn Pearsall, ed. *Women and Values: Readings in Recent Feminist Philosophy,* pp. 124–127. Belmont, Calif.: Wadsworth, 1986.

Beck, Evelyn Torton, ed. *Nice Jewish Girls: A Lesbian Anthology.* Watertown, Mass.: Persephone Press, 1982.

Bulkin, Elly, Minnie Bruce Pratt, and Barbara Smith. *Yours in Struggle.* New York: Long Haul Press, 1984.

Califia, Pat. "Feminism and Sadomasochism." *Co-evolution Quarterly,* no. 33, Spring 1981.

————. *Sapphistry: The Book of Lesbian Sexuality.* Tallahassee, Fla.: Naiad Press, 1983.

Goodman, Gerre, George Lakey, Judy Lashof, and Erika Thorne. *No Turning Back: Lesbian and Gay Liberation for the '80s.* Philadelphia: New Society Publishers, 1983.

Grier, Barbara, and Colette Reid, eds. *The Lavender Herring: Lesbian Essays from "The Ladder."* Baltimore, Md.: Diana Press, 1976.

Johnston, Jill. *Lesbian Nation: The Feminist Solution.* New York: Simon & Schuster, 1974.

Myron, Nancy, and Charlotte Bunch, eds. *Lesbianism and the Women's Movement.* Baltimore, Md.: Diana Press, 1975.

Rich, Adrienne. "Compulsory Heterosexuality and Lesbian Existence." *Signs: Journal of Women in Culture and Society* 5(4), Summer 1980, pp. 631–690.

Rule, Jane. *Lesbian Images.* Trumansburg, N.Y.: Crossing Press, 1982.

Samois. *Coming to Power: Writings and Graphics on Lesbian S/M.* Palo Alto, Calif.: Up Press, 1981.

Critiques of Radical Feminism

Cocks, Joan. "Wordless Emotions: Some Critical Reflections on Radical Feminism," *Politics and Society* 13(1), 1984, pp. 27–58.

Elshtain, Jean Bethke. *Public Man, Private Woman.* Princeton, N.J.: Princeton University Press, 1981, pp. 204–228.

Jaggar, Alison M. *Feminist Politics and Human Nature.* Totowa, N.J.: Rowman & Allanheld, 1983, pp. 249–302.

Lorde, Audre. "An Open Letter to Mary Daly." In Cherríe Moraga and Gloria Anzaldúa, eds. *This Bridge Called My Back: Writings of Radical Women of Color,* pp. 97–97. Watertown, Mass.: Persephone Press, 1981.

PSYCHOANALYTIC FEMINISM

The Roots of Psychoanalytic Feminism

Bernstein, Anne E., and Gloria Marmar Warna. *An Introduction to Contemporary Psychoanalysis.* New York: J. Aronson, 1981.

Cohen, Ira H. *Ideology and Unconscious: Reich, Freud, and Marx.* New York: New York University Press, 1982.

Erdelyi, Matthew Hugh. *Psychoanalysis: Freud's Cognitive Psychology.* New York: W. H. Freeman, 1984.

Erikson, Erik. *Childhood and Society.* New York: W. W. Norton, 1963.

————. *Identity: Youth and Crisis.* New York: W. W. Norton, 1968.

Freud, Sigmund. *Civilization and Its Discontents.* New York: W. W. Norton, 1962.

————. *Dora: An Analysis of a Case of Hysteria,* ed. Philip Rieff. New York: Collier Books, 1963.

————. "Femininity." In Sigmund Freud. *The Complete Introductory Lectures on Psychoanalysis,* trans. and ed. James Strachey, pp. 576–599. New York: W. W. Norton, 1966.

————. "On Narcissism: An Introduction." In Sigmund Freud. *General Psychological Theory,* ed. Philip Rieff, pp. 56–82. New York: Collier Books, 1963.

————. "The Passing of the Oedipus Complex." In Sigmund Freud. *Sexuality and the Psychology of Love,* ed. Philip Rieff, pp. 176–182. New York: Collier Books, 1968.

————. "The Sexual Aberrations." In *The Basic Writings of Sigmund Freud,* ed. A. A. Brill, pp. 135–172. New York: Modern Library, 1938, vol. 7.

————. "Some Psychical Consequences of the Anatomical Distinction Between the Sexes." In Sigmund Freud. *Sexuality and the Psychology of Love.* New York: Collier Books, 1968.

————. *Totem and Taboo.* In *The Standard Edition of the Complete Psychological Works of Sigmund Freud,* trans. and ed. James Strachey, pp. 1–161. New York: W. W. Norton, 1966, vol. 13.

Hall, Calvin Springer. *A Primer of Freudian Psychology.* New York: New American Library, 1954.

Izenberg, Gerald N. *The Existentialist Critique of Freud: The Crisis of Autonomy.* Princeton, N.J.: Princeton University Press, 1976.

Joes, Ernest. *The Life and Work of Sigmund Freud.* New York: Basic Books, 1961.

Laplanche, Jean. *The Language of Psychoanalysis.* New York: W. W. Norton, 1973.

Lichtman, Richard. *The Production of Desire: The Integration of Psychoanalysis into Marxist Theory.* New York: Free Press, 1982.

Mannoni, Maud. *The Child, His "Illness" and the Others.* New York: Pantheon Books, 1970.

Reppen, Joseph, ed. *Beyond Freud: A Study of Modern Psychoanalytic Theorists.* Hillsdale, N.J.: Analytic Press, 1985.

Roazen, Paul. *Freud: Political and Social Thought.* New York: Alfred A. Knopf, 1968.

Voloshinov, V. N. *Freudianism: A Marxist Critique.* New York: Academic Press, 1976.

Standard Feminist Critiques of Freud

Adler, Alfred. *Understanding Human Nature.* New York: Greenberg, 1927.

De Beauvoir, Simone. *The Second Sex,* trans. and ed. H. M. Parshley. New York: Vintage Books, 1974, pp. 48–58.

Firestone, Shulamith. *The Dialectic of Sex.* New York: Bantam Books, 1970, pp. 41–71.

Friedan, Betty. *The Feminine Mystique.* New York: Dell, 1974, pp. 95–116.

Millett, Kate. *Sexual Politics.* Garden City, N.Y.: Doubleday, 1970, pp. 176–203.

Pursuing Psychoanalysis
in Feminist Directions

Chesler, Phyllis. "Patient and Patriarch: Women in the Psychotherapeutic Relationship." In Vivian Gornick and Barbara K. Moran, eds. *Woman in Sexist Society: Studies in Power and Powerlessness,* pp. 251–275. New York: Basic Books, 1971.

_____. *Women and Madness.* Garden City, N.Y.: Doubleday, 1972.

Chodorow, Nancy. "Family Structure and Feminine Personality." In Michelle Zimbalist Rosaldo and Louise Lamphere, eds. *Women, Culture, and Society.* Stanford, Calif.: Stanford University Press, 1974.

_____. *The Reproduction of Mothering.* Berkeley: University of California Press, 1978.

Deutsch, Helene. *The Psychology of Women: A Psychoanalytic Interpretation,* vol. 1. New York: Grune & Stratten, 1944.

Dinnerstein, Dorothy. *The Mermaid and the Minotaur: Sexual Arrangements and Human Malaise.* New York: Harper Colophon Books, 1977.

Eisenstein, Hester. *Contemporary Feminist Thought.* Boston: G. K. Hall, 1983.

Engel, Stephanie. "Femininity as Tragedy: Re-examining the 'New Narcissism.'" *Socialist Review* 10(5), September-October 1980, pp. 77–104.

Ferguson, Ann. "Motherhood and Sexuality: Some Feminist Questions." *Hypatia* 1(2), Fall 1986, pp. 3–22.

Gallop, Jane. *The Daughter's Seduction: Feminism and Psychoanalysis.* Ithaca, N.Y.: Cornell University Press, 1982.

Garrison, Dee. "Karen Horney and Feminism." *Signs: Journal of Women in Culture and Society* 6(4), 1981, pp. 672–691.

Gilligan, Carol. *In a Different Voice.* Cambridge, Mass.: Harvard University Press, 1982.

Horner, Matina. "Femininity and Successful Achievement—A Basic Inconsistency." In J. Bardwick, E. Douvan, M. Horner, and D. Gutmann, eds. *Feminine Personality and Conflict.* Belmont, Calif.: Brooks-Cole, 1970.

Horney, Karen. *Feminine Psychology.* New York: W. W. Norton, 1973.

_____. *Neurosis and Human Growth.* New York: W. W. Norton, 1950.

Janeway, Elizabeth. *Man's World, Woman's Place.* New York: Dell, 1971.

Kahn, Arnold S., and Paula J. Jean. "Integration and Elimination or Separation and Redefinition: The Future of the Psychology of Women." *Signs: Journal of Women in Culture and Society* 8(4), 1983, pp. 659–671.

Kerber, Linda K., Catherine G. Greeno, Eleanor E. Maccoby, Zella Luria, Carol B. Stack, and Carol Gilligan. "On *In a Different Voice:* An Interdisciplinary Forum." *Signs: Journal of Women in Culture and Society* 11(2), Winter 1986, pp. 304–333.

Klein, Viola. *The Feminine Character.* London: Routledge & Kegan Paul, 1971.

Kofman, Sarah. *The Enigma of Woman: Woman in Freud's Writings.* Ithaca, N.Y.: Cornell University Press, 1985.

Kohlberg, Lawrence. "FROM IS TO OUGHT: How to Commit the Naturalistic Fallacy and Get Away with It in the Study of Moral Development." In T. Mischel, ed. *Cognitive Development and Epistemology,* pp. 151–233. New York: Academic Press, 1971.

Lorber, Judith, Rose Laub Coser, Alice Rossi, and Nancy Chodorow. "On *The Reproduction of Mothering*: A Methodological Debate." *Signs: Journal of Women in Culture and Society* 6(3), Spring 1981, pp. 482–514.

Miller, Jean Baker, ed. *Psychoanalysis and Women*. Baltimore, Md.: Penguin Books, 1978.

Mitchell, Juliet. *Psychoanalysis and Feminism*. New York: Vintage Books, 1974.

Ortner, Sherry B. "Oedipal Father, Mother's Brother, and the Penis: A Review of Juliet Mitchell's *Psychoanalysis and Feminism*." *Feminist Studies* 2(2-3), 1975, pp. 167–182.

Person, Ethel Spector. "Sexuality as the Mainstay of Identity: Psychoanalytic Perspectives." *Signs: Journal of Women in Culture and Society* 5(4), 1980, pp. 605–630.

Raymond, Janice. "Female Friendship: Contra Chodorow and Dinnerstein." *Hypatia* 1(2), Fall 1986, pp. 24–36.

Ross, Cheryl Lynn, and Mary Ellen Ross. "Mothers, Infants, and the Psychoanalytic Study of Ritual." *Signs: Journal of Women in Culture and Society* 9(1), 1983, pp. 26–39.

Thompson, Clara. *Interpersonal Psychoanalysis: The Selected Papers of Clara Thompson*, ed. M. P. Green. New York: Basic Books, 1964.

Van Herik, Judith. *Freud on Femininity and Faith*. Berkeley: University of California Press, 1982.

Webster, Brenda S. "Helene Deutsch: A New Look." *Signs: Journal of Women in Culture and Society* 10(3), 1985, pp. 553–571.

Weinstein, Naomi. "Psychology Constructs the Female." In Vivian Gornick and Barbara K. Moran, eds. *Woman in Sexist Society: Studies in Power and Powerlessness*, pp. 133–146. New York: Basic Books, 1971.

Williams, Juanita. *Psychology of Women: Behavior in a Biosocial Context*. New York: W. W. Norton, 1977.

SOCIALIST FEMINISM

Bartky, Sandra L. "On Psychological Oppression." In Sharon Bishop and Marjorie Weinzweig, eds., pp. 33–41. *Philosophy and Women*. Belmont, Calif.: Wadsworth, 1979.

———. "Narcissism, Femininity and Alienation." *Social Theory and Practice* 8(2) Summer 1982, pp. 127–144.

Berch, Bettina. *The Endless Day: The Political Economy of Women and Work*. New York: Harcourt Brace Jovanovich, 1982.

Caulfield, Mina Davis. "Imperialism, the Family, and Cultures of Resistance." *Socialist Revolution* 20(4), October 1974, pp. 67–85.

———. "Universal Sex Oppression?—A Critique from Marxist Anthropology." *Catalyst*, nos. 10-11, Summer 1977, pp. 60–77.

Delphy, Christine. *Close to Home: A Materialist Analysis of Women's Oppression*, trans. and ed. Diana Leonard. Amherst: University of Massachusetts Press, 1984.

Easton, Barbara. "Socialism and Feminism I: Toward a Unified Movement." *Socialist Revolution* 4(1), January-March 1974, pp. 59–67.

Ehrenreich, Barbara. "Life Without Father: Reconsidering Socialist-Feminist Theory." *Socialist Review* 14(1), January-February 1984, pp. 48–57.

———. "What Is Socialist Feminism?" *Win*, June 3, 1976, pp. 4–7.

Ehrenreich, Barbara, Berkeley-Oakland Women's Union, Michelle Russell, and Barbara Dudley. "The National Conference on Socialist Feminism." *Socialist Revolution* 5(4), October-December 1975, pp. 85–116.

Ehrenreich, Barbara, and Deirdre English. *For Her Own Good: 150 Years of the Experts' Advice to Women.* New York: Anchor Books, 1979.

––––––. "Microbes and the Manufacture of Housework." *Socialist Revolution* 5(4), October-December 1975, pp. 5–40.

Eisenstein, Zillah, ed. *Capitalist Patriarchy and the Case for Socialist Feminism.* New York: Monthly Review Press, 1979.

Ferguson, Ann. "The Che-Lumumba School: Creating a Revolutionary Family-Community." *Quest* 5(3), February-March 1980, pp.

––––––. "Women as a New Revolutionary Class." In Pat Walker, ed. *Between Labor and Capital*, pp. 279–309. Boston: South End Press, 1979.

Ferguson, Ann, Ilene Philipson, Irene Diamond, Lee Quinby, Carole S. Vance, and Ann Barr Snitow. "The Feminist Sexuality Debates (Forum): Viewpoint." *Signs: Journal of Women in Culture and Society* 7(1) 1981, pp. 158–199.

Foreman, Ann. *Femininity as Alienation: Women and the Family in Marxism and Psychoanalysis.* London: Pluto Press, 1977.

Haber, Barbara. "Is Personal Life Still a Political Issue?" *Feminist Studies* 5(3), Fall 1979, pp. 417–430.

Hartmann, Heidi. "Capitalism, Patriarchy, and Job Segregation by Sex." *Signs: Journal of Women in Society and Culture* 1(3), part 2, 1976, pp. 773–776.

––––––. "The Family as the Locus of Gender, Class, and Political Struggle: The Example of Housework." *Signs: Journal of Women in Culture and Society* 6(3), 1981, pp. 366–394.

––––––. "The Unhappy Marriage of Marxism and Feminism: Towards a More Progressive Union." In Lydia Sargent, ed. *Women and Revolution: A Discussion of the Unhappy Marriage of Marxism and Feminism*, pp. 1–41. Boston: South End Press, 1981.

Hartmann, Heidi, and Ann R. Markusen. "Contemporary Marxist Theory and Practice: A Feminist Critique." *Review of Radical Political Economics* 12(2), Summer 1980, pp. 87–93.

Hartsock, Nancy. *Money, Sex, and Power.* Boston: Northeastern University Press, 1985.

Jaggar, Alison M. *Feminist Politics and Human Nature.* Totowa, N.J.: Rowman & Allenheld, 1983, pp. 123–163.

Martin, Gloria. *Socialist Feminism: The First Decade, 1966-1976.* Seattle: Freedom Socialist Publications, 1978.

Mitchell, Juliet. *Woman's Estate.* New York: Pantheon Books, 1971.

––––––. "Women: The Longest Revolution." *New Left Review* 40, November-December 1966, pp. 11–37.

Nakano, Evelyn, and Glenn and Roslyn L. Feldberg. "Clerical Work: The Female Occupation." In Jo Freeman, ed. *Women: A Feminist Perspective*, 2nd ed., pp. 316–336. Palo Alto, Calif.: Mayfield, 1979.

Nicholson, Linda J. *Gender and History: The Limits of Social Theory in the Age of the Family.* New York: Columbia University Press, 1986.

––––––. "'The Personal Is Political': An Analysis in Retrospect." *Social Theory and Practice* 7(1), Spring 1981, pp. 85–98.

Nussbaum, Karen. "Women Clerical Workers." *Socialist Review* 10(1), January-February 1980, pp. 151–159.

Padgug, Robert A. "Sexual Matters: On Conceptualizing Sexuality in History." *Radical History Review* 20, Spring-Summer 1979, pp. 3–23.

Page, Margaret. "Socialist Feminism—A Political Alternative." *m/f* 2, 1978, pp.

Petchesky, Rosalind Pollack. "Reproductive Freedom: Beyond 'A Woman's Right to Choose.'" *Signs: Journal of Women in Culture and Society* 5(4), Summer 1980, pp. 661-685.

Phelps, Linda. "Death in the Spectacle: Female Sexual Alienation." *Liberation*, May 1971.

———. "Patriarchy and Capitalism." *Quest* 2(2) Fall 1975, pp. 35-48.

Phillips, Anne. *Hidden Hands: Women and Economic Policies.* London: Pluto Press, 1983.

Rapp, Rayna, Ellen Ross, and Renate Bridenthal. "Examining Family History." *Feminist Studies* 5(1), Spring 1979, pp. 174-200.

———. "Family and Class in Contemporary America: Notes Toward an Understanding of Ideology." *Science and Society* 42(3), Fall 1978, pp. 278-300.

Rowbotham, Sheila, Lynne Segal, and Hilary Wainwright. *Beyond the Fragments: Feminism and the Making of Socialism.* London: Merlin Press, 1979.

Rubin, Gayle. "The Traffic In Women: Notes on the 'Political Economy' of Sex." In Rayna R. Reiter, ed. *Toward an Anthropology of Women*, pp. 157-210. New York: Monthly Review Press, 1975.

Sargent, Lydia, ed. *Women and Revolution: A Discussion of the Unhappy Marriage of Marxism and Feminism.* Boston: South End Press, 1981.

Sennett, Richard. *The Fall of Public Man.* New York: Alfred A. Knopf, 1977.

Trimberger, Ellen Kay. "Women in the Old and New Left: The Evolution of a Politics of Personal Life." *Feminist Studies* 5(3), Fall 1979, pp. 432-450. (See also the response by Peggy Dennis in the same issue, pp. 451-461.)

Vogel, Lise. "The Earthly Family." *Radical America* 7(4-5), July-October 1973, pp. 9-50.

———. *Marxism and the Oppression of Women: Towards a Unitary Theory.* New Brunswick, N.J.: Rutgers University Press, 1983.

Weinbaum, Batya. *The Curious Courtship of Women's Liberation and Socialism.* Boston: South End Press, 1978.

Weinbaum, Batya, and Amy Bridges. "The Other Side of the Paycheck: Monopoly Capital and the Structure of Conscription." *Monthly Review* 28(3), July-August 1976, pp. 88-103.

Working Papers on Socialism and Feminism. Chicago: New American Movement, n.d.

———. "Socialist Feminism and the Limits of Dual Systems Theory." *Socialist Review* 10(2-3), March-June 1980, pp. 169-188.

EXISTENTIALIST FEMINISM

Sartre's *Being and Nothingness:*
A Backdrop to *The Second Sex*

Aron, Raymond. *Marxism and the Existentialists.* New York: Harper & Row, 1969.

Caws, Peter. *Sartre.* Boston: Routledge & Kegan Paul, 1979.

Chiodi, Pietro. *Sartre and Marxism.* Atlantic Highlands, N.J.: Humanities Press, 1976.

Grene, Marjorie. *Dreadful Freedom: A Critique of Existentialism.* Chicago: University of Chicago Press, 1948.

———. *Sartre.* New York: New Viewpoints, 1973.

Kaufmann, Walter Arnold, ed. *Existentialism from Dostoevsky to Sartre.* New York: New American Library, 1975.

Novack, George, ed. *Existentialism vs. Marxism: Conflicting Views on Humanism.* New York: Dell, 1966.

Sartre, Jean-Paul. *Being and Nothingness,* trans. Hazel E. Barnes. New York: Philosophical Library, 1956.

———. *The Emotions: Outline of a Theory.* New York: Philosophical Library, 1948.

———. *Existentialism,* trans. Bernard Frechtman. New York: Philosophical Library, 1947.

Simone de Beauvoir:
Existentialism for Women

Ascher, Carol. *Simone de Beauvoir: A Life of Freedom.* Boston: Beacon Press, 1981.

De Beauvoir, Simone. *Adieux: A Farewell to Sartre.* New York: Pantheon Books, 1984.

———. *The Ethics of Ambiguity.* New York: Citadel Press, 1967.

———. *Memoirs of a Dutiful Daughter,* trans. James Kirkup. Harmondsworth, England: Penguin Books, 1963.

———. *The Prime of Life,* trans. Peter Green. Harmondsworth, England: Penguin Books, 1965.

———. *The Second Sex,* trans. and ed. H. M. Parshley. New York: Vintage Books, 1974.

Jardine, Alice. "Interview with Simone de Beauvoir." *Signs: Journal of Women in Culture and Society* 5(2), 1979, pp. 224–236.

Keefe, Terry. *Simone de Beauvoir.* Totowa, N.J.: Barnes & Noble, 1983.

Kuykendall, Eléanor H. "Linguistic Ambivalence in Simone de Beauvoir's Feminist Theory." In Iris Young and Jeffner Allan, eds. *The Thinking Muse,* pp. 1–30. Bloomington: Indiana University Press, 1989.

McCall, Dorothy Kaufmann. "Simone de Beauvoir, *The Second Sex,* and Jean-Paul Sartre." *Signs: Journal of Women in Culture and Society* 5(2), 1979-1980, pp. 209–223.

Schwarzer, Alice. *After the Second Sex.* New York: Pantheon Books, 1984.

Simons, Margaret A., and Jessica Benjamin. "Simone de Beauvoir: An Interview." *Feminist Studies* 5(2), Summer 1979, pp. 330–345.

Whitmarsh, Anne. *Simone de Beauvoir and the Limits of Commitment.* Cambridge: Cambridge University Press, 1981.

Critiques of Existentialist Feminism

Elshtain, Jean Bethke. *Public Man, Private Woman.* Princeton, N.J.: Princeton University Press, 1981, pp. 306–308.

Lloyd, Genevieve. *The Man of Reason: "Male" and "Female" in Western Philosophy.* Minneapolis: University of Minnesota Press, 1984.

POSTMODERN FEMINISM

Some Major Influences on
Postmodern Feminist Thought

Derrida, Jacques. *The Post Card: From Socrates to Freud and Beyond,* trans. Alan Bass. Chicago: University of Chicago Press, 1987.

_____ . *Spurs: Nietzsche's Styles*, trans. Barbara Harlow. Chicago: University of Chicago Press, 1978.

_____ . *Writing and Difference*, trans. Alan Bass. Chicago: University of Chicago Press, 1978.

Lacan, Jacques. *Écrits: A Selection*, trans. Alan Sheridan. New York: W. W. Norton, 1977.

_____ . *The Four Fundamental Concepts of Psychoanalysis*, ed. Jacques-Alain Miller and trans. Alan Sheridan. New York: W. W. Norton, 1978.

Postmodern Feminism: Three Perspectives

Brée, Germaine. *Women Writers in France*. New Brunswick, N.J.: Rutgers University Press, 1973.

Burke, Carolyn Greenstein. "Report from Paris: Women's Writing and the Women's Movement." *Signs: Journal of Women in Culture and Society* 4(4), Summer 1978, pp. 843–854.

Cixous, Hélène. "Castration or Decapitation?" *Signs: Journal of Women in Culture and Society* 7(1), 1981, pp. 41–55.

_____ . "The Laugh of the Medusa." In Elaine Marks and Isabelle de Courtivron, eds. *New French Feminisms*, pp. 245–264. New York: Schocken Books, 1981.

_____ . "Sorties." In Elaine Marks and Isabelle de Courtivron, eds. *New French Feminisms*, pp. 90–98. New York: Schocken Books, 1971.

Clément, Catherine. *The Lives and Legends of Jacques Lacan*. New York: Columbia University Press, 1983.

Conley, Verena. "Missexual Mystery" [review of Cixous' and Clément's *La jeune née*]. *Diacritics* 7(2), Summer 1977, pp. 70–82.

Diacritics: Special Issue. "Textual Politics: Feminist Criticism." *Diacritics*, 5(4), Winter 1975.

Duchen, Claire. *Feminism in France: From May '68 to Mitterrand*. London: Routledge & Kegan Paul, 1986.

Fauré, Christine. "Absent from History." *Signs: Journal of Women in Culture and Society* 7(1), 1981, pp. 71–80.

_____ . "The Twilight of the Goddesses, or the Intellectual Crisis of French Feminism." *Signs: Journal of Women in Culture and Society* 7(1), 1981, pp. 81–86.

Gallop, Jane. *The Daughter's Seduction: Feminism and Psychoanalysis*. Ithaca, N.Y.: Cornell University Press, 1982.

_____ . "The Ladies' Man." *Diacritics* 5(4), Winter 1976, pp. 28–34.

Irigaray, Luce. "And the One Doesn't Stir Without the Other." *Signs: Journal of Women in Culture and Society* 7(1), 1981, pp. 60–67.

_____ . *This Sex Which Is Not One*, trans. Catherine Porter. Ithaca, N.Y.: Cornell University Press, 1985.

_____ . "When Our Lips Speak Together." *Signs: Journal of Women in Culture and Society* 6(1), 1980, pp. 4–28.

Kristeva, Julia. *Desire in Language*, trans. Leon Roudiez. New York: Columbia University Press, 1982.

_____ . *Powers of Horror*, trans. Leon Roudiez. New York: Columbia University Press, 1982.

_____ . *Revolution in Poetic Languages*, trans. Leon Roudiez. New York: Columbia University Press, 1984.

_____ . "Women's Time." *Signs: Journal of Women in Culture and Society* 7(1), 1981, pp. 13–35.

Kuykendall, Eléanor H. "Toward an Ethic of Nurturance: Luce Irigaray on Mothering and Power." In Joyce Trebilcot, ed. *Mothering: Essays in Feminist Theory*, pp. 263–274. Totowa, N.J.: Rowman & Allanheld, 1984.

Marks, Elaine. "Review Essay: Women and Literature in France." *Signs: Journal of Women in Culture and Society* 3(4), Summer 1978, pp. 832–842.

Marks, Elaine, and Isabelle de Courtivron. *New French Feminisms*. New York: Schocken Books, 1981. [Bio/bibliography and bibliography provide references to untranslated French titles not listed here.]

Mitchell, Juliet, and Jacqueline Rose, eds. *Feminine Sexuality: Jacques Lacan and the Ecole Freudienne*, trans. Jacqueline Rose. New York: W. W. Norton, 1982.

Moi, Toril. *Sexual/Textual Politics: Feminist Literary Theory*. New York: Methuen, 1985.

Wittig, Monique. *Les guérillères*. New York: Viking, 1971.

CONCLUSION: STANDPOINTS AND DIFFERENCES

Cornwell, Anita. *Black Lesbian in White America*. Tallahassee, Fla.: Naiad Press, 1983.

Gillespie, Marcia Ann. "The Myth of the Strong Black Woman." *Essence Magazine*, August 1982, pp. 58–60.

Harding, Sandra. *The Science Question in Feminism*. Ithaca, N.Y.: Cornell University Press, 1986.

Hartsock, Nancy C.M. "The Feminist Standpoint: Developing the Ground for a Specifically Feminist Historical Materialism." In Sandra Harding, ed. *Feminism and Methodology*, pp. 157–180. Bloomington: Indiana University Press, 1987.

Herman, Alexis M. "Still . . . Small Change for Black Women." *Ms.*, February 1979, pp. 96–98.

Hood, Elizabeth F. "Black Women, White Women: Separate Paths to Liberation." *Black Scholar* 9(7), April 1978, pp. 45–56.

Hooks, Bell. *Ain't I a Woman: Black Women and Feminism*. Boston: South End Press, 1981.

———. *Feminist Theory: From Margin to Center*. Boston: South End Press, 1984.

Hull, Gloria T., Patricia Dell Scott, and Barbara Smith, eds. *But Some of Us Are Brave*. Old Westbury, N.Y.: Feminist Press, 1982.

Jaggar, Alison. *Feminist Politics and Human Nature*. Totowa, N.J.: Rowman & Allanheld, 1983.

Joseph, Gloria, and Jill Lewis. *Common Differences: Conflicts in Black and White Feminist Perspectives*. New York: Anchor, 1981.

Lorde, Audre. *Chosen Poems, Old and New*. New York: W. W. Norton, 1981.

———. "Scratching the Surface: Some Notes on Barriers to Women and Loving." In Alison M. Jaggar and Paula S. Rothenberg, eds. *Feminist Frameworks*, pp. 432–436. New York: McGraw-Hill, 1984.

———. *Sister Outsider*. Trumansburg, N.Y.: Crossing Press, 1984.

———. *Zami: A New Spelling of My Name*. Watertown, Mass.: Persephone Press, 1982.

Lugones, Maria, and Elizabeth V. Spelman. "Have We Got a Theory For You! Feminist Theory, Cultural Imperialism, and the Demand for 'The Woman's Voice.'" In Marilyn Pearsall, ed. *Women and Values: Readings in Recent Feminist Philosophy*, pp. 19–32. Belmont, Calif.: Wadsworth, 1986.

McCandless, Cathy. "Some Thoughts About Racism, Classism, and Separatism." In Joan Gibbs and Sara Bennett, eds. *Top Ranking,* pp. 105–115. New York: February Third Press, 1979.

Moraga, Cherríe, and Gloria Azaldúa, eds. *This Bridge Called My Back: Writings of Radical Women of Color.* Watertown, Mass.: Persephone Press, 1981.

Morrison, Toni. *Beloved.* New York: Alfred A. Knopf, 1987.

———. "Cinderella's Stepsisters." *Ms.,* September 1979, pp. 41–42.

———. *Song of Solomon.* New York: Alfred A. Knopf, 1977.

———. *Sula.* New York: Knopf, 1974.

———. "What the Black Woman Thinks About Women's Lib." *New York Times Magazine,* August 22, 1971, p. 55.

Omolade, Barbara. "Black Women and Feminism." In Hester Eisenstein and Alice Jardine, eds. *The Future of Difference,* pp. 247–257. Boston: G. K. Hall, 1980.

Rich, Adrienne. "Disloyal to Civilization: Feminism, Racism, and Gynephobia." *Chrysalis: A Magazine for Women's Culture* 7, pp. 9–27.

Russell, Michelle, and Mary Jane Lupton. "Black Women and the Market." *Women: A Journal of Liberation* 2(3), 1971, pp. 14–15.

Shange, Ntozake. *A Daughter's Geography.* New York: St. Martin's Press, 1983.

———. *For Colored Girls Who Have Considered Suicide/When the Rainbow Is Enuf.* New York: Macmillan, 1975.

———. *Nappy Edges.* New York: St. Martin's Press, 1978.

———. *Sassafrass.* San Lorenzo, Calif.: Shameless Hussy Press, 1977.

Smith, Barbara. "Notes for Yet Another Paper on Black Feminism, or Will the Real Enemy Please Stand Up?" *Conditions: Five—The Black Women's Issue* 2(2), Autumn 1979, pp. 123–127.

Spelman, Elizabeth. "Theories of Race and Gender: The Erasure of Black Women." *Quest* 5(4), 1980, pp. 36–62.

Steele, Norma, and Margaret Prescod-Roberts. *Black Women: Bringing It All Back Home.* Bristol, England: Falling Wall Press, 1980.

Tate, Claudia, ed. *Black Women Writers at Work.* New York: Continuum, 1983.

Walker, Alice. *The Color Purple.* New York: Harcourt Brace Jovanovich, 1982.

———. *In Search of Our Mothers' Gardens.* New York: Harcourt Brace Jovanovich, 1984.

Index